P9-BYB-658

ALSO BY ANN RULE

If You Really Loved Me
The Stranger Beside Me
Possession
Small Sacrifices

EVERYTHING

→ A TRUE STORY

SHE EVER

◆ OF OBSESSIVE LOVE,

WANTED

→ MURDER, AND BETRAYAL

Ann Rule ◆

SIMON & SCHUSTER

NEW YORK   LONDON   TORONTO   SYDNEY   TOKYO   SINGAPORE

SIMON & SCHUSTER
Simon & Schuster Building
Rockefeller Center
1230 Avenue of the Americas
New York, New York 10020

Copyright © 1992 by Ann Rule

All rights reserved
including the right of reproduction
in whole or in part in any form.

SIMON & SCHUSTER and colophon are registered trademarks
of Simon & Schuster Inc.
Designed by Carla Weise/Levavi & Levavi
Manufactured in the United States of America

10 9 8 7 6 5 4 3 2 1

Library of Congress Cataloging-in-Publication Data

Rule, Ann.
    Everything she ever wanted : a true story of obsessive love, murder, and
betrayal / Ann Rule.
        p.   cm.
    1. Murder—Georgia—Pike County—Case studies.   I. Title.
HV6533.G4R85   1992
364.1′523′09758453—dc20   92-21541
                                                              CIP

ISBN: 0-671-69070-1

All photographs are from the author's collection.

To My Best Friend
In Loving Memory
Richard W. "Dick" Reed

Seattle Police Department
Homicide Unit (Retired)

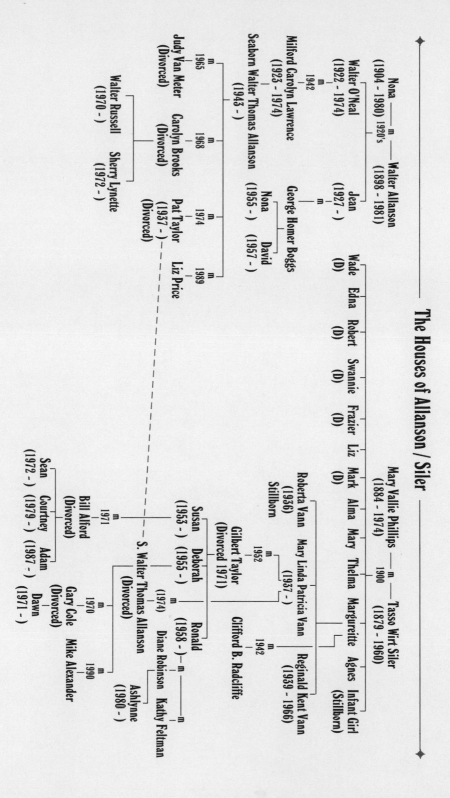

The Houses of Allanson / Siler

Express Malice is that deliberate intention unlawfully to take away the life of a fellow creature which is manifested by external circumstances capable of proof.

Malice shall be implied where no considerable provocation appears, and where all the circumstances of the killing show an abandoned and malignant heart.

—Georgia statute

ZEBULON

1

Zebulon, the seat of Pike County, fifty miles south of Atlanta, is little more than a town square, the four streets surrounding it, and some houses radiating beyond. Like scores of other small towns in this part of Georgia, it is sheltered by a green blur of trees—pine, dogwood, magnolia, and oak. On a hot summer's day, their branches form a leafy dome that traps the sodden heat, and everything beneath grows as if in a hothouse. Shade gives only an illusive promise of surcease from the sweltering summer temperatures. Cosseted in a perfect environment, the kudzu vine creeps along the orange earth, smothering each thing it covers, an innocuous-looking blanket of pointed leaves, an emerald parasite.

The courthouse in Zebulon is red brick, with white gingerbread trim and an alabaster bell tower gleaming against the sky. Magnolias, oaks, and maple trees dot the broad lawn, and each of the courthouse's four entrances is flanked by blood red geraniums in stone urns. A tilted, graying stone memorial sits in one corner of the courthouse grounds, its purpose to honor seventeen white Zebulon boys who died in World War II, including two Marshalls, two Pressleys, and a Pike. Only one name is listed under the chiseled COLORED in the lower right corner. E. R. Parks remains segregated even on a heroes' memorial.

The businesses across from the courthouse hide behind contiguous—but totally different—stone facades with squared-off rooflines of varying heights: a clothing outlet store, some antique shops, a furniture store, a hardware store. The *Reporter*, Zebulon's weekly newspaper, has its offices at the end of the block. There are Coca-Cola and Dr. Pepper machines every seventy-five feet or so along the sidewalks. Vehicles—mostly pickup trucks—park diagonally along the street. A yellow dog, in no danger, ambles casually across the carless road.

When Hollywood producers were looking for a typical southern town as a filming site for *Murder in Coweta County* starring Andy Griffith and Johnny Cash, they chose Zebulon. Pat Taylor and Tom Allanson also chose Zebulon to live out a fantasy of their own. It was 1973 when they came to town, first living as lovers, then as man and wife. She was a slender woman with emerald green eyes and a pile of bouffant curls. He was a tall, tanned man. She was beautiful, he was handsome, and together they seemed to have the kind of love that could survive any adversity. Pat described her feelings in a note she wrote to Tom on the back of their wedding picture:

We are joined together as one for life—What greater thing is there for 2 human souls than to be joined together for life, to strengthen each other in all our labor, to lean on each other in time of need, to rest on each other in time of sorrow, to minister to each other in time of pain, to be with each other always with our memories and our ONENESS LOVE to sustain us. . . . I feel that in loving My Tom I am nearest to heaven. . . . When I came to you, My Tom, I put me within your hand—my body, heart, and soul. You are my love, and you make me wholly yours in all the ways there are; this sweet bondage is more enduring than locks or bars. I will never leave your breast to dream of other things for I have found in My Tom the "end-of-my-quest." . . . My body blooms all over from every vien [sic] because I'm Tom's Pat. Behold, I left the old me far behind and shed my old life leaf by leaf. . . .

And so she had.

Pat and Tom set out to create from their perfect love a perfect world. And yet, within that paradise lurked the possibility of jealousy and rage, of adultery, fornication, incest, rape, and even murder, grim and violent intrusions from the real world. Each of them had family ties far too strong to let loving commitment grow unstunted. Back and back and back, old slights magnified rather than diminished. Pride, like the kudzu covering the dry earth, only scabbed over deep and painful wounds that had never healed. Untangling the story of their lives is akin to following the verdant convolutions of that parasitic vine that eventually kills every living thing that sustains it.

2

They had come to each other from the cold ashes of failed marriages. At thirty, Tom was younger than Pat by six years; he had two short, bad marriages behind him and she had one long one in which she had felt trapped and smothered. Both of them had sought perfect love most of their lives. Despite the odds, they truly seemed to have found it in each other, although —at least on the surface—they had nothing more in common than potent sexual passion.

Tom was strong as an ox, and Pat was tiny boned and fragile, often ill. He was a blacksmith; she loved doing dainty handwork, embroidery and painting. He had a college education, and she had married first when she was in the tenth grade and dropped out of school. He was calm and soothing, and she sometimes seemed anxious and frightened.

It didn't matter. All he had to do was open up his huge arms, and she would crawl up on his lap and hide in the safety of his strength. Tom always told Pat, "Remember, Shug, 'First things first'—and the first, most important thing is that I love you more than anything in this world."

And she would answer in the soft little girl's voice that belied her thirty-six years, "I love you, Sugar. I love you, Shug."

Pat Taylor had known Tom for years before she really *saw* him. Her whole family—her parents, retired army Colonel Clifford Radcliffe and his wife, Margureitte; her children, Susan, Deborah, and Ronnie; as well as Pat herself—was deeply involved in the horse show world of Atlanta. The Radcliffes' stables boasted some of the area's finest horses. Pat, who was living with her parents, taught riding to an exclusive clientele, and both her daughters were champion equestriennes.

Tom Allanson had worked with their horses and sold them feed when he was employed by Ralston Purina. The son of an attorney, he had set out to be a veterinarian, although he had not quite reached that goal. Tom had been a friend to Pat's family, nothing more, but any woman who watched him at work, naked to the waist, his muscular torso glistening with sweat, would have noticed him. Shoeing the Radcliffes' prize Morgan horses, he lifted their hooves in his hand as easily as if they were lambs' feet.

And then, a series of events in the fall of 1973 brought Tom and Pat together. Pat was free of romantic commitments, and Tom, who was seeking a divorce from his second wife, needed a temporary place to live. The Radcliffes had plenty of room at their horse farm on Tell Road in East Point south of Atlanta, and they invited him to stay. He could sleep on the sofa in their den, and they could use his help with their horses.

To a pragmatist, their coming together was expedient; to a romantic, it was fate. Whichever, Tom Allanson and Pat Taylor soon spent every waking moment together. He loved everything about her, and she continually surprised him. He knew almost nothing of her life before he met her and didn't care to. She, however, was insatiably curious—about his family and the women whom Tom had loved before he loved her.

In spite of the fact that Tom was still married, they had a wonderfully romantic courtship. Tom could not believe his good fortune at having found Pat, and he was awed that she loved him back. His biggest fear was that her health would completely break down and he would lose her. When she was taken with one of her fainting spells and hospitalized, he was desolate, standing helplessly beside her bed with her pale hand in his huge work-gnarled fist. He lay single roses on her pillow and gazed at her with tears in his eyes.

Pat tried to send him away, warning Tom she wouldn't be good for him, that he deserved a "whole woman." She begged him to face the truth. "You don't want me, Tom," she sobbed. "I can never give you children—I've had a hysterectomy. I'm just an old woman with a scar down my stomach. Nobody would want *me*."

It only made him love her more. He didn't need more children; he and Pat would raise *his* two children and, of course, her boy, Ronnie, was still only in his teens.

Pat and her family became everything to Tom. They had given him shelter—and love—when no one else would. Pat's mother, Margureitte, was the kindest woman he had ever known; she would do anything to help her children and grandchildren, and Tom respected the colonel for his army service and for his dignity and military bearing. He pleaded with Pat to marry him as soon as his divorce was final.

Pat couldn't take stress or dissension or disappointments. When Tom listened to her speak of her longings, he realized that what she wanted in this world wasn't that much; she just wanted it so badly. He vowed to do whatever he could to make her life so happy and calm that she would regain her health.

Pat had one special dream—a dream that no man yet had been able to make come true. She longed to live on her own plantation. More than a century had passed since the Civil War, but Pat yearned for the genteel life of a southern belle as it was evoked in Margaret Mitchell's novel *Gone with the Wind*. She wanted her own Tara; she wanted to *be* Scarlett O'Hara. Somehow, someday, she believed Tom was going to get her her own place, a spread of land where she could hold her head up proudly. A place where she could grow the roses she loved so.

"I'm like a rose, Tom," she explained softly. "And like a rose, I'm selfish. I want all the sun for myself, all the rain. Roses need everything so that they can bloom and be beautiful."

She wasn't really selfish, he knew. It was only her appetite for life, for love, she spoke of. That was one of the things he admired about her: she reached out for life with her two hands, grasping all its wonder and clasping it to her breasts. She made him see what could be—*should* be—for them.

Together, that first October, they came across a place that seemed meant just for them. Pat was having a good week, feeling strong and healthy, and she and Tom went deer hunting. He was so proud of her. The way she tramped around the woods with him, cooked over a campfire, and loaded her own gun, shouldering it as well as any man, amazed him. "She knew more about guns than most men," he said later. "She had me buy a .44 carbine so she could go deer hunting with me—that's a powerful carbine."

She was such a remarkable woman. Pat could do just about anything. They cuddled together through the long cool Georgia nights, warming themselves with a sexual fervor that had not diminished with familiarity, but had only grown more intense. So it seemed a good omen for their future together when they found the red brick house with a porch all around it in Zebulon during their hunting trip. There was a For Sale sign on it, and they learned it was the old "Hoyt Waller place" and that Waller was selling it because he was divesting himself of some of his many real estate holdings.

After Pat pointed out the tremendous potential just waiting to be tapped in the sprawling farm, what *they* could do with it, Tom was as wild to have it as she was. The place was right on Highway 19 a few miles north of Zebulon. Its four hundred feet of road frontage was fenced in with freshly painted white horizontal boards. There were soaring pine trees beyond the roadside meadow and a curving drive wound between tall Georgia holly bushes all the way back to the brick house and the barn.

"It was just perfect," Tom remembered. "I wanted to stay there until the day I died. It had everything I ever wanted. The house was a brick ranch-style house. It had a twenty-five-acre pecan grove plus twenty-seven more acres. It had everything you could ask for. It was the most beautifully landscaped place. It had the orchards. It had the garden spots. It had the vineyards. Apple trees. Pecan trees. Pear trees. Catalpa trees. Rose gardens. It had a beaver pond on the back side of it, and the pastures, the deer, the quail. It was just a beautiful place. . . ."

All they had to do was figure out a way to buy it. Waller wanted forty-two thousand dollars for the spread, and it would take some fancy financing for Pat and Tom to swing that. There was money in Tom's family, all right. His father was a successful

East Point attorney who had made a bundle of money in land deals. Still, Tom knew his father wasn't likely to help him out. He couldn't remember the last time he had done anything his parents approved of. They were still so angry about his second divorce, there was no point in even asking them for help. Anyway, it seemed that his father *enjoyed* watching him fail.

Tom was the last of three Walter Allansons. Old "Paw"— Walter Allanson—was the first, and then came Tom's father, Walter O'Neal Allanson, and finally Tom himself, Seaborn Walter Thomas: "Tommy." Paw and Nona, Tom's grandparents, were well up in their seventies, but they had always been more like his parents than Walter and Carolyn Allanson ever were. Paw still farmed his place over on Washington Road in East Point. He had made a small fortune over the years and he was frugal—but he wasn't stingy, the way his son was.

Tom figured and figured until he came up with what might be a way to buy the Waller place for Pat. He had long wanted Nona and Paw to live near him, especially now that they were older. His grandmother was in failing health, and Paw couldn't go on forever. Tom took Pat over to meet them, and left her chatting with Nona while he and Paw went out walking around the farm to discuss "business."

Paw and Nona were polite to Pat, although they were a little puzzled to see Tommy with his third woman in a decade. She was obviously older than Tommy by several years, and Nona thought she dressed awfully flashy. The old woman was surprised when Pat told her she had three children and that both of her daughters were already married. Nona, whose speech was compromised by a stroke, and who was too polite to speak what was on her mind anyway, listened quietly as Pat rattled on about her wonderful plans with Tommy. Despite Nona's earlier misgivings, she couldn't help but like Pat—and catch her enthusiasm. Meanwhile, Tom explained to Paw about the place in Zebulon: the fifty acres and the house and barn and all that went with it that could be had for only forty-two thousand. It was a buy that Tom couldn't just walk away from—not without consulting Paw.

The two men worked out a plan. Paw would give Tom the money for twenty-five acres, and that money would serve as a down payment for the whole place. Tom would find a way to make the balloon payments due down the road. Tom said he would like either to build or move a house onto that acreage for his grandparents. That sounded good to Paw; since Nona's stroke, he had been doing both the outside chores and the inside work. He prided himself on the fact that he took excellent care of his wife, but it would be nice to have a woman around to spell him and cook a meal once in a while. Tom assured Paw that Pat already loved both him and Nona. He had told her how good they had always been to him.

Colonel and Mrs. Radcliffe, Pat's parents, also helped Pat and Tom with the down payment on the Zebulon property. Their only request was that they call their farm Kentwood in memory of Pat's brother, Kent, who had died when he was in his mid-twenties. Although Pat would have much preferred something more romantic and evocative—like Rose Hill Farm or Holly Hedge Stables, or even Tara Orchards—they called it Kentwood Morgan Farm.

At long last she had her love *and* her piece of earth, a fine brick house, and a barn big enough for all the horses she and Tom would raise. They would make it a showplace where they could host grand riding competitions. Tom could shoe horses and she could teach riding and, afterwards, they could stroll hand in hand through her own rose garden. There could be nothing more perfect than the hushed twilight of a soft Georgia night, and being in love.

Pat and Tom moved onto the wonderful property on Highway 19 in late 1973, and Tom immediately began to work on the place, sure his divorce from his second wife was imminent. When he was truly free, he would marry "his Pat." Making the house just right for her was a labor of love and, as he was able to afford materials, he remodeled and refurbished. "I redid it just like we planned," he said. "We got lumber out at Fort McPherson and redid the barn and the pastures. I had such great expectations."

Pat proved to be remarkably unhandy at home improvements and although she picked up a paintbrush from time to time, the bulk of the work was Tom's. He didn't mind. He was euphoric just to be with her and to have Kentwood.

Ronnie, fifteen, moved in with his mother and Tom, although he was certainly welcome to stay with his grandparents. Pat loved her son. She indulged him too. She bought him anything he wanted and let him do whatever he asked—except visit his father. He missed a lot of school, and Pat didn't push him to go. He was both spoiled and neglected. When Tom tried to explain that boys needed some discipline so that they would grow into good men, Pat gently reminded him that Ronnie was *her* child, and that she knew best.

Ronnie adored his mother; there were no lengths to which he wouldn't go to please her. If she voiced a wish, Ronnie would carry out her bidding. His devotion didn't stop him from getting into trouble, like getting drunk and wrecking cars and doing other things not sanctioned by the law, but he didn't want any of it to disturb his mother. If she was hurting too bad and needed pain medication, Ronnie always found a way to get it for her. If someone wounded her feelings and needed a reminder not to do that, Ronnie took care of that too.

Not everything in their new life went smoothly, of course— but Tom was so happy nothing much bothered him. On Christmas Day 1973, he went to take a big gelding out of the barn and it came out running full tilt. He held on, but even *his* weight didn't stop the spooked horse and it dragged him along, fracturing his right collarbone. For a blacksmith, it was a bothersome injury and kept him off work.

Pat was jealous of Tom's wife, whom everybody called "Little Carolyn" since his mother's name was Carolyn too. Of course, she was called "Big Carolyn." If the truth be told, Tom was kind of proud that Pat was so jealous of him, even though, Lord knew, she had no cause to be. Little Carolyn was pretty, but she was nothing compared to Pat. Pat was a perfect lady and was beautiful and fiery and her kisses tasted like honey. He was eager to get his divorce.

Pat refused to have anything around her that might remind Tom of Little Carolyn. "I remember I came home once," Tom said later, "and something came flying out the door and shattered on the sidewalk. It was a brand-new J. C. Penney's radio. It had been in my bedroom and it belonged to me, but as far as Pat was concerned it belonged to Carolyn, and she wasn't having anything of Carolyn's in the house. She just pitched it out. She hated Carolyn so bad, she even tried to say once that my children weren't mine—that they were my *father's* children, that they'd had an affair while I was married to Carolyn."

Tom didn't believe Pat meant that about his kids. She often talked about bringing Russ and Sherry to live with them and how she would be their mother. It was just that Pat was so high-strung that she sometimes said things she didn't mean.

Still, she wouldn't allow Tom to display pictures of his children in her house.

The divorce from Little Carolyn dragged on and on, and Pat cried with frustration. She wanted to be married to Tom, not just living with him. But a hearing in early spring of 1974 ended, not in Tom's final decree, but in another postponement. After realizing that Tom and Little Carolyn Allanson were far, far apart on monetary agreement, the judge said, "I will not grant a divorce at this time." Hearing that, Pat turned white and dug her fingernails into Tom's arm. She made it out of the De Kalb County Courthouse but she fainted on the front lawn. Someone screamed and paramedics were summoned. Gradually she came around and Tom half led, half carried her out of the crowd that had gathered. He wondered how much more of this kind of strain she could take.

And then, suddenly, it was all right, as if Pat and Tom's love was somehow blessed. On May 9, 1974, Tom had yet another divorce hearing. He expected one more delay and the hearing seemed mostly an irritant. Tom and Pat were scheduled to be at a Morgan horse show in Stone Mountain, Georgia, that evening.

Pat had decreed that they would go to Stone Mountain as "Scarlett and Rhett" and had busied herself making their costumes. Dressing up and slipping into another persona never failed to cheer her up; it was almost as if she could step out of her own life into an existence she craved. And everyone always raved about how clever she was as a seamstress. She knew she and Tom would be the hit of the Stone Mountain show. She had chosen royal blue as the Kentwood Morgan Farm's show colors, and their chairs, tents, and blankets all matched.

Pat's gown was white with a sweetheart neckline, puffed sleeves, and a voluminous hoop skirt. She would wear white gloves, white feathers in her hair, and she would suspend her favorite gold-rimmed cameo from a moiré ribbon around her slender neck. When she posed for Tom in her costume, he stepped up and circled her tiny waist with his two hands. She had never looked more beautiful, and she knew it.

Tom felt a little foolish when he saw his costume, but he

shrugged and tried it on: a black cutaway coat with tails, a white satin vest over a shirt with ruffles at the neck and wrists, and a top hat. Pat even had a fake moustache for him to stick on. Standing in front of a long mirror together, they looked as if they had just returned to Zebulon through some dusty curtain in time. They also looked incredibly like Scarlett and Rhett, and Pat was elated.

They were both thrilled beyond words when Tom's divorce, at long last, was granted that very day. They quickly reserved a chapel at Stone Mountain for their wedding. But nothing in Pat's life ever seemed to happen without fanfare. Her wedding to Tom was no exception. It made headlines. A slightly sentimental reporter for the *Griffin Daily News* related that Pat and Tom had not only met "cute," they had married "cute." Under the headline THEY WERE DETERMINED TO GET MARRIED, a three-column spread described the nuptials:

"Pat Radcliffe and Tom Allanson had an unusual wedding, to say the least. . . ."

Pat had explained to the reporter that she and Tom had known each other for fifteen years—ever since the day she had called Tom as a last minute replacement for her regular blacksmith. They had not gotten along at all, Pat laughed, since she was a specialist in Morgan horses and Tom preferred quarter horses. However, she had won him over.

"When Pat was stricken and confined to bed, Tom became a regular caller," the reporter wrote. "And from that came wedding bells. 'She moves about so much that it was the first time I had to catch her,' Tom beamed the other day."

The Griffin feature story did not mention that Tom's divorce was brand spanking new. It didn't mention *any* other marriages for either the bride or groom, only the romantic and chaotic details of May 9, 1974. Pat and Tom had engaged the chapel for a 2:00 P.M. wedding, and rented *"one* motel room" for that night.

"Tom was taking a van loaded with horses to the show when he had a blowout. Another tire went and he was stranded on a busy interstate near Atlanta," the paper reported. "He made his way to a service station. As chance would have it, someone passing by knew where he could get two large tires for the van.

"Tom's bride-to-be was waiting at the chapel in Stone Mountain when the ceremony time arrived. He sent word that he had run into trouble and would be late. By the time word reached Pat, she already had guessed that something had gone wrong. The ceremony was canceled.

"When Tom finally got the van repaired and to the horse show, word had spread among show people about what had happened. They suggested since the show tents already were beautifully decorated, that one of them be used for the wedding. Tom and Pat agreed. The Rev. William Byington, a Baptist minister, was called. He said that in all of his many years in the ministry, he never had been called on to perform a wedding ceremony under such circumstances. But he agreed to do so. With show people looking on in one of the tents, he asked Tom and Pat to pledge their love to each other in a standard and simple ceremony."

Pat managed to get in several plugs for their new Kentwood riding facilities and mentioned that she would continue teaching riding at Woodward Academy on the Riverdale campus. She and her horses would commute both ways daily.

"But back to the wedding story," the Griffin newspaper continued, obviously pleased with such fascinating new residents of nearby Pike County. "The couple stopped at Western Sizzlin' Steak House for a Sunday night meal. When they had finished, Tom took the van and his bride was to follow. He pulled onto the expressway and moved slowly into traffic. He checked the rearview mirror to look for the vehicle his wife was driving. Tom heard a noise that sounded like a wreck. He stopped.

"Someone had had a collision with his wife and she lay injured in the vehicle. She was taken to the Griffin-Spaulding Hospital for examination and treatment. She was strapped up and told it would be all right for her to go home. But the pain in her shoulder persisted. Next day, she went to an Atlanta hospital, where it was learned she had a broken collarbone. She came home in a cast and has been in one since. . . . The newlyweds have managed to smile through it all and are looking forward to establishing their farm home here."

The picture accompanying the piece was, of course, perfect for the story. Pat and Tom, as Scarlett and Rhett in their antebellum finery, smiled for the camera as they were united in marriage in a huge flower-bedecked building: the lovely slender woman with feathers in her hair and an ivory fan open in her small gloved hands, the huge man with the tremendously proud grin.

Why Pat had pulled directly into the path of an oncoming car remained a mystery. She might have been blinded by the sun, but she was probably only careless. She was not a particularly good driver, and she was easily distracted. Driving a truck and pulling a horse trailer behind cut most of her side and rear vision. She may well have been exhausted after three whirlwind days at the Stone Mountain horse show, but it was an exhilarating fatigue; she had gone from being "left at the chapel" to being a bride whose wedding was the focal point of the whole show. It had turned out better than even she could have envisioned.

It was even kind of romantic that she and Tom had both suffered broken collarbones—they shared everything. His own injury was long since healed, but Tom remembered how painful it had been, and he was especially tender with Pat, never letting her lift anything heavy or reach for something if he could get it for her.

Gradually, she resumed her riding lessons, and Tom divided his time among his work at Ralston Purina, shoeing horses, and fixing up their place. As their fortunes increased, they planned to buy more and more Morgan horses. They would have the finest Morgan stables in the state of Georgia. They already had the finest marriage. That, Tom was sure of. "Two human souls joined together for life . . ."

3

There was only one cloud over their happiness. While Pat's family was pleased with her marriage to Tom, and Tom's grandparents found Pat a sweet and thoughtful woman, his parents were another story entirely. Walter and Big Carolyn Allanson wanted nothing to do with Tom's third wife. In fact, they had sided with Tom's *ex*-wife during the divorce, and resisted all his efforts to let them see what a fine woman Pat was.

Hoping to ease the situation a little, Margureitte Radcliffe made overtures to the Walter Allansons. She called and invited them to join her and Colonel Radcliffe for dinner at the officers' club at Fort McPherson. "They were not interested," Margureitte later said, "and I thought, How *can* they not be interested when they do not know us?"

Margureitte, who always prided herself on her sense of propriety and her impeccable social grace, was shocked to find Tom's parents so hostile. Using a phrase she often sprinkled through her conversations, she sighed, "I never in this whole wide world thought people could act like that."

Then Tom lost his job at Ralston Purina, and he suspected it was his father's fine hand interfering in that too. He tried to make up for his lost salary with his blacksmith work, but that caused a bit of a problem in his relationship with Pat. He was surprised to find that his bride was not only jealous of his ex-wife, she was jealous of any woman who might cast an appreciative eye on him. She plain didn't want him around other women, not unless she was with him. He tried to explain to her that horse barns were not exactly prime spots to find other women and that he spent 95 percent of his life around men, but it did no good. Pat insisted on accompanying Tom on his farrier rounds.

He was proud of her, but she sure put a damper on male conversation. Instead of jawing easily with the good old boys who hung around as he shod horses, Tom worried whether Pat was comfortable and feeling okay. Her presence made his customers uneasy too. But he loved her too much to ever feel smothered by her attention. If she wanted to be with him, then she was always welcome.

He wouldn't have dreamed of telling her to stay home.

Lavished with Tom's love, Pat's health improved—at least enough so she was able to help on the elaborate grounds of Kentwood; she could manage the riding mower. She gave a few horseback lessons, and they sometimes rented their surrey or the sulky and their horses for shows and parades. She and Tom went often to horse shows. But they both soon realized that they would have to budget tightly and work harder to make Kentwood the kind of place they visualized. Pat wanted everything *now,* and Tom had to gentle her down and explain they just couldn't afford all that—a bigger barn, a grandstand for horse shows, more roses, chandeliers, more horses and more buggies, more elegant livery for their drivers.

All of it took money, and the money would have to come from somewhere outside their household. Without his job at Ralston Purina and with the broken collarbone that had kept him from shoeing horses for a couple of months, Tom had lost ground financially. Now he could work, but his blacksmith business was going downhill instead of up—mostly because of Pat's insistence that she always be present, or because he so often had to drop everything and rush home when she had a spell of fainting.

Tom could never tell when Pat was going to pass out. Sometimes she would be driving their jeep around the place and she would just faint at the wheel and fall out the driver's door; sometimes he would race home to find her lying by the telephone. No, it was impossible to even think of Pat working full-time; he didn't want her to do that anyway. He wasn't even sure she should be giving so many riding lessons.

Tom wanted to get his grandparents moved onto the place too. He had promised to do that, and that promise, he thought, should be honored before the big expansion of Kentwood. But even with worries about money and feuds with his parents, Tom was happy. When he and Pat saddled up their horses and rode over their own land, he thought he was probably the luckiest man who had ever lived. Sometimes Pat wore one of her costumes for a ride around their place, and the sight of her with the burgeoning spring trees behind her was enough to make him want to weep with joy. They called each other "Sugar" and eventually that was abbreviated to "Shug." They had special songs and little sayings that were just for them to know about. "First things first, Shug," they would say. They would see to what was important and the rest of their plans would fall into line.

✦ ✦ ✦

Tom had never told Pat how bad things were with his parents —especially with his father. Walter Allanson could have a crude mouth, and he had used it to talk about Pat. Although he had never met her, his father detested Pat. When Tom was first living with her, he had told his son she was a slut, a woman whose bad reputation was common knowledge. "She'll lie down with any man with a truck and a horse trailer. You damn fool, can't you see that?"

Pat had had affairs that were no secret, Walter Allanson had pointed out. If Tom had anything to do with her, he was a bigger idiot than he had already proved he was. "Stay away from that, Tommy," Walter had argued. "That's bad stuff there."

Of course, his father's warnings had only made Tom want Pat more. It wasn't true what he said about Pat; Tom didn't believe a word of it. That was his father's way of ruining things for him, the way he always had managed to tarnish those things that meant the most to him. Pat would be heartsick if she heard what Walter Allanson had said about her, and Tom wasn't ever going to tell her.

It was difficult though, because Pat kept urging Tom to make peace with his family. She suspected—correctly—that there was money in Tom's family, even though—except for his aunt Jean Boggs, Walter's sister—they lived rather austerely. Tom had told her that Paw was shrewd and had hidden money stashes all over his place on Washington Road.

The way Pat understood it, Paw had sold the back part of his land to Tom's father, and Walter had seen to getting it zoned for multidwellings, then sold it to builders who had put up the Forest Apartments, the Gray Estates, and the Club Candlewood Apartments. There had to have been a great deal of money coming into the family from those transactions. Tom didn't seem to care a hoot about it, but he *was* the Allansons' only son, and Paw and Nona's favorite grandson, and eventually, she figured, it would all belong to him. Heaven knows they were never going to make Kentwood what it should be if Tom didn't get his rightful inheritance.

Tom's aunt Jean Boggs and her husband, Homer, had a fine house in East Point and she dressed as if she were a wealthy woman. Tom told Pat that Jean hadn't had anything to do with her brother Walter after some fuss over their father's property— not for seven or eight years. She had children too, but they hadn't been raised by the elder Allansons, the way Tom was; he was almost like Paw and Nona's own son.

Now that she and Tom were married, Pat was sure Walter and Big Carolyn Allanson would accept her. She came from the Silers on her mother's side, a fine old family. She had parents to be proud of—Papa was, after all, a retired colonel. Pat considered herself far superior to Tom's ex. She was a *lady,* whose children were riding champions, a lady who had met Governor Jimmy Carter *and* the Japanese royal family personally. The Allansons had to recognize that and be *grateful* that she had married their son. It would all work out.

Tom wasn't optimistic about that happening anytime soon. He knew how muleheaded his father could be, but it was impossible for him to explain to his bride why they couldn't go calling on his parents. As much as he loved her, he had already learned that Pat had a way of aggravating people, of speaking without thinking and saying the wrong thing at the wrong time. And then there was her appearance. Personally, he loved the way she looked and dressed, but seeing Pat through his father's eyes, he shuddered. She showed too much leg and too much bosom. The little old-fashioned clips she used to hold her halter tops together had a way of working loose. She was a magnificent-looking woman, but the sight of her would only give his dad more ammunition to talk against her.

He wouldn't subject Pat to that.

And now that he was married to her, he saw that Pat was even more impetuous and sensitive to slight than he had realized. Her grandmother Siler had died the spring they married and the Siler clan gathered in North Carolina to bury her, most of them meeting Tom for the first time. There was a ruckus as the funeral procession was organized. Pat's aunt Mary Adams and her husband, Charles, pulled their Cadillac just behind the hearse and waited for the procession to begin. But Pat had a fit. "Mama Siler would have wanted me to be first," she sobbed. "I was her favorite. Tom, just you pull the truck in there—right there in front of the Cadillac."

Bewildered but obedient, Tom jockeyed the farm pickup with the round Kentwood emblem featuring a Morgan horse on the door into line, edging out the Cadillac. Nobody stopped him. He was fascinated to see the way the Silers parted the waters for his beloved.

Pat calmed down some as they led the endless string of vehicles to the cemetery; her sobs halted and she sat up straight and almost proud. She explained to Tom how special she had always been to her grandmother, and he could see that everyone loved Pat, her folks, her daughters and Ronnie, his grandparents—everyone but his parents, who were as stubborn as hogs in a sweet corn patch.

Pat was too smart not to realize that her in-laws wanted nothing to do with her. She was hurt and angry. It wasn't fair—she hadn't done anything at all to harm them. Was it a crime for her to love their son more than life itself? She was six years older than Tom, but no one could consider that *that* was robbing the cradle. Why did Walter and Big Carolyn have to be so petty?

Their relationship with his parents—or rather their lack of

relationship—became a constant irritant to Pat. Although she and Tom still had wondrous, dreamy days in Kentwood, tiny fissures began to break through their seamless joy. Pat complained to anyone who would listen about Tom's father and his ex-wife, Little Carolyn. She insisted they were somehow responsible for Tom's losing his job at Ralston Purina: "Somebody called up and told them there was a countersuit [to the divorce] and they were going to put [Tom] in jail and all this, and Purina has a *very* strict law about that—so Tom lost his job. . . ."

Furthermore, Pat felt Walter was making it his life's mission to see that Tom never got a job again. "He has had several applications in for good jobs," she said, "but each one his father has managed to put a kink in. Tom wanted to be on the mounted patrol, and his father stopped that too."

It may well have been true. Walter Allanson's animosity toward his only child was as bitter as gall. He would not accept Tom's divorce and remarriage, and Pat had a right to feel resentful. But Tom soon realized that his new wife was no peacemaker and that she had precious little tact. She was always on his side—and that was good—but she talked far too much and her comments got back to his father, and things only got worse.

As the spring of 1974 edged toward full summer, Pat Allanson was a woman on fire. It was a side to her personality that Tom had never seen before. He had known her to be loving and passionate, wistful and sad, and as frightened as a child. He had not seen her rage. Instead of being content that she and Tom were finally man and wife and letting the rest of the world go by, she nagged at him constantly to "do something" about his father. "You call yourself a *man?*" she taunted Tom. "If you were a man, you wouldn't let him treat us like he does!"

Her tears hurt Tom far more than her words—it tore him up to see Pat cry—but he had never been able to win in confrontations with his father. He had no idea what Pat expected him to do. He wanted to run his own life, his own farm, and his own marriage—but Pat seemed to be in his face whichever way he turned. He couldn't make her see that they didn't need his father, *or* his father's money.

Pat persisted. She wanted Tom to work things out with his parents, and she demanded to be welcomed into his family—not to be treated like trash. They were insulting her and embarrassing her, not to mention her parents. Any husband who truly cared for her wouldn't stand still for such treatment. Their marriage was only a little more than a month old, but their bliss was souring like apple cider turned to vinegar.

Pat began to withdraw from Tom. The newlyweds already had fifteen-year-old Ronnie living with them, and now Pat started asking her daughters, Susan and Deborah, or other relatives to visit. Her aunt Alma Studdert and Alma's granddaughter, Mary Jane Smith, were frequent overnight guests. Pat and Alma would rock for hours on the back porch glider and watch the sky turn dark over the fields of Kentwood when Alma thought Pat would have chosen to be in bed with her new husband. Pat's daughters and relatives couldn't help but notice that Pat was avoiding being alone with Tom. This struck them as decidedly odd since she and Tom were technically still on their honeymoon and should have been in the googly-eyed stage of marriage.

Having family close by was not new for Pat; she had always needed them for security. But now that she had Tom to keep her safe, her relatives were puzzled by her obvious reluctance to be alone with him. Maybe she didn't want to say something she would regret. She seemed quietly heartbroken, and, in spite of her beauty, her family knew that Pat had always required continual emotional support. Tom's parents' total rejection had crushed Pat. It had leached joy from her life, leaving her marriage flat and sere.

4

Tom and Pat's honeymoon was over far too soon, and the situation only grew worse when Pat's mother, Margureitte, received an unexpected phone call at the office of the children's dentist where she worked. It was from Walter Allanson himself. "Perhaps you have some influence with Tom," he began without preamble. "Would you please tell him to stop doing the things he's been doing—and to do what he's supposed to do?"

Margureitte Radcliffe was a woman who remembered long, complicated conversations verbatim. Her most common mien was one of indignation and shock over the behavior of less refined people, particularly those who misunderstood her daughter, Patricia. Pat could do no wrong in her mother's eyes.

And, ironically, Tom could do no *right* in his father's.

Her voice full of disbelief, Margureitte later described the bizarre conversation she had had with Walter Allanson. "He told me that Tommy had come into his ex-wife's apartment and put formaldehyde in some milk! [I said,] 'Did you call the police?' He said they did and they had it tested and there *was* formaldehyde in it. They were pouring the milk out into a glass for the little girl. He—Mr. Allanson—said, 'Well, I'm sure Tom did it.' "

Margureitte was appalled. It didn't make sense. It wasn't like Tom to do such a thing. He loved his children. He would never have harmed them. Of course she told her daughter about the call, and when she heard about Walter Allanson's accusations, Pat became almost unhinged with frustration. How could Tom allow anyone to lie about him that way? He was permitting his father and his ex-wife to ruin his reputation with vindictive lies.

Margureitte Radcliffe decided she had had enough. She would not allow anyone to hurt Patricia this way. She spoke to Paw and Nona, Tom's grandparents, about the trouble between Walter and Tom and Pat, but there was nothing they could do about it. They explained stoically that their son was a "cold person. He's never been wrong in his life, never made a mistake in his life, and he's never admitted he was sorry for anything . . . not since he was a child."

Never famous for minding her own business, Margureitte took it upon herself to straighten out her daughter's new father-in-law. On Monday, June 21, 1974, she went to Walter Allanson's law offices without an appointment and asked to be announced. Mary McBride was his receptionist; her granddaughter Becky had gone to school with Pat's daughters and she asked how they were. Margureitte was shocked to realize that Mary didn't even know that Tom and Pat were married. The Allansons were certainly ones for keeping secrets.

When Walter got off the phone, Margureitte marched into his office, undeterred by his astonished stare. Her memory of their first meeting remained crystalline in her mind ever after. "Mr. Allanson," she said. "I didn't want to come and see you, but I *had* to come . . . because I've tried to have you all meet us. I couldn't believe all the things I've heard—that you were a stern man and a hard man—and I just can't believe any father could be like that. . . . Tommy's not said anything, but I can see his heart has to be breaking inside from the attitude that you and his mother have with him. . . ."

Walter Allanson was hardly cowed by the indignant words of the woman before him. "Mrs. Radcliffe," he said ominously. "Let me tell you something. I'm Scotch, I'm a strict disciplinarian, and I'm a stern man. I have schooled myself that when I'm finished with someone, I'm finished with them. I don't *have* a son."

"Mr. Allanson," Margureitte said, "you don't mean that. Deep down inside you, this is some kind of front that you are putting on. Deep down inside you, you have to have some feeling."

"No, Mrs. Radcliffe, I do not. . . . If Tommy would drop dead today, I would not go to his funeral, and if he was dying and would ever call me, I would not lift a finger to help him. In fact, I would do everything I can to ruin him."

"Mr. Allanson! Have you always felt this way about him?"

"No. About a year ago, he changed. I think the boy has a tumor."

Margureitte drew herself up. "Well, if I thought a child of mine had a tumor, rather than accusing him of things, I think I'd do everything I could to persuade him to seek the proper medical advice."

"He won't pay any attention to me," Walter Allanson said. Then he mentioned the formaldehyde in the baby's milk again, and added that Tom had also put sugar in the gas tank of his car on May 9.

"That couldn't be," Margureitte countered. "Tom was in Stone Mountain getting married on that day; there were at least three hundred people at his wedding. Really and truly, Mr. Allanson, you must have something back in your cases and you should be looking there instead of thinking that everything that happens is Tommy's fault."

"Well," Allanson said, leaning across his desk and glaring at Margureitte, "I want to tell you what he did. Yesterday morning, sometime between nine A.M. and one-thirty P.M., someone broke into our house and stole three guns."

Walter Allanson wanted the weapons back and he instructed Margureitte to have Tom *mail* them to him. "He's not to come and bring them to me, because I'll kill him when I see him. If he doesn't mail them to me, or the police department doesn't make the case against him, then I'll get him."

Margureitte blanched. "Mr Allanson, you can't mean that. . . . Even though your son hasn't done anything to you? If he came to you and said, 'Dad, I don't know what this is about, but can't we sit down and talk it over and let bygones—let it be over with,' Mr. Allanson, . . . you couldn't forgive your son?"

"No. I'm finished. I don't have a son. I don't have a daughter-in-law either. Your daughter is not my daughter-in-law."

Her face stiff with horror, Margureitte Radcliffe left Walter Allanson's office. Her visit had only made things worse. Everyone in the family felt it. The atmosphere at Kentwood in late June was thick with tension.

Liz Price, an old friend of Tom's and a horse show acquaintance of Pat's, owned a farm seven miles south of Kentwood. Her daughter, Johnette, exercised their horses three or four days a week and occasionally rode the Morgans in shows. Liz was present when Tom walked into the kitchen one evening with an onion from the garden and presented it to Pat with a flourish. Liz was surprised to see Pat frown and brush his hand away fretfully. "She was always fussing at him," Liz recalled.

Pat's daughter, Susan Alford, who was twenty-one that summer and often came out to Kentwood with her baby son, Sean, had always been able to gauge her mother's moods; she saw that Pat was strung out to a fine thread. She picked at Tom for having no backbone. She demanded that he defend her honor, go to his parents and *force* them to welcome her into the family circle as his wife. Susan saw that Tom was so completely smitten with Pat that he would do anything to please her, at least anything within his power.

But Tom knew he had no power at all with his father. He never had.

Pat's aunt Alma rocked on the porch glider one velvet night in June, but she couldn't relax. "I can't put my finger on it," she commented to Liz Price, "but something bad's fixing to happen."

✦ ✦ ✦

On June 28, Pat was alone at Kentwood. Tom had gone over to Barnesville to shoe horses, and Ronnie had said he would be in Zebulon on a painting job. It was a glorious sunny day and Pat was finally feeling well enough to do a little more work around the place. She got out the riding mower to cut the grass. In a statement she later gave to a Pike County deputy, she described the terror she had endured that afternoon.

"I was there by myself and we have a great big huge yard; we have fifty-something acres there . . . and I was cutting way up the very front part of the road—which is a long way from the house. I was on the small riding mower and I was just nonchalantly cutting around. I had just started cutting . . . and I saw a truck go by. It looked just like our truck, a blue camper truck. I knew it wasn't ours because the camper top was off. . . . You know how something just goes through your mind and it just sort of sticks? I went on around—it was a good acre—and there is a big tall hedgerow about fourteen feet high between our farm and the field next to us and . . . I could see the top of a camper. . . . I thought, Well, gee, that man must have had trouble with his truck. . . . And all of a sudden I got right at the end of the hedgerow where we have a great big tall tree. And there he stood. Sleeves rolled up, and he just dropped his pants. . . . I didn't know what to do. I slammed the brakes on the tractor and it seemed like I was frozen for an hour, but I know it wasn't but a second."

Pat told the deputy the most shocking part of her ordeal. She recognized the man. She had seen him for years around East Point, and lately his picture had been in all the papers and on political signs. The man who had exposed himself to her was Walter Allanson, her husband's father!

"I was sure it was him. The only thing that threw me off—there was a cigar in the man's mouth. . . . I had never seen his daddy smoke a cigar. . . . I have never seen him with anything except a cigarette in his mouth. . . . I slammed the tractor into third gear. It doesn't go very fast. I headed across to go to the neighbors next door, and there were no cars over there, so I headed back up my long, winding driveway and another acre to get back to the house. I ran straight into the house."

Tom always kept his "shoeing book" right there in the house so that Pat would know exactly where he was all the time in case she had a "sinking spell." Pat hadn't called the sheriff first; she called Tom. She was in such a panic that he could barely understand her, but then she blurted out that his father had stood right out there in their hedgerow and exposed his penis to her. Tom could scarcely take in what she was saying, but one thing was certain—she was hysterical. "He said, 'Shug, for crying out loud, stop and hang up the phone and call the sheriff!' "

And Pat had done just that. The sheriff told her he was on his way, and before Pat could dial again, the phone rang. It was Ronnie, calling from Atlanta, where he was visiting Margureitte. She was so frightened that she really wasn't sure *where* Ronnie was, she told the sheriff later. She had thought he was in Zebulon painting a house.

But then, who knew where Ronnie was half the time? He and his friend, Cecil "Rocky" Kenway—who often stayed at Kentwood with him—were like most teenagers, taking off for God knows where whenever they pleased.

Ronnie told his mother that he had had a sudden presentiment about her. "Mom, I don't know why—I just wanted to call and see if everything's all right."

Pat began to tell her son what had happened, when Ronnie stopped her and said, "Mother, are the doors locked?"

"Oh, my God, I don't know. Wait a minute. I'll call you back."

She set the phone down and ran to lock all the doors in the house, but then she was struck with a terrible thought: *Oh my God, what if I've locked him in the house with me? He could have come up the hedgerow that lines the back of the house. . . .*

Ronnie held on the line until Pike County's chief deputy sheriff, Billy Riggins, raced the two and a half miles from the courthouse in Zebulon to Kentwood. Riggins found an attractive but hysterical woman standing at the kitchen phone, clutching an unloaded .22 rifle. Since Riggins didn't know it was unloaded, he gingerly removed the gun from her grip and she handed the phone to him. "Please talk to my son and reassure him that you're here with me."

After Riggins spoke to Ronnie and hung up the phone, he was assaulted with a torrent of words as Pat told him how horrified she had been to see her own father-in-law standing there in the hedgerow waving his private parts at her. "I've been ill," she told Sheriff Riggins. "I have a lot of trouble with blood clotting, and what have you, and I have to have oxygen. I have high blood pressure and all from an accident I was in—I just got out of the hospital. This was the first day I felt well enough to mow.

"My son said for me to ask you to load the gun for me, so I'll have something to protect myself after you leave—at least until my husband gets home."

"Where are the shells for this .22?" Riggins asked.

"I don't know."

Tom called back just then and told Riggins where the keys to the gun cabinet were. The deputy chambered the rounds and showed Pat how to shoot the gun. She wasn't unknowledgeable about guns. She could load and shoot a .22 rifle, and she had used a much more powerful gun when she went deer hunting with Tom the previous fall. But she was apparently too frightened to think straight, and her hands shook.

Riggins noted that she also seemed terribly embarrassed, and, hell, what woman wouldn't be? It was a humiliating thing to have to turn in your own kin for showing off his privates. It wasn't natural.

"Can you describe the man you saw?" he asked.

"Yes," she began slowly. "Of course—I mean I knew it was his father. . . . There he stood wearing that same kind of hat that he wears, that kind of floppy hat, and his shirtsleeves rolled up like he does, and just dropping his pants. Yet at the same time I was thinking, How *could* it be his father? You know? But I know it was him."

The Pike County deputy managed to calm Pat down and suggested that she talk with her husband about whether they wanted to bring charges against his father. Pat seemed composed enough when he had to leave on another call.

This was, in fact, Riggins's second visit to Kentwood Morgan Farm. In early April, Tom Allanson had called him to report that somebody had shot one of his cars full of .22 bullet holes. The car was parked out in back of the barn, and it looked as if somebody had used it for target practice. Riggins had never been able to pin the shooting on a suspect, and Tom had had no suggestions. There were a lot of visitors coming and going at Kentwood, and then there was fifteen-year-old Ronnie Taylor living there with his mother and stepfather, and from time to time *his* teenage friends. But this time, a suspect had been positively identified.

When Tom got home a few minutes after Riggins left, he listened in icy shock to Pat's accusations against his father. His father was a mean SOB on occasion, but Tom couldn't even imagine Walter Allanson as an exposer. His father was much too controlled to do such a thing, or had always seemed so to Tom.

Still, his dad had done about everything else he could to make their lives miserable.

Tom called his father's law offices and no one answered. His life seemed to be spinning out of control. It was one thing to have his father angry with him. Lord knew he was used to it. But every day brought some new shock. Margureitte had told him his father didn't care if he lived or died and wouldn't even spit on his grave if he did. His father had accused him of putting poison in his own baby's milk and of stealing guns from him. And Pat believed his father had ruined him in the job market, and would actually kill him if he got the chance. That was exactly what he had told Mrs. Radcliffe. Even Nona and Paw had warned Tom that he might be in danger.

But *this*. His father had done the unforgivable. Walter Allanson, an attorney at law, candidate for judge, had exposed himself to his wife.

Tom was enraged. Poor Pat was so sick she could barely move, her collarbone hurt her all the time, and still she had been out there trying to help by mowing the lawn. How dare his father frighten and shock her that way? It made Tom realize that Pat had been right; he couldn't let his father get away with it. Neither of them could stand for such shabby treatment. As much as he dreaded the prospect, Tom knew that he would have to confront his father.

5

Walter O'Neal Allanson and his wife, Milford—but called Carolyn—were both fifty-one in late June of 1974. They had been married for thirty-two years, more than half of their lives. They lived in East Point, a gracious suburb adjacent to Atlanta's southwest border. Theirs was by all accounts a comfortable marriage, although some said that Walter had strayed a bit in his forties. If he had, Carolyn had let it go. The woman involved was long dead. In his fifties, Walter Allanson had grown almost puritan in his opinions about the sanctity of marriage, as virtuous as a reformed hooker. If there were children involved, he was inflexibly against divorce—a sometimes difficult stance for an attorney whose practice was general law.

Walter was a handsome man with iron gray hair and clear blue-gray eyes, a compactly trim man—save for a slight falling away of his chin line as he moved through middle age. "Big Carolyn" was a plain woman who rarely wore makeup. Her hair was brown and combed back from her face into nondescript waves. She was neither slender nor fat; rather, her figure was full breasted and solid.

The months ahead promised to be as challenging and exciting as any in the Allansons' lives, ever since Walter had announced his candidacy for a civil judgeship. He had a good reputation, and there was every reason to think he would win in the fall elections. Carolyn truly enjoyed her job as a nurse in a local doctor's office, but both she and Walter came home for lunch every day. They were always together. If the early fire had gone out of their relationship, they were companionable.

Walter came from simple people, uneducated but with native intelligence. His childhood had been hardscrabble, and it was important to him to have money against tomorrow's uncertainties. He was shrewd when it came to real estate. He had bought the house at 1458 Norman Berry Drive in East Point for a good price. The neighborhood was prime then, with Norman Berry Drive a pleasant boulevard divided by a green strip of young trees and shrubbery in its center island. Russell High School, Walter's alma mater, was almost directly across Norman Berry.

The house was built in the forties of dun-colored brick and white siding with peaked dormers. It was a solid house, set on a plateau so high above Norman Berry Drive that a man could get winded just walking up the driveway. Oaks, pines, laurel hedges, and rhododendrons grew thick, shutting out the noise of the street below and separating the Allanson house from neighboring properties.

Carolyn's mother—"Mae Mama" Lawrence—owned the property to the west of them, but you could hardly see her house through the foliage between them. Walter planted a grape arbor out back, and it thrived. He laid down a strip of concrete smack dab in the middle of the backyard so he could turn around and not have to back up the 194 feet to the street. It didn't add much aesthetically to the yard but it was practical. And Walter Allanson, if anything, was a most practical man.

His pragmatic view of life had cost him any relationship with his sister Jean, even though she and her husband lived only a few blocks away. And now his rigid moral views had shut his son out too. Walter detested Pat, and he would far rather lose Tom than bend even a little toward his new wife. Walter didn't need anyone in his life who questioned his authority. Tom had known that since he was a little boy.

A number of people had reason to resent a man like Walter Allanson. Lawyers make enemies, often unaware. Over the years, he had represented the usual assortment of clients who felt they hadn't been given proper attention. But Walter didn't run scared. He had always considered himself fully capable of defending himself. Still, his partner, Al Roberts, his law clerk, and his secretary had noticed that he was jumpy and tense in the last weeks of June 1974—not at all like himself.

✦ ✦ ✦

On Saturday, June 29, 1974, Carolyn and Walter Allanson left the house on Norman Berry Drive a little after nine, driving their 1963 white Ford station wagon. Walter wanted to check on one of his real estate purchases. It was a beautiful morning, with only the edges of the day betraying the heat to come, and they headed northeast of Atlanta toward Lake Lanier in Forsyth County, where Walter had picked up a piece of waterfront property. There were no buildings on it yet, but the land was prime, and neighboring lots already had attractive cabins and year-round homes. He and Tommy had built a good boat dock up there. Then they had had a bad winter in '71 and the dock got so much ice on it, it had sunk itself. Tommy dove and dove and put lines on it and they had hauled it up. With the help of Walter's best friend, Jake Dailey, they had cleaned it off and started all over. Tommy had been there working on the new dock until Walter washed his hands of him over Pat. Now, he would have to finish the last of it himself.

The lake was an hour's drive at most, but Forsyth County might have been a world away from Atlanta: wherever you went you could find huge platters of fried catfish and hush puppies, collard greens, yams, cornbread, biscuits, and barbecue for only a few dollars. It was well known that Forsyth County still banned blacks after sunset. The crude warnings weren't posted anymore, but the sentiment was the same. It was said the Ku Klux Klan was active in the county.

The Allansons' old Ford station wagon, rusting out on the doors, wasn't a suitable vehicle for a hopeful judge-to-be, but it was a good work car. Walter and Carolyn rode with the windows down, smelling hot pine needles and baked red clay. The kudzu was halfway up telephone poles and creeping higher as it choked out weeds and fences and anything else in its path. They crossed the Chattahoochee and the thickets of spindly pine trees grew denser. Cement spillways waited in the dry earth for a deluge to fill their hollows with rain. In June, they were as useless as Christmas tree ornaments. It was too dry even to remember rain.

The atmosphere changed with each mile beyond Atlanta. There were signs advertising sorghum syrup, boiled peanuts, and chewing tobacco. In Cumming, the county seat, old men in overalls talked of other, better days and spat brown streams of that tobacco from the front porches of the aged red brick buildings of Main Street.

Walter slowed at the four-way stop at Hammond Corners, paused, and went straight ahead on Route 306 until it dead-ended on Highway 53. He had driven this route so many times he barely noticed the signposts. He turned onto 53, and they came to the Y where they would veer off to the left toward the lake on Truman Mountain Road.

Walter stubbed out a cigarette in the glass ashtray that perched precariously on the dashboard and glanced over at J. C. Jones's store. It was quaint and jerry-built, but it was a gold mine for J. C.: white-painted concrete blocks, gas pumps out front, and the old signs—PEPSI, ICE, and FISH BAIT. Jones was a shrewd old boy, rotund and cheerful. Walter knew he had bought up a whole mile of land along 53 when it was cheap. He and his pretty wife worked from six in the morning until nearly midnight, selling everything anybody might conceivably need— from fishhooks to thick homemade sandwiches and lemonade. They were always threatening to retire, but hadn't made any move to do it.

Walter thought about stopping and then figured they could come back down the few miles from the lake if they needed anything. He eased the station wagon left and headed up narrow Truman Mountain Road. The oaks and pin oaks and pines were dense here, enough to throw the road into shadow. The sunlight was only a blurry yellow haze as it was swallowed up in the trees. It was so quiet they could hear the whir of tires two hundred feet away as Highway 53 passed by the back of the narrow strip of woods. Walter lit another cigarette and turned to say something to his wife.

The shots came absolutely without warning—from somewhere in the woods up the six-foot bank to their right. There was no question of defending themselves or of evasive driving. Walter and Carolyn Allanson were helpless, caught in their fish-bowl of station wagon windows.

"What!" Carolyn cried out, before her husband pushed her down and gunned the motor.

They were hit, or rather the station wagon was. Once, twice. More. No—*they* were hit. Walter felt a trickle of blood on his face and had the sense that they were both bleeding. The splat of bullets hit the car again and again. The windshield spider-webbed in front of Carolyn, then in front of him, and then the wing window struts bulged and the glass inside exploded.

He kept driving and heard the back window disintegrate.

When it was finally quiet, Walter could hear again the wind in the trees. He looked back and saw no one at all in the woods. With a shaky hand, he helped his wife off the floor and kept on driving. Both of them were cut and dappled with blood.

But they were alive.

The call came in to the Forsyth County Sheriff's Office in Cumming at 11:20, and Sheriff Donald Pirkle and Deputies Jim Avery, Randall Parker, and Richard Satterfield responded to J. C. Jones's store. The station wagon had been hit nine times, and the officers retrieved four bullet fragments from inside the vehicle.

Back up toward the lake, the sheriff and his men located an area that could only be a carefully prepared ambush site. Branches had been cut off a pine tree and arranged as a shield to hide a shooter from the road. There was a beer can on the ground with a half inch of beer, still cool, in the bottom, and six .22-caliber bullet casings. Behind the blind of limbs, the investigators detected a trail through the woods that led back to Highway 53. There were faint tracks in the dirt shoulder of the highway, zigzagging impressions, indicating that a large vehicle had been parked there recently.

Someone had apparently waited quietly in the burgeoning heat of the June morning for this particular vehicle to head up Truman Mountain Road. The space between the severed tree limbs had given the shooter a perfect straight-arrow look down the road toward the Joneses' store. It was a miracle that the Allansons had not been hit by at least one of the bullets. Or maybe the shooter had only meant to scare them.

Whoever it was had certainly done that. Walter Allanson's hand trembled as he lit a cigarette. Yes, he answered Satterfield's question. He did have an idea about who had ambushed them. "My son. I think my son did it. We had trouble before. He stole guns from me a few months ago."

Allanson offered his son's name: "Tommy. Walter Thomas Allanson. He lives in Zebulon, Georgia."

✦   ✦   ✦

Pat and Tom were having dinner that night with the colonel and Margureitte at their Tell Road horse ranch in East Point around 6:30. It was there that they received the message that Nona and Paw had to talk to them at once, and that was how they learned that someone had shot up Tom's parents' station wagon near their Lake Lanier property.

Tom wondered why his life was growing steadily more bizarre and violent. He had no idea who might have wanted to take a bead on his father's car. It might even have been an accident, some damn fool poaching deer. But Pat wasn't all that concerned about the ambush incident. Since Walter Allanson treated her like trash, his misfortunes didn't distress her. He was an evil man, she reminded Tom, and he probably had a lot of enemies. He might even have exposed himself to somebody's wife or daughter—somebody too angry to waste time going through legal channels to punish him.

But Tom—Tom did things by the book. On Monday, July 1, Pat and Tom appeared at the East Point Police Department at 5:15 P.M. Pat, extremely agitated and tearful, did most of the talking. She demanded that a warrant be sworn out for the arrest of Walter O. Allanson, charging him with public indecency and threatening telephone calls. Sergeant Charles Butts informed Pat and Tom that he had no jurisdiction over incidents occurring in Zebulon and directed them to either the Pike County sheriff or the Zebulon Police Department.

Tom stood quietly behind Pat until she completely broke down in tears, and then he stepped forward and told Butts, "My father's running for a judgeship in this county. This kind of man doesn't need to be running for any office." Butts swore later that he had heard Tom say softly that "if this kind of stuff keeps up, I'll kill the bastard."

Very likely, Tom did say that. And now both father and son had threatened each other. But Tom did not yet know that his father had accused *him* of the Lake Lanier shooting. Nor did Walter Allanson know that Pat had accused him of indecent exposure.

On Tuesday, July 2, Margureitte was in her office when the phone rang. She was amazed to hear Walter Allanson's voice. She had not expected him to call her again. Right after her first meeting with him in his office, she was so wary of Allanson that she had gone to the East Point police to try to tell someone he was dangerous—especially to Tom. She had also told the women in her office that she was afraid of Tom's father. Now, here he was, calling her again.

"This is Mr. Allanson."

"Yes, Mr. Allanson."

"Mrs. Radcliffe, what time do you go to lunch?"

She told him that she usually had lunch between twelve and one, depending on the patient load. "I'll be a little late getting out today."

"I want to tell you something, and show you something."

"Well, Mr. Allanson, I'll be glad to talk with you."

"You'll come to my house?"

She agreed to go, but as soon as she hung up, her office staff surrounded her, aghast that she would even consider such a thing. The man was obviously unhinged and she would be putting herself in frightful danger. After all, he had already "shown something" to Pat. "You are *not* going over to that man's house," one fellow worker said vehemently. "If you try to go, I'll have to call Colonel Radcliffe and tell him."

As it turned out, Walter Allanson was quite willing to come to the dentist's office. He drove up in a station wagon whose windshield was crisscrossed with tape. It looked as if it had been through World War II. He motioned to her to look at it, and Margureitte was terrified being so close to such a dangerous man.

Walter told Margureitte that he blamed Tom for the shooting. She quickly replied that she knew for a fact that Tom and Pat had been in Lithonia shoeing horses at the time Allanson gave for the ambush, and that there were witnesses to prove it. "Mr. Allanson, I told you before. Why don't you look for someone else?"

Allanson opened the station wagon door and beckoned her in.

"I was really shaking inside by that time," Margureitte said later. " 'No sir, Mr. Allanson,' I told him. 'It's hot and I'm not going to have much time to talk with you.' . . . And then I said, 'Mr. Allanson, I've met Tom's ex-wife one time, but I've talked to her numerous times. . . . Tell me really. What kind of a person is she? Is she a nervous person? Is there any reason she would want to do you harm? Is there any way she would benefit . . . other than to hurt Tom?"

"Well," Allanson allowed, according to Margureitte, "she's a nervous person and she has a quick temper, but I don't know why she would want to do anything like this."

Margureitte continued to try to help him ferret out the real culprit in the ambush shooting. Fighting to stay calm, she once again suggested that he must have a former client who hated him enough to do these things. And then she brought up the incident at Kentwood the previous Friday, although it was painfully embarrassing for a lady to discuss the exposure of male privates with someone she knew so slightly—much less the alleged exposer himself.

Allanson stared at her as if she had taken leave of her senses. "Mrs. Radcliffe," he sighed. "As a Mason and a gentleman, I swear I did not come out to Pike County on Friday and expose myself to your daughter. I have not *been* in Pike County for some time. . . . Lady, I have high blood pressure and I am under a doctor's care. I take medicine for that, and when you do this it affects your sexual life. I have not had sex for some time. So why in the world would I go out there and expose myself to your daughter? In fact, Mrs. Radcliffe, if I were going to be on display at a flower show, I would have to go as a dried arrangement!"

As Margureitte Radcliffe retold it later, the whole meeting with Tom's father was thoroughly shocking, horrifying, and distasteful to a woman with tender sensitivities. But she was fighting for her child, and her child's marriage. She could scarcely force herself to keep talking to Allanson after his crude revelations about sex, but she did it.

"Then just as I had to go, he turned around to me and said, 'Mrs. Radcliffe, you tell Tommy that I will get him because in my heart I know that no matter what you say, no matter what witnesses he's had, that he is the one that is doing these things.

And I will kill him the first chance that I get. You know what? I think it will be this weekend. I think he'll try to get me. Tell him that he had better be able to duck better than he can shoot, because I'm not afraid to die. Yes, I think the whole thing will be finalized this weekend."

Margureitte returned to her office and informed her fellow workers that she felt Walter Allanson was a sick man, that *he* probably had a tumor, and that he was very, very dangerous.

That was Margureitte's way. If she could not reconcile other people's behavior with her view of the world, she invariably suggested "professional help." Now the only thing "in the whole wide world" she wanted to do was to protect Pat, and she had just spent an hour of "absolute terror" with a person she considered a madman. Perhaps Pat should have waited before marrying into such a family. But even so, Margureitte would fight to the death to protect her child. There wasn't a thing she wouldn't do to see that Pat was happy.

Not one thing.

✦ ✦ ✦

Margureitte reported this latest encounter to Pat and Tom, but despite all the uproar, or maybe because she and Tom needed a diversion so desperately, Pat continued to look forward to an Independence Day parade in which she and Tom were scheduled to ride, in costume, on two of their finest Morgans. She loved pageantry. Tom smiled at how childlike she could be sometimes, how she enjoyed dressing up and pretending.

To please Pat, he had agreed to ride beside her, but by July 3 Tom was fully expecting to die in the Atlanta parade, to be held July 6, the Saturday after the official holiday. He felt in his gut that his father was going to shoot him right off his horse and all of Atlanta was going to see it. It didn't make any kind of sense —especially not with his daddy running for judge—but what else could Tom think? Mrs. Radcliffe said his father wanted him dead, Pat said his father wanted him dead, and Nona and Paw were of the same mind.

Tom was thirty-one years old, and he was deeply, desperately in love with Pat. But after only seven weeks of marriage, what the hell good did it do him? His life was draining away from him because of his father. He was probably going to be the top story on the weekend news, only he wouldn't be around to watch it.

6

July 3, 1974, was a coolish rainy day in Zebulon, hardly propitious for the holiday ahead. On the one hand, things seemed completely normal; Pat measured Tom for alterations to his costume for the parade and tacked together the long skirt and bodice she would wear. She chattered happily about what a great showcase the parade would be for Kentwood Morgan Farm. But on the other hand, nothing was normal. Pat and Tom *had* gone down to Pike County to get a restraining order against his father. But the police and sheriff in Zebulon didn't take them seriously. "Everybody knew him in these parts," Tom said later. "So that went nowhere."

Tom no longer felt safe in leaving Pat alone on the farm. She had him just about convinced to go see his father and have it out. They had to find some way to come to a meeting of the minds. Tom dreaded the prospect. He knew for a certainty his father would try to kill him, but Pat kept urging him to do *some*thing. They couldn't go on the way they were.

Walter Allanson and his friends were edgy too, and had been for months. Jake Dailey had lent Walter his own .32-caliber pistol earlier that spring—just in case there was trouble. At 10:00 on that Wednesday morning, July 3, Jake had driven up the Allansons' driveway with a new battery for one of Walter's boat engines. He wasn't there more than a minute or so when Lee and Mary Dorton—who lived two doors down—hurried over. They hadn't recognized his truck and they knew Walter and Carolyn were at work.

Everybody was jumpy. Dailey and the Dortons grinned nervously as they recognized each other, but they decided to check the house out as long as they were there. Lee Dorton and Jake Dailey noticed that there was a light on in the basement. That was peculiar, and Jake suggested that they walk around the house and check all the doors. They did that, and found them all locked.

Everything seemed as usual.

At Kentwood Farm in Zebulon, the atmosphere was also laced with apprehension. Pat had been ill all during the night of July 2. She told Tom she had exacerbated the injuries to her collarbone trying to saddle a horse. And she had a new torment. "Your father—or if it wasn't him, *someone*—called all night long and just breathed on the phone. Didn't you hear it ringing?" she asked Tom incredulously. "Between that crazy man and my collarbone, I didn't get any sleep."

They had a horse show to go to on Friday and the parade on Saturday, and Tom insisted that Pat see a doctor. She demurred at first—she had to finish her parade costume—but Tom insisted and Pat finally agreed. "I hadn't had any sleep since his father had started threatening our lives," she said later. "Tom said I just couldn't keep going on like this, not with the high blood pressure and all the other problems I had."

Pat couldn't get an appointment with her regular doctor, but Tom said she should go to her orthopedist, Dr. Thompson, anyway. His office was on Cleveland Avenue just off Norman Berry Drive, not more than two blocks from Tom's parents' house, but almost sixty miles from their place in Zebulon. Pat said she would call there.

Tom finished his horseshoeing that morning before they left for East Point, and he made a decision. The way to make peace with his father would be to talk with his mother. But that wouldn't be easy either. He had tried to call her at the doctor's office where she worked and she just got upset with him. He couldn't call her at home because his father was usually home when she was. Tom would have to go to see her before his father got home from work. If he was lucky, he would have perhaps an hour's window of time to try to talk some sense to her.

✦   ✦   ✦

Exactly what happened on Norman Berry Drive on July 3, 1974, would be the subject of conjecture for almost two decades. Certain things were unarguable: Big Carolyn and Walter went, as usual, to their jobs that Wednesday, she in her white nurse's uniform and he in bluish gray striped trousers, a white business shirt, and a dark gray tie. They ate lunch together as always, promptly at noon. Big Carolyn got off work shortly after four, and Walter was supposed to leave his office by six.

The only thing unusual on that day was that Walter had left his office from 2:45 to 3:00 P.M. When he returned, he showed his secretary, Mary McBride, what he had purchased. It was a Marlin .45/70 lever-action rifle with a box of ammunition to go with it—the largest caliber made. He had paid Berryman's Sports Center in East Point $201.15 for the gun. In the space of just a few months, Walter had obtained two weapons—the .32 pistol Jake Dailey had lent him and the new, powerful rifle.

It was an hour's drive or more from Zebulon to East Point and Pat and Tom left Kentwood well before midafternoon, with Tom driving carefully because the rain had brought up the oil slick on the roads; he didn't want to risk any further injury to Pat. Pat said goodbye to Tom at Dr. Thompson's office on Cleveland Avenue about 3:30 P.M. and watched him walk off toward his bank, where he had some business.

At about the same time, Horace Smith, a fire fighter with the East Point Fire Department, was driving one of the department's fire rigs on a test run down Norman Berry Drive. He noticed the tall man striding along the south side of the street, a man with long light brown hair who wore Levi's and cowboy boots. Suddenly, Smith recognized the man; he was an old friend.

Smith yelled, "Hey, Tom!"

But the tall man didn't answer.

✦ ✦ ✦

A second unusual event took place that afternoon, varying Walter Allanson's heretofore precise schedule once more. First he had bought the rifle, and then he left for home early. His staff recalled that he had received a call at his office sometime around 5:30 from a woman who didn't give her name. She had been brusque. "You'd better tell Mr. Allanson to get home as fast as he can," she said. "His son is headed over there to cause trouble."

Allanson ran to his car and drove home.

Big Carolyn was already home with her grandchildren, Russ and Sherry, whom she had picked up at the day-care center. She carried in a case of Cokes she had bought for the next day's picnic—and a blowup plastic blue dinosaur for the kids' wading pool—and set them down on the dining room table. When Walter walked in, he unwrapped the new rifle and left the box it came in beside the Cokes.

"Daddy," Big Carolyn told him, "it's the oddest thing. It wasn't lightning at all today, but the lights won't go on, and the television's dead."

Walter ran down the basement steps and found that someone had pulled the main switch. He pushed the circuit breaker over and back and all the lights came on and the refrigerator started to hum.

Within minutes, Little Carolyn—or as Walter called her, Junior—arrived. Suspecting that somebody had been in the basement, Big Carolyn stayed upstairs in the kitchen with the youngsters while Walter and Junior searched the house inside and out. They checked all the windows and doors to be sure they were locked, and looked to see if anything was missing.

That was when they discovered that the phone line had been cut.

Walter said he also missed two items: an old leather suitcase and an Excel 20-gauge shotgun he had had for years. He went to Lee and Mary Dorton's house, two doors down, and called the East Point police. The Dortons came back to his house with him, and while they were waiting for the police, he showed them where the telephone line had been neatly sliced in two.

According to the Dortons, Walter didn't seem anxious or even very concerned. He was more matter-of-fact about the situation. After all, it was daylight, early on a summer's evening. And, Lord knows, it wasn't as if he hadn't been expecting trouble.

Sergeant C. T. Callahan of the East Point police pulled up the long driveway on Norman Berry at one minute after seven and Walter Allanson met him outside. He wanted to report a burglary. "I can't tell where he got in," he said, "but he took a suitcase and my twenty-gauge Excel shotgun—"

"He?"

"My son, Walter Thomas Allanson."

Callahan moved toward the house and said he would check it out, but Allanson blocked his path. "No need. I did it myself. I've checked it once, and there's no one there."

Despite Callahan's concern about a citizen doing the job *he* was trained for, Allanson was adamant. He had once served as a reserve police officer himself; he knew what to do. There was no need for the police to bother coming inside. He only wanted official confirmation that the phone line had been cut, and he led Callahan around to the east side of the house and pointed out the dangling wire. It had obviously been cut deliberately; whoever did it would have had to wade through thick rhododendron bushes to get to it.

Allanson went into the house and returned with the .45 rifle to show Callahan. "I got this rifle here," he said. "I know who it is, and I'm going to take care of it myself."

"Don't do anything drastic," Callahan warned. "Call us first."

Shaking his head, Callahan backed down the drive. You never could tell about family beefs. But you didn't argue with Walter O'Neal Allanson; he was an outstanding citizen in East Point. Probably half of the East Point police force knew him. Callahan couldn't force police protection on him if he didn't want it.

Walter walked back in the house and put the new .45 in its box on the dining room table. Then, leaving Big Carolyn and the kids at the house, Little Carolyn drove him over to her nearby apartment to be sure that no one was waiting inside to attack her when she came home, and to see if anything had been stolen. The place was just as she had left it that morning on her way to work.

They drove back to Norman Berry Drive. On the way, Little

Carolyn spotted a blue jeep with a Pike County tag on it in front of them and said, "Daddy, that's Pat!"

"Well, just follow her, Junior, and see where she goes."

They followed the jeep as it turned onto Norman Berry Drive and then into the driveway right next door to the Allansons'. That was Big Carolyn's mother's house. Mae Mama Lawrence was getting on in years, and they certainly didn't want her upset. The jeep sat there for a moment, but as Walter leaped out of his car and started toward it, Pat quickly backed down Mae Mama's driveway and disappeared down the street.

"You go look for her!" Walter called to Little Carolyn. She did as he said and drove slowly around adjacent streets, but the blue jeep had vanished. When she came back, Walter instructed her to stay in the front yard and watch to see if Pat came back again. She walked to the crest of the sloping lawn and scanned both sides of the boulevard for Pat.

But then Sherry started crying and Little Carolyn hurried into the kitchen to see what was wrong. Later when she tried to reconstruct what came next, Tom's ex-wife saw the scene in agonizing slow motion. Big Carolyn had turned toward Mary Dorton, who was standing nervously in the dining room. "Well, where's Walter?" she asked.

"He went to the basement," Mary answered.

"Whatever for?"

Mary shrugged. "I don't know."

Although he had searched the basement before, "Daddy" Allanson, carrying his borrowed pistol, had clomped downstairs again. The three women huddled together with the crying children and thought they heard another man's voice—or maybe it was just Walter—muttering to himself in the basement.

Suddenly, Carolyn heard her father-in-law yell up the stairs, "Junior! Get the kids out of the house! I have him cornered in the cubbyhole!"

Both Carolyns pushed the children toward Mary Dorton, who clutched them in her arms and ran toward her own house.

Walter called up the stairs once more. "Mother! Bring me that new gun!" Still in slow motion—or so it seemed in retrospect— Big Carolyn took the .45-caliber rifle from the box on the dining room table and headed toward the basement. Little Carolyn begged her not to go downstairs.

✦ ✦ ✦

At 8:04 P.M.—almost exactly an hour after he had first responded to a call from the Allanson residence—Sergeant Callahan's radio crackled and he heard a familiar address. Too familiar. This time, the complainant was a neighbor: Mary Dorton.

"Car 26—Evening: Signal 6—Holding: 1458 Norman Berry Drive."

"I'll take it, " Callahan responded. "I was just there an hour ago."

To the East Point police, "Signal 6" meant there was a burglar in the house, and "Holding" meant that a citizen was detaining the suspect by physically holding on to him. It was definitely an emergency designation, intended for the B (burglary) car on the evening watch. Other cars moved in to back that unit up.

Callahan arrived in two or three minutes—his was the first car on the scene. As he pulled up the driveway and around to the rear of the Allansons' house, a young woman came running toward him, her eyes wide open, screaming. Callahan couldn't make any sense out of what she was saying; she was a hair away from complete hysteria.

He called for backup, and for detectives. Lieutenant Gus Thornhill, Jr., a nine-year veteran with East Point, was supervising the evening watch. He headed for the scene, right behind the patrol units that had been dispatched.

Callahan edged cautiously around the house. There were two cars parked out in back, a 1963 Ford station wagon with several shattered windows, and a 1964 Chevrolet sedan. Most of the windows of the house were six or eight feet above ground, but in the rear there were several ground-level windows in the basement. The cellar door was ajar, but Callahan avoided that entry until he had some backup. Instead, he crouched down and shielded his eyes as he peered into one of the basement windows.

He gasped involuntarily at what he saw. A middle-aged woman dressed in some kind of white uniform sat upright near the bottom of the steps descending into the middle of the basement. There was a great splotch of blood across her breasts, and she didn't move at all.

Had she been there all along? Callahan wondered. No, she

couldn't have been—not unless Walter Allanson had shot her and that was why he hadn't allowed him to search the house on the prior call. The first rule of crime scene investigation was "Don't assume *anything*."

Callahan had no more time to ponder what might have happened. There was a cacophony of sirens approaching, and East Point police units raced up the driveway and parked along Norman Berry Drive. Officers surrounded the house. They had no idea who might be inside, alive or dead. They knew only that there was a burglar in the house and a dead woman was sitting on the basement steps. Officers peering in the basement windows could make out sprays and droplets of blood on many walls and items in the cellar. There was blood everywhere. Whatever had happened in this house, it had been horrific.

✦ ✦ ✦

Patrol Officer Cecil McBurnett, Jr., was working a "wreck car" (accident investigation) that evening and heard the Signal 6 go out on the burglary on Norman Berry. He was only three blocks away, so he responded to give backup to Callahan. He turned off Martin and headed east on Norman Berry. He was checking house numbers when he saw a man leap from the lawn near Mae Mama Lawrence's house and hit the sidewalk running. The man turned to look at the patrol car, not once but several times, and McBurnett saw him full-faced.

McBurnett did not yet have a description of the burglary suspect, but a running man near a crime scene couldn't be ignored. He had just spun his car around and was heading back to apprehend the man when he heard a "Help the officer" call on the radio: "I've got a woman shot. The perpetrator is in the basement holding a hostage."

McBurnett's natural response was to go to the aid of his fellow officer, so he left off his pursuit of the running man and turned into the Allansons' driveway just behind another patrol unit. Still, the image of that man stayed in his mind. He was wearing Levi's, boots, and a green and brown striped shirt. McBurnett had no fix on the man's size; he had been running hunched over. He could have been five feet ten inches tall—or six feet six.

When McBurnett arrived at the Allansons' house, he found

incredible chaos. A young woman was screaming and out of control; more and more police and EMTs were arriving, with their blue and red whirling bubble lights giving the night a psychedelic glow; and the falling rain made it seem like anything but the eve of the Fourth of July in the suburbs of Atlanta.

Sergeant William Vance and Detective J. E. Lambert noted gouge marks on the open basement door; it had probably been jimmied. They also saw a light on at the top of the steps, the bulb eerily spotlighting the body of the dead woman. The rest of the basement was bathed in shadows of black and gray. Lambert peered toward the heating and air-conditioning unit and thought he saw an arm protruding from behind it. Spooked, he fired his pistol in that direction.

The round hit something metal and clanged loudly, but there was no human movement. The arm had been only a shadow.

Captain J. D. Lynn ordered a canister of tear gas to be thrown into the basement, and all the doors were sealed. If there had been a burglar in the house on Callahan's first visit an hour before, he might very well still be inside. The men surrounding the house fully believed they had a hostage situation.

They waited, officers poised at each of three exterior doors of the house and at all the windows. Five minutes. Ten minutes. No one bolted from the house, vomiting and blinded by the gas. After fifteen minutes, Lieutenant Thornhill, Detective Lambert, and Sergeant Vance donned oxygen masks provided by the East Point Fire Department and edged into the basement.

It was so hard to see; tears ran down their faces despite their masks and the fans the fire fighters had set up to air out the cellar. They stumbled over lumber and tools, a half-finished boat, a surfboard, a miniature railroad track mounted on a sheet of plywood. It was like anyone's cellar, a repository for things to be used later, or things once used and no longer needed.

They could make out the white-clad body sitting on the basement steps, and, just opposite, behind the heating system, there was the brick base of a fireplace. It had a large rectangular hole in it—three feet high by about a foot and a half wide—easily large enough for a man to hide in. They had no idea how far back it went.

Outside the hole they found a bloodstained flashlight, turned off, and a .32-caliber pistol wedged between a surfboard and the plywood that held the electric train. Their own flashlights picked up a profusion of still-liquid puddles and droplets of blood on the floor around the hole in the base of the fireplace.

Back toward the stairs they located a .45/70 rifle and a crowbar near a stack of interior doors. Their tear-gassed eyes burned and blurred, but behind the doors they discerned what looked like a leg clad in blue pants.

They moved closer with their guns drawn.

7

Captain Lynn ordered the uniformed division to fan out on foot to check the neighborhood for a suspect. At that point, they knew only that an older woman was dead. The young woman on the scene was too hysterical to be of much help, although they knew now that she was Carolyn Allanson, the ex-daughter-in-law of Walter Allanson. She repeated over and over that someone had been in the basement and Daddy Allanson had gone down to "get him." She continued to babble about "Daddy" and "Mother." Daddy had had someone "caught in the hole" and she had begged Mother Allanson not to go down in the cellar. Almost as an aside, the distraught woman said that she had seen "Tom's new wife" driving around the block in her blue jeep. Beyond that, she was no help at all. When they tried to probe deeper, she lost control again. They couldn't count on much of anything the woman said in her current state.

It was no secret to the East Point police that Walter Allanson and his son, Tom, had been feuding. They had heard rumors about an ambush up at Lake Lanier and Tom and Pat had been in to the police station only a few days before, trying to charge his father with indecent exposure. If Pat Allanson *was* in the neighborhood, the East Point police wanted to find her as quickly as possible. They had so little to go on as Captain Lynn, Sergeant R. W. Jones, and Sergeant Callahan drove their police cruisers in ever-widening circles around Norman Berry Drive, looking for anything that seemed unusual, for someone running, and for either Tom Allanson's blue pickup truck or the blue jeep Pat had been seen driving.

The King Professional Building occupied the triangle of land just between Bayard Street and the point where Norman Berry Drive bisected Cleveland Avenue about three-tenths of a mile from the Allanson house. It was new construction, a many-storied concrete structure whose white fretwork panels made it resemble an out-of-place mosque. The wide cement parking apron was almost empty of cars at 8:20 on a rainy night, but the East Point officers spotted the blue jeep they were looking for parked there.

They suspected this was the vehicle Carolyn Allanson said she had seen; there was already a statewide want out on it—and on its alleged driver, Patricia Taylor Allanson. Callahan noted the license plate number, CY 242, a 1974 Georgia-issued plate. A quick radio check with "Wants and Warrants" elicited the information that the plate had been issued for a new jeep, purchased three months before in Marietta, Georgia, and that it indeed was registered to Patricia R. Taylor of the Kentwood Morgan Farm in Zebulon.

In the rapidly dimming light, the three policemen could make out the form of a woman sitting in the jeep. There was no way of knowing if she was alone, or if someone was crouching down beside her or behind her.

They leaped from their police unit and approached the jeep from behind with guns drawn. The woman in the vehicle didn't move at all—not even to turn her head to glance at them.

"Get out of the jeep!" Callahan shouted. "Get out of the jeep with your hands up!"

For a moment there was no movement in the little blue ragtop jeep, and then a pretty, slender woman wearing a miniskirt and a halter top poked one bare leg out, slid to the ground, and turned to stare back at them. She held up one arm and gestured that she could not raise the other because it was injured.

"Anyone else in there?" Callahan called.

She shook her head.

"You sure?"

"I'm all alone."

Callahan and Jones moved to either side of the woman they presumed to be Pat Allanson and led her into the police car. She didn't resist, but she winced as if her shoulder hurt her.

"What is going on?" she asked. "What has *happened?* Where is Tom?"

"Are you Mrs. Allanson?"

"Yes."

"Well, he shot his mother."

Pat sagged a bit, and then said forcefully, "No, he couldn't have shot his mother. Not *Tom. Not my Tom!*"

"Well, his ex-wife said he did."

Pat didn't care about what Tom's ex-wife said. She insisted that if anybody did any shooting, it wouldn't have been Tom.

At this point, they couldn't argue with her. The only thing they could be sure of was that the elder Carolyn Allanson was dead. For all they knew at this point, Tom might be dead too and, as improbable as it seemed, they might be looking for *Walter* Allanson. The basement up the street had been so obscured by walls, doors, and junk that they couldn't be sure of anything, and they hadn't yet been informed about what the investigators back at the house might have found.

None of the police units circling the area had made any definite sightings of Tom. His new wife seemed to be in shock. All she knew was that she had been waiting for him for hours. She was worried sick—so much so that she had called her parents, Colonel and Mrs. Clifford Radcliffe, to come and be with her. She would, of course, be glad to talk with the officers about anything they wished—if only she could wait for her mother and daddy to get there.

She appeared panicked that the officers would remove her from the parking lot before her mother and father arrived. "Please don't take me away. They're on their way, and they won't know where to find me if you take me away from here."

She said she had no idea where her husband might be at the moment. He had been wearing a brown shirt, blue jeans, and cowboy boots when she last saw him.

"How tall is your husband, ma'am?" Lynn asked.

"Tall. Real tall—six foot three or better. He's a very large man—but very gentle. I believe he weighs over two hundred pounds."

Captain Lynn got on the radio and broadcast a BOLO (be on the lookout for) on Tom Allanson, giving the additional descriptive information on his appearance. The details fit the running man that Officer Cecil McBurnett had observed just after hearing the report of "Burglar in the house" at 1458 Norman Berry Drive. The man had been running toward the intersection of Cleveland and Norman Berry, and, incidentally, the King Building.

Of course, that man had been hunched over and no one knew how tall he was. Had it been Walter? Or Tom? There was no way Lynn could be sure. Tom had last been seen in blue Levi's and Callahan had said Walter was wearing blue trousers when he talked to him earlier.

Lynn, Jones, and Callahan had far too much to do to wait for Pat Allanson's parents. They took Pat with them as they drove slowly around the neighborhood. They stopped now and again to check garages where a shooter might be hiding.

Pat heard the radio chatter constantly and tried to understand the police codes. They had told her only that Tom's mother was dead. Shot. They hadn't said anything about Tom's father. Or Tom. She bit her lip and stared nervously out the squad car's window.

They turned from Cleveland onto Stewart Avenue and drove right past the very spot—Nalley's Chevrolet—where Pat's brother, Kent, had died eight years earlier. Shot too. Pat looked away, her thoughts known only to herself.

After a while the police took Pat back to the King Building, where the colonel and her mother were waiting for her. Her mother took her hand, and the colonel demanded to know just what was going on and why his daughter was being detained.

The police retrieved Pat's pocketbook and sewing things from the jeep, and they instructed the Radcliffes to follow them to the East Point Police Department. And there they waited, the three of them. The police were too busy even to talk to them.

Pat thought about sewing on her Fourth of July parade costume—just to keep her panic down—but there didn't seem much point. Probably she and Tom wouldn't be riding in the parade Saturday after all. She didn't even know if Tom was alive.

The blue jeep was towed into the city garage. The detectives saw a container of take-out fried chicken in the front seat, and noted it along with their other observations.

✦ ✦ ✦

Back at 1458 Norman Berry Drive, East Point officers had completed their search of the basement. Milford Carolyn Allanson still sat on the basement steps, shot through the heart. They had found another body there too. Walter Allanson lay on the floor parallel to the steps; his body had been hidden by the stack of doors. His new rifle was on the floor four feet from his body, and a few feet from the body of his wife. There was no way of telling which of them had fired the rifle, or if, indeed, either had. One round had been fired from it, and it was partially cocked with a live round half into the chamber.

Walter Allanson had obvious gunshot wounds in his face, neck, and torso. In all likelihood, it was his blood that had left trails of gore over half the basement—particularly near the hole in the base of the fireplace and then pooled beneath him as he bled out.

After Detective Marlin Humphrey, Jr., took photographs, Lambert, Vance, and Patrolman Bob Matthews removed the bodies of Walter and Carolyn Allanson, carrying the victims up the steps to be laid out on the wet grass of their side yard for more police photographs and to await transportation to South Fulton Hospital. They could not be declared legally dead without a physician; the bodies would then await postmortem examination.

Bob Matthews, who worked as an identification officer, bagged the .45/70 carbine rifle and the .32 pistol, which had six empty chambers. The investigators could not hope to do a thorough crime scene investigation until daylight, which was still hours away. Lieutenant Thornhill ordered the property cordoned off and stationed patrolmen to guard it until morning. They now knew what had happened. It would take them a long, long time before they knew how and why.

✦ ✦ ✦

Jean Boggs, Walter Allanson's sister, hadn't felt well all day. She was standing at her stove fixing something to eat at 8:30 on the night of July 3 when a neighbor came to the back door. "I don't want to frighten you, but I think something's wrong at your brother's house. Maybe you'd better call him. There are ambulances and police cars and everything up there."

Alarmed, Jean heard the phone at Walter's house ring six, ten, twelve times with no answer. She didn't know, of course, that the phone line was severed and the rings she heard were silent in her brother's house. When she called Mae Mama's house, a policeman answered and suggested that she had better go on down to her brother's house. He wouldn't tell her anything else, nor would the desk sergeant at the East Point police station. That scared her. Her husband wasn't home, but her neighbor said he would drive her over to Walter and Carolyn's place.

"When we got up there," Jean said later, "I remember seeing oodles and oodles of people going up and down the bank where my brother lived and up and down the driveway—many strangers. I also remember seeing a television station there . . . Channel Five."

Jean walked up to a policeman who was holding people back with his extended arms. When she told him who she was, he summoned Captain Lynn, who listened quietly to her concerns.

"Ma'am, all I can tell you is that he [Walter] has been shot."

"*Shot?* . . . What about Carolyn—Carolyn, Walter's wife?"

"She has been shot too." Jean Boggs's knees buckled as she heard Lynn say, "They have been carried to South Fulton Hospital and I would recommend that you go there."

Jean didn't get much more information at the hospital, which was only two blocks away. The receptionist summoned a nurse and Jean begged, "Please tell me something. Just not knowing is killing me."

The nurse turned and went down a corridor, and another nurse appeared.

"Could I *see* my brother and sister-in-law?"

"No. Two bodies are just arriving back there and they have not been identified, and that is all I can tell you. You'll have to wait for a detective to get here." Both nurses seemed upset, and they evaded all Jean's desperate pleas for information.

It was a nightmare. Jean demanded to see Lieutenant Thornhill, who she had been told was in charge. She knew Gus Thornhill. Surely he would be straight with her. *She* would identify her brother and sister-in-law. Who else was there? Her parents were too old to go through this, and she didn't even know where her nephew Tommy lived now.

Thornhill hurried over, and when Jean saw him he was holding Carolyn Allanson's driver's license in his hand. Her heart turned over. "Are Walter and Carolyn back there dead?" she breathed.

"Yes."

"Can I see them?"

"Mrs. Boggs." Thornhill looked away from her and took a deep breath. "I have known you a long time, and I feel like a friend of yours. I'm going to ask you out of friendship not to go and look."

"What happened?"

"Tom killed them. . . ."

No. *NO!* Tommy wouldn't do that. It didn't make any sense to Jean. Vaguely, she was aware of a television set in the background. The shootings were already on the news. Everyone was looking for her nephew, Tommy, who was believed to be wounded. All Jean could think was, My Lord, I will have three to bury instead of two.

And then Jean realized that she had to get to her parents and tell them before they turned on the television. It would kill Paw and Nona to hear it like that. Gus Thornhill said he would drive her to the elder Allansons'.

As Thornhill and Jean Boggs left the hospital, they passed an ambulance parked at the ER doors. One of the two back doors was open and Jean saw a body covered by a bloodied sheet. One bare foot stuck out. Transfixed with horror, she was drawn toward the ambulance. It took both Thornhill and her neighbor to pull her away. "Gus, I want the truth," Jean said. "Is that Walter? Is that my brother?"

"Yes, ma'am, but I must still ask you not to look."

When Jean and Gus Thornhill reached the elder Allansons' place on Washington Road, she asked her father to sit down, but he stood, resolute, braced, an old man who had known tragedy before and survived it.

"Paw," Jean said softly. "Walter and Carolyn have been killed

—I don't know any way to break this to you any gentler—and they're looking for Tommy, Paw."

Paw's first words were hollow. "Well, I have been expecting something like this."

When they told Nona, she began to scream and scream. Her physician, Dr. Lanier Jones, came over to give her a shot so she could sleep.

Paw was worried sick about what might have happened to "the boy." He called down to Kentwood and the phone rang twenty times, an empty sound in an empty house. He would keep trying until he got Tommy on the line. When Jean finally got home, she realized that she was still clutching an envelope they had given her at the hospital. She stared at it blankly, wondering what it could be. "I dumped the contents of the package I had into my hand," she later recalled, "and it was my sister-in-law's rings and they were just coated with blood, and with that I said, 'Oh my God, I just can't stand any more!' "

8

Gus Thornhill called Detective George Zellner at home at 9:30 P.M. on the night of July 3 and asked him to come in to the station to interview two subjects: Carolyn Allanson the younger and Patricia Taylor Allanson. When Zellner arrived at East Point police headquarters, he was given a rundown on what was known so far about the double murder—which wasn't much. Zellner had been with the East Point department for two and a half years, and he had been a detective for only a year. He was a thin—but muscled—young man.

It was ten minutes to eleven before Zellner could turn his attention to Patricia Allanson, who was waiting nervously on one of the station's long oak benches. He saw a very attractive woman with startling green eyes. She wasn't crying; she looked exhausted and apprehensive. The older couple with her were being very solicitous.

Zellner explained to Pat that under the *Miranda* decision he had to read her her rights as she was—at least nominally—a suspect and/or a material witness in the shooting deaths of her husband's parents. Pat signed the waiver with only a trace of concern.

With Detective Lambert standing by as a witness, Zellner began to interview Pat. "Mrs. Allanson, I wonder if you would start with this afternoon?" he asked. "What happened leading up to your husband's disappearance?"

Pat spoke rapidly and breathlessly; she had waited so long to talk to someone. Zellner had only to ask a short question here and there to keep the flow of her thoughts channeled into some sort of order.

She began with her own numerous physical problems, her sleep deprivation, and Tom's absolute insistence that she see a doctor. "We finished shoeing horses in the morning. . . . Then Tom brought me in and took me to Dr. Thompson's office like he always does, 'cause I can't drive without it hurting me. . . . He walked up to the door with me like always. . . . It must have been three-thirty—something like that. I got through at the doctor's and Tom still wasn't in the waiting room, so I went outside and the jeep was there. . . . When he left me, he walked in the opposite direction toward the C&S Bank. I thought he was going up there to talk to them about a loan he has there. He was trying to get an extension on it because he had been having to pay so much alimony and so much court costs and all and his father had made him lose a couple of jobs he had, and he had been begging and pleading with his father to leave us alone. His father would call and make threats and his father came out to our house last Friday when I was cutting grass . . . and *exposed himself!* . . . Then he [Walter] called and told my mother to tell Tom that he was going to kill him. . . . Tom had said several times he was going to see him, and I said, 'No, just leave him alone. . . .' "

Pat shifted gears suddenly. "I waited and waited for Tom and he didn't come, and he has *never* left me like that."

"What time did you come out of the doctor's office?"

"They took me so soon . . . they weren't very busy today. I went in and he took the X ray of my shoulder. I don't think I was in the doctor's office over an hour at the very most. . . . I went outside and Tom wasn't in the jeep . . . and I had the skirt for the costume and I started working on it. I kept looking at my watch and I went back in the office and asked if I could use the phone. I was going to call over to my daughter's. . . . It wasn't like him at all and I was beginning to get worried about him because of the threats his father had made to him. The first thing that entered my mind was that just maybe . . . his mother and father had driven by and maybe he was talking to them, or maybe he had gone to talk to them. . . . I waited and waited and waited. Then I really started getting nervous. . . . It was really getting late. . . . It must have been six because all those cars from across the street in the professional buildings—everybody was coming out of there. I was trying to figure where there was a telephone. . . . The only telephone I knew of was in the King Professional Building. I got in the jeep and drove there. . . . Tom knew I couldn't drive that thing any great distance without it hurting me. So I tried to call his mother's office and there was no answer—"

"Where does she work?"

"At Dr. Tucker's office. I looked that number up. I had to go into that chicken place and get some change. . . . I was so nervous . . . I didn't know whether he got run over by a car or something! I started thinking, Now just stop and think. I called the hospital first to see if there had been anybody hit by a car or anything. I knew he had his wallet in his pocket. . . . He had his jeans on."

"Were there any guns with him or anything?" Zellner asked.

"He didn't have any guns with him. . . . Tom couldn't kill anybody."

Pat explained that Tom's parents and maternal grandmother lived very close to her doctor's office. "Tom . . . told me he was going to talk to them one more time: 'I am going to beg and plead with them,' [he said]. I said, 'Don't beg and plead with your father. Just leave him alone. Maybe if we just leave them alone, they will leave us alone.' All we were trying to do was just start over again."

Pat said she had called everyone she could think of—Tom's parents' house, his mother's office—but she didn't know Mae Mama's number, so she had gotten in the jeep and driven around looking for Tom, becoming more and more concerned. She called her own house in Zebulon, although Tom would scarcely have had time to travel all the way to Pike County. She even called Liz Price and told her Tom was missing. Pat said she had finally called her mother and father to come and help her.

Zellner noted that Pat Allanson was highly dramatic as she described her terror.

"I sat there and started working on the skirt . . . out in the open lot. I didn't want to get too close to the building. I knew it would get dark up there, and I didn't know anything about who might be hanging around up there."

"You never did actually go to his mother and father's house?"

"No. I drove into his grandmother's drive. . . . I was going to try to talk to her but I chickened out at the last minute. . . . I thought, No, this is stupid. They won't talk to me anyway. They will probably just shoot me because they have threatened to kill us both."

The picture Pat painted was of two young people in love, besieged by wicked in-laws and a vindictive former wife. Zellner heard at least a half-dozen times about the "excessive" alimony, the lecherous exposing father-in-law, the threats and the strange calls in the middle of the night. It sounded as if she had been living in hell. She appeared to be a helpless, ill, and injured woman who had spent hours gripped by anxiety when her husband failed to meet her at her doctor's office.

"Do you have any idea where he might have gone?" Zellner asked about Tom.

"I don't know unless he has gone home. But how *could* he go home. I don't know how—"

"Where are you-all living now?"

"We have a farm in Zebulon. I bought a farm down there. When Tom and I were married, we moved out there. . . . Everybody knows it by 'the Pat Allanson farm.' I have had a Morgan farm for over fifteen years in Georgia and I am known for my horses. I moved down there to get away from up here— for us to start again."

"Is anybody at home now?"

"No. In fact, the farm is unlocked. Everything is wide open because we expected to come right on back. We have horses that haven't been fed, cows—or anything."

"Did you say you don't think Tom would be capable of anything like that?" he asked, meaning murder.

"Listen to me," Pat said fervently. "The only way Tom could

hurt anybody is if they tried to hurt him first. Tom couldn't go in there and do something to somebody just out of the clear blue sky. No way. Not Tom."

"Even if all this back pressure had built up on him?"

Pat shook her head impatiently. The police were wasting time by not questioning Tom's ex-wife Carolyn Allanson further.

"Tom wouldn't have gone off and left me there unless it was vitally important or unless he was *forced* to go . . . or they did something to him. I don't know. But if he went back to their house with them, I'll guarantee Carolyn would not have wanted them to talk. . . . If they listened to Tom, then they would have found out that she parties and that she leaves those children— and all kinds of things that she didn't want them to know. . . . Tom didn't shoot anybody unless somebody tried to hurt him first, and I still don't believe he even shot anybody then." But she said she would not put.it past Carolyn to use a gun. She has shot at Tom before—when they were living together. . . . I still remember him being late to shoe horses at my place because of that. . . . But if he was caught in the middle of it—if everything has tried to be pinned on him—"

Pat drew herself up as if she were about to make a most important pronouncement. "If he is running, he is running because he is scared because *somebody* is going to try to put it on him."

"Would you have any idea where we might find him?"

"Where would a man go with no money—if he even has a dollar? He would listen to me, but I don't know where to look for him. Do you think I don't *want* to find him?"

"If you should hear from him, be sure and let us know."

"Listen," Pat said earnestly. "Is there any way? I don't know if he is near a radio or television. Isn't there any way? If I could just tell him to come in!"

"We'll see what we can work out," Zellner said. "If we can do it." Pat Allanson was eager to go on television to give a dramatic plea to her fugitive husband—if that was what it would take to get him back. "If they haven't killed him," she said bitterly, and Zellner wasn't sure whether she was referring to his parents or the police.

"No," Zellner assured her. "Nothing like that—yet. But it could come to that if we don't get him."

Pat, supported tenderly by the Radcliffes, was allowed to leave the East Point police station after Colonel Radcliffe posted a thousand-dollar bond. She would be staying with her parents at their Tell Road stables until Tom was found.

Zellner interviewed Carolyn Allanson next and failed to make much sense out of her story. She was still in shock. She kept repeating that Daddy Allanson had been searching for a burglar in the house, that he had gone down to the cellar and called to Mother Allanson to bring down his new rifle. Through tears, Carolyn told Zellner that Daddy had saved her life and her babies' lives by ordering them out of the house. She did not mention a shooter—or shooters—by name. Zellner decided to talk with her again when she had regained a modicum of control.

9

Chief Deputy Billy Riggins of the Pike County Sheriff's Office was at home late in the evening of July 3, 1974. Five days before, he had shown a panicky Pat Allanson how to load a gun to protect herself from further sexual advances from her father-in-law. Her complaint was certainly peculiar, but it hadn't seemed to be a major incident, and Riggins hadn't expected to hear from the Kentwood Morgan Farm again soon, although the sheriff's office had received an inordinate number of calls from the Allansons in the short time they had occupied the property. Riggins had half a suspicion that the lady was one of those nervous types. For all he knew, she'd seen a stalk of corn waving in the wind and imagined an ear of corn right into a man's pecker.

But then it had been the very next day, just four days ago, when Riggins went out to Kentwood again at the request of the Forsyth County Sheriff's Office. Walter O'Neal Allanson, the alleged exposer, and his wife had been ambushed near Lake Lanier in that county. Riggins had checked out the Allanson farm on June 29 and reported back that no one was home.

The new residents were proving to be anything but boring. Nevertheless, Riggins was shocked on this rainy Wednesday night when he got a call forwarded by the Pike County dispatch center. The East Point police wanted him to send deputies out to Kentwood Farm and see if there was any activity there. Most particularly, they asked him to be on the lookout for Walter Thomas Allanson, the owner, who was being sought for questioning in the murder of his parents.

Riggins sent deputies out to sit on the place, and they waited in the drizzling rain. They reported back that the house and barn were apparently empty, and that there were no vehicles on the premises. Riggins asked them to call him back the minute they caught sight of Tom Allanson.

Sometime after 2:30 A.M., Riggins's phone rang. Deputies had just seen Tom walking into his house. Riggins called the GBI (Georgia Bureau of Investigation), the sheriff's office in Spalding County—which adjoined Pike County—and the Griffin Police Department and asked for assistance in apprehending Allanson. Tom had always seemed like a real pleasant fellow, but he was huge and, if the East Point police had their suspicions right, had just blown his mother and father away. Riggins was not about to go in with his tiny squad of men to arrest Allanson. Next, Paw Allanson called Riggins to say Tom was home.

Riggins dialed the Allansons' number and was more than a little surprised when Tom himself answered the phone. Tom sounded exhausted—but quite rational.

"You know we're good friends, Tom," Riggins began. "I got a warrant here for your arrest, and your granddaddy has called us and said you were home. I don't want any problems or anything."

"That's okay," Tom said. "It was me who told Paw to call. I won't cause you no problems."

And he didn't. Tom Allanson walked out the front door of his house at 3:00 A.M. and was arrested for murder.

Riggins read Tom his rights under *Miranda* and advised him that there were two warrants charging him with the murder of his parents. He studied Tom Allanson's face for a reaction. He saw no tears. Nor did he see surprise. The man before him seemed mostly very, very tired—and quite possibly in a state of shock.

Riggins didn't question Tom. Rather, he held him in the Pike

County jail for the hour or so it took for Detective George Zellner and Sergeants C. T. Callahan and Bill Vance to arrive to transport the prisoner back to Atlanta. Outside, the gray rain drummed against the courthouse in Zebulon and the wind scattered scarlet petals from the geraniums in the stone urns.

It was just before dawn in Zebulon when the East Point officers arrived. "You've already been advised of your rights, but we have to do it again," Zellner explained to Tom. "We've got two warrants here charging you with the murder of your mother and your father—"

"And that's about as ridiculous as it can be," Tom answered, his voice flat with fatigue. He turned around willingly and waited while the East Point investigators looked for a pair of handcuffs big enough to circle his massive wrists.

They drove back to East Point in a deluge. It was officially the Fourth of July now. The tape of the East Point investigators' conversation with their suspect was blurred by the loud drum of rain on the police unit's roof and the steady *swish-swish-swish* of windshield wipers.

"What happened this afternoon?" Zellner asked.

Tom explained that he and his bride had had a "big disagreement" two nights before—July 2—and that they had continued their "fussing" during their trip to her doctor's appointment. "I finally just told her I was gonna leave, give her the money, the house, and everything else—I wasn't any good for her—I wasn't doing anything but hurting her—and I just left and started for home."

Tom estimated he had left Pat about 5:00 P.M. the evening before and walked and hitchhiked his way back to Zebulon. "But I mostly walked."

Tom told Zellner that he had realized how bad he was for Pat, that it must be him who was making her so unhappy and sick. It didn't seem to matter how much he loved her. But then he had changed his mind. "About halfway home, I realized that was the worst thing I could do, 'cause she couldn't get along without me."

His story was simple. He had fallen asleep from sheer exhaustion once he got home. He wasn't running from anyone, he said, because he had done nothing wrong. He hadn't even known his parents had been killed until his grandfather had called him.

Tom was voluble about his problems with his father, recounting all the acrimony and infighting over his recent divorce. Tom hadn't seen his father outside a courtroom, he said, since he had been kicked out of the family home the winter before. He hadn't wanted to see him, and he certainly wouldn't go over to his parents' house when his father would just as soon shoot him as say "Howdy."

He suggested his father had had enemies—someone out to get him ever since he had announced for judge. "But I don't know why *anyone* would want to kill my mother," Tom said quietly. "She's a good woman. She's always been a good woman."

Tom told Zellner—just as Pat had—that his ex-wife Carolyn was a woman completely out of control, particularly when she drank. "But they've taken her under their wings—since the divorce. They paid for her lawyer, and she works at the office with Mother. But she gets drunk now and then, and calls and tells me, 'I want to see you dead.' "

For a man in his precarious position, Tom talked too much, coming up with theories and obscure suspects. He couldn't seem to bear the silences. His drawl was laconic and slow, nothing like Pat's rapid-fire speech, but he talked a lot.

"There was a girl that committed suicide on my granddaddy's farm," he suddenly remembered. "She was an alcoholic. I flat know my daddy was playing around with her. My granddaddy said Daddy got all her stock in her company when she died. But I know for a fact my daddy was playing around with her—that old gal would get drunk and she'd just talk and talk and talk. That's back when I was in college."

The woman had been married, Tom explained. "She used to come over to the house all the time, get drunk, and crawl all over him all the time. My mother wasn't there, and I don't think [her husband] knew anything about it. . . ."

Tom paused in deep thought. "You know, I still loved him as a father, but it was kinda hard to understand at the same time what he was doin'."

Tom denied that he had a bad temper. He had never had a fight or hit anyone—"off a football field."

"Paw called me tonight," Tom said, recalling his conversation with his grandfather. "I asked him to call the sheriff's back there, and let them know I was here. He said, 'Are you all right?' and I said, 'Yeah, except for I'm going to jail.' He said he heard I was shot, and I said, 'Well, I'm not.' "

Tom had a scrape on one leg. That was all. He figured he had got that somewhere while he was walking home from East Point. Sixty miles. A very, very long walk.

Tom was adamant that he had *not* been at his parents' home earlier in the evening, or anytime in the past several months. He himself had begun to wonder—after talking to Margureitte Radcliffe—if maybe somebody was trying to set both him *and* his father up, some unknown enemy stalking them. Both Tom and Walter had been getting weird, threatening phone calls.

Could that be possible? Was there someone who didn't care if both Tom and Walter Allanson died, someone who might even have something to gain from their deaths? It was a far-out theory. Too far out. A dozen hours after the murder, the East Point detectives were almost positive that they had the right man in custody.

Tom Allanson.

As soon as Tom arrived in East Point, he learned that Pat had hired an attorney for him: Calhoun Long. On his attorney's—and his wife's—advice, he had nothing more to say to detectives.

✦ ✦ ✦

All murder seems senseless. But this double murder seemed more so than most. Two responsible, well-known citizens of East Point were dead and their son was in jail. He wasn't a man with a criminal background, nor a man on drugs or on the street. He was a man with a new marriage, a fine farm, a good reputation among horse people and with everyone he had worked for. He was a good old boy, easygoing, likable, and kind. Nobody but his ex-wife and his parents had ever had a bad word to say about him. Why would Tom Allanson throw all of that away in a moment of blind rage?

Even Tom's demeanor on the long ride back from Zebulon warred with the image of a man given to blind rages. Rather, he had showed no emotion at all. His parents had not been dead twelve hours, and yet the three detectives had seen no tears nor heard any choking up in his voice as he discussed their deaths.

That bothered them.

✦ ✦ ✦

Susan and Bill Alford were far away from Atlanta when they heard the devastating news of the double murder of Pat's in-laws. They were headed to Colorado to pick up some prize Morgan horses for Kentwood Morgan Farm. Before dawn, they received a call at their motel telling them to come back home at once; there had been a tragedy.

Both Susan and her great-aunt Alma had had some foreboding of disaster, a sense that "something bad was fixing to happen," but this news was beyond anything they might have envisioned in their worst nightmares. Pulling a still-empty horse trailer, Bill and Susan Alford turned around and headed home.

✦ ✦ ✦

The East Point police investigators would not sleep for another day. Nor would they celebrate the Fourth of July in the traditional way. At the first clear light of day, they were back at the crime scene. Detective George Zellner, Sergeants Maulin Humphrey and C. T. Callahan, searched the interior of the house, and Sergeant Bill Vance and a uniformed squad combed the sodden yard.

As Vance and his crew worked their way through ivy and underbrush between the Allansons' house and the house to the east, Vance found a shotgun 135 feet from the basement steps. It lay where it had apparently been dropped, its stock protruding along the fence line on a dirt path that ran between the Allansons' side yard and that of Paul and Harriett Duckett, who lived next door. The gun was 40 feet from the sidewalk. It was an Excel single-shot shotgun, exactly like the gun that Walter Allanson had reported stolen when Callahan answered Allanson's first complaint the night before.

It was fully cocked and loaded.

As they were searching the area, the officers moved into the Ducketts' yard. "There's no need for you to be pulling up geraniums and stomping through there," Harriett Duckett scolded. Vance and Patrolman Bob Matthews apologized, but geraniums were expendable at the moment.

The Ducketts said they had both seen a tall man running down the dirt path about 8:00 the night before. Their dog Roman had barked frantically. Later, Paul Duckett had attempted to alert the police swarming over his neighbors' property, but the scene had been one of such confusion that he had been waved back toward his own house.

"My first sight of him was nothing but legs because of the dogwood trees," Duckett said. He weighed close to 250 himself, so he was a good judge of size when he described the man's appearance as he broke into the open. "I saw his right profile when he hit the street. There was a police car there, kind of keeping pace with him. Then it turned around and came back next door. The man was tall, probably weighed over two thirty, and he had on dark pants and a light shirt. He was holding on to himself."

Duckett demonstrated by clutching his own side.

Harriett Duckett, who was still surveying the damage to her garden, had seen the man too. He had run off the path, breaking into the clearing right at their driveway, and then headed east past the Pilgrim Press Building on the corner.

Both of them were a little annoyed that their tips to the police had been ignored, and Harriett recalled that she had finally managed to get a patrolman's attention about 10:30 the night before and said, "Look, you missed your man. He went around the corner on Harris Street."

Neither of the Ducketts had met the Allansons, so they had no idea if it was Tom they had seen. They had heard no shouts *or* shots before they saw the running man; only later, when the tear gas was fired into the Allansons' house, did they hear a sound of shots.

They agreed to attend a lineup on July 6.

✦ ✦ ✦

Inside the Allansons' basement, the lingering smell of tear gas droplets stung the eyes of the investigators. In the daylight filtering from the windows, Sergeant Callahan and Patrolman Bob Matthews could see that most of the bloodshed was near the stairway where both victims had been found *and* back at "the hole" in the brick fireplace wall. The basement floor was spattered brown-red with now-dried blood all around the furnace and the area in front of the hole. The hole in the brick wall led to an area about six feet by ten feet, large enough for a man to hide in—not comfortably, but it was possible. Looking out, the line of sight would be straight ahead to the stairway down from the kitchen.

The hole itself had a dirt floor and was partially filled with junk—an old lemonade cooler, burlap sacks, paper bags full of nails. With flashlights held at an oblique angle, the investigators could see seven marks on the bricks *inside* the hole that had been left by ricocheting bullets. Fragments of those bullets were also visible, along with chips of concrete.

And yet they found no blood at all in the hole. There *was* blood on the wall outside the hole, and the trail of blood on the floor led from the opening in the wall all the way to the bottom of the steps eighteen feet away, where blood had spurted and cascaded until the body that contained it could no longer stand upright. They scraped samples for typing, but it seemed obvious that it was Walter Allanson who had bled here. His wife had never moved after she sat down on the stairs.

Carefully, Matthews and Callahan bagged the fractured chunks of bullets they found on the dirt floor of the hole. There were no bullet casings in the hole itself, but a dark blue shotgun cartridge lay on the floor just outside the rectangular aperture. Vance found one shotgun pellet inside the hole too. And when Matthews lifted a piece of wood in front of the hole in the wall, he found a second 20-gauge shotgun cartridge. This one was yellow.

The one vital bullet they never found was the single round that had been fired from the .45/70 Marlin rifle that Big Carolyn had carried down the stairs, obeying, as she always had, her husband's orders. The spent casing was there all right, next to the rifle itself. The slug was gone.

The detectives were also puzzled that there was no blood inside the hole; firing into that hole would be akin to shooting fish in a barrel. And hadn't Little Carolyn Allanson said that Daddy Allanson had called out, "I've got him trapped in the hole"? If Tom Allanson was the one in the hole, he was lucky to be alive. In fact, he had no wounds, nothing beyond a quarter-sized abrasion on his left leg.

Ballistics—bullets, cartridges, casings, fragments, line of fire, angles, ricochets—were tedious, but in a case like this one, they were essential to finding the truth. This basement had been a shooting gallery where two people died, and it was highly unlikely that they had shot each other. That meant that at least one person had survived. To reconstruct, the East Point detectives had to find everything they could, everything—tangible and intangible—left behind by the guns involved.

It seemed obvious that the Excel shotgun had been fired two times, the .32 pistol six times, and the new Marlin .45/70 rifle only once. The question was, who had shot which weapons?

And *why?*

✦   ✦   ✦

Belatedly, Pat Allanson was given a paraffin test on her hands to see if *she* had recently fired a gun. The test was designed to turn up primer residue—*if* the subject had not washed her hands, smoked a cigarette, used toilet tissue, or performed other normal human functions. It was not the most accurate test for gunshot residue, and Pat was not given the test until early July 4.

The test results were negative.

Tom Allanson was also tested for gunshot residue. He remarked to the officers who were administering the test that he had done some target shooting a few days before. Even so, his test—like his wife's—was negative.

✦   ✦   ✦

Tom was being held in the East Point jail and Pat was staying with her parents on their Tell Road farm. Their neighbor Liz Price and Pat's son, Ronnie, tended to the animals at Kentwood Farm, the paradise Tom and Pat had created in Zebulon. They had been married only fifty-four days. It was perhaps inevitable that when the *Griffin Daily News* printed the story of the Allanson murders under the headline NEW RESIDENT OF PIKE COUNTY HELD IN DEATH OF HIS PARENTS, it once again featured the picture of Pat and Tom on their wedding day, dressed as Scarlett and Rhett.

10

While investigators swarmed over their home, the late Walter and Carolyn Allanson awaited autopsy by Dr. Robert Rutherford Stivers, chief medical examiner of Fulton County. In the six years since Stivers had come to Fulton County, he had performed some thirty-eight hundred autopsies, and on this gloomy Independence Day, he set about to do two more.

He noted that Walter O'Neal Allanson weighed two hundred pounds and measured sixty-nine inches tall; like most humans in late middle age, he had shrunk a few inches since his youth. Dictating into a tape recorder as he worked, Stivers described what he found:

"The body is clothed in a white shirt, blue and white pants and underwear, black shoes and socks. . . . The body temperature is cold and rigor mortis is present in the extremities. The examination of the exterior . . . shows multiple entrance gunshot wounds. These are present in three rather distinct patterns. They number twenty entrance wounds altogether. . . . There is a cluster of wounds within a five-inch-in-diameter circle on the left side of the face and neck, with the center of this circle overlying the angle of the mandible [the back edge of the jaw], and there are ten entrance wounds in the left side of the face extending from the area of the nose and the upper lip and down across the neck. . . . There is, secondly, a cluster of wounds in the back of the left wrist and hand extending for a total distance of four inches. . . . These number five wounds.

"Then there are five wounds in a scatter pattern over the chest of the decedent, one each in both shoulders, one over the lower portion of the sternum—ahh, central upper abdomen—and then one each in the right and left abdominal quadrants. . . ."

Dr. Stivers determined that the wounds to the hand, the shoulders, and the abdomen had not passed through any vital organs. The deadly trauma had come from the wounds to the face and neck.

"There is a path of destruction extending . . . in a slightly upward from left to right direction . . . passing through the left carotid artery and causing massive hemorrhage into the left side of the neck and into the larynx [voice box] . . . with destruction at the base of the tongue. Death was caused by gunshot wounds to the face and chest."

Walter Allanson had bled to death when the carotid artery, which ran up the left side of his neck, was severed. But in Dr. Stivers's opinion, he could have moved about, walked forty or fifty feet, and even fired a pistol after he sustained the wounds he did. He could not, however, have spoken or shouted. His tongue and larynx had been virtually obliterated.

Carolyn Allanson, Dr. Stivers recorded, had been five feet five inches tall and weighed 130 pounds. She wore a white nurse's uniform, blouse and pants.

"There are perforations of the clothing of the left upper and anterior panel of the blouse. . . . Upon examination . . . there are multiple perforating wounds of the left upper chest within a four-inch-diameter circle with fourteen entrance wounds . . . [that] include the left breast of the decedent. . . . There are multiple missile tracts of destruction which pass through the tissue of the left breast, the sternum, the upper heart, and the right lung. . . . Death is determined to have been caused by a shotgun wound to the chest."

Carolyn Allanson had died almost instantly. "The upper portion of the heart is totally destroyed, as well as a portion of the right lung. . . . There may have been a moment or so of consciousness until the lack of oxygen to the brain cells would take place, but for all practical purposes, she died immediately. The top of the heart is essentially missing."

Dr. Stivers speculated that Carolyn Allanson might have had some spasmodic muscular movement for a short period of time. Could she have cocked a rifle? Possibly. Could she have pulled the trigger? Possibly.

✦ ✦ ✦

Pat went to the East Point jail and insisted on seeing her husband. She was led into a visiting area and was disappointed because she had intended to give him a big hug to show him that everything was all right. Instead, the officers pointed to a chair in front of a glass panel. She would not be allowed to touch Tom; she could only talk to him on the phone that hung on the cubicle wall.

Tom looked terrible. He had stubbly whiskers and she could tell he hadn't slept.

"I have everything taken care of, Shug," she began. "Now you just remember that I'm handling this. Don't say anything. I've got you a good lawyer. You just trust me and you don't talk to anyone else, you hear me, Sugar?"

He nodded. She was so brave. When he began to ask her something, she glanced sideways at the cops and put her finger to her lips, shushing him.

"Shug, just you hush. I'll be back."

✦ ✦ ✦

Still reeling from shock, Jean Boggs struggled to hold what was left of her family together. She was an attractive, slender brunette, but her face was drawn with tension now. She went to the East Point city jail a little later in the day on July 4. The police were not eager to let her see Tom, but finally George Zellner told her she could do so—if he was allowed to be in attendance.

Jean had not seen her nephew Tommy in a year or two—an indication of how alienated this family had become. She offered to get him an attorney, and Tom replied, "Well, you will have to get in touch with Pat. She'll be handling all that. She probably already has someone picked out."

"Pat? Pat who?" Jean asked, mystified.

"My wife."

"Aren't you married to *Carolyn?"*

"No. We got divorced, and I married Pat Taylor."

For the moment, Jean was dumbfounded. Just as Mary McBride, Walter's secretary, hadn't known Tom was remarried, neither had his own aunt.

Tears rolled down Tom's cheeks as he assured his aunt he had not killed his parents. "You know how it was. I was frightened to death of Daddy, but I would have no reason to shoot and kill Mother."

Tom explained to his aunt—as he had to the three detectives on the long ride back from Zebulon the night before—that he had walked away from his new wife because he felt he only brought her unhappiness. "I made up my mind that I was leaving her, so I hitchhiked." He didn't know how many rides he had gotten or how many miles he had walked as he headed south to Zebulon. Later in their conversation, Tom was adamant that he didn't want to take a lie detector test. He didn't trust their results.

Jean Boggs was deeply troubled, but she believed in Tommy. She loved him; he had grown up with her own children. She could not fathom that he would hurt his parents. She wondered what kind of person Pat was, this new wife whom she had never heard of.

The rest of Jean Boggs's day was taken up with arranging for her brother and sister-in-law's funeral. They would be buried out of Hemperley's Funeral Parlor, just as Kent had been, and just as almost everyone who lived in East Point was. Mae Mama inexplicably demanded that her daughter be buried in a blue dress in long sleeves.

"I won't look at her otherwise," the old lady said.

✦ ✦ ✦

A solemn party went to Walter and Carolyn's house: Jean Boggs, Nona (in a wheelchair), Paw, their preacher, and their doctor. The house was locked, but Jean steeled herself and went down the outside steps into the basement, averted her eyes from the profusion of bloodstains, and climbed to the kitchen up the stairs where her sister-in-law had died. All those doors were unlocked.

The house still reeked of tear gas. Choking, she saw that all the storm windows were in place, trapping the gas despite the fire department's fans. Frantically, she kicked out two storm windows to get air, cutting her heel. Then she let her parents in. Jean maneuvered her mother's wheelchair to the open front door, where she could breathe, and then carried Walter's suits to Nona and let her choose which one to bury him in. Jean couldn't find anything blue for her late sister-in-law to wear; she would have to buy a new dress in a color Big Carolyn apparently had never worn.

It was nightmarish. It wasn't happening. Carolyn's woven straw purse still sat open on the dining room table. The case of Coca-Cola was there too. The inflatable blue dinosaur shivered and bounced as they walked near it.

But it was real enough. Reporters from the Atlanta papers pushed to get in and take pictures, and perfect strangers walked up the driveway, trying to peek in the windows to see what they could see. They acted as if they had every right to be there. Didn't people have any consideration at all? Jean and the preacher got Paw and Nona out of there as soon as they could.

✦ ✦ ✦

Al Roberts, Walter's law partner and his friend since high school, called at the elder Allansons' home on Washington Road to offer his condolences. After speaking with Paw and Nona, he and his wife and daughter moved on to the den. The doorbell rang and Roberts saw two women walk in. The younger woman immediately began to sob and scream.

"Paw!" she cried, clutching at the old man. "He didn't do it!"

Roberts's daughter, Martha, spoke to the newest visitors, calling them by name. "Hey, Miz Taylor—er, Allanson. Hey, Miz Radcliffe." She explained to her father that this was Tom's new wife and her mother. Margureitte and Pat walked back to Nona's bedroom, and Pat's hysterical sobbing could be heard all over the house.

Roberts knew Walter's mother couldn't stand much more, and he hurried back to urge Pat Taylor Allanson to leave Nona's room. After his second, more urgent request, Pat walked to the kitchen, where the table was laden with pies, cakes, and covered-dish casseroles from the Allansons' friends and fellow church members.

Pat answered the kitchen phone, spoke briefly, and then, apparently recovered from her hysterics, dialed a number herself. Roberts, who sat a few feet away, was astounded as he heard Pat's conversation with Calhoun Long, apparently Tom's attorney. Oblivious of her surroundings, Pat said in a loud voice, "He did not do it—he went to the doctor with me. When I came out of the doctor's office, he was gone. He walked to Zebulon."

And then, right in front of the late Walter Allanson's law partner, Pat told her husband's legal counsel about the incident of the previous Friday. As Paw sat at the kitchen table trying to eat some soup, Pat rattled on about how his dead son had exposed himself to her only six days earlier, on June 28. She recalled her terror to Calhoun Long, and then proceeded to give alibis for Tom for the ambush incident at Lake Lanier the next day. "My mother, Mrs. Radcliffe, is on the extension in the bedroom, and she will tell you the very same things I have."

Tommy's new wife certainly had no sense of time and place, and Al Roberts wondered how she could even *imagine* that Walter had exposed himself to her. Roberts knew Walter Allanson would be incapable of such an act, and furthermore he knew exactly where Walter had been on the day she was talking about —right there in their law offices with him. Walter had arrived for work at 9:10 on that morning and had stayed there all day long—with the exception of the fifteen minutes around 3:00 P.M. when he went to pick up the deer rifle. If Tom Allanson *had* shot his own father because he was outraged that Walter had exposed himself to Pat, it was all for naught. There was no way he could have been showing his penis to his daughter-in-law in the hedgerow at the plantation in Zebulon, sixty miles away, on June 28. No way at all. If Pat had told Tom his father had done that, she had made a terrible, tragic mistake.

The doorbell rang again and Paul Vaughan, Walter's law clerk, arrived. Roberts asked Vaughan to go out with him for a glass of iced tea. He was perplexed—shocked—by this woman Tommy had married.

Vaughan verified Roberts's recall; he had seen Walter on June

28 too. They discussed the Lake Lanier ambush, but there were things Al Roberts hadn't heard about. Vaughan said that Walter had told him his boat engine had suddenly exploded but that he had managed to get to shore without sinking. The clerk also recalled a phone message left for Carolyn and Walter from a man identifying himself as their son. "He said to tell them he had missed them—but that he would get them."

Al Roberts didn't know what to think. Pat Allanson and her mother, Mrs. Radcliffe, seemed so at home in Paw and Nona's house, and Pat herself had seemed overcome alternately with grief and hysteria, a woman not quite in control. She had been almost vulgarly specific about the exposing incident and then had forced herself to be coldly businesslike. Perhaps she had been so shocked that she couldn't see what effect her words were having on the old couple who had just lost their only son.

Mrs. Radcliffe dressed and acted like a proper lady. But Pat was something else again. She was a fine-looking woman, all right, but she was obviously older than Tommy, and her clothing was flamboyant; the dead man's partner saw why Walter Allanson had not approved of her.

It was also apparent that Pat and her mother were a team— that no matter what Tommy's wife said, Mrs. Radcliffe backed her up. Her head began to nod almost from the moment Pat opened her mouth.

11

As their investigation continued, Detective Zellner and Sergeant Callahan followed up on the ambush shooting in Forsyth County on the Saturday before the Allansons were killed. In fact, Mary Rena Jones, who ran the J. C. Jones store with her husband, was sure she had seen Tom near the gas pumps, standing next to his blue pickup truck, on Friday the twenty-eighth, around 5:30 P.M. She had seen the Kentwood Morgan emblem on the door, and, of course, both Joneses remembered seeing Walter Allanson the next morning after he had been shot at. He and his wife had come in with cuts all over their arms.

"I told him that before I'd let someone shoot me, I'd shoot them first," J. C. put in. "He told us it was his son who had shot at him."

Mary Jones picked Tom's picture out of a laydown of suspects.

Zellner and Callahan knew about the sugar in the Allansons' gas tank. They knew about the exploding boat, the phone calls. Either Tom Allanson was guilty of it all, or someone had done a dandy job of setting him up to look guilty.

✦ ✦ ✦

On July 5, George Zellner typed up a probable-cause affidavit requesting a search warrant in Pike County. The East Point investigators wanted to search the premises of Kentwood Farm and a 1971 GMC pickup truck (license plate RL 7223) for certain items:

One .22-caliber semi-automatic rifle;
One man's shirt, color brown and green striped;
Blue jean pants;
Boots having soil and blood stains.

The investigators located several pairs of jeans, but none with bloodstains. Two pairs of jeans were in the washing machine with a still-damp load of otherwise white items of clothing. A woman would never have mixed the jeans with white clothes. A man might have—especially a man trying to wash blood away. The Allansons had a gun rack at Kentwood Farm with several rifles and shotguns. The investigators found a .22-caliber Remington Model 66 rifle, loaded with Federal copper-clad bullets. The empty cartridges recovered in the shooting at Lake Lanier had been the same type.

They didn't find the striped shirt. When a neighbor told them that he had seen Tom walk down the road in the wee hours of July 4 and that he had been wearing only a T-shirt and jeans, they figured they would never locate the green and brown shirt; it could be anywhere between East Point and Zebulon.

✦ ✦ ✦

Elizabeth Thomason, a forensic serologist with the Georgia State Crime Laboratory, received blood samples from Dr. Stivers on July 5. The vials of blood retrieved at autopsy showed that both the Allansons had the same type of blood: O positive. All the blood samples from the basement—from the floor, light switch, gun, holster, boards—were type O positive. But then the prime suspect—the man who waited in the East Point jail—was the natural son of Walter and Carolyn Allanson. He would have type O positive too.

It was a moot point. The only wound Tom had was the scrape on his left calf, and it had barely bled.

The normal physical evidence that is usually so helpful to homicide detectives—hairs, fibers, blood, fingerprints—has greatly diminished worth in a "family murder." Both the victims and the accused have reason to occupy the premises where the crimes take place. Their fingerprints could be expected, and so could their clothing fibers, hairs, blood, urine, saliva, even semen. It didn't matter that Tom Allanson had not lived in the Norman Berry Drive home for six months; fingerprints last for years, even for decades. *Alien* physical evidence would be of use in this case if the killer proved to be someone outside the family and not a regular visitor to the Allansons' home.

The fingerprint question didn't matter anyway; Detective Marlin Humphrey, Jr., had dusted for prints in the Allansons' basement to little avail. He failed to raise any prints on the fuse box, basement doors, or furnace. Walter's borrowed .32 revolver had a partial latent as did a light bulb; both proved to be those of East Point police officers, an embarrassing discovery but not surprising in light of the chaotic terror that had reigned in that basement on the night of July 3.

The mystery behind the deaths of Walter and Carolyn Allanson probably would not be unraveled through forensic science; the answers would come from a more imprecise area: human behavior.

✦ ✦ ✦

The Saturday after the murders was a day that seemed forty-eight hours long. Tom Allanson appeared in a lineup at the East Point police station on July 6. He was by far the tallest man present. All the subjects wore white T-shirts and either jeans or work pants. Some were fire fighters, some were cops, and one was a friend of Tom's, a tall man who volunteered to join the lineup so that Tom wouldn't stand out so conspicuously.

Viewing the lineup were Harriett and Paul Beauregard Duckett and Patrol Officer C. L. McBurnett, Jr., the only eyewitnesses who had seen the fleeing man just after the murders. The Ducketts and McBurnett walked in separately, checked off the form without speaking, and left the lineup room.

Each had checked space No. 2: Tom Allanson.

Things looked bad for Tom. His aunt Jean was offering to help, but he didn't dare tell his wife about that. Pat assured him continually that *she* was taking care of everything. He wasn't to worry; she would see that he had the best legal defense money could buy. He just had to remember not to talk to *anyone* but her. When he argued with her that to him the truth seemed the best route, Pat shushed him. No, he must not even suggest such a thing; anybody knew that a man who tried to handle his own defense was a fool. He had to believe in her, she explained, because no one loved him the way that she loved him.

And no one ever would.

✦　✦　✦

That same Saturday, Walter and Carolyn Allanson had a joint funeral in the chapel at Hemperley's in East Point. Their caskets were side by side, and they were closed. Mae Mama Lawrence's insistence on a blue dress with long sleeves for her daughter was moot; no one could tell what Carolyn wore. Mae Mama commented tearfully that it was just as well that her daughter and son-in-law had "gone together. They were always together. Neither one of them could have lived without the other."

The chapel was full to overflowing, and floral tributes filled it with an almost suffocating sweetness.

Pat was too ill to go, but she wanted her family to be represented at the chapel. She called her daughters, Susan Alford and Deborah Cole, and begged them to go to the Allansons' funeral. Susan was twenty-one and Deborah was nineteen and they were horrified at the thought of walking into Hemperley's in front of the deceased's friends and relatives. They hadn't even *known* the Allansons.

"You're going to be there for Tom," Pat insisted. "If you don't go, I'll have to get up out of this sickbed and go myself. You just walk right in with your heads up high, and you show him you care—that we all care."

As far as Margureitte and Colonel Radcliffe were concerned, they backed Tom to the limit, but they felt no allegiance to his parents. They had issued gracious invitations to the Allansons in life and all their overtures had been rudely refused. They did not now feel it was incumbent upon them to join the mourners for people who were virtual strangers—by their own choice.

Pat's two daughters went to Hemperley's, their faces aflame with embarrassment when they realized there was no way they were going to go unrecognized. They were further mortified when the chapel began to buzz and heads turned to gawk at them. Their arrival had actually produced a massive gasp. They could feel disapproval and curiosity from every side.

Suddenly, there was the sound of chains clanking at the back of the room, and eyes finally turned away from them. Tom Allanson had been allowed to attend his parents' services, but George Zellner and C. T. Callahan had brought him in both handcuffs and leg-irons. The leg-irons were removed, but still handcuffed, Tom stood with his head bowed. Susan and Deborah saw that tears streamed silently down his cheeks. They managed to catch his eye and smiled wanly. And then they left. Their few minutes in the chapel would remain one of the more hideous memories of their lives.

The Allansons were buried side by side in Westview Cemetery.

✦　✦　✦

Shortly before 5:00 P.M. at police headquarters that Saturday, Detective Zellner interviewed Mrs. Clifford B. Radcliffe, the woman Pat Allanson affectionately called "Boppo." If he had found her daughter talkative, Zellner didn't know what "stream of consciousness" was until he interviewed Margureitte Radcliffe. There seemed to be no pauses in her conversation, and she had much to tell him. She spoke in a perfectly modulated "society" voice. She was a daunting woman who gave the impression that never, ever, *ever* had she—or anyone she was related to, or even *acquainted* with—had occasion to be involved in a criminal investigation. She would be glad to help Zellner, of course, if only to straighten out this ridiculous predicament Tom was in as quickly as possible.

Yes, indeed, she had spoken—not once, but twice—with the deceased Mr. Allanson. He *had* confided in her that he suspected Tom of all manner of mischief and misbehaving—from putting formaldehyde in his own children's milk to the theft of suitcases. The dead man had made his son's life utterly miserable. For what reason, she could not say.

Why, even Bill Alford—"my granddaughter's husband"—had called her from one of Tom's many divorce hearings as he struggled to be free of Little Carolyn Allanson. "Mr. Alford's getting ready to study law, you see—and he said, 'You will not believe what is happening. I'm here and I'm seeing it and hearing it, and *I* don't believe it. Tom is not being allowed to present anything. . . . But yet Mr. Allanson is getting on the stand and saying his son is a drunkard!' All these horrible things about his son, yet he—Tom—doesn't even drink and he doesn't even smoke."

Mrs. Radcliffe explained that Tom had been their feed man for years, "but we have only known him in recent months in the capacity we do now. His wife is our daughter. We have known him as a very nice, clean-cut young man—never anything bad about him from anyone."

"You ever heard him say anything negative about his father?"

"Never! Never have I! Nor have I heard him say anything about his father at all."

Mrs. Radcliffe told Zellner that the most unpleasant person she had had contact with through Tom was his ex-wife, who would call constantly at all hours to harass Tom and Pat for money. Sighing, she murmured, "What *did* she do with all of the money? Because she had gotten a tremendous amount of money—and was [still] getting her money."

"Did they stay with you often? Tom and his wife, your daughter?" Zellner put in.

"They were there until they were married, in our home. He slept on a sofa in our den."

Margureitte Radcliffe explained that she had had very little contact with Tom's parents, who had been quite rude generally. Walter Allanson had frightened her too, she said, as he accused Tom of all manner of theft. In the next breath he had told her he would "get" Tom.

Zellner didn't have to ask questions. Margureitte seemed eager to get all of her contacts with Walter Allanson out in the open. "He acted to me like he thought I knew something that I didn't know and that he was trying to justify himself to me— which wasn't necessary. . . . I came away firmly convinced that this man was dangerous, that he was very devious, that he was very cunning, and I couldn't figure out why. I could not figure out his purpose."

Pat's mother confided that she had been so alarmed by Walter Allanson's behavior that she had gone to the East Point Police Department and pleaded for advice about what to do. "I told them, 'I really feel that the man is ill, really and truly ill.' "

She had never even seen Big Carolyn Allanson. "I had only one conversation with Mrs. Allanson and that was when I called her at her office—several months ago—hoping she would accept our invitation, at her convenience, for her and Mr. Allanson to have lunch or dinner with Colonel Radcliffe and me."

Mrs. Radcliffe recalled her fear when Walter Allanson had driven his shot-up station wagon to her place of employment and insisted she view what he said Tom had done. "I saw three places with some kind of tape or something over them on the windshield . . . and there were some shatters around it. . . . He said, 'Do you know that on Saturday, on our way up to the lake, Tommy got out on that road and built an ambush up on an embankment, and then when Carolyn and I were on [the road], he shot at us?' I said, 'No, he didn't—because he was out shoeing horses.' He said, 'Well, it has to be him,' and I said, 'No. It does not have to be—because everything you have accused him of, he has had lots of people around him at the time that these things have occurred—' "

"Did you really, *personally,* know where Tom was that day?" Zellner asked.

"On that day?"

"Yes, ma'am."

"He had called us, and there are people who know he shod horses at their place," she explained.

Colonel Radcliffe sat beside his wife as she explained her unnerving encounters with the late Walter Allanson. "Really and truly," she confided. "I tell my husband, it seems to be like the Lawrences—all of them—had some kind of feud. I felt like we were kind of in on the tail end of something here."

"Caught in the middle?" Zellner offered.

She nodded. "Right. But I'll tell you—perfectly frankly— that I don't feel like there's one way in this whole wide world that Tom Allanson could, *would,* kill his parents. . . . I have two theories on him. Am I supposed to tell my theories?"

Zellner nodded. "You can if you want to, yes."

Margureitte Radcliffe hinted broadly—and incredibly—that she suspected the dead man and his daughter-in-law might have been romantically involved. It was, of course, only her own theory. "I really and truly feel like this thing was set up and I feel like Mr. Allanson and Carolyn planned to do something to Mrs.

Allanson and blame it on Tom and perhaps—at the last minute
—it backfired on him and that Carolyn did the whole bit."

Mrs. Radcliffe was confident that there was no way "in the
whole wide world" that Tom could be guilty of murder. If that
should be true, she would be "the most absolutely shocked person in the entire world."

"But you said earlier," Zellner reminded Margureitte Radcliffe, "that it is your nature to see the good side of everybody."

"Well, I was *trying* to see the good side when I was speaking
to Mr. Allanson. . . . I still don't feel that anybody can be that
hard—"

"Pretty much changed your mind at the end, didn't you?"

"That's why I came to the police department, and I said [to
myself], Oh my God, I hope that nothing happens to that man,
because if it does . . . Tom will be the one that will be blamed
for it. . . . I was terrified of that man . . . and I think his parents—the elder Mr. and Mrs. Allanson—were afraid of him too.
. . . Yesterday, she [Nona] said she could say it for the first time
—she never could say it while they were alive—that they were
never parents, never 'mother' and 'father' to Tommy. I've heard
a lot of [other] things, but they were hearsay."

Zellner asked about Pat's first marriage, and Margureitte explained that she had been married very young and that it had
never worked out. "Her father and I—Colonel Radcliffe and I
—supported them for sixteen, seventeen, eighteen years. Right,
honey? She got *nothing* out of the divorce. . . . She's got fine
children too, I'll tell you that."

It had been quite a day. A lineup with a positive ID of Tom
Allanson. A double funeral. And a long, long interview with
Mrs. Clifford Radcliffe. According to her, the late Walter Allanson had been a monstrous, fearful man with a heart as cold as
death. And "Tommy," like herself, saw only the good in everyone. He had been a dutiful son, a fine son-in-law, and had alibis
for every incident his father accused him of.

For all but that very last, fatal encounter.

✦ ✦ ✦

In the weeks that followed, the investigators learned that Tom
would inherit nothing from his parents. Tom had known that
for months. He knew that both his father and mother had cut

him out of their wills the previous Valentine's Day. In fact, Tom was specifically eliminated in codicils to their existing wills. He had tried to explain that to Pat, but she never seemed to understand; she thought that he would, of course, be declared their natural heir. Each of his parents' wills had designated Carolyn's brother, Seaborn Lawrence, as their executor. Walter and Carolyn were each other's heirs and then they stipulated that, should they die together, their estate would go to Tom's children. Item Eight of Walter Allanson's will read:

> The provisions of this Will are made for the purpose of omitting my son, Seaborn Walter Thomas Allanson, completely, due to his disowning of the family and his failure to support his children, and I figure that his part of my estate was [already] used [by me] for the purpose of supporting his children. The trustee and executors are specifically instructed that, under no circumstances, is he to receive anything from my estate, and they are to oppose his appointment as Guardian of these children by any Court whatsoever, and in the event that he should succeed in being appointed as Guardian, then the trustee is not to pay any funds whatsoever to the grandchildren or to him as Guardian, but shall retain the funds until the payment age of twenty-five (25) is reached by the grandchildren.

It was a slap from beyond the grave. Tom had been paying five hundred dollars a month toward his children's support, and he would dearly have loved to have them back with him. He had had high hopes that one day soon he would be able to raise them on the grounds of Kentwood. He had left their mother in desperation—sick at heart in a loveless marriage.

Clearly, his father had never forgiven him. The only thing that Walter had forgotten about was an insurance policy in which Tom was still named as beneficiary—but Tom wouldn't know about that until months after his parents had died.

The house on Norman Berry Drive was cleaned and put up for sale. Despite the horror that had exploded there, it sold rather quickly. Paul and Harriett Duckett, right next door—and eyewitnesses to the fleeing gunman—bought it.

None of the financial mopping up mattered to Tom; all he had ever dreamed of had come true when he married Pat and they lived together at Kentwood. As it turned out, he had lived with her on that wonderful spread of land for less than a year; their time as man and wife had ended in less than two months. Tom would celebrate their two-month anniversary in court— being arraigned for double murder.

Their love had burned as white hot as any iron ingot, and now their lives were as cold and gray as the steel such an ingot might become. The glory was all gone, and he could not, for the life of him, fathom why.

PART TWO

TOM

12

Seaborn Walter Thomas Allanson—Tom—was born out of time, if not place. He would have made a far more satisfactory son for his grandfather than he ever had for his own father. Paw Allanson had never known quite what to make of *his* son, the austere and ambitious Walter O'Neal Allanson, and Walter always seemed to look at his Tommy as an impediment and an irritant.

Actually, Carolyn and Walter had been reluctant parents to begin with, not thrilled when Carolyn became pregnant in 1942. Both Carolyn and Walter were only nineteen and he was in the Army Air Corps, serving in World War II. Perhaps they had not planned to have *any* child, and they would never have another. Carolyn gave birth to Tommy on April 22, 1943, in Ocilla, Georgia, where Paw and Nona lived at the time. The baby was very large, a precursor of the size he would be as a grown man.

In their early years, it often seemed to Walter and Carolyn that every possible obstacle had been placed in their way. Like so many young men who graduated from high school in 1940,

Walter had to go to war. When the war was over, he came home and went to Georgia State University. Next, he received his law degree from Atlanta Law School and his master's in law from John Marshall Law School. Carolyn worked as a nurse to put him through.

Just when Walter was finally ready to practice on his own, the Korean War came along and he was called up again. He was over thirty before he could really begin his life. A decade of his prime years gone, he was home and in practice in East Point, with offices across the hall from his high school friend, Al Roberts. Walter and Carolyn had a lot of catching up to do. Walter worked as a justice of the peace in East Point from 1952 to 1956, and he joined all the organizations that a young man in a hurry needed: the East Point Masonic Lodge, the Optimist Club, the American Legion, the First United Methodist Church of East Point.

Carolyn was the choir director and taught piano to students at home. One Sunday, it was Walter's turn to teach the young marrieds' Sunday school class, and he rose and surveyed the group somberly before he said, "I'm Scotch, I'm stubborn, and I want things my way."

It was a disclaimer, a prelude to his lesson that morning on how Christians could be all different kinds of people. You could, he explained, be stubborn or meek or aggressive or a darned fool and still be a good Christian. Stubborn was as apt a description of Walter Allanson as anyone could ask for. No excuses. No apologies or promises to change. He was who he was.

Carolyn kept on working full-time for Dr. Tucker in East Point, and things gradually got better and better for them. They made up for all the wasted years. In March 1959, Walter and Al Roberts moved into a larger suite of offices and continued their law practice. They did well. Walter wasn't a rich lawyer with an estate in Atlanta's exclusive Haines Manor section, but he made a comfortable living. He practiced general law: wills, divorces, contracts. His staff found him almost unfailingly cheerful and pleasant to work with. He joined the Coast Guard Auxiliary and worked his way up in the East Point Masonic Lodge No. 88 to become a Thirty-second Degree Mason. He loved boats and he liked to fish but he liked to do it in solitude, without the nuisance of taking Tommy along

From young Tommy's viewpoint, his father had been either

studying or working his whole life. Indeed, both his parents had worked for as long as he could remember. Walter was a man who seldom showed emotion. Tommy was humiliated the few times he tried to relate to him. His father was closed in and rigid. He had a set way of doing things. His expectations for his son were just as unyielding. Carolyn Allanson was warmer, but she deferred to her husband when it came to dealing with Tommy and in the matter of getting ahead in the world. Their home wasn't built around the boy; the boy would have to fit in wherever he could.

It was not surprising that Tommy looked to Paw for the love and attention he didn't get at home. He spent the happiest days of his childhood on his grandparents' farm. He was proud when he went into the feed store with his grandfather and Paw winked at him as he announced to the clerk, "This is my son, Tommy." He loved to hang around with his grandfather as they worked with the horses and other farm animals. The old man and the husky blond boy both loved animals.

Tommy went to the Harris Street School in East Point until he was nine and then his parents enrolled him in the Georgia Military Academy in College Park. He attended that private and prestigious school until he graduated in 1961. The military discipline wasn't that different from the rules his father set down. But between the military academy and the many weekends he spent with his grandparents on their farm on Washington Road, Tommy didn't see that much of his parents. He went hunting with Paw, and Paw cooked breakfast for him. The two of them would scrounge through waste bins in back of the supermarkets for outdated vegetables to give to the cows and pigs. They would tease his grandmother when they came home with their boxes of brown lettuce and mushy tomatoes, saying, "Look what we brought for supper!" Nona was a pretty, green-eyed woman and she ran the household. Paw let her; in his taciturn way, he idolized her. And, like Paw, she loved Tommy and loved having him around.

Paw Allanson was an old-fashioned southern man. He had a fourth-grade education and he had labored as a steelworker for fifty-five years. He had lived through the Great Depression and never really trusted banks again; he salted away most of his cash in hiding places on his property.

Nona and Paw had bought the property on Washington Road

in 1934. The house on the property in East Point was little more than a shack then. But the farm proved to be a canny buy, and as the Atlanta area boomed over the years, it appreciated many, many times over its purchase price. Both Walter and his sister Jean were expected to work hard doing farm chores, since their father was often off hefting steel girders for buildings all over America. They had horses, cows, hogs, and chickens and there was always work to do in the fields; they sold their beef, pork, and produce—steel work was sporadic—and the farm took up the slack in their income.

When Walter was about twelve, he contracted rheumatic fever. His survival became the focal point of his parents' existence. Nona was always exhausted because she was up day and night turning Walter so he wouldn't get bedsores. Penicillin had yet to be discovered, and strep infections of any kind were often fatal. Paw and Nona didn't mean to neglect Jean, but her needs took second place in their fight to save their son.

Walter and Jean had never had a solid brother-and-sister relationship. Walter was four years older than Jean, and their personalities were on entirely different tracks. Walter's illness distanced them even more. When Walter got out of bed after his long siege with rheumatic fever, their parents were so grateful he had survived that they gave him everything he asked for. To Jean's eye, her brother was always greedy. A greedy boy and a greedy man.

Many years later, when Walter persuaded Paw to sell him the back half of the thirty-four acres he owned on Washington Road, Walter resold it and made a handsome profit. But Jean had asked her father first, and she was both outraged and humiliated when she learned that Paw had sold her brother the acreage she wanted. Her efforts to please her parents had always failed. Walter came first because he was a son, and her father doted on her mother, but Jean was left out.

The Allanson family relationships would always be distant and strained. Paw had become a gnarled, ornery old man, but he was devoted and gentle with his wife, Nona, and he loved Tom. As for his own offspring, he might do business with his son, but he didn't really care for either Walter or Big Carolyn. He often ignored Jean.

Jean and her husband, George "Homer" Boggs, had two children, David and Nona. They were quite a bit younger than Walter's Tommy and as cousins they would never be close. The Allanson line had continued, but only grudgingly. Tommy was it for a long time. The last Allanson to carry the name unless he had a son.

Years would go by when Jean wouldn't see Walter. And yet he was her brother. She may not have liked him very much, but she loved him. She had always assumed that, one day, they would settle their differences.

And then, suddenly, it was too late.

✦ ✦ ✦

Tom Allanson had often shivered in the emotional chill of his childhood home. "That's why I grew up being such a sucker for love," he remembered years later. "I never had any. I can never remember—even once—hearing my parents say 'I love you' or feeling them put their arms around me. . . . They showed they cared about me by giving me a good education, they fed me, they took care of me, but that was their form of love. I understood that, although I found out later in life that I wasn't exactly planned when I came along. I wasn't exactly a blessing. But I was the kind of kid that thrived off of love. I needed to be *told*. I needed to be *shown*."

Tom grew into a huge teenager who towered over his parents. He looked like a big old country boy and that suited him fine. All his life he would hide his intelligence and his education and speak with a deep southern drawl. He was happiest in the country, competing in a rodeo or working in a horse barn. Teenage girls—and not a few grown women—watched Tom Allanson longingly from the rodeo stands. His jeans fit him like second skin, and he exuded masculinity.

One of the women was Liz Price, who would move in and out of his life for years to come, and she laughed as she remembered knowing Tom. "He was my ideal man coming up. A big rodeo star and—oh, how he fit those jeans! You hear about his jeans? I thought he was God's gift to women. . . . One day I was walking across the horse show grounds with a bucket of water in my hand, and somebody says, 'There goes Tom!' and I turned around, looking for him, and I ran right into a guy wire with my neck and I poured all my water in my boots!"

Tom didn't know women looked at him that way. He had had few compliments in his life and his self-esteem was wrapped up only in his skill with horses. While he was still in high school, he learned to shoe horses and worked as a farrier when he was only sixteen. He had a crush on Liz, who was a few years older than he. But he never mentioned it to her; he was much too shy. "I won't say I was all that good on my first horse or two," he remembered. "Liz was my first horseshoe customer and I like to ruined her horse."

After Tom graduated from the military academy, he enrolled in the University of Georgia in Athens. He played football; he was a line coach's dream at six foot four and 250 pounds. But he was forced to drop out of football—and the university—in 1963 when a rodeo accident ended his playing career. He transferred to Truett McConnell Community College and graduated with an associate degree in science. Then he returned to the University of Georgia.

Despite his father's vehement opposition, Tom married for the first time while he was in college. He was mesmerized by a tall, slender, raven-haired girl with clear blue eyes, Judy Van Meter. "I fell in love with this young girl up there in Athens," he said. "She was beautiful. She looked absolutely beautiful— like Lynda Carter, 'Wonder Woman.' You couldn't tell me anything as far as my parents goes. I was in *love*. My dad said, 'You can't get married until you get through with your college.' And I said, 'Well, *you* can't stop this love I've got for this girl.' He said if I got married, they'd cut off all my funds for college. Well, I got married and he cut it off just like he said he would. There wasn't another penny. So I had to make it on my own."

Tom's marriage to Judy didn't work out. "She had a champagne appetite," Tom recalled ruefully. "And I had a beer pocketbook. I was trying to go to vet school and work, and she was working too. She started playing games. . . . If I didn't do what she wanted me to do, there was no more sex." He would later admit that it would be a long time before he had good sense about women. When his first wife shut the bedroom door on him, his eye soon wandered to an even more unsuitable choice. "You couldn't tell me anything then—no more than you can tell any young man in love."

Tom's next love was, unfortunately, his wife's best friend, Carolyn Brooks. Carolyn was a delicate-appearing woman who swept her blond hair back into a chignon. "She looked like Grace Kelly," Tom said, shaking his head. "All my women were real pretty."

Carolyn was in her twenties and also married—to a man almost fifteen years her senior.

"She gave me attention, and I wasn't getting that in my marriage," Tom said. "My wife was withholding sex and Carolyn was free with it. We started going to the Moose Club together—and that was out of character for me. I didn't drink—never have." Tom said Carolyn enjoyed dancing and drinking, and it didn't concern him in the beginning.

Two divorce suits would be filed when Tom's wife and Carolyn's husband discovered their romance. Tom had yet to distinguish between love and sex. He believed that he had finally found what he was looking for and that Carolyn would make a good wife as soon as their divorces were final.

Despite his romantic misadventures, Tom managed to stay in college and he graduated from the University of Georgia in 1966 with a bachelor of science in agriculture, with emphasis on veterinary medicine. He went to work after graduation for the Beaver Dam Angus Farm in Colbert, Georgia, near Athens, and stayed there for three years as cattle manager over an eighteen-hundred-head herd of Angus. He then attended Graham's School for Cattlemen and Horsemen in Garnett, Kansas, and was certified to perform artificial insemination.

If Tom Allanson didn't understand women, he most definitely did know horses. He was now a farrier who specialized in "corrective shoeing" and worked with quarter horses, thoroughbred Morgans, and Arabians. By this time, he had bred, trained, and shown quarter horses and Morgans in halter, western, trail, reining, and fine harness classes. He was soon a judge in western horse shows. He was a working fool. Stripped to his jeans and an undershirt to offset the heat of a Georgia summer and the flames of his blacksmith rig on wheels, Tom was larger than life. His shoulders were ax-handle wide and his hugely bulging arms matched those of any professional wrestler. But, for all his physical power, he was the gentlest of men, who truly believed the lyrics of romantic country and western songs.

Given the right woman, he would have undoubtedly remained faithful for fifty years. But Tom had an uncanny talent for picking the *wrong* woman.

Tom and his bride-to-be, who was soon called "Little Carolyn," were not well matched. He had a college degree and she
had left school in tenth grade. He was noncombative and she
had a fiery temper. But Carolyn was attractive and sexy, and
Tom wanted so much to be married and create a family of his
own. He married Carolyn with high hopes on October 25, 1968.
"I had this idea," he said, "that I could change her. I could stop
her drinking. I could sober her up and she wouldn't never have
a problem, 'cause I was going to take care of her. You can't do
that if they don't want to change."

They moved back to Atlanta and Tom went to work for Ralston Purina. The fourth Walter—Walter Russell Allanson,
called Russ—was born in 1970. When he was just a baby, Carolyn and Tom had so much trouble getting along that they
separated, and Tom asked his father to file divorce papers for
him. He moved Carolyn and Russ up to Athens and figured his
second marriage was over. "But I just couldn't stand being away
from my baby boy," Tom remembered. "I went back up to
Athens and got her and brought her back home, and then a year
passed and another baby was born. My daddy had the divorce
papers in a drawer; he'd never filed them."

Tom's second child, Sherry Lynette, was born in 1972.
Though Tom's parents didn't particularly approve of Carolyn,
either as a wife or as a mother, they did want to see him settled
down. Big Carolyn and Walter were pleased to have grandchildren. However, when Little Carolyn wrecked her mother-in-
law's car, Walter was livid. Why couldn't Tom have picked a
wife with at least a lick of sense?

Tom himself was beginning to rethink his reconciliation. All
he had wanted was a peaceful home to come to after a hard day's
work, but what he got was a complaining nag. The house was
messy and the kids were crying. He found it difficult even to
remember the pretty little blonde he had fallen in love with.

One night, Carolyn drank too much and, according to Tom,
she started waving a gun around. Worried for Russ and Sherry,
Tom tucked a baby under each arm and headed out the front
door. He was in the doorway when his wife pegged a shot at him
with his own .357. The doorframe splintered beside him and he
took flight, his long legs landing the three of them beyond the
front porch.

Nobody was hurt, but his stomach turned over when he thought of what might have happened. Tom knew he couldn't go on in the marriage, but he had no idea how he was going to escape it without hurting his kids. He didn't want to file charges against Little Carolyn, though, and wondered what he was going to do. He wasn't yet thirty years old, and the love he longed for was still somewhere off in the distance, tantalizing and elusive and always beyond his grasp.

13

By the summer of 1973, Tom had finally come to a place where he knew he had to walk away from his five-year-old marriage or die trying, *literally* die. In his mind at least, that was well within the realm of possibility. The fragile blond he had married who "looked like Grace Kelly" regarded him with unveiled disinterest if not frank malice. Anytime a woman sights down on a man and pulls the trigger, he has to figure the magic has gone out of their relationship. Tom was going to have to stop picking his women for the way they looked and concentrate on more permanent attributes. He acknowledged that he had made another major mistake with Carolyn. Their marriage had been dead for a long time.

On September 23, 1973, Tom left Carolyn. He couldn't support two households; he had nowhere to go for the moment but back to his boyhood home on Norman Berry Drive. He dreaded it. He was a head taller than his father, but Walter could still diminish him with a word or even a scornful glance. Tom didn't expect to find shoulders there to cry on or someone who felt concern for his situation. The most he hoped for was some breathing space to get his feet on the ground and figure out his future. He didn't find what he needed.

Tom's parents had not been much upset by his first divorce. He was a college boy then, and the marriage was over quickly. But when he went to his father asking for legal advice about his plans to divorce Carolyn, he found that the rules had changed. Walter disapproved mightily. Tom had children, and that made it a completely different situation. Walter leveled his cool blue-gray eyes at his son and intoned, "You can get a divorce any day in the week as long as you don't have children. If you have children, you live in it [your marriage]—no matter what the circumstances are. I don't care if your *life* is threatened, you live in it."

Walter refused to listen to any of Tom's quite cogent reasons for wanting to be free. He didn't care if Carolyn sometimes drank too much, and he didn't care if she had fired a gun at Tom. Hell, he didn't care if she ran over him with a truck. Tom was a big boy and he should have been able to handle his wife.

"I want no part of a divorce case for Tom," Walter confided to a lifelong friend. "I wouldn't touch it. I told Tom's wife, 'You're twenty-one years old. Get you an attorney of your own. I won't have a voice in it this way or that.' "

At length, Walter had grudgingly said he would look into the divorce matter for his son. But in truth, Walter did everything he could to *block* a divorce, even while he kept promising Tom he would file for him. He was actually trying to delay long enough so that his son might change his mind. He had spent more than half his life supporting Tom, and he didn't relish supporting Tom's ex and his two children. Walter knew it would come to that; he wasn't the kind of man who let his kin go on welfare, and Little Carolyn surely couldn't keep herself and the kids afloat alone. Walter would take care of his own if he had to, or at least those who couldn't do for themselves. His grandchildren would never go hungry, but he would seethe at the imposition and resent the son he blamed for it.

He hadn't been happy to have Tom back in their house anyway. His son was thirty years old—a grown man. Tom tried to help around the place, and he had gone up to Lake Lanier and worked on the dock "just like a horse," according to Jake Dailey,

Walter's old friend. But almost everything else Tom did aggravated his father.

Tom's only emotional support came from his grandparents—Paw and Nona. And when he found out that his father had done nothing about his divorce papers, he went to another attorney, who filed for his divorce. His father was furious. Still working for Ralston Purina selling feed, and shoeing horses in a second job, Tom contributed as much as he felt he could to his family, but not enough, in his father's estimation.

Just before Thanksgiving, 1973, Walter ordered Tom to move out of his house. After saying he would not take sides in his son's dispute with his estranged wife, it was apparent that he had done just that. Tom's parents declared Little Carolyn the injured party and rallied around her.

Fortunately—or so it seemed at the time—Tom had had somewhere to go. He had known and worked for the Radcliffes for several years, but until recently he had known their married daughter, Pat, only slightly. Now she was unmarried, and he had been pleasantly surprised when she let him know that she was interested in him. They had begun to date. Tom liked her whole family. The Radcliffes approved of him, probably more so because they felt the need for some kind of stability in Pat's life. Tom wasn't literally single, but he was the next best thing to it.

When his father and mother ordered him out, the Radcliffes said Tom could stay at their place temporarily. He could sleep on the sofa in their den. It was, allegedly, an arrangement of convenience. Of course it was a smoke screen. Pat had declared her intention to marry Tom Allanson six months earlier, long before he had any idea of even dating her. She had dedicated herself to seducing him and captivating him and he had been a sitting duck. For all his headlong rushes into marriage, Tom was essentially naive. Pat was six years older than he was, had grown children and a twenty-year marriage behind her, but she knew how to cajole and steer a man over the jumps of any emotional obstacle course she devised.

"I guess you could call her an aggressive/assertive woman," Tom said many years later. "She was very much aggressive in that she knew what she wanted and she'd go after it. In a way, I kind of admired that in a person."

Tom had been just about the lonesomest man in Atlanta when Pat decided she wanted him. By his own admission, he was virtually "starving" for affection. "Pat was so cool about the way she did things that you didn't know what was happening to you," he remembered. "You were in quicksand really before you realized you'd got your feet wet. Because of the way she did. I'm just sayin' . . . so nice, so gentle, so calm, and so innocent. And then this little piece went here, this little piece went here, and this one went here, and everything—and then all of a sudden you were not in control. And she turned it a little bit tighter, a little bit tighter. . . . You didn't feel it as it was turning, but then— And I never knew what hit me."

During their courtship, Pat displayed an absolute devotion to his needs, and Tom reveled in it.

✦ ✦ ✦

On New Year's Eve, 1973, Tom and Little Carolyn Allanson's custody and support hearing was on the court docket. Tom was shocked to find that his parents not only were not going to testify *for* him, they took the stand on behalf of his wife. They never mentioned Carolyn's accident that wrecked their vehicle, but Walter hinted on the witness stand that *Tom* sometimes drank too much. In fact, Tom neither drank nor smoked. He listened incredulously as his own blood relatives convinced a judge that he was at fault, and that he should pay what he considered excessive and impossible support and alimony to his nearly ex-wife.

Later that night, Tom stormed over to Norman Berry Road to confront his wife and parents. He was no angel; he could be a real hothead when he felt he had been injured. Walter later claimed that Tom had "cussed out" Big Carolyn that night. It was more likely that his epithets were directed toward his father. They had a major blowup, and Walter again ordered him out of the house.

When Tom left that night, it was the end of something. He would never again have even a civil relationship with his own father. It was as if his father had disowned him and adopted the woman who'd tried to blow his head off. Tom couldn't understand that. Carolyn was the one who had wrecked his mama's car, but his daddy now seemed to want her around all the time.

She had a perfectly good apartment of her own to go to. Tom remembered Little Carolyn's smug smile as she watched his banishment. He was hurt and he was mad, and his future seemed like a long, grim tunnel ahead of him. All he had left of his blood kin were Paw and Nona. He had no one else he could count on—only Pat and her parents, the Radcliffes—and he was grateful for all of them.

✦ ✦ ✦

The fact that his father had warned him about Pat, had called her a slut and a harlot, only made Tom want her more. He saw his father as a jealous hypocrite. "I wouldn't listen," he said. "That was like telling a teenage boy to not think about sex. I'd look at Pat in those little miniskirts and halter tops and . . . all I can say is she would have corrupted a preacher. I was vulnerable. She needed someone that was good with horses, and somebody who could shoe her horses free and somebody who could sell her feed free. I was just an easy mark. Some woman comes along and tells me she *loves* me, and of course I said, 'You *love* me? Well, all right! You've got me.' By that time, I didn't think anyone would love me ever again."

And so in 1973, Tom chose to see an entirely different Pat than the woman his father had warned him about. Beyond his recognition that she was a woman who marked her territory and took what she wanted, he had found her kind and gentle and as frail as a rose battered in a storm. She wasn't well, but she fought desperately to keep going. She fainted easily, slipping to the ground so softly. When that happened, Tom felt helpless and protective. All he could do was pick her up and carry her into the house and lay her down as gently as possible on the sofa.

There was another attraction. Pat had introduced Tom to sex unlike anything he had ever known before. When they were together, she seemed to forget how sick she was and strived only to pleasure him. No other woman had done that for him. He was besotted with Pat.

Pat's daughter, Susan Alford, and her husband, Bill, returned from a trip once to find their apartment occupied. They saw first a huge pair of boots and then a triumphant Pat and a sheepish Tom, who was hastily tucking his shirt into his jeans.

"*There*, Tom!" Pat said for everyone to hear. "You've had sex before, but you've never had anyone teach you how to make love until *I* came along!"

All of them, save Pat, were embarrassed, and Susan bustled around to make iced tea while Bill made awkward conversation. Tom was glowing like a teenager in the grip of a consuming crush.

✦ ✦ ✦

Two days after the New Year's Eve custody hearing, Tom's father wrote him a curt letter on his law office stationery.

January 2, 1974

Tommy:

This is to inform you that I talked to Mr. Turner this morning and he informed me that your wife was awarded all of the furniture and household appliances, including the refrigerator and freezer in Mrs. Lawrence's basement, and that you not be allowed to remove the same. Your wife also asked me to look after this refrigerator and freezer for her; so this puts me in the position of being her bailee. Therefore, I have put my own lock on this basement to insure that these two appliances will not be removed until such time as I get a Court Order instructing me to do otherwise.

If you intend to be your usual bull-headed self and remove them . . . I intend to file charges against you and anyone who assists you . . . for breaking and entering and theft. . . .

While you have some help I suggest that you move your junk from the garage and my backyard, and return the fan that was loaned to you. Any of your junk, equipment or otherwise that is left . . . after January 15, 1974, will be placed on the street for the City to pick up.

You will please give Mrs. Lawrence your back door key as you are forbidden to enter the house.

Walter O. Allanson

Allanson also sent a letter to the East Point police, warning them that he would file charges against his son and anyone who might help him try to remove appliances from his grandmother's basement.

Tom didn't want furniture and appliances; he wanted only a few of his more portable belongings. But he had to be careful about what he chose to retrieve from his former life. If ever there were an acrimonious divorce, Tom's divorce from Carolyn was it. According to Margureitte, Carolyn bombarded the house on Tell Road with calls. "I'd only met her once at a horse show some time ago—never thought anything about her one way or the other—and [she] called us and called us at all hours of the night and day."

Tom didn't make that much money to begin with, and he had to give five hundred dollars every month to Carolyn, a fact of life that Pat resented fiercely. Carolyn just wouldn't let them be. Pat and Margureitte complained that if the money didn't arrive, or even if it did, they were *still* being plagued with harassing calls from Tom's ex-wife demanding more money.

Pat detested Little Carolyn because she had once had Tom and because, technically at least, she was still married to him. Pat had begun to call him "my Tom" or "Pat's Tom." And Tom thrived on her all-enveloping possessiveness; he had never had a woman love him like that before. He was overwhelmed by the syrupy writings she composed for him. All her *o*'s were carefully traced hearts.

Pat was convinced that Little Carolyn was consumed with jealousy when Tom bought the Zebulon farm for her, and again when they were married at Stone Mountain.

Margureitte agreed with her. Without coming right out and saying it, after the murder Margureitte tried her best to let Detective Zellner know her personal theory about Tom's daddy and his daughter-in-law. If that wasn't cause for murder, she didn't know what was. And that, she felt, would explain why Walter hated Tom enough to just as soon kill him as look at him. Walter had purely terrified Margureitte. She shuddered to think about Pat out there all alone at Kentwood when he had come down and blatantly exposed himself to her.

If ever a man had a right to be bitter and resentful toward his father, it was Tom. But Tom was gentle; his hurt went inside. He would never have murdered his own parents. Never in the whole wide world. It wasn't fair that he was locked up. If there was anyone behind the shooting of Walter and Big Carolyn, Pat and Margureitte both insisted they saw the fine hand of Little Carolyn Allanson. They could not understand why the police weren't using the information they had given about her. They were convinced that they had all but handed the investigators a blueprint for murder, and they were annoyed that none of them recognized it.

14

There is nothing neat about murder; its untidy ravels can never be woven back into the fabric of time perfectly. Blood can eventually be scrubbed away and property disposed of. But questions seem always to be left begging for an answer. Even with a suspect in jail accused of the murders of Walter and Carolyn Allanson, the East Point police investigators still had a great deal of work to do.

On Sunday evening, July 7, George Zellner received a call from Little Carolyn. She had remembered something that she heard the night of the murders, something she had not told them before. Talking at the police station with Zellner and Gus Thornhill, Carolyn was considerably calmer than she had been in their earlier sessions. Her version of the events just before the shooting had not changed substantially, but she now remembered more. She had heard Daddy Allanson yell upstairs that he had "him" cornered in the hole, but she had never remembered a name for "him" before.

"Did you ever see your father-in-law while he was in the basement?" Zellner asked.

"No, sir."

"But you heard him?"

"Yes—only when he said for Mother to bring the gun down and when he said, 'Junior! Get the hell out of here!' "

Carolyn recalled that she saw her mother-in-law start down the steps with the gun and that she had wrestled with her, trying to take it away from her.

"Why?"

"I didn't want her to go—I didn't want her to get killed."

Mother Allanson had been distraught. Carolyn had heard her say, "If I see him, I'll shoot him!" Then she told the detectives that Mother Allanson had said something while she was going down the stairs.

"What?"

"Just before she was shot, she cried out, 'Tommy! Tommy! Tommy, don't hurt Daddy!' "

The detectives stared at her. How could she forget that for days? And then Zellner asked quietly, "Did you hear anything else?"

She nodded. "I heard a man's voice—not Daddy's—shouting, 'Shut up! Shut up! Shut up!' "

"Was it Tom's voice?"

"I can't swear that it was."

Carolyn said that Mother Allanson had been carrying the hunting rifle in front of her as if she was ready to fire it. It was at that point that everything had exploded. Little Carolyn had started down the steps after Big Carolyn, Walter had shouted to her to "Get the hell out of here," and she had heard a blast. She saw her mother-in-law just sit down, and a burst of red begin to blossom over her left breast. Little Carolyn had known her mother-in-law was dead; there was so much blood and she just sat there like a wax figure.

Carolyn said she had fled, but that she heard what seemed like five or six consecutive shots. "Pop! Pop! Pop! . . ."

And then she thought she had heard another blast.

The noose was tightening around Tom Allanson. His former wife must have had reasons to want to incriminate him, but would she deliberately "remember" details to make him look even more guilty, or was she simply coming out of her shock and telling the truth? Detectives doubted that she was the killer herself, despite the Radcliffes' suspicions.

✦   ✦   ✦

Tom Allanson was arraigned on Monday, July 8, 1974, before
East Point Municipal Court Judge R. M. McDuffie. There
would be no bail. On August 2, the Fulton County grand jury
returned a true bill charging Walter Thomas Allanson with two
counts of murder. If convicted, he could face the death penalty.

On August 8, Judge Charles Wofford heard arguments over
whether bond should be granted to Tom Allanson. Tom had
new counsel. Although Cal Long was a perfectly adequate attorney who had successfully represented the Radcliffes in lesser
matters in the past, Pat wanted Tom to be represented by the
top criminal defense lawyers in Atlanta. But that would take a
great deal of money—ironically, it would take more money than
she had originally planned to spend to turn Kentwood into a
showplace.

Tom had needed four thousand dollars by July 15 to retain a
new law firm. His aunt Jean had lent him two thousand dollars,
but he had to pay that back within a week. Pat paid Jean back
with a check that, to her chagrin and Jean's anger, bounced. To
raise money for Tom's defense, the Radcliffes mortgaged their
Tell Road farm for as much as they could get: thirty-five
hundred dollars. Then they put the farm up for sale.

Tom wrote to his grandparents, Nona and Paw, begging them
to help Pat. Despite his own predicament, it was Pat's desperation that seemed to eat at him. "Please help my Pat." She had
no money to pay the utilities on the farm, and no "spending
money." Paw and Nona were slow to respond with money, although they were backing Tom emotionally. The elderly Allansons were the only resource Tom had. Pat had quickly managed
to alienate Jean Boggs by dismissing any of her suggestions
about how to help Tom. Tom explained to Paw that Pat would
go to work in a minute if she could, but a job would kill a woman
in such delicate health. She was already selling off her precious
antiques to help him.

Still Paw held tight to his cash.

Unsure of where the money for legal representation would
come from, Pat nevertheless retained the firm of Garland, Nuckolls and Kadish, assuring them that she had adequate funds. She
wanted Tom free, and somehow she would find a way. Reuben

A. Garland was the canny, grand old man of the firm, and his son, Colonel Edward T. M. Garland, was a brilliant and colorful man in his late thirties. You couldn't do any better in Atlanta than to have the Garlands represent you.

Father and son would be assisted by John Nuckolls, who now pleaded for Tom's release while he awaited trial. Pat was there in the courtroom, along with Margureitte and the colonel and old Paw Allanson. Nuckolls argued that Tom had absolutely no record of violent behavior prior to the crimes he stood accused of. And he was sorely needed at home. "Your Honor," he pleaded. "There's a serious financial problem in connection with that stable [Kentwood] due to a mortgage. The farm was purchased five months ago. It was purchased on a down payment with a balloon and that balloon is coming due, and they are fixing to lose that farm because of the inability to meet the notes."

Even worse, Nuckolls pointed out, both Tom's wife and his grandmother were in very poor physical condition, and his continued incarceration wasn't helping. "Your Honor, I have two letters from doctors concerning his [Tom's] wife's condition." Nuckolls explained that Pat was suffering from pulmonary emboli, a release of clots into the bloodstream that would ultimately pass into her heart and lungs. "She has had open heart surgery and has an umbrella valve implanted in the heart. Her condition is reported by her doctors at Emory Hospital and her private physician, Dr. William J. Taylor, as undoubtedly terminal with a life expectancy of two years or less."

Pat certainly appeared to be ill. Since the shootings, she had lost so much weight that she looked like a skeleton. Her mother and her aunts had tried everything they could to get her to eat; if she did eat, she threw up. Her aunt Thelma made her special homemade soup, and Pat couldn't even hold that down.

The defense had a number of prestigious character witnesses, including Colonel and Mrs. Radcliffe, standing by to vouch for Tom's gentleness. Nona and Paw wanted him out on bond too. If he were to be released, his counsel assured the court that he would go straight to Kentwood and stay there, leaving only to assist his defense team from time to time.

William Weller, for the Fulton County District Attorney's Office, quickly erased the picture of Tom Allanson as gentle, describing him as "a mountain of a man" who was charged with "blowing his mother's heart out." Although he had known Tom and his family for years, Judge Wofford reluctantly agreed with the state that there would be no bond and that Tom would remain in jail, but he set the earliest trial date possible, the first Monday morning after Labor Day: September 9, 1974.

Tom's defense team had lost only the first round, but already Ed Garland could sense trouble. Although she obviously hadn't the foggiest grasp of the way the law worked, Pat Allanson clearly didn't trust her husband's lawyers. She would not allow Tom to confer with Garland unless she were present. She watched him like a hawk, monitoring and editing his responses even as they emerged from his mouth. She spoke *for* him whenever possible. Why was she so concerned about what her husband might say? She was almost hysterical about losing "her Tom."

Garland detected that Tom ached to talk to him alone, that the man had a heavy load on his mind. There might well be extenuating circumstances, something a top defense lawyer could build a case on, but Pat seemed to be afraid to let Tom speak freely. In her zeal to protect him, she became a defense lawyer's nightmare.

Worse, Ed Garland could see that Tom trusted his wife implicitly. The man was addled by love, consumed by love; he would gladly die for her. Ed Garland sincerely hoped it would not come to that.

15

In less than a year, Pat had fallen in love with Tom, married him, they had purchased Kentwood Morgan Farms, and now it was all gone. She was far too ill to live in Kentwood alone, and she couldn't possibly do the chores or handle the horses by herself. What was the use? They were probably going to lose Kentwood anyway. Without Tom, she could never meet the balloon payments. When fall came round again, Pat was back living with Margureitte and the colonel on Tell Road, while Ronnie stayed on in Zebulon so the place wouldn't be empty and a target for vandals. He wouldn't be sixteen until November, but he had always hastened to help his mother. He never refused anything she asked of him.

Tom Allanson awaited trial in a sweltering jail cell.

◆ ◆ ◆

Margureitte Radcliffe traced all the misery in her family to 1974—to the passionate alliance between Pat and Tom and the violence that followed so soon after. Once things started to slide, it was like an avalanche. A pebble or two at first, and then the flowers and grass from the hillside, and finally the very foundation of their lives.

As it was in most felony cases of such importance, there was a delay in going to trial. Tom's pretrial motions wouldn't be heard until October and Pat told him she had hit bottom. She had no money and no strength to go on. She couldn't bear it that the trial had been delayed. She told him she really needed to be in the hospital. "But I won't go, Sugar," she said softly. "Because that would mean I couldn't see you at all, couldn't come and visit you—and that would surely kill me. Besides, the premiums on the medical insurance are past due and I can't pay for that or for my medicine."

There could have been no more degrading purgatory for a man like Tom than to be caged and see this fragile woman he adored reduced to poverty and illness gone untreated. Pat had become the only person who mattered to him. Her moods, worries, opinions, and well-being determined his own. Her fears and sorrows had the power to leave him twisting in the wind.

Tom's attorneys would far rather have seen him plead guilty to lesser charges than innocent to murder. Pat would not have it. She came to every lawyer-client conference, attached to her husband's side, it sometimes seemed, like an annoying growth. It was almost as if she had a secret fear that Tom would tell the Garlands and John Nuckolls something that would endanger *her*. But that was ridiculous.

Ed Garland finally got a chance to talk with Tom alone, and he seized it. "Tom, *listen to me*. I cannot defend you unless I know the truth. I'll defend you on what you say to do, but I've got to know . . . because all this stuff *cannot* be true."

Tom would later admit that he did finally tell Ed Garland what had happened that night in the basement of his parents' house. But he would not let Garland repeat what he had said—not to anyone. Tom exacted a promise that Garland would not use that information in defending him. He had promised Pat. She, of all people, loved him more than anyone on earth. And they would do it her way. Garland was supremely frustrated; he was one of the best criminal defense attorneys in the state of Georgia, and he was ethically bound to proceed with one legal arm tied behind his back.

Pat was distraught when she learned what Tom had told his attorney. "I thought she was going to divorce me right there," Tom remembered. But they did what Pat wanted. She absolutely refused to consider a plea bargain that would dictate that Tom would go to prison, if only for a few years. She would die without him. He *had* to be free, and he would be, she promised him. She would brook no compromise.

It was agreed that Tom would plead innocent to all charges. And that left his attorneys precious little ammunition with which to defend him. They had character witnesses who admired Tom, and witnesses who would demean the character of those who testified against him. Hardly the stuff of which a powerful defense is constructed.

Private investigators for the defense had tried to find someone who had seen Tom far away from the shooting scene. They had even advertised for such a witness in the *Atlanta Journal* personals:

REWARD

ANYONE SEEING TOM A., 6 FT 4, 250
POUNDS, LIGHT HAIR, 2 WEEKS AGO,
WEDNESDAY, JULY 3RD BETWEEN 4:30 AND
9:00 ON CLEVELAND AVENUE BETWEEN
S. FULTON HOSPITAL AND I-75 OR GIVING
HIM A RIDE ON I-75 FROM CLEVELAND TO
CENTRAL, PLEASE CALL 344–5729, 436–8435.

URGENT! URGENT!

The ad backfired, and became State's Exhibit No. 102.

✦ ✦ ✦

It was an endless hot summer and fall as they waited for the trial, and a relief when October 14, 1974, finally came. Both Pat and Tom seemed to believe that he would be found innocent and they would be together again, perhaps in time to save their plantation. Hoyt Waller expected a balloon payment by December or he would repossess their paradise. Tom thought he could find some way to scrape the money together, if only he were free before the end of October.

Tom's divorce skirmishes had been held in small county court-houses; his murder trial would be held in the Fulton County Courthouse in downtown Atlanta. Outside the massive white marble courthouse, the oak trees of Atlanta glowed golden, the dogwood's leaves were tinged with red, and the maples turned a clear bright coral. Inside, as in all courtrooms, there was no sense of season, only the dust of many seasons, many years.

"The court calls for trial," Judge Charles A. Wofford, white-haired and benign, intoned, "the case of *The State of Georgia v. Walter Thomas Allanson,* charged with murder, Indictment No. A-22765, Colonel Edward T. M. Garland for the defendant and Colonel William Weller for the state."

Customarily, relatives of the accused sat behind the gallery divider, but Pat insisted on sitting at the defense table. That was fine with Tom, but Garland threw up his hands. Dressed in a dazzling new outfit each day, sewn by her own hand, Pat was the picture of the anxious, devoted wife standing by her man. Her vantage point at the trial also allowed her to instruct Garland and to nudge and whisper to Tom.

It took only a day to pick a jury, although they went through more than four dozen candidates before both Ed Garland and William Weller accepted a panel of seven men and five women, eight blacks and four whites, with two alternates. An inordinate number of the prospective jurors had relatives in law enforcement, or knew either the prosecutor or the defense team, or had very strong feelings about the death penalty. In the end, Tom Allanson's fate would be decided by a Sears Roebuck store manager, a retired teacher, two postal employees, an insurance analyst, a grocer, a physical education teacher, a phone company clerk, a retired waitress, a payroll administrator, a housewife, and a retired airline pilot.

✦   ✦   ✦

As Assistant D.A. William Weller called his witnesses one by one, they painted a devastating, unrelenting picture that would be hard for Ed Garland to erase. Sergeant Butts of the East Point Police Department testified that Tom had been so angry two days before the killings—as he sought to charge his father with public indecency—that he had said, "If this kind of stuff keeps up, I'll kill him!" Deputy Richard Satterfield of Forsyth

County, an investigator into the abortive ambush at Lake Lanier four days before the murders, described how Walter and Carolyn Allanson had almost died in a storm of bullets. Mary Rena Jones of the Jones store said she had seen a blue pickup truck with a round decal on the door the morning of the ambush.

Weller called Walter Allanson's employees and neighbors, and then all of the East Point police investigators who had pored over the house and the yard on Norman Berry Drive or who had gone to Zebulon and arrested Tom. Twenty-two convincing witnesses for the state, none of whom had particular axes to grind. Step by step, Weller built his case, implying to the jury that Tom Allanson was not only guilty of shooting his parents on July 3, but that he had been present at all the earlier attacks and harassments.

Tom sat frozen at the defense table, his longish hair cut now above his ears and his shoulders straining at a tailored navy blue sport coat. When Mary Jones testified that she had seen him drive by her store on the morning of June 29, 1974, in a blue pickup with a canopy and a Kentwood Morgan Farm circular seal on the door, he shook his head slightly. He knew that seal hadn't been on the truck since Pat's accident in Stone Mountain two months before. Pat's reaction was much more obvious to the jury. Frowning and grimacing, she wrote a note and shoved it dramatically across the defense table to Ed Garland.

On cross-examination, Garland got Mrs. Jones to admit she hadn't recognized the driver of the blue truck, nor had she mentioned seeing the truck on the day of the ambush. Her testimony warred with her first police report. She had first recalled seeing Tom the day *before* the ambush at Lake Lanier. Garland fought to have Mary Jones's testimony thrown out, but he lost. For the second time in two days, he asked for a mistrial, and for the second time, Judge Wofford denied his request.

There would be many legal tussles between the defense and the prosecution during the trial, times when the jury would be banished from the courtroom. Judge Wofford was an easygoing, folksy jurist. He invited the male members of the jury to remove their jackets and even their shoes if they were pinching. Ashtrays would be provided for those who cared to smoke. He apologized for the delays and explained that "if you're inclined to blame anyone, blame the court."

Little Carolyn Allanson was probably the biggest gun the prosecution had. She was right next door to an eyewitness, and television mysteries had made eyewitness testimony seem infallible. Carolyn had never said she saw Tom that rainy night in July, but in her third interview with George Zellner, she *had* recalled that she heard her ex-mother-in-law scream out, "Tommy! Tommy! Tommy!" She was on the witness stand for much of the third day of trial, examined and cross-examined.

The Allansons' next-door neighbors, the Ducketts, and Officer McBurnett were, of course, *true* eyewitnesses to a tall running man who fled the crime scene. All of them pinned Tom Allanson a little tighter to the wall.

Hampered as he was by Pat's refusal to allow her husband to plead guilty to lesser charges, Ed Garland could only try to stem the damage. He was good. He elicited an admission from McBurnett that he had glimpsed Tom in the police station *before* he identified him in the lineup. McBurnett had, like most of the East Point officers, made it a habit to glance into the identification room to wave to a particularly attractive female clerk who worked there. On June 6, Tom had been sitting in the ID room as McBurnett passed.

Several of the investigating officers had not saved their notes or reduced their interviews to written reports. Garland was agile, a fencer poking tiny holes in the fabric of the state's case with his rapier. But only tiny holes. The state's eyewitnesses included a police officer and a fire fighter. The Ducketts both described the huge man who had run past their house even as the first sirens howled through the Norman Berry neighborhood. It would be a herculean task for any attorney to overcome that kind of testimony. Ed Garland was further handicapped by Pat's courtroom behavior and her continued insistence that she and not her husband's attorney should decide how his defense would be handled. When Pat was dissatisfied with the way things were going, she punched Tom in the ribs. She seemed to hover just at the edge of hysteria, watching and listening for some danger to Tom. It drove Garland nuts.

On Wednesday morning, October 16, Ed Garland, his jaw tight, asked Judge Wofford for a conference in chambers out of the jury's hearing. The opposing attorneys were both present, as was the court stenographer.

"Judge, I think it's necessary, to protect my reputation and the integrity of the judicial process," Garland began, "[to note] that I find substantial disagreements between the defendant's wife and myself concerning how the case . . . should be conducted. . . . There are certain witnesses that I decline to put on the stand, *will* not put on the stand . . . because of my investigation in the case.

"I also find there's an inability to communicate with my client effectively because of his desire to have his wife present, and I find that his wife is unstable. His wife is affecting his judgment insofar as my ability to communicate with him."

His exasperation obvious, Garland told the judge that Pat wanted to select which witnesses would testify, and that she was telling Tom that he must testify. Almost always, a competent criminal defense attorney chooses not to put his client on the stand; once he does that, he opens the defendant up to cross-examination from the prosecution and devastating questions often ensue. Pat apparently felt she could coach Tom in the proper way to testify.

"I want the record to show," Garland continued, "that I requested that she remain out of the courtroom during the case. She has refused, and the defendant has demanded that she be allowed to be present. . . . I feel like the approach I have taken is the best I know how to do. That's all I wanted to put on the record, Judge."

"Would you like me to bring her in here—have Mrs. Allanson brought in?"

"I think it will just get into her crying and gnashing of teeth, Judge," Garland sighed.

"Colonel Garland, I have watched her—her facial expressions —a number of times," Judge Wofford said. "Now, she has not made any audible statements in the courtroom. . . . She's made no truly noticeable gestures—unless you were watching her carefully. . . . I have felt for the days this has been proceeding that she has been a detriment to the trial, but she committed no action that was sufficiently overt . . . for the court to take action. I recognize that her presence is definitely a stumbling block to the harmonious proceedings that we still have ahead."

Ed Garland, fighting for his client, was truly stymied. "What has occurred has occurred outside the presence of the jury and the court," he said. "I asked her to leave yesterday where I could talk to him alone, to remove him from her suggestive influences. . . . She went across the courtroom and faked a heart attack— in my opinion—to get the attention."

Judge Wofford nodded. Pat Allanson had gasped and fainted the moment he had walked out of the courtroom, and the sheriff's deputy had informed him of it.

Ed Garland explained further. "When I tried to talk with him . . . gave him my uninterrupted counsel, and got him to reflect on it, she pulled a heart attack . . . and demanded that she be present with him in all my discussions. . . . I find that with her acting the way she acts, that he doesn't think clearly."

Nobody in Judge Wofford's chambers could argue with that. But there didn't seem to be anything they could do about it. In her near-hysterical fight to save Tom, Pat continued to disrupt his trial, but she always managed to stay just within the bounds of courtroom propriety. The judge had warned against demonstrations, and her grimacing and whispering remained on the edge of what he would allow, barely restrained. Her visits to Tom left him unsettled and worried. She wanted him to testify; she warned him Ed Garland wasn't doing right by him. Outside the courtroom, Pat often fainted and clutched her heart. On one occasion during a break, she pointed out a policeman to Tom and whispered desperately, "Oh my God, Tom! That man raped me!"

And then she fainted once again.

"What did she expect me to do?" Tom later asked futilely. "Deck a cop right there in the courthouse hallway? I couldn't do anything."

Tom Allanson descended further into his own private hell. The way things were going, he now figured he would probably be found guilty and executed. Who would look after Pat? He was so in love with his wife that his biggest worry was not his own bleak future, but hers. What would she ever do in this world without him?

✦ ✦ ✦

Ed Garland trudged on, feeling Pat Allanson around his neck like an albatross. He attempted to have her description of what Tom was wearing on the day of the shootings excluded. It didn't help his client's case one bit to have his own wife corroborate the state's eyewitnesses. Garland's objections were overruled.

The jury saw dozens of pictures of the blood-drenched basement and heard Sergeant Callahan describe the scene he had found on the night of July 3. But had Tom been one of the people in the basement? If Garland could convince Pat that he had to keep Tom off the stand, the case would come down to ballistics. Ballistics were not nearly as emotional or fraught with danger as Tom's testimony could be.

Three guns had been present: a .32 revolver, a brand-new Marlin deer rifle—really an "elephant gun," high-powered as they come—and a 20-gauge shotgun. Could anyone prove *who* had fired which guns? Garland was able to establish on cross-examination that Tom's hands had been clean of gunpowder residue when he was tested, and that no fingerprints had been found on any of the weapons.

Kelly Fite, a criminalist and microanalyst from the Georgia State Crime Lab, was called to the stand as an expert witness for the prosecution. He testified that the shotgun cartridges, one blue and one yellow, found in the "hole" itself and on the basement floor just beneath it had come from the Excel shotgun, the "stolen" gun. They had once contained approximately twenty pellets—No. 3 buckshot, the same gauge as those found in Walter and Carolyn Allanson. The buckshot itself was consistent with the type used in the empty cartridges, although lead pellets, unlike bullets, bear no definitive markings that can identify the weapon from which they have been fired.

Fite's laboratory tests indicated that the shotgun had been about ten feet from Carolyn when it was fired. Whoever shot Walter Allanson had been over forty feet away, and the angle of the deadly buckshot had been from left to right. Some of the pellets had "skipped" as they hit a flashlight Walter had carried and the overhead light fixture. The closer a shotgun is to a target, the smaller the circle of damage it will leave in the target —or in the victim. Carolyn Allanson's wounds had been centered in her left chest area; Walter's wounds were widely scattered from his face to his hand, wrist, and abdomen.

Fite concluded that only two shots had been fired from the Excel shotgun in the Allanson basement, one hitting Carolyn and one striking Walter. He had test-fired the gun and found that a cartridge would eject directly back about six to eight inches and fall at the feet of the shooter. Reconstructing from the physical evidence, he could speculate with accuracy what had happened. Someone had fired the shotgun from the hole or just in front of the hole. Someone had fired a pistol into the hole, not once but six or seven times. Someone had fired the Marlin once—from an area near the stairs. Fite had determined that the empty casing found near Walter and Carolyn was from the Marlin .45/70—the "elephant gun"—but the slug itself had never been found.

It appeared that there had been at least two shooters in the basement that night. There could have been three. But if Tom was that third shooter, would he be capable of murdering his own parents?

To establish a pattern of vindictive behavior, Prosecutor Weller continued to focus on the harassment of Walter Allanson —principally the Lake Lanier ambush—before the fatal night, and Ed Garland fought like a tiger to keep it out. Connecting Tom to all those bullet holes in his parents' station wagon would only bury him deeper. Weller, of course, insisted that the ambush shooting was only part of a "total continuous transaction" from June 29 to July 3. And countless hours would be spent arguing over when the Morgan Kentwood seal had been removed from Tom Allanson's pickup truck. In fact, it had not been there since May, but witnesses from Jones's store still claimed to have seen Tom driving a truck with that seal on the morning of the ambush. Garland wanted that false identification excluded from the jury's consideration, but Judge Wofford ruled against him.

And he lost again when he attempted to keep word of Walter and Carolyn's rancorous wills from the jury's ears. The jury heard of them in Mary McBride's testimony as Walter Allanson's secretary.

"They have accomplished their motive," Garland complained to Judge Wofford. "They wanted to hit the jury over the head with a sledgehammer and then tell them, 'Now you ignore the headache.' That's what we have here. We have thrown horse manure in the jury box and want to ask them not to smell it. . . . We have flashed wills here and said, 'Oh, there were wills. There must be motive. He must have killed for financial gain.' "

Perhaps the biggest defense loss of all was Ed Garland's attempt to have a mistrial declared over Carolyn Allanson's altered recollections of what she had heard the night of the murders. Her firm voice testifying that she remembered hearing screams of "Tommy! Tommy! Tommy!" before the fatal shots might well be a death knell for his client.

16

The state rested, and Ed Garland rose to present the case for the defense. It would be an arduous uphill climb and he knew it, but he gave no sign of that as he questioned his first witness.

Garland and his investigators had located a number of people who knew Tom Allanson well, and who had seen him on Saturday, June 29. The shots had hit his parents' car a little after 11:00 A.M. as it headed up Truman Mountain Road. If Garland could show that Tom was someplace else at that time, it would neutralize the continual testimony about the man in the blue pickup with a canopy attached and with the Kentwood seal on the door. In the best of all possible worlds, he might even produce someone who had seen Tom on the night of July 3, far, far away from his parents' home.

Garland began with the Saturday before.

James Strickland, a Kayo Oil gas station attendant, saw Tom and Pat Allanson in his station in Barnesville—some ninety miles south of Lake Lanier—on the twenty-ninth between 10:15 and 10:30 A.M. They were driving a blue truck with a green horseshoeing trailer on the back. Strickland remembered no emblem on the truck's door.

Bobby Jackson, a man who had been "rodeoing" with Tom for a dozen years, saw him on June 29. Jackson was on his way to a "jackpot steer roping" in Madison, and heading east on I-20, just east of Atlanta, when he recognized Tom's shoeing rig pass him. He testified it was between noon and 12:30, and Tom had exited at the Lithonia off ramp.

Edgar Milton Smith, president of Voice Communications, Inc., of Atlanta, had horses pastured in Lithonia, and Tom had arrived shortly after 12:30 the afternoon of June 29 to shoe them. He had stayed until approximately 6:00 that evening.

Robert Warr, Tom and Pat's next-door neighbor in Zebulon, had seen them come home at eleven o'clock on the night of June 29, driving the blue pickup with the green horseshoeing rig on the back.

Donald Cooper, a potential horse buyer, had been to Kentwood on June 29 and found Tom and Pat gone. He *had* seen the canopy of the blue truck on blocks in the yard.

Liz Price, Pat and Tom's neighbor and friend, verified that the Kentwood Morgan emblem had not been on their blue pickup since Pat's accident just after their wedding.

Garland was doing the best he could with what he had, and yet he hadn't even touched on Tom's whereabouts on the murder night. Pat had brought Garland the next witness, and the defense attorney approached him warily.

The witness's name was Bill Jones, and he was employed at a liquor store located on Cleveland Avenue at the I-75 freeway. He recalled that, yes indeed, he had met up with Tom Allanson at twelve minutes to eight on the evening of July 3 when Tom came in to ask for change to make a phone call.

"Some people want change for the telephone—which is outside on the parking lot against the post," Jones testified, "but ever since I have been there, no one has asked me for change to make a *long-distance* call. . . . He even added Zebulon, Georgia. . . . The only reason why I would have remembered that—his wife came in the next night after and asked me was there a man in there that evening, and I told her what had happened. . . . See, when he said 'telephone,' the light bulb went on in my mind because my wife goes to sleep on the sofa at night—

roughly at eight o'clock. I have to call her by eight. . . . When he said 'telephone,' I looked at my watch."

The voluble Mr. Jones estimated that his store was located about two miles from Norman Berry Drive in East Point.

The state demolished Mr. Jones as Weller took over cross-examination. Jones admitted that, while he had told Sergeant Callahan that Tom had been in the store at 4:30 P.M., he had later told a private investigator that he didn't know if Tom had been in at seven or eight—or nine, for that matter. Jones recalled, after being prodded, that Pat Allanson had been in the liquor store to see him at least three times, and after that he had been visited by defense investigators on several occasions. He denied vigorously that he had seen a reward for information posted in the *Atlanta Journal.*

He was not a credible witness—undoubtedly one of "Pat's witnesses" that Ed Garland had told Judge Wofford he did not want to put on the stand. But he was the *only* witness who placed Tom away from the slaying scene. And he was far from impressive.

Mrs. Clifford B. Radcliffe was. Dressed impeccably, her beautiful gray hair perfectly coiffed, she made her way gracefully to the stand.

Ed Garland approached her, smiling. "And what is your husband's occupation?"

"My husband is with the federal government with—in a security support branch. He's a retired lieutenant colonel."

"He's here today, is he not?"

"Yes, he is." She smiled serenely.

"Right there?"

"Yes."

"The man who just took his glasses off?"

"The most distinguished man in the courtroom," Margureitte replied proudly.

Garland had let her go a bit too far. He wanted the jury to see what fine people the Radcliffes were, but he didn't want to leave them with the impression that they were holier-than-thou. He quickly changed the subject. "All right. Now, Mrs. Radcliffe, is your daughter present in the courtroom?"

"Yes, she is."

"She's the defendant's wife?"

"That is correct. That is our daughter."

Garland hurried on before the witness could point out that Pat was the "most beautiful woman in the courtroom."

Margureitte disputed the ridiculous idea that the Allansons' truck had *ever* had an emblem like the one the Lake Lanier witnesses described. Next, she verified that Pat and Tom had come for dinner on June 29, and had been summoned from there to Nona and Paw's.

Garland leapt ahead to the evening of July 3. Margureitte testified that Pat had called them, worried sick, around 7:30. "I told her that me and her father would meet her, to stay exactly where she was. . . . I told her to stay at the King Professional Building at the parking lot, to park away from the building. . . . We'd be there and we were there."

Garland moved into Margureitte's two strange and frightening encounters with the late Walter Allanson. Bill Weller objected. "Your Honor, it seems to me we're going into an awful lot of hearsay. . . . It's too bad I couldn't have poor . . . Mr. Allanson here to come and say what he said or didn't say—but I'm sort of in a peculiar situation . . . Your Honor. . . . If it's all right for him to go into hearsay of a man resting six feet under, it's all right for me to go into something the wife said to her also."

Judge Wofford refused to let either lawyer bargain for future rulings. He nodded to Garland, who asked the witness what Walter Allanson had said to her.

Margureitte's tone was dramatic as she recalled her last conversation with the late victim. "He said, 'I think it will all be over by this weekend, that Tommy will either be jailed or he will be dead,' and I was terrified."

"Did he say anything in response to your statement that Tommy didn't do it [the ambush]? . . . Did he say anything about whether it could be anybody else that could have done it?"

"Your Honor," Weller objected. "I think we are leading a little bit."

Garland grinned ruefully. "I think we are, Your Honor."

Bill Weller questioned the defendant's mother-in-law. Even on cross-examination, Margureitte Radcliffe was a most forthcoming witness. She was, however, disturbed by quotations attributed to her from her July 6 interview with Detective Zellner. Even when told that they had come directly from a transcription of an audiotape, she felt sure that words had been added or left out. A comparison to the original tape showed no such omissions or additions. "[The night Pat called you] she had no idea where her husband, Tom, was at that time, did she?"

"She said he had gone to talk with his mother," Margureitte replied.

"Oh, she told you that?" Weller sounded surprised.

"Yes."

"She didn't tell you that she didn't know where he was and she was frantic waiting on him?"

"No."

"She told you that he had gone—"

"He had gone there. . . . I was frightened."

Garland fought back with hearsay objections and was sustained.

"Now, Mrs. Radcliffe," Weller continued. "Tom Allanson's final decree on his divorce from the second wife, Carolyn, was on the ninth of May, 1974, wasn't it?"

"To my knowledge, yes, sir."

"And they [Tom and Pat] got married when—the latter part of May 1974?" Weller led the witness smoothly into a trap.

"They were married on the evening of May 9."

"Oh, they got married the very evening that the divorce decree went into effect?"

"That is correct." Margureitte sat up straighter and fixed the prosecutor with a thin smile.

"Now, isn't it a fact that the late Mr. and Mrs. Allanson would not accept your daughter?"

"I don't know. They did not know her."

"Well, I didn't say that. I said, they did not *accept* her as a daughter-in-law, would they?"

"He said that . . . he didn't have a son, so therefore, how *could* he have a daughter-in-law?"

"Yes, ma'am."

"That's right." Margureitte fixed her eyes triumphantly on a chastened-appearing Weller. She was a disaster as a witness on cross; she offered too much information and she came across as supercilious. On balance, Garland's case would have been better off without Margureitte's testimony. She was more help to the prosecution.

It had been a very long day, this fourth day of trial, and Judge Wofford released the jury at 6:00 P.M. Ed Garland asked for yet another mistrial and was again denied. Each request, of course, would add to the likelihood that an appeal for a new trial would be granted. He was a cunning attorney; he knew exactly what he was doing. The lawyers wrangled over legal points in chambers long after the jury had dispersed.

✦ ✦ ✦

On Friday morning, October 18, the first witness was Fred Benson, a blacksmith and longtime friend of Tom Allanson's. Garland hoped to throw doubt on Tom's identification in the police lineup three days after the murders. Benson had been a voluntary participant in the lineup of July 6. He explained why. "I went in to see Tom, see, and Detective Thornhill was real nice—took me back to the cell to talk to Tom. . . . All these officers were in there [the police station] . . . and they were fixing to have a lineup. They brought these two car theft boys out. They were little bitty short guys, looked criminal—criminal-type-looking people—with moustaches."

"You don't mean to say that just because they had a moustache—" Garland cut in quickly. Several of the jurors had moustaches.

"You *know*. What I'm trying to say—they didn't look like Tom. If you've seen Tom, he's twelve foot tall, only man in the world I have to look up to."

Two other lineup members were fire fighters, who had stripped down to their T-shirts and trousers. Benson volunteered to stand in the lineup so that Tom would have a better chance. He was a big man too, and he figured he would offset the "little bitty" criminal types.

Benson had also known Tom's ex-wife for many years, and Garland elicited his opinion of her. "Mr. Benson," he asked. "Do you—from your knowledge of Carolyn Allanson of Athens, Georgia— Did you hear what people generally said about her in reference to her reputation for truthfulness and honesty?"

"Most anybody in Athens—"

"Answer yes or no."

"Yes, sir."

"Was that reputation good or bad?"

"It was very bad."

"And based on that reputation, would you believe her on her oath?"

"I wouldn't believe her if she was standing on a stack of Bibles. I told Tom—" Benson was just getting warmed up.

"Just answer the questions," Garland stopped him. "All right, your witness."

Weller dispatched Tom's fellow farrier quickly. Looking chagrined, Fred Benson turned to the judge. "Your Honor, I didn't get to say all I wanted to say—"

"You have said all they will allow you to," Judge Wofford explained.

Pursuing his strategy to cast doubt on Tom's identification in the lineup, Garland called Hugh Maples, a private investigator working for the defense team, to the stand. He recalled the circus atmosphere that Fourth of July weekend at the East Point police station.

"Did you have occasion," Garland asked, "to be at the East Point jail in the presence of Tom Allanson on an occasion when there was a disrobed hippie girl?"

The jurors exchanged glances. Every day there seemed to be a surprise or two in the testimony.

"Yes, sir."

"Tell the jury about that incident."

"This was on a Saturday prior to the lineup. . . . Pat was back there . . . talking with Tom. . . . Chief of Police Godfrey was up at the other end of the hall talking with this hippie girl . . . she had just taken a shower and was complaining about no towels."

"How was she dressed?"

"She *wasn't* dressed."

"Did that attract any attention from the policemen?"

Several jurors smiled and a few gallery members tittered.

"Several. Yes, sir. . . . Detective Zellner leaned around the corner. He called someone to come there, and I turned and saw it was Officer McBurnett."

"And could Officer McBurnett see the defendant, Tom Allanson?"

"Yes, sir."

Garland ended his questioning there. Had the jurors understood that this prior viewing would have *further* contaminated McBurnett's identification of Tom in the lineup?

Ed Garland knew in his bones that Pat had concocted a story

for Tom to tell, believing her version would fly better than what he might say. Garland didn't want Tom on the stand, and he certainly would not put Pat on the stand; she was so unstable emotionally that he couldn't predict what she might do. So Garland was left with a defense that only nibbled at the edges of the questions in the jurors' minds.

Bill Weller kept making sarcastic references to the fact that most of Tom's witnesses were "horse people," as if that would automatically make them lie for him. Bill Jones, the liquor store eyewitness, had been pretty well tainted as a defense witness. So Garland could only chip away at the lineup and at Carolyn Allanson's reputation for honesty.

None of it was really enough to fight double murder charges.

✦ ✦ ✦

There was a hush in the courtroom as an old man made his way to the witness stand. Walter Allanson—Paw—had come to testify for his grandson in a murder trial where his own son and daughter-in-law were the victims. He had loved Tommy since the day he was born. He didn't look like a sentimental man. Actually, he appeared to be a weather-beaten old cuss whose expression reflected no discernible emotion.

"Did you have occasion, Mr. Allanson," Garland asked, "to have a telephone call from Carolyn Allanson?"

"Yeah . . ."

"When did Carolyn Allanson call you?"

"About six weeks ago."

"In that conversation, what did she say to you?"

"She wanted to come out to the house but I had company coming. I asked her to wait till Sunday to come. Then in talking to her, she's telling me she loved Tom, and I asked her what all went on out at the house at the killings. She said, 'Mother Allanson got killed.' That's what she called her mother-in-law, see, and then [she said], 'But we didn't mean for Walter to get killed—' "

What could she have meant: that there had been a plot to kill her mother-in-law, and her father-in-law was killed by mistake? It was doubtful that young Carolyn had been romantically involved with her husband's father, as Margureitte had suggested. Was this simply the testimony of a very old man who would do anything to save his grandson? Quite possibly. Paw had no further observations or remembrances to offer on Carolyn, and the jury seemed oblivious to any spicy connections his testimony might have evoked.

Weller seemed to think that the old man was fabricating. "Mr. Allanson," he began on cross-examination. "You want to do everything you can to help your grandson, don't you?"

"I want to be fair with the world."

"Yes, sir. You want to help him and do everything you can to help him?"

"If it takes anything to help him, the truth is what I'm telling."

"And really," the prosecutor asked, "it's pretty well your philosophy that the dead are gone and the living are still here, isn't it?"

"Yeah."

"Nothing further."

On redirect, Garland elicited Paw's opinion of Tom as far as violence went.

"I've known him and he's a fair, square boy," he replied.

"Wait a minute. I'm asking you about his reputation for peacefulness."

"Good." Paw did not waste words.

While questioning Paw, Bill Weller had, for the third time in the trial, managed to get the information on the record that Tom Allanson was a quick-draw expert. He had, the prosecution maintained, once shot himself in the leg while practicing in college. Paw Allanson agreed that Tom was a "pretty good quick-draw" shooter.

Nona Allanson, who could barely speak due to a stroke, entered the courtroom in a wheelchair. She testified that she had heard her son Walter threaten to kill her grandson.

"Did you tell your grandson that?"

"Yes, I told him."

Weller had no questions. Lawyers rarely make points with the jury by cross-examining such a vulnerable witness.

✦ ✦ ✦

The long week of testimony was over. Next would come the summations. The members of the jury would hear neither Tom nor Pat Allanson speak. They had watched their interplay and wondered about them, seeing the pretty woman whisper passionately to her husband and his attorneys, seeing the man on trial gaze at her with such longing in his eyes. The jury had not seen Tom and Pat kiss and hold each other as they did during court recesses, but they had picked up on the sexual tension between them. They had been curious, and undoubtedly wished they *could* have heard Tom and Pat testify. There seemed to be so much about this case that remained unexplained. But both sides had been represented by extremely able attorneys, and now it was time for final arguments.

Bill Weller contended that Tom Allanson had killed his parents deliberately. "Everything points to him. He has no reasonable hypothesis. The only reasonable hypothesis, the only reasonable circumstances—this man murdered his mother and his daddy in cold blood. He's the only one had a motive. No phantom involved in this."

Weller came as close to naming Pat Allanson as an accomplice as he dared under the law. She had not been formally charged with any crime because the D.A.'s office wasn't sure just where she fit in—if at all. Weller asked the questions the D.A.'s staff had asked one another. "What's she doing way up from Zebulon fifty or sixty miles away driving around the Allansons' home—if not to let him off to do his little deed? Is she the fly in the ointment? Is she the rejected woman that the parents would not accept because they had another daughter-in-law and two children? And the constant needling—constant needling—crying . . . about somebody exposing himself and here she is a grown woman. . . . Every time you hear some witness, 'Yes, she was with him.' . . . *This wife's everywhere.* She's here waiting for him. She's there. She's driving around the house. He's walking to Zebulon. She's next door looking for him at his grandmother's house thirty minutes before."

Weller reminded the jury that Tom had been seen on Norman Berry Drive. "Three eyewitnesses. . . . That policeman looked him flat in the face three or four times. Mr. and Mrs. Duckett saw the police car running down the road with him. They described him, jeans, boots, Tarzan hair, tannish shirt—or brownish green, all the same color scheme." Weller ended his summation with a call to the jury to simply add up the established facts. It was all there.

Ed Garland contended in his final arguments that the case

against Tom Allanson had not been proven to a moral certainty, and that was what was needed to convict. "That is what this case is about. There *is* no moral certainty in it. There's no firm piece of evidence you can plant your foot on and say, in fact, in that house that the defendant fired that weapon and killed those two people. It does not exist—but there's this *assumption, speculation*. There's positive proof to the contrary that *someone else* did the shooting on the twenty-ninth of June. . . .

"There's not one piece of evidence that puts this defendant in that basement—not one—and if you consider a guilty verdict, you have to speculate—you have to assume. . . . In this case you're dealing with circumstantial evidence. Lots of bits and pieces of circumstances. The law sets an even higher standard. It says this, that the circumstances must exclude every other reasonable theory—*must exclude every other one!*"

And it was true. There was no physical evidence that placed Tom in that charnel house of a basement.

"It's just not there," Garland continued. "Was there a boot print, a bloody boot print walking from this basement through that blood where the man was lying in the trail of blood? *Somebody* had to go right through it. Was there . . . one bit of blood on an item of clothing this defendant had?" They went there to his home and arrested him. There was not and there's a reasonable doubt. . . .

"If you can meet the challenge of the law, then you will stand up and write a verdict of not guilty in this case because there are *hundreds* of reasonable doubts."

Ed Garland's voice dropped as he spoke the final sentences of his argument. He would not be allowed to speak again. Bill Weller would; the onus of proving a case is always on the state and the prosecutor is allowed a rebuttal statement after the defense finishes. "I ask you to write a verdict of not guilty," Garland pleaded. "In this case—*not proven*—to follow your duty as jurors . . . and return a verdict that says this case has not been proven. . . . I now give the burden of Tom Allanson's life to you. Please look after it."

Step by step, in rebuttal, Weller went over the case the state had built, asserting that the defendant had pried open the door into his parents' basement and then waited coldly for them to come home so he could murder them. It was a good argument, and plausible, and Weller was persuasive. "I want to quote one thing from the Scriptures, from the Book of Proverbs, and I'll leave it with you," Weller concluded. " 'He that curseth his father and mother, his lamp shall be put out in the midst of darkness.' "

The jury could find Tom guilty of murder, not guilty of murder but guilty of voluntary manslaughter, or they could find him not guilty, period. In a two-count indictment such as this, they had to return a separate verdict on each count.

The jury retired to deliberate at 6:00 P.M. on Friday, October 18. At 8:27 P.M. they buzzed the courtroom and asked to come before the court. Judge Wofford understood that they had a question. But it was not a question. Joseph Thackston, the payroll administrator, had been elected foreman by his fellow jurors, and he said, "We have reached a decision, Your Honor."

"You *have?*"

"Yes, sir."

Judge Wofford immediately sent the jurors back into the jury room and placed a call to Ed Garland and Bill Weller. No one had expected a verdict so soon. Tom was brought over from jail, and the colonel and Margureitte supported Pat with their arms as they entered the courtroom.

By 8:44 P.M., all the principals were present. Pat stared at the jury, her face full of hope.

"Mr. Foreman," Judge Wofford asked, "has the jury reached a verdict?"

"Yes, Your Honor."

"Mr. Weller, will you receive and publish the verdict, and Mr. Allanson, will you and your attorney stand right out here, please, and face the jury?"

Assistant District Attorney Weller unfolded the piece of paper and began to read, "Dated October 18, 1974. We the jury find *for* the defendant—"

Tom sighed with relief, and Ed Garland started to smile—but only as long as it took to take half a breath. Weller continued to read. "We the jury find for the defendant *guilty* on both counts of murder . . ."

The jurors had mistakenly used the wrong terminology. They had found Tom guilty, but the term "find for the defendant" meant, of course, that he had been acquitted. The relief and then the letdown were excruciating.

"You will go back in the jury room and correct your verdict,"

Judge Wofford explained to the jury. "It will be, 'We the jury find the defendant guilty.' In other words, you have one word too many in there." They returned with the word deleted.

Ed Garland asked for a polling of the jury. Tom stood as if made of stone, as pale as marble, showing no emotion at all. Pat watched the jury in utter disbelief, her chin trembling and her eyes filling with tears. As each juror spoke the word "guilty" aloud, she swayed as if she could collapse at any moment.

Georgia justice was swift; there would be no wait before sentencing. Tom Allanson would know his fate before he left the courtroom. He could be sentenced to death—twice. He might now be facing the electric chair.

Weller asked to address the court. Those watching expected to hear him ask for the death penalty. Instead, he began, "I have spoken to the family of the late Mr. Allanson and . . . I think I can state that they do not wish the state to press for the death penalty in this case because of the emotional involvement between the defendant and his late parents. Because of the family's wishes, we will waive the death penalty and request the court to direct the jury to sentence the defendant to two concurrent life sentences."

A few moments later foreman Thackston handed the sentence to Bill Weller. On the judge's orders, he had hastily written in his own hand the words that charted Tom Allanson's future.

"Your Honor, shall I publish the sentence?"

"If you will, please, Mr. Weller."

"We the jury," Weller read, "fix the sentence of the defendant at life imprisonment on both counts, the sentence under Count II to be served concurrently with the sentence on Count I."

Tom and Ed Garland stood before Judge Wofford as he read the sentence again. "It is hereby the verdict of this court that these be your sentences, a life sentence on Count I of Indictment No. A-22765, and to run concurrently with that, a life sentence on Count II of Indictment No. A-22765, and may God's love sustain you now and in the days that are to come. The court is now adjourned."

It was 9:00 P.M., only sixteen minutes since they had all been summoned there.

Pat threw herself into Tom's arms and kissed him on the mouth, clinging to him desperately until deputies stepped in to handcuff Tom and lead him away.

"Tom?" she called after him, and he stopped and looked back at her, his expression one of blank despair.

She blew him a kiss and said, "I'll see you tomorrow?"

He nodded.

"Good." Pat smiled brilliantly—for Tom's sake.

Margureitte, who sat in the front row of the courtroom watching, called out, "I love you, Tommy!"

He had been so thankful when he became involved with Pat and the Radcliffes and they had welcomed him into their home and their hearts. They had transformed his life. How could everything have gone so terribly wrong?

Technically, Tom would become eligible for parole in seven years. It didn't matter. Seven years without Pat was like imagining a thousand years without air. Pulling slightly against his handcuffs, he struggled to get one more glimpse of her. If he had wanted to, Tom could have flung the deputies beside him against the wall, but he never thought of it. He watched Pat walk out of the courtroom, borne on her parents' arms, and then let his guards lead him away.

Tom didn't know that Judge Wofford himself had come down from his bench to speak with the Radcliffes and Pat's daughter, Susan. Susan Alford had wiped away her own tears and listened as the judge comforted them. "You know, it's really sad, Mr. and Mrs. Radcliffe. That boy didn't get a fair chance. That boy *was* there in the basement that day of the killings. Something happened. Maybe a terrible argument. But it wasn't a premeditated shooting. Why in the world wasn't this done another way?"

Judge Wofford was only echoing the unspoken question on everyone's lips. How could it be that a nice guy, a good old boy like Tommy Allanson, was on his way to prison for life for the cold-blooded shootings of his own mama and daddy? How could it be that the perfect love he had finally found in his Pat had ended in death and despair?

PART THREE

PAT

17

Mary Linda Patricia Vann was the name they gave her at birth. She would have many names in her life. Patricia, or rather Pat, was the only one that would stay with her. She was born into a southern family whose roots were so deep in the earth that no hurricane of scandal could tear them loose.

She was a Siler. And Silers took care of their own. They were the Silers for whom Siler City, North Carolina, was named. Her maternal grandfather was Tasso Wirt Siler, born November 3, 1879. He had studied to become a Lutheran minister but changed his religious allegiance and became instead a fire-and-brimstone Baptist preacher. A tall, strong man with an expansive wit and a kindly heart, he combed his thick white hair into a subdued pompadour and wore round wire eyeglasses. Tasso Siler was highly respected in the close-knit community he served. A truly good man.

In 1900, when he was twenty-one, Tasso Siler married Mary Vallie Phillips, five years his junior. She was a slender, almost ethereal girl, quite beautiful, who seemed too frail to serve her husband and the Lord as a preacher's wife. Mary Siler seldom betrayed her own deepest emotions. She was given instead to reciting optimistic sayings and poems, and to recording her journal. ". . . We were so happy," she wrote of her days as a bride. "It did not seem our lives could be made so sad in times to come. But it's best that people can't see ahead. If so, some of us might give up."

Six decades later, she lamented the passing of another year. "What we have done will soon be a sealed book. If it's been good or bad, we can't change it. It will stand as it is. It is sad, for some of us will have marked up pages in our book from many unkind words to someone, or maybe [we] did not try hard to make others' lives happy."

The Rev. Silers would live in countless parsonages around Wilmington and Warsaw, North Carolina, in their more than fifty years together. Mary was dutiful, dedicated, and fecund. She gave birth to thirteen children. Later to be dubbed "the Righteous Sisters" by an irreverent younger generation, the girls were Edna Earl, Swannie Lee, Florence Elizabeth, Alma Mehetibel, Mary Louise, Thelma Blanche, Myrtle Margureitte— subsequently just Margureitte—and Agnes Fay. The boys were named Mark Hanna, Wade Hampton, Robert Winship, and Floyd Frazier. Mark died in infancy, as did an unnamed infant girl. When a minister's salary could no longer stretch to feed more children, the Silers chose the only certain birth control available to them in the 1920s; Mary moved into a separate bedroom and their conjugal pleasures ceased. She was only thirty-seven and Tasso just forty-two.

Margureitte was particularly attentive to Siler family history. By 1991, she would proudly list her parents' 241 descendants— down to the sixth generation. They had 13 children, 47 grandchildren, 95 great-grandchildren, 84 great-great-grandchildren, and 2 great-great-great-grandchildren. Over the years, tragedies occurred, as they do in all families: babies died, young soldiers never came back from war, and children succumbed to cancer and rheumatic fever and, one, impalement on a bedpost. A young wife disappeared, leaving her children to be raised by whomever, another threw her baby away in a trash can (it survived), and a few descendants—or their mates—went to prison for violent crimes. Such negative minutiae were never officially acknowledged, and bad marriages were simply ignored in the recitation of the family tree.

"We are all so fortunate," Margureitte wrote in a booklet she typed herself in 1991 to give out at the twenty-fifth anniversary of the Siler Family Reunion, "to have had such a wonderful heritage. None of we children can blame any of our mistakes on our childhood. . . . I remember when we had a bad storm how Mother would gather us all around and sing 'Nearer My God to Thee,' while Daddy went to the door and watched the storm. Mother said Dad was daring the Lord to hit him."

Perhaps more than most families, the Silers had their idiosyncrasies, and they were all very strong-minded. Thelma, who was a perfectly healthy child, refused to walk until she was five years old. When the Rev. Tasso Siler dropped dead in his own yard in 1960 at the age of eighty-one, hundreds of mourners attended his funeral and his widow took to a wheelchair in her grief. She was not ill; like Thelma, she simply decided not to walk. Although she eventually got back on her feet, she never got over his death. But while there might be eccentricities, arguments, recriminations, and even banishments that took place *inside* the Siler family, no one on the outside must know. Under the most intense pressure, the Siler women stared back at the world with a look of inflexible serenity that was inviolable: "the crystal gaze."

✦　✦　✦

Myrtle Margureitte was next to last in birth order, and arguably the most beautiful of the Reverend and Mrs. Siler's children. She had a heart-shaped face with a high rounded forehead, huge blue eyes, and full lips. Coming into puberty in the darkest years of the Great Depression in the sexually repressed household of a Baptist minister, Margureitte was something of a rebel. Her rebellion and her fertility would cause her gentle and loyal mother pain.

According to family lore, Margureitte ran off to Wilmington with Robert Lee Vann when she was only fifteen and became pregnant. Vann was a slight youth, some five years older than Margureitte. It is not clear whether they ever lived together, but on March 16, 1936, when Margureitte was sixteen, she gave birth in her parents' house to her first child, a ten-pound still-born girl.

She wept and named her dead baby Roberta.

Bereft, she soon became pregnant again. Margureitte felt that somehow the dead Roberta might have lived if she had only been born in a hospital. She was insistent that her next child would be, and so, indeed, she was. The baby was born on August 22, 1937, in the J. W. M. Hospital in Wilmington, North Carolina, a city that stands just where the Cape Fear River widens into the Cape Fear inlet on the Atlantic Ocean. The baby girl came into the world at 6:18 that morning and her young mother rejoiced that she was alive and healthy. Margureitte labored long to bring forth her second ten-pound female child. This was Patricia, a replacement, some said. The lost Roberta found, some said.

Margureitte gave her maiden name as Myrtle Margureitte Siler on the birth certificate, and her age as twenty. She was really just eighteen when Patty was born. She said that she had been married for three years to the listed father, Robert Lee Vann, twenty-three, and that he was employed in a radio store. But some family members wondered whether the Vann boy was really Patty's father.

If they ever existed, the records of Margureitte's marriage and divorce to and from Vann were lost. One of Vann's brothers, younger by a decade, could not recall that Robert Lee was *ever* married to Margureitte. He remembered that his brother worked on the railroad but never in a radio store. His memory may well have been faulty; he would have been under ten when his older brother was with Margureitte.

Although Margureitte has said that Vann was her husband and the father of her children, Robert Vann may have been an expedient red herring. Some of her family believed that Margureitte had fallen in love with a married man. He was a farmer and carpenter in Warsaw, North Carolina, and his name was John Cam Prigeon, a huge young man with blond hair, full lips, and protruding ears. And he was a terror. Prigeon was as wild as Margureitte's father was pious. A drinker of spirits and a brawler on occasion, he walked along any path he chose. His wife knew of Margureitte, the preacher's beautiful daughter, but she said nothing. Her husband had a violent temper.

In her strict Baptist household, Margureitte's latest misadven-

ture must have been greeted with dismay. But the family undoubtedly rallied around her, thinking she would get "Cam" out
of her system. She was, after all, a Siler, and the teenage mother
and her new baby girl returned to Warsaw in that strange blazing
summer of 1937 to live with her parents. The headlines had
been full of disasters and tragedies for months: five hundred
Texas children perished in a school explosion, Amelia Earhart
was lost over the Pacific Ocean, the *Hindenburg* dirigible melted
in a fireball of burning hydrogen gas, the king of England abdi-
cated, movie sex queen Jean Harlow succumbed to uremic poison at twenty-six, and war was brewing in Europe and Asia.

It was also the year that Margaret Mitchell won the Pulitzer
Prize for *Gone With the Wind,* at once a historic re-creation of
the gracious life of the Old South and a terrifying tale of its
destruction during the Civil War. Its beautiful heroine, a survi-
vor and woman of intricate wiles, would become Patricia's life
model.

Margureitte had to work, and so Mary Siler raised Patty for
the first five years of her life. Patty called *her* "Mama," and her
grandmother Siler doted on little Patty to the point of obsession.
Patty shared Mary's life and Mary's bed. She had only to voice
her every wish and it was granted.

The little girl was exquisite. She grew thick taffy-colored curls
and her eyes were bigger even than Margureitte's and as green
as new leaves in April. Mama Siler kept her in ruffly dotted
swiss dresses, sunbonnets, and white Mary Janes. Her aunt
Edna—who was so much older than Margureitte that she was
more like a mother than a sister—sewed every stitch of the
child's clothing. Everyone who saw her said she was much pret-
tier than Shirley Temple.

And she was.

Mary Siler made Patty the center of her life. Each of her own
thirteen children paled beside her golden grandchild, "Next to
God," she often said, "I love Patty more than anything in the
world." There was always fruit from the orchard and vegetables
brought by parishioners, but Patty would eat nothing but pancakes. Her grandmother gave up trying to feed her vegetables,
eggs, and cereal, and served her flapjacks three times a day.

Of all the grandchildren living in or visiting at the parsonage,
Patty was special. When the other youngsters clamored for

Cokes, Mary explained, "No one can have it—because there's only one." And then she would beckon Patty into the back room and surreptitiously give *her* that single Coca-Cola. When the children were naughty, they were sent out to find their own switch and were whipped. But Patty was never spanked. Instead, her grandmother picked her up gently and whispered, "Now bend over, and be sure and cry real loud." She could not bring herself to strike Patty, so she only pretended to hit her.

While her mother cared for Patty, Margureitte worked at a number of jobs, looking for a career that would lead her into the life-style she sought. Born into the country preacher's world of meager circumstances and self-sacrifice, she yearned for gracious living, fine things and a lovely home. She was clever and quick, and she had always wondered what it would be like to be part of the horsey set, riding to the hunt, performing in shows with jodhpurs and a well-cut jacket. She longed for romance and true love, but her days were spent working at a dull job as a clerk. As fertile as her mother, Margureitte once again conceived, her third pregnancy before she was twenty.

This time, Margureitte made no pretense of a husband. She agonized over the few choices open to her. She had to work and Mama Siler couldn't take care of *two* toddlers. Margureitte would have to give this baby up for adoption. She arranged to stay at the Florence Crittendon Home at 4759 Reservoir Road in Washington, D.C. Required to work both before and after her delivery to pay for her board, room, and medical care, Margureitte chose to take the training the home offered in practical nursing. It was hard work and arduous for a pregnant girl, but she was then and always would be a woman who put the best face on things. "I have nurse's training," she explained confidently even fifty years later. "I'm not a registered nurse, you understand, but I have two years' training."

On October 10, 1939, Margureitte was at full term. She was given a shot of Pituitrin to start labor. "Pit" usually triggers hard and frequent contractions. After twenty-four hours, a drained Margureitte gave birth to a nine-pound six-ounce son. The baby's hair was white blond and his features were bold and masculine. He looked nothing at all like her delicately pretty daughter. Some people thought he was the image of Cam. She named him Reginald Kent Vann and would call him Kent.

She loved him, and could not give her baby boy up, not once

she had held him. That was so like Margureitte; right or wrong, she would always love her children to distraction, and when her mind was made up she was resolute. No one could legally force her to hand her infant son over for adoption. But she had to stay in Washington and work at Florence Crittendon until she paid off her debt. She carried bedpans and changed sheets until her arms and feet ached—but she kept her baby.

Although Margureitte gave her last name as "Vann" on Kent's birth certificate, the line for a father's name was left blank. On the line that asked "Legitimate?" someone had crossed out "Yes" and "Unknown," leaving "No." When Margureitte returned to her family in Warsaw, locals who saw the husky blond toddler marveled at his resemblance to John Cam Prigeon and chortled knowingly, "There goes little Cam."

Margureitte had few assets and no reason to think that her life would be any easier in the future, but she was young and healthy and very beautiful. She was a sweet young woman but determined. Wanting so much to make a home for Kent and Patty, she vowed she would spend her life "helping" her children, creating for them the most perfect of all worlds.

She tried to be with them almost all the time, possibly to make up for the early years when she was not with Patty. They had never had an opportunity to truly bond with each other. She had handed her baby daughter over to her mother, and that had hurt Margureitte even though she idolized her mother. In the world Margureitte grew up in, the perfect woman was long-suffering, patient, soft-spoken, and lived a life of gentle servitude to her family. She sometimes wondered how her mother managed, but vowed to emulate her. Looking back over her years as a mother, Margureitte would murmur, "We're on earth to do for our children—to help them any way we can." She half believed in reincarnation and her own place in a stream of reborn souls. "The doctor I worked for for so many years always told me, '*You* came back to help someone.' "

✦　✦　✦

At last disillusioned with her love life, Margureitte looked elsewhere and, quite suddenly, her luck changed. Just as the rest of the world was gripped in the bleakness of World War II, Margureitte's world blossomed.

Whether she met the man who would be her lifetime love in

the romantic way they recalled, or in the more mundane manner her sisters remembered, didn't really matter. Margureitte described meeting Second Lieutenant Clifford Brown Radcliffe in 1942 at a party in Washington, D.C. Her retelling of that encounter makes it as idyllic a meeting as any starry-eyed schoolgirl might envision. "That never happened," one sister snorted. "Margureitte was working as a waitress at the Lobster House near Fort Bragg in Fayetteville, and Clifford came in, and that was it."

Whichever, their eyes *did* meet and lock across a crowded room. It *was* love at first sight. The young army officer was a half-dozen years older than Margureitte and very handsome with classically aquiline features, dark hair and eyes. In fact, he looked like the movie stars who were portraying gallant army officers in films of the forties. He wasn't terribly tall, but at five feet ten inches, he was certainly taller than Margureitte. Clifford was from an old family in Westchester County, New York, whose ancestors had come over on the *Mayflower*. He had a deep and cultured speaking voice and he gazed at her as if he were utterly fascinated.

As indeed he was. He was not deterred by the fact that she had two small children. Not at all. They were married on January 8, 1942, in the Fort Bragg chapel, and Margureitte broke the news to her mother that now she could raise her own babies. She had a husband and they planned to take both Kent and Patty with them wherever Clifford was stationed.

When Cliff was transferred to Texas, it was time for Patty to leave Mama Siler and be her real mother's little girl. It was stunning news. Margureitte's sisters begged her not to do it. "Don't hurt Mama like that—she has a bad heart," they cried. "You'll kill her if you take that child away from her."

But Margureitte was obdurate. She had worked and waited years for this moment. She and Clifford took the children with them when they left by train for Clifford's duty station in Mineral Wells, Texas. Patty was five and a half and had very firm ideas of her own. She turned up her nose at everything on the menu in the dining car. She wanted pancakes. She wouldn't eat anything else. Margureitte was afraid Patty would starve if she didn't relent. Patty got her flapjacks. That was all she ate for the entire trip across America. And for weeks after.

She still cried for "Mama."

Back home in Siler City, Mama Siler was inconsolable. They had taken her baby away. She lay in bed for days, mourning her loss. But she didn't die; she lived for many decades more. Margureitte now had her little daughter back and, if she was sometimes willful, the young mother would blame Mama Siler for that. "It wasn't natural for my mother to be so obsessed with Patty."

18

Although Patty and Kent were only two years apart in age, they were vastly different in temperament. Patty was stubborn and spoiled rotten, used to having her own way. Everyone in her small world had always catered to her. First her grandmother and her aunts, and now her mother. It was hard not to. She was such a dainty, beautiful child. Her mother liked to use a southern expression to describe her: "Patty's so pretty she can't whistle." When she was happy, her laughter was like bells. When she cried, she could break your heart. It was impossible to say no to Patty.

Kent was a sensitive, studious boy. He was blond as a Scandinavian and his big ears stuck out. He was never cute—his bone structure was too rough-hewn—but he was an endearing little boy whose gaze was straight on. He willingly took a backseat to his sister.

Patty had scant patience with her little brother. In her mind, she was meant to be an only child, and she grew cranky when attention moved away from her. Those first five years in Mama Siler's house had ruined her for sharing. She needed her spotlight, and she felt cold without it. She looked upon her brother as an interloper. It was more than the normal sibling infighting. "She hated him," one relative said flatly. "She always wanted him gone."

He almost went. Kent, who had been born perfect, contracted meningitis shortly after the family arrived in Mineral Wells. The army base was in the grip of a massive epidemic. Kent's fever raged above 105 degrees for days and he came very, very close to dying. When he finally recovered, the doctors told Margureitte that he was almost totally deaf. After that, Kent always wore hearing aids, but he became adept at reading lips. People could not sense how profoundly deaf he was unless they turned away as they spoke to him. Then he was lost.

Margureitte and Clifford Radcliffe let Patty and Kent grow up believing that he was their natural father. He had accepted her children so readily that it seemed the reasonable thing to do. After all, Margureitte *was* Patty and Kent's mother, and Clifford was the only father they had ever known. There was no point in bringing up Patty and Kent's real father. It would only confuse them.

When "Daddy Cliff" was away in the war, Margureitte often took the children and stayed near his family in Mamaroneck in Westchester County, New York. Her in-laws accepted her only grudgingly, not pleased to have their son marry a woman they thought was divorced, but they eventually admitted she was a gracious and refined young woman who took marvelous care of her children. She was an utterly devoted mother. It is quite possible that they, too, believed Clifford was Patty and Kent's natural father; they often remarked on certain physical traits the children shared with their son.

The children were all any grandparents could ask for. Patty always looked perfect, like a child in the society pages in her starched pinafores and black patent-leather Mary Janes or in a bowler hat and fitted coat. His mother put Kent in the proper clothing too. Photos show him with a Buster Brown haircut grimacing into the camera as he wore a tailored tweed coat and a matching Eton cap. His knobby knees look ridiculous above long dark stockings. He wasn't a boy meant to be dressed up like a fancy pants kid, and he looks uncomfortable and self-conscious.

Kent idolized his stepfather. Although he was a rather small-boned man, he was larger than life to Kent. Clifford was often far away fighting a war, and when he was home he was an awesome figure in his impeccable uniform, an austere—even cold—man who had little patience with small boys. Clifford Radcliffe's own father had been just such a cold man, and generation unto generation it had continued.

Clifford did enjoy little girls because they could be dressed up as pretty as dolls and carried around. He remonstrated with his wife if their clothes weren't perfect and clean; he hated to find tears or holes in their dresses or panties. He found no such charm in rough-and-tumble little boys. But Kent desperately wanted Clifford's approval. He was an intense boy. Early on, he set impossible goals for himself. And even as he set such high standards, he seemed to know already he would never meet them.

✦   ✦   ✦

The Second World War was a lonely time for Margureitte Radcliffe, but not nearly as lonely as the years before she met Clifford. While he was in Germany, she knew he would come back to her—if he could. She believed in her heart that Clifford had been telling her the truth when he said he had adored her from the very beginning, and that he always would. And she was grateful that it was so.

And then Clifford Radcliffe was listed as missing in action, and Margureitte didn't know if he was alive or dead. Word finally came that he had been injured in Germany; he had suffered a facial wound. She would love him no matter how he looked, of course, but Clifford had been *so* handsome that it seemed especially tragic that he would be disfigured. Margureitte was told only that her husband had been sent to a hospital in England.

His homecoming was as romantic as a love song. One day, she heard a cane rattling against her door. She ran to open it and it was Clifford. Home safe! He had grown a moustache and it completely hid any remaining scars. Everything was all right after all.

Margureitte had a place in the world. She was a married woman, an officer's wife, and she had her foot on a solid rung in the social hierarchy of service wives. Together, she and Clifford moved up through the army ranks. After the war, the family was transferred from one duty station to another as Clifford's orders came through—to Germany, Japan, Atlanta, Alabama, and back to Germany. They had no children together, but even though Margureitte never bore Clifford's natural child, he always treated Patty and Kent as his very own.

Clifford would eventually become Colonel Radcliffe; he worked in military intelligence, the most elite and mysterious specialty in the army. He was well suited for it, with his keen mind and a certain natural distrust of the obvious. When he strode the streets of Frankfurt, Germany, in his trench coat, the wind slightly ruffling his iron gray hair, Colonel Clifford Radcliffe looked as if he had stepped from the screen of an Alfred Hitchcock movie. And woe be unto any underling who couldn't adhere absolutely to his interpretation of army regulations.

Margureitte was the ideal colonel's lady. She never lost her southern accent and her voice was dulcet-toned and graciously modulated. When Clifford and Margureitte stepped out for an army social function, they looked like a million dollars. Her figure was perfect for her strapless chiffon evening gowns, her gorgeous legs looked even more so in her ankle-strapped shoes with three-inch heels, and Clifford was imperiously handsome in full dress blues.

Margureitte would recall later to her granddaughters that, wherever they were stationed, men made passes at her. "Your grandfather was insanely jealous of me at the officers' club—if I danced with another man, he would become quite upset. It was just easier not to dance with other men, even if they were friends of ours. . . . I loved Papa and I did not want to upset him—I had to lavish all the attention on him."

Patty seemed to thrive on the peripatetic life-style of an army family. She was such an enchanting child that she was welcome wherever they went. People made a fuss over her just as her grandmother and aunts back home in North Carolina had. Margureitte couldn't bring herself to cut Patty's golden brown hair and it grew past her waist. Usually, she wore it in tight, long braids looped up with ribbons and barrettes. Sometimes she coaxed Margureitte to let it hang free in thick waves. When they were stationed in Japan, the Japanese reached out shyly to touch Patty's radiant hair with wonder.

The Colonel Radcliffes moved in rarefied circles in the Far East. It was in Japan where Patty became the tennis partner of the young crown prince. Margureitte and Cliff were thrilled to see their lovely daughter accepted by royalty. Patty herself took it for granted; she had *always* been treated like a little princess. She was not awed by the young prince. When the Radcliffes were reassigned, the royal family presented Patty with a full ceremonial Japanese kimono, obi, and sandals. The heavy satin garments rested in tissue paper in her bureau drawer wherever she lived. Patty loved costumes.

When she reached puberty, she didn't get chubby or sprout pimples. She moved gracefully into her teens and became, if anything, more flawless. At thirteen, the planes of her face changed subtly from the roundness of childhood to the classically defined cheekbones of a genuine beauty. She posed for a snapshot wearing a white organza gown and stole, the fitted party dress held up by two narrow spaghetti straps over creamy white shoulders.

Patty's hair was cut, finally, and swept back from her face in shimmering waves and then combed under in a pageboy. She wore bright red lipstick and her green eyes were arresting in their intensity. She had a slight overbite but it scarcely detracted from her beauty. Rather, it gave her a pouting, sensuous look. She was fully developed, a southern beauty blooming early.

She looked at least eighteen.

Patty was sweet and loving with adults, but she could sometimes be artless, even cruel, with her peers. She was far and away the prettiest of the many girl cousins in the Siler clan, and she knew it. She had heard it often enough. Once, when she noticed an ugly-duckling cousin staring at her as she combed her hair, Patty turned and whispered, "You might be as pretty as I am someday." She pretended to be shocked when the girl ran away crying. But she seemed to be adroit at finding the other girls' sore spots. Early on, there was something in Patty that went for the jugular, detecting weakness in an adversary and moving in relentlessly.

Patty had never been much of a student, although she was smart enough. She loved sewing and crafts, and she was very talented artistically. She preferred reading romantic stories and poems and, in her mind, *she* became the heroine. She was Scarlett O'Hara and she was Elizabeth Barrett Browning. She was the Highwayman's sweetheart waiting at her window in the dark of the moon for her lover to come take her away.

Not surprisingly, Patty was fascinated with boys. And they with her. Most of the eighth-grade girls were flat chested and gawky, but Patty Radcliffe looked like a movie star. And, as always, Kent took a backseat to his sister. He was shy and hesitant about asserting himself. His hearing loss, although very well hidden, made him just a little slower on the uptake than his peers. Patty still detested him. Everything he said or did seemed to irritate his older sister.

✦ ✦ ✦

When Patty was in her early teens, Colonel Radcliffe was ordered back to Fort McPherson in Atlanta. It was a happy move for the family; the Atlanta area had become home. And there, history would repeat itself. The Siler women all seemed to blossom early. It was more usual than not for them to bear their first children in their mid-teens. When Patty was fifteen, Margureitte was only thirty-three and nervously aware of the dangers of having a beautiful teenage daughter who looked years older than she was. But what could Margureitte do? Patty had never had any rules to follow, no brakes at all to slow her impetuous pursuit of whatever caught her fancy.

She met eighteen-year-old Gilbert Taylor at a party on the Fort Mac base; he was an army brat too, a lanky, skinny young man whom Patty found terribly handsome. She put all her romantic fantasies into the relationship and Gil fell hard for the lovely and seductive teenager. Suddenly she stepped from childhood to womanhood. She would not answer to "Patty" any longer; she was Pat, or, when the moment called for it, she asked to be called Patricia.

Pat became pregnant almost immediately. She didn't mind; it meant she could get married. Gil was both proud and jealous. He wanted to believe this was his baby, but he knew Pat had been dating another young man too, a soldier. It *was* Gil's baby, but his insecurity with Pat never quite went away. As much as he wanted to believe in her, she kept him slightly off-balance, letting him wonder.

Her parents would have preferred that she marry into an officer's family. A hearty, boisterous man, Gil's stepfather, Mike Downing, was only a sergeant and his mother, Eunice, a buxom, flamboyant woman—not the kind Margureitte would have picked as a friend. Eunice dressed to show off her hourglass figure. She was pretty in a flashy way, a great cook, and good-hearted, the very antithesis of the properly reserved colonel's wife Margureitte had become.

The sergeant worshiped his wife. "I thank God every night for Eunice," Mike often said. He showered Eunice with presents, including diamonds and a new Cadillac every four years. Eunice had beautiful things, nicer than a lot of officers' wives. Privately, Margureitte found it all a little vulgar, but there it was. Colonel and Mrs. Radcliffe accepted the inevitable. It could have been worse. Eunice was very well thought of in enlisted circles, and active in projects to benefit army dependents.

A wedding was hastily planned, to be held in the Fort Mc-Pherson chapel on September 6, 1952. "All they had in common was physical attraction," Margureitte later commented ruefully. "Pat was vastly superior in IQ." The colonel had wanted her to go to a fine school to study art; she was so talented. He felt Pat's future was ruined by this unfortunate marriage.

Pat wore a white satin gown with a three-quarter-length skirt and an off-the-shoulder neckline edged in net ruching. A short veil fell from her Juliet cap and she carried white orchids. Her white satin pumps matched her gown. She looked lovely and at least twenty-two. The bridegroom was less regal in a suit two sizes too big for him, a white carnation boutonniere, and saddle shoes—which he had forgotten to change before the ceremony. Gil looked like a kid dressed in his dad's clothes.

The newlyweds had very little time together. To support his growing family, Gil—whom Eunice called Junior—enlisted in the army. He was sent almost immediately to Korea, and Pat moved back home with her parents. Nothing had really changed. Margureitte and Clifford took care of her, and she used her allotment check for things she wanted.

Of course, there *was* a baby on the way. Pat was adamant that she wouldn't go to an army hospital. She didn't want to be on an assembly line and have some doctor she didn't even know walk in at the last minute to deliver her baby. She had heard the army even made the new mothers get up and take care of their own babies and eat their meals in the cafeteria! She saved her own money so she could have her baby in a nice civilian hospital, Georgia Baptist. Unfortunately, she thought she was in labor twice and was rushed to the hospital each time. As a result, Pat had spent all her savings before she was really ready to have her baby, so she ended up having to go to an army hospital anyway.

When Pat went into actual labor on March 4, 1953, Junior Taylor was far away, but her mother and the colonel drove her to the hospital. She rolled in the backseat, sobbing about how cruel Gil was to put her through such pain. After assuring the doctors that she had extensive nurse's training, Margureitte was allowed to be right there in the delivery room with Pat. It was, perhaps, the first time that Margureitte was unable to absorb all her daughter's pain.

The child was finally born, a dark-haired baby girl. Susan. Her mother was sixteen, her grandmother thirty-four. "How I loved that baby," Margureitte recalled in a gentle, pained voice nearly four decades later. "I don't know what happened. Susan just became pure evil. Just evil. Of course, I can't forgive that."

But the early affection between Susan and her grandmother was mutual. For the first three decades of her life, Susan found Margureitte the "sweetest, kindest person in my whole life. I thought she was perfect."

19

Unlike his sister, Kent was a diligent student and got excellent grades. He was thirteen when Pat and her baby returned from the hospital. He adored his little niece and gingerly held Susan, grinning with delight at how small she was. Pat let him play with the baby, but she was vaguely annoyed whenever he was around. Pat was a married woman and a mother, only visiting in her parents' house, marking time until Gil came home; it wasn't really her home anymore. But she didn't see it that way. As always, she viewed her brother as the interloper.

Kent's presence grated on Pat because he took so much of her mother's time away from her and her baby. If it weren't for him, things would have been perfect. Margureitte did the cooking and the housework and rocked Susan when she was fussy. It was almost as if Pat hadn't gotten married at all, and she liked the cozy feeling of being a little girl again.

When she became a grandmother, Margureitte took on another name. Clifford still called her Margureitte or "Reit," or sometimes "Reichen" with a German touch of endearment. Her sisters continued to call her Margureitte. But soon tiny Susan would call her "Boppo."

The colonel was called "Papa." Boppo and Papa fell easily into the role of matriarch and patriarch of an expanding family. It became them, and they seemed transformed overnight from youth to late middle age even though they still made a handsome pair. They would have been happy to stay on permanent assignment at Fort McPherson in Atlanta.

Pat liked everything about the home Margureitte and the colonel made. No matter how many times they were reassigned by the army, Margureitte always managed to decorate with taste and élan. Sometimes they lived in big old barrackslike barns, and sometimes on bases where the officers' housing was splendid. The Radcliffes had collected exquisite pieces in their travels around the world—fine china, paintings, objets d'art, Japanese screens, silver tea sets, thick rugs, and gleaming furniture. Later, when the colonel's mother passed away, her full china closets and family heirlooms came to the Radcliffes.

Margureitte had vowed to live graciously a long time back, and she had succeeded. Wives of younger officers saw her charm and poise as a goal to aim for. Why wouldn't Pat want to live in her family home, instead of in a cramped apartment or some tinny trailer somewhere? She had grown up with the very best. She had been groomed her whole life for elegance. Moreover, she had been imbued with the absolute belief that she was special. She was, after all, a colonel's only daughter.

And Kent—as far as he knew—was a colonel's son. There was nothing he wanted more than to enlist one day in the army himself. He thought that would please his father.

Kent shot up like a young sapling in his mid-teens. Almost overnight, he went from being a little blond boy to an awkward, acne-scarred teenager. With his thick glasses and the burr haircut that accentuated his protruding ears, his appearance gave scant promise of the good-looking man he would become. He competed on the swimming team in high school; he had the wide shoulders and flexible muscles for it. He was much taller then the colonel, but he still looked to Cliff for approval.

He rarely got it.

✦   ✦   ✦

After a year, Gil Taylor came home from Korea unscathed and reclaimed his family. He moved Pat and Susan to Shirley, Massachusetts, to his next post. There, they lived in a minuscule apartment, and Pat seemed to enjoy playing at being a housewife. Like most young service families, they had almost nothing in the way of furniture or possessions: a cheap orange and avocado upholstered couch with maple-stained arms, triangular Formica end tables, and Melmac dinnerware.

Gil had filled out. He was tanned and muscular and probably thirty pounds heavier than the skinny kid Pat had married, an attractive man. Pat soon became pregnant again. On June 14, 1955—just over two years after Susan was born—she gave birth to a second daughter, Deborah Dawn.

Boppo and Papa were stationed in Gary, Indiana, and Margureitte worried herself sick about how her little girl was doing. Pat was only seventeen, with *two* babies to take care of; it seemed she faced one traumatic situation after another. She had always had a flair for the dramatic; she experienced no emotion moderately. If she and Gil ran low on food toward the end of the month, she translated their predicament into abject poverty and called home for help. There were many "emergencies," like the time Pat was "overcome" by paint fumes when she tried to brighten up her apartment. She wrote her mother that they didn't have enough to eat—that sometimes it got so bad they had to scavenge for windfalls in apple orchards. "If we can afford meat at all, it's only a half pound of hamburger or one pork chop. . . . If there's one piece of bread, the kids get it." That just tore Margureitte up inside, the thought that her daughter and the babies might be hungry.

It seemed as though Boppo was constantly burning up the highways between Gary, Indiana, and Shirley, Massachusetts. She was horrified on her first visit to see where Pat and Gil were living; their apartment was in a building whose other residents looked highly suspicious to her. She reported to the colonel, "Cliff, I believe they're living in a whorehouse. It's not a fit place for them."

She had returned home alone only reluctantly that time. But then Pat called and said she had almost choked to death on a pork chop—served at one of her "single pork chop" meals—and Margureitte drove all night to get to her. This time she insisted that Pat and the babies must come back to Indiana with her, and Gil let them go. Margureitte told her husband that there were rats running all over the place, that Pat and the babies were in "terrible condition. They were the most pitiful sight when I got there." Susan remembered how happy they all were to see her grandmother arrive, a one-woman army to the rescue. "We adored her. When Boppo showed up, we knew that things were going to be under control again."

When they arrived back in Gary, Kent gave up his bedroom to his sister and moved into the living room. It would be a thoroughly entrenched pattern. Rescuing Pat from danger was gradually becoming the entire thrust of Margureitte Radcliffe's life. With her mother's enthusiastic support, Pat would spend the next several years traveling back and forth between her parents' home and Gil's duty stations.

Gil was sent to Iceland, Germany, and Washington, D.C., and he usually went by himself. There was a plethora of emergencies, each one only serving to convince Margureitte that Pat and the children should stay with her. Pat was driving one day when Deborah accidentally hit the door handle and fell out into the street. Luckily, there were no cars behind them.

Susan's baby book bears a cryptic notation. "Age 3. Susan run over by a truck. Not injured." Susan does not remember being hit by a truck. How odd that all of her baby presents, all of her measurements, her first words, were listed in her baby book, but something as potentially tragic as being "run over by a truck" has no details at all.

✦ ✦ ✦

When Susan was four and Deborah two, Gil was assigned to the Philippines and he persuaded Pat to bring their little girls and join him there. Things would be better; he would make her happy. He adored his beautiful young wife and was thrilled that she would leave her mother behind and come to him.

While they were in the Philippines, Deborah caught a fungus infection from her cat and all her hair fell out. She was partially bald for the next three years, but Pat designed clever hats to cover her hair loss. Every dress had its matching hat. She was a superb seamstress and made most of the two little girls' clothes. Susan and Deborah always wore either matching or contrasting outfits for special occasions—dressed not unlike the way their mother had dressed as a child. Pat took scores of pictures of her daughters and of the events that marked the passing years of their lives. Susan and Deborah in Easter coats and bonnets, Valentine's Day dresses, Christmas dresses—two brown-eyed little girls looking like dolls. To glance through the Radcliffe and Taylor family albums was to see Christmas dinners, Halloweens, Easters, and birthdays right out of *Good Housekeeping*. Everyone was smiling. Everyone was dressed precisely right. Boppo and Pat, of course, wore frilly aprons as they carved a turkey or carried in a birthday cake. "It was strange," Susan recalled. "At that time, Mom didn't care how she dressed—but she always wanted us to look perfect."

Pat went through a period when her clothes were almost matronly. Gone were the soft dreamy dresses of her early teens. In her twenties, she wore high-necked blouses and long skirts in muted colors. She parted her hair on the side and pulled it back in severe tight curls. Heavy harlequin glasses hid her green eyes, and her shoes were Cuban heeled and sensible. And all the while her figure was as slim and attractive as always. But it was hidden beneath those clothes, her sensuality blunted.

Despite Deborah's miserable fungus, they all enjoyed the Philippines for a while. But then it began to unravel. Pat wrote her mother that she had suffered two miscarriages and she needed Boppo to come help her. "I was four or five months pregnant, and I was all alone. I didn't know what to do, so I just sat on the toilet and flushed them away."

But this time her mother couldn't come; she was in Europe with her husband at his duty station and she had to choose. For once, she chose Cliff.

Susan had a vague memory of being injured while they were in the Philippines. "Somehow, my hand was crushed. I don't know if it got shut in a car door or what happened. I only know it was Christmastime and I was in the hospital and I heard them singing carols in the hall. My mother came to see me, but I wouldn't look at her. Children remember things oddly. I heard the carols and I turned my face to the wall until my mother went away."

Pat wrote again to her mother, saying her doctor had told her that Gil was an animal and was wearing her out with his insatiable demands for sex. Margureitte was horrified, and when Pat became pregnant again, her mother insisted that she return to the States. Once more Pat and the girls went back to "family." Boppo and Papa were still in Germany, but Pat and the girls lived in North Carolina with Mama Siler, who was delighted to have her precious Patty back.

This time Pat gave birth to a boy. Ronnie Taylor was born in November of 1958. Pat was twenty-one, immature, indulged, and seemingly incapable of taking care of her husband and her children without the support of her family. She also tended to embroider on the truth a little and was given to hysteria and histrionics. But her family considered her only a little high-strung. And, in upper-class southern women, being high-strung was almost an admirable trait, bespeaking fine genes. The Silers had produced a number of "high-strung" females. When their antics became tiresome, the rest of the family intoned, "She needs professional help." Otherwise, they scarcely noticed a tizzy or two.

✦ ✦ ✦

In 1959, Pat and the children again tried living with Gil—in the Magnolia Gardens Apartments in Falls Church, Virginia. "I think we were too much for her—without my grandmother to help," Susan recalled. There was a new, frenetic quality about Pat. She fought constantly with a woman who lived in an upstairs apartment. Margureitte, by now back in the States, was appalled when she visited and heard Pat screaming insults. "You're acting like a fishwife, Pat," she gently remonstrated.

Pat kept the door locked all the time, frightening her children with warnings that someone was trying to get in. Susan yearned to breathe fresh air and escaped outside whenever she could. She wandered all over the neighborhood—alone—but felt safer than when she was locked in with her mother's fears.

There was no one trying to break into the apartment; Pat simply wanted Gil to come home and help her, and her stories usually got her what she wanted. She *was* often hysterical, but that too served a purpose. When she was small, she had only to stamp her foot and pitch a fit to get her way. Now, she was using the same methods. And what Pat really wanted was to go home, to live with Boppo and Papa and have all the onerous burdens of parenthood lifted from her shoulders.

She also wanted to be rich.

Pat still dressed her children with exquisite good taste. She fixated on the way Jackie Kennedy dressed John-John, and she wanted Ronnie to look just like him. She saved her money to buy her babies the very best. But on at least one occasion, she was apprehended for shoplifting in a Falls Church department store. She had hidden some Feltman Brothers toddlers' outfits in her clothes. Among the most expensive children's clothing made, Feltman Brothers' garments were far beyond Pat's budget. Margureitte was aghast. "That terrible, terrible, *rude* store detective took her to the front office and just treated her very, very badly. We could have sued them, but we decided not to."

Things in Falls Church were not going well. Ronnie was having convulsions, which would continue regularly until he was almost twelve, and Pat wrote that no one in the entire state of Virginia was even civil to her. When Margureitte heard her daughter's version of her life in Falls Church, she insisted that she move home to Atlanta at once.

Of Margureitte's two children, her son was the one who truly needed some bolstering, but he rarely asked for help and Pat's demands drowned him out. Now a handsome and powerfully built young man, Kent had come home from Germany with a broken heart. He had fallen completely in love—the all-out, no-protective-walls first love that happens only once. The girl was German, tall and flaxen-haired. Her name was Marianne Krauss. She loved Kent too. She was an extremely nice girl and she wanted to marry him. But she couldn't even imagine leaving her parents to go off to America forever. Nor could Kent face never going home again. In the end, when he left Germany he was as alone as he had ever been.

His troubles piled up and he occasionally drank too much. Sober, Kent was as gentle as most really big men are; he had nothing to prove. His strength was awesome. Even a little tipsy, he was good-natured. But if he drank a few bottles of beer or too many rum and Cokes over his limit and someone put him down, he went wild. Kent could level a bar in no time.

But that really wasn't him. The episodes were aberrations. Kent, when in emotional pain, was far more likely to turn inward—to blame himself for whatever went wrong.

20

If there were secrets among the members of the Siler clan, and indeed there were, the world was allowed to see only their staunch loyalty and sense of family. Charity toward others and religious devotion were also prominently on display. Susan and Deborah, as very little girls, delighted in car trips with their great-aunts. "They sang—oh, how they sang," Susan recalled. "We'd be going to Sneads Ferry for a fish dinner and the car was always alive with music. Hymns, you know—like 'The Old Rugged Cross,' and 'We Will Gather at the River,' and 'Amazing Grace.' We loved those times. Each aunt would try to outdo the others, and it just made us feel safe and happy."

Their aunts—"the Righteous Sisters"—often made Susan and Debbie giggle. Susan's favorite was her great-aunt Thelma, who generally did and said what she felt at the moment—even to complete strangers. She said grace at the lunch counter at Rose's Dime Store in Jacksonville, because that was the Christian thing to do and she didn't care who snickered. Thelma often went up to fat women and said, "I know I'm a stranger, but I just have to tell you that you have such a pretty face it's a shame you went and let yourself get so stout." She had been known to offer intimate marital counseling to couples at her church when they hadn't asked for it. She never failed to be amazed when people did not seem to appreciate her Christian concern. "But I loved her so," Susan recalled. "She didn't think she was pretty at all—not like my other aunts—but she was just so *good.*"

Hospital visits and funerals were always a large part of the Silers' social life. The Rev. and Mrs. Siler had, of course, raised their brood to care tenderly for the sick and to give the recently deceased a properly somber—but loving—goodbye. "I know it sounds awful," Susan said, "but I never saw Boppo happier than when she was on her way to do for the sick. She'd go sit all day in the hospital with people she barely knew, but she'd always say they were practically her best friends. Of course, if they were sick too long, it got to be old and she lost some of her enthusiasm. And she *always* took a hot dish to the house when somebody died. I was mortified once when she stood there and gave the whole recipe for the escalloped corn she brought—it had to be shoe-peg corn and all—to these people who were *grieving.*"

Since the Silers lavished such caring on strangers, they were absolutely steadfast in their support of one another. Pat Taylor's closest relatives were a brick wall against the outside world—her mother and stepfather, her grandparents, her aunts. Whatever pickle she got herself into, they came running.

There were those in her extended family, however, who looked upon her with slightly less enthusiasm. Pat's peers in the Siler family thoroughly disliked her. Beginning in August 1966, the huge Siler Family Reunion would be held in White Lake, North Carolina. It was an annual tribute to the late Rev. Siler and a celebration on a grand scale, with mouth-watering barbecue, fried chicken, potato salad, "heavenly hash," biscuits, and every pie known to mankind. Women cooked in shifts, and family members brought handcrafted items to be auctioned off in the Siler Auction. The proceeds were used to put fine young men through Baptist Bible colleges.

Pat's things always drew the highest bids at the auctions and perhaps that was cause for some resentment. But over the years Pat's female cousins had stored away anecdotes about her that gradually became Siler folklore. Little Patty Radcliffe, the "beautiful" cousin, apparently managed either to anger or to hurt the feelings of most of her plainer kin. When Susan and Deborah grew older, they were invariably buttonholed at the Siler reunions by someone still smarting from Pat's cruel—but deft—tongue.

"No one ever seemed to forget whatever it was Mom did to them," Susan said. "They'd always want to tell us all about it. And Debbie and I'd say, 'Wait a minute. We weren't even born at the time you're talking about.' Mom just had a way of riling people, and getting under their skin. The aunts still loved her like they always did—but, well, you have to understand the Silers. The cousins would *say* they loved her too, but they didn't *like* her. Nobody in our family would ever, ever admit they didn't love another Siler."

Everybody liked Kent; he was as noncombative and lovable as a big Saint Bernard puppy. He never caused a fuss. In college, he studied engineering and played varsity football. Then he suffered another crushing disappointment, which everyone else had seen coming. Despite his hearing loss, Kent had clung to his belief that he would one day be a soldier. But when the time for his physical examination came, there was no way he could pass the stringent hearing tests. His profound deafness kept him out of the army. All the men in his life were career army, and he had wanted so to move into that world. But he couldn't hear. It was that simple, and that final.

That disappointment added to the loneliness he still felt from the loss of Marianne. It helped when he made a firm platonic friend in Cindi Alan.* Both of them were uncomfortable with their fathers, who were both colonels and as unbending and unemotional as stone. Their mutual problems drew Cindi and Kent together. It wasn't a romance, but it was a haven.

After a while, Kent wanted more than a buddy and he began dating another girl. Cindi wasn't hurt when on July 3, 1961, Kent, now almost twenty-two, married Meta Raye Crawford, the daughter of yet another colonel stationed at Fort Mc-Pherson. Meta Raye was a dainty, dark-haired girl, very pretty, and both sets of parents smiled on the match. Kent was the

---

* The names of some individuals have been changed. At their first mention in this book, these names are marked with an asterisk.

second of Margureitte and Cliff's children to be married in the chapel at Fort McPherson. But sadly for Kent, the union lasted only a year. There were no recriminations; the marriage simply wound down. Kent had never forgotten Marianne and he could not have Marianne.

After graduating from college, Kent worked as a draftsman for a construction company, and he was as talented with a pencil as Pat was with a needle and thread. His huge hands could produce the most precise and delicate drawings. But even with his parents back in the States, Kent's life became free-floating. He would have liked to be with them more. But he often felt that he was crowding people at their house. Pat and her children lived there most of the time. Her crises and emotional tizzies had begun to accelerate; whenever she was far away from home, something went wrong.

Gil's parents were assigned to the Orlando/Lakeland, Florida, area—where they would eventually retire—and they were understandably eager to see their grandchildren. From time to time, Pat gave in to Eunice Downing's pleas and agreed to bring the children down for a visit.

Susan remembered that visits to her other grandparents were fraught with scenes and high drama. "Grandma Downing loved my mother and us and she was a wonderful cook—I got my love of cooking from her—but we hardly ever got to eat there. Somehow, my mother always took offense at something that was said, or she'd get into fights with my dad's brothers' wives. She'd tell us to get into the car because we were leaving. We'd cry because we were hungry and we wanted to eat, but we'd end up driving around and around the block while Grandma Downing would be out on her front porch begging us to come back."

On one of the ill-fated visits to the Downings, Pat called home for help, relating a bizarre story about her mother-in-law: "I think she's trying to poison me!"

Pat's cries of murder never failed her. Although Margureitte and the colonel were on overseas assignment, Margureitte's sister, Aunt Lizzie Porter, drove all night from North Carolina to Florida to "rescue" Pat once again.

Aunt Lizzie Porter was a slender, patrician woman who worked for the telephone company and raised her son, Bobby, by herself after her husband left her. Bobby commented that no matter how many times his cousin insisted someone was trying to kill her, no one ever called the police or paramedics—or any authority. Instead, Margureitte or one of the Righteous Sisters would leap into a car and drive great distances to save Pat.

Eunice Downing was bewildered; she never could figure out what she had done to upset her daughter-in-law, but she kept trying to bridge the communication gap—and was invariably left with a table laden with rapidly cooling food and the sight of her small grandchildren sobbing out the back window of a disappearing car.

✦ ✦ ✦

In 1963, Gil Taylor was transferred to Germany, to Bad Tölz —and then to Bad Aibling, near Frankfurt. Pat agreed to go with him. For a while, things went well, but soon Pat was embroiled in feuds with the neighbors. She almost seemed to seek out confrontations deliberately. On occasion, she fought physically with neighbor women, scratching and pulling hair. She told Gil that their husbands were flirting with her and hinted that some had gone further. She was furious when he seemed doubtful.

A theme was emerging. More and more, Pat portrayed herself as an innocent beauty besieged by sex-crazed males who couldn't keep their hands off her. Gil had heard so many of his wife's dramatic stories and seen the most minuscule of problems blown into huge scenes too many times. That was just Pat. She craved upheaval, hysteria, and emotional fireworks. And she had to be the center of it all. He was an unsophisticated man and at a loss to know how to deal with her. Usually things blew over if he just ducked and sought cover.

They seldom had a pleasant family outing. When they took weekend trips to Lake Kimsey, Pat accused Gil of drinking. Actually, he scarcely drank at all—and if he did, he had to sneak off to drink one beer. Or they would be in the midst of a happy picnic in an Alpine meadow when Pat would cry out that she had eaten bad mushrooms and been poisoned, probably fatally. It was not the stuff of which happy memories are made. Invariably, their holidays ended in shambles.

When her parents were nearby for backup, Pat could maintain a tentatively even keel, but alone, she invariably turned day-today life into chaos. She begged Boppo and Papa to get a transfer back to Frankfurt. She needed them.

Of course they would come. Clifford Radcliffe put in at once for a new assignment. But things continued to go wrong until they arrived. A huge grandfather's clock fell over on Susan, but luckily she was just far enough past it when it fell that she was scarcely hurt. Her mother explained that the uneven floors of the army housing had caused it to tilt.

The Radcliffes were soon in Frankfurt. Their headlong rushes to come to Pat's rescue were, in a sense, their finest hours. It seemed to them that it was what they were meant to do. If it also meant that Margureitte had to give up any semblance of a life of her own, well, she would make the sacrifice. Her daughter came before anything. This time, however, even her mother conceded that Pat was out of control and had her committed to a hospital for a psychiatric evaluation. But not for long. Indignantly, Margureitte proclaimed the doctor "as cuckoo as anyone I ever saw! He actually asked Pat if she saw pink elephants! Imagine . . ."

With her parents nearby, Pat seemed much better. Then there was a blowup with Gil, and Pat and the children moved in with Boppo and Papa in their house in Falkenstein. She expected that Gil would come to beg her forgiveness, and she would eventually relent and give him one more chance. When he didn't, she was furious. "Your father's no good," she told Debbie and Susan. "He lost your German shepherd gambling."

Boppo bought two poodle puppies for Susan and Debbie, but they both died. Their grandmother felt so sorry for them as they sobbed, bereft, that she bought them two more. "I can't stand to see your brokenhearted little faces," she said.

This time, the puppies survived.

21

Pat wrote to Gil and told him he should come get her. The children missed him and they were too much for her to handle without him. More than that, the men in her parents' neighborhood frightened her. She hinted that someone was trying to kill her. She wrote her husband that she lived in terror of being raped. She prophesied that Gil would live to regret it if he left her alone.

There was no question that men noticed twenty-six-year-old Pat Taylor. With her clear green eyes, pouty lips, and slight overbite, and the sensual recklessness she exuded, men always looked twice—even though their second look elicited only a cold stare from her. But it was doubtful that she was being sexually stalked. It was even less likely that anyone was plotting to murder her. She had cried wolf too many times.

Susan and Debbie liked Germany and, at ten and eight, they weren't particularly disturbed by their mother's mood swings. They had never known anything else. However, one day Susan and a German friend Dorte, also ten, returned to her grandparents' house earlier than they were expected. Dorte skipped up the path ahead of Susan but stopped suddenly. When she whirled back toward Susan, she had a bewildered look on her face. She pointed toward a bedroom window and said, "Your mutta—your mutta."

"What about my mother?" Susan asked.

"Look—in the window." The little girls peeked in the window and saw Pat, alone, hitting herself all over her body with pots and pans. Hard. Susan was embarrassed. She couldn't explain it to Dorte because she didn't understand it herself.

Soon they heard sirens and saw German police cars with their lights flashing screech to a halt outside the house. The next morning, Pat's body was a mass of bruises, scratches, and welts. She looked as if she had been run over by a truck. She gave a statement to the German detectives about a salesman who had forced his way in, beaten her, and then sexually attacked her.

"Boppo and Papa took her to the hospital and notified my father," Susan recalled. "I guess he believed that men had been hurting her. He showed up the next day, and we went back to live with him." But there were no physical signs that Pat had been raped. No semen. No labial or vaginal contusions, none of the characteristic inner thigh bruising that is found in rape victims.

Susan said nothing about what she had seen in the window. She was ashamed, but she didn't really know why.

✦　✦　✦

Pat and Gil had been married over a decade. He was no longer a teenager in love. He had been through the mill with Pat's theatrics and bizarre stories—but he loved her, and he loved his three children. When Pat was sweet to him, no man could ask for more. If anything, she was even more beautiful than when he married her.

It seemed sometimes to Gil that if he could find out what it was that would make Pat happy and serene—and then give it to her—they could have a good marriage. He knew she needed to be around her family, and that was a start. When they left Germany in 1965 and flew to Fort Dix, New Jersey, for reassignment, Margureitte and Clifford Radcliffe remained in Germany, finishing the colonel's tour of duty there. Gil wondered how Pat would manage without them. After all, they had asked for the Frankfurt post so they could be near her, and now she was heading back to the States.

But it worked out all right. Pat was delighted when they were sent to Fort Bragg in Fayetteville, North Carolina. Mama Siler was there and all of her beloved aunts. If her mother and stepfather weren't close by, she had, at least, the second string.

Gil and Pat even bought a little brick house near Fort Bragg. The house, of course, wasn't anywhere near what Pat had envisioned. She had become increasingly obsessed with having her own estate—a plantation, a lavish spread of green fields and horse barns with a main house where she could entertain. She had never been able to take care of even an apartment without her mother's help, but she knew she would be happy if she could only live the way Scarlett O'Hara had lived at Tara before the Civil War.

While driving through the countryside near Warsaw one day, Pat saw the house she really wanted. It was a Victorian mansion surrounded by a wrought-iron fence. The porch roof was supported with tall columns, there was a fountain in the front yard, and even a carriage house—but it was in terrible condition, with peeling paint and a sagging roof. The rose garden was overgrown with weeds and the foundation listed to one side.

Pat had to have it. Gil checked it out and, despite the house's decrepit condition, the asking price was far beyond anything an enlisted man could manage. He tried to explain that to his wife, but Pat sulked: If only she could have that house, she would be happy. If he loved her, he would find a way to get it for her.

Whatever Gil did for her, it wasn't enough.

Later, when Pat showed the house to Margureitte, her mother paled and said, "Pat, are you crazy?"

The house was a stone's throw from where John Cam Prigeon still lived with his family. Pat probably did not know the significance of that proximity at the time, but her mother was vehement that Warsaw, North Carolina, was no place for her to even think about living.

There is no evidence that Pat Taylor had had anything but imaginary encounters with men other than her husband. She used her stories of men's unwelcome attentions to keep Gil in line. But at Fort Bragg, she ran into her old boyfriend. He was now a captain, while Gil was only a sergeant. Gil had always been jealous of the man, even though he had long since been convinced that Susan was his own offspring.

That evening there was a terrible scene when Pat and Gil went out to eat with her aunts at Sneads Ferry. Hearing that the captain still found their niece fascinating, the aunts urged her to encourage his interest. In the long run, they advised, she would have a much more solid future than with an enlisted man. They dismissed the fact of her marriage to the father of her three children with the wave of a hand. If being married to an officer would make Pat happy, then that was what they wanted for her.

Gil might as well have been invisible.

Pat *was* miserable. She didn't like marriage, and she didn't like being alone either. She wasn't interested in the captain. What she really wanted was to be home with Boppo and Papa.

✦ ✦ ✦

The Radcliffes left Germany and were reassigned to Fort McPherson, their last duty station before the colonel's retirement. They bought a small house near Atlanta, but when they realized that Pat and the children were again planning to move in with them, they knew it wouldn't be nearly large enough.

They found a house in East Point that Margureitte fell in love with, a low brick rambler with white shutters. It was set far back from the street—Dodson Drive—and the half acre of land that came with it was dotted with pine and maple trees. After all the years of fixing up and making do with army housing, Margureitte at last had her own home. She would have been happy to live on Dodson Drive for the rest of her life. The house was lovely and the neighborhood was very upper-middle-class.

Kent came to live with them, at least part of the time, and a familiar pattern was soon reestablished. Every time Pat and her children appeared to stay with Boppo and Papa, Kent obligingly moved out of their way. Space was always maintained for Pat.

Kent loved Pat's kids, but he tried to avoid her. If she had been known to hurt her cousins' feelings, she invariably aimed directly at Kent's very gut. "He tried to stay away from her," Susan recalled. "But she'd follow him from room to room, and if he went outside, she'd find him there too. I think she was trying to drive him out of the house forever. He was so kind and nice, and all my girlfriends had crushes on him. They were only about twelve, but they could see how handsome he was and they just followed him around."

Pat had no women friends. She had never really had girlfriends, and she had never missed them. She really didn't like women. She had Boppo and Papa, and she spent a lot of time with her daughters. Susan and Debbie's friends could not believe that Pat was a mother; she looked like a teenager, and she was so pretty. To young visitors, the ambience at the Radcliffes' house seemed wonderful: the great-looking uncle, the darling young mother, and the grandma and grandpa who were so kind. Susan and Debbie were the envy of their friends.

Both of Pat's daughters would remember her as a good mother. She led a Brownie troop and she delivered her children to Sunday school and picked them up afterward. She gave wonderful birthday parties, and she loved to decorate the house for special occasions. And, of course, she sewed for them. She often told them how wonderful they were, and that they could achieve anything they wanted in the whole wide world.

The one thing Pat wouldn't allow was anyone interfering with her three children. No one could discipline them but her, not even Boppo. Susan and Debbie and Ronnie belonged to her and she would see to their raising. But Boppo belonged to her too, and she wasn't going to allow anyone to interfere with that. Subtly but steadily, Pat began to edge Kent out. "She set him up so many times," Susan recalled. "If she wanted him out of the house, she'd start a fight and then make it look as though he was at fault. Then Papa would say, 'Kent, why don't you just leave?' "

Kent knew all too well that his presence aggravated Pat. His mother seemed incapable of opposing her. Margureitte was pulled in too many directions, and she was not a woman comfortable with direct confrontation. She had other ways of letting her family know she was unhappy. She would slam the kitchen cupboard doors loudly and mutter under her breath. This never bothered Pat; it made Kent terribly ill at ease. Driven too far, Margureitte also had a histrionic side. She would drop to her knees, hold out her arms, and cry, "What about *me*? Why doesn't anyone ever ask me what *I* want?"

Kent took every word to heart. He would gladly have given

her what she wanted—if only he could have. He knew, he told Susan, that if he could just be as good and kind as Boppo was, he would be a better person. Susan and Debbie believed it too. Their grandmother was the most selfless person they had ever known.

Kent usually assumed that his departure would ease things in the house, and so he would leave. Kent could look out for himself, but Pat was so helpless. Boppo *had* to take care of Pat; anyone could see that.

Choices are like dominoes, one tumbling against the next and then the next until events go out of human control. Margureitte would never really have dominion over her life again. That her own choices had set the scene for tragedy would never occur to her. She would only cry out again and again, "Why doesn't anyone ever ask me what *I* want?"

No one ever would.

✦ ✦ ✦

In 1964, Kent had reestablished his relationship with Cindi Alan, and this time their friendship had blossomed into a romance. At twenty-five, Kent was probably happier than he had been since he fell in love with Marianne in Germany. Cindi was attractive and blond and she always had a smile on her face. They were not physically intimate, but Kent believed they soon would be. They had fun together. Cindi was so proud to be seen with Kent. Her parents approved. His parents approved.

They didn't see each other as often as they would have liked. Cindi worked in Alabama and Kent worked in Atlanta, but they wrote all the time and exchanged photographs. Kent sent her a picture of himself pensively staring into the distance. He had pasted the words "Love" and "Future!" over the snapshot.

In November of 1964, he sent a picture and wrote on the back,

> Cindi,
> Your long slim "Echo" continues to look for that
> very special day! The day of beginning our lives
> together—May it come soon and bring us our happiness.
> > Loving you!
> > Kent

Another time he wrote, "I am missing you very much, Cindi. Hurry home—so I can smile again."

One weekend when they were together, they put ten dollars' worth of quarters into a "Three Photos for a Dollar" booth and posed together, with Cindi perched on Kent's lap. The last picture was of a tender kiss.

They talked about getting married and even planned on having a little girl. They would call her Jessica. Sometimes when Kent wrote to Cindi, he sent a message to "Jessica," their secret child of the future. "Jessica, I know you are somewhere waiting out there. . . ."

A local paper featured a picture of Kent and Cindi and her parents on the society page. The copy read,

Cindi Alan of Birmingham, Alabama, who has been visiting her parents, Lt. Col. and Mrs. Bertram Alan* in Atlanta, was invited by a reporter to pose for a picture. She in turn invited her date, Kent Radcliffe, to stand by her side. Just as the camera shutter snapped, she extended her hand, displaying a handsome ring.

And that is how the Alans learned that their daughter was engaged!

It was the stuff that warms the hearts of society reporters, but things were not exactly as they seemed. Cindi wanted so much to love Kent completely, and she *did* love him, but not in the way he needed. She had kept a secret side of her life away from him. She thought she could make the relationship work and she tried, but she couldn't. Without telling Kent the real reason, she gently broke their engagement. They were still friends and he still loved her. He tried pleading and he even got angry at her, but nothing worked. He could not understand how she could just walk away from everything they had planned. He was desolate.

Kent went to Houston to stay with his uncle Frazier—to get away and to find a job he could lose himself in. As always, Kent assumed it was some defect in *him* that had made still another romance crumble. He was in as vulnerable a state as he could possibly be, but he was trying to put the torn seams of his life back together when he received two oddly urgent messages. One was a phone call from a female voice he couldn't place and the other was a letter.

The message was the same: "Get back on the bus and get back to Atlanta."

Kent did not know who initiated the call and letter, but when he returned to Atlanta, he walked into an onslaught of crushing news. His sister Pat told him an ugly, unbelievable story. If Kent had harbored even the slightest hope that he and Cindi would get back together, she smashed it. "Your girlfriend prefers women," she said flatly. "I don't know why she ever got engaged to you—maybe to cover up her real life. She's a lesbian."

It was true, but Cindi had never wanted Kent to know. This was 1965, and she loved him enough to let him go with less devastating truths.

Reeling from that disclosure, Kent was in despair. And yet within a short time Pat chose to hit him with an even more stunning revelation. Kent had always believed that he was the natural son of Clifford Radcliffe, and no one had even hinted otherwise. Although Kent had yet to prove himself to the man he admired so much, he was proud to be his son. But, of course, he was not. According to his birth certificate, he had been born out of wedlock long before Margureitte ever met Radcliffe.

Again it was his sister who lacerated him with the truth. In a moment of rage, Pat turned her fury on her brother and spat out, "You're not our kind, you know. You don't even know who you are! You think Papa's your father but he isn't. You're a bastard, and you're so stupid you don't even know it!"

It was such a cruel thing for her to do. The little boy who had endured deafness, the teenager who had survived a broken heart, the man who saw one marriage and his hopes for another fail, had everything he believed in taken away from him in those appalling sentences.

Pat could hardly have believed that *she* was Clifford Radcliffe's true issue. She was older than Kent; in all likelihood, she and Kent had both been fathered by the same man. However, she clearly saw herself as superior to Kent; in her mind, she was aristocracy and he was an interloper from a lower stratum of society. Once she had opened the Pandora's box of Kent's genetic heritage, she reminded him of his true roots every chance she got. There were witnesses who heard her do it.

Kent was never the same. He dated again, but his heart wasn't in it. He drank too much and his ability to deal with loss was

Mary Linda Patricia Vann—"Patty"—two and a half in 1940, the most beautiful baby in Warsaw, North Carolina.

Patty's mother, Margureitte, 22, married Captain Clifford Radcliffe, 29, in January 1942. Patty and her little brother, Kent, grew up believing Radcliffe was their real father.

Patty, who now insisted on being called Pat, was 15 when she married 18-year-old Gilbert "Junior" Taylor in Atlanta, Georgia, on September 6, 1952.

The young Taylor family: (left to right) Pat, 20, Debbie, 2, Susan, 4, and Gil, 23. In the army, Gil was transferred often. If she did not care to move with him, Pat was welcome to stay at home with her mother.

Pat at 26. Now the mother of three, she was a skillful seamstress and dressed her children beautifully.

Margureitte and Colonel
Radcliffe step out to a
formal dance on the base.
But her social life always
came second to the needs
of her daughter, Pat, and
her grandchildren, who
called her "Boppo."

Pat's brother, Kent, 26,
a quiet and gentle man,
in one of the last pictures
taken of him.

Pat on a rare vacation with Gil in Hawaii in the late '60s.

Pat and Gil pose with their daughter Susan at her wedding in Atlanta on March 27, 1971. Pat's expression gives no hint of the dramatic announcement she is about to make.

Susan Taylor Alford, five months pregnant and pinned into her mother's favorite burnt-orange velvet costume. Both Susan and her sister, Debbie, were accomplished horsewomen, a source of great pride to Pat and Boppo.

Five generations of Siler women in 1971. Standing from left: Margureitte, 51, Pat, 33. Sitting from left: Mary Siler, 86, Debbie, 15, holding her daughter, Rachel Dawn, one month old.

Newly divorced in 1972, Pat, determined to lead the life she really wanted, changed everything about herself—clothes, makeup, hair.

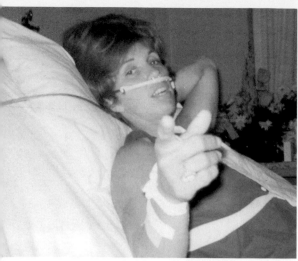

Always in delicate health and subject to frequent fainting spells, Pat suffered pulmonary emboli (blood clots in the lungs) and was hospitalized in 1973. Suitors filled her room with roses, but the one suitor she wanted most backed away.

(INSET) Pat, 1973, when Tom Allanson fell in love with her and they moved to Zebulon, Georgia, to build their dream plantation: Kentwood Morgan Farm.

(BELOW) It was a high point in her life when Georgia Governor Jimmy Carter rode with Pat, costumed in velvet, in one of the Kentwood Morgan Farm surreys.

Pat and Tom's *Gone With the Wind* wedding on May 9, 1974. She was "Scarlett" and he was "Rhett."

Tom, an only child, was 11 in this picture with his parents, Carolyn and Walter Allanson, taken in 1954.

Tom (in the background) was 15 when he posed with both sets of grandparents: (left to right) "Paw" Allanson and his wife, Nona, and "Mae Mama" Lawrence and her husband, Tom. On prickly terms with his own father, Tom adored Paw and Nona.

On June 29, 1974, bullets smashed
into the windshield of the car Walter
and Carolyn Allanson were driving
to Lake Lanier, Georgia. Walter
accused his son Tom of firing
the shots.

"The Hole" in the basement of 1458
Norman Berry Drive on the night
of July 3, 1974. The bullet-riddled
corpse of Walter Allanson was found
nearby, and Carolyn Allanson was
sitting upright on the basement steps,
shot through the heart.

Three guns were discharged in a hail
of bullets that night, one the .32
pistol found lying in a pool of blood.

Pat was in despair when Tom was convicted of the murders of his parents. And after the barns and house at Kentwood Morgan Farm burned to the ground, leaving only the sweeping entrance, her perfect world was in ruins.

Tom's intelligence and education put him much in demand as a lieutenant's clerk in Jackson Prison. Meanwhile, Pat and her mother, Margureitte, were taking care of the ailing Paw and Nona Allanson, Tom's grandparents.

Pat's daughters, Debbie Cole (left) with her daughter, Dawn, and Susan Alford with her son Sean, visited Tom at Jackson Prison. They were forbidden to visit him again.

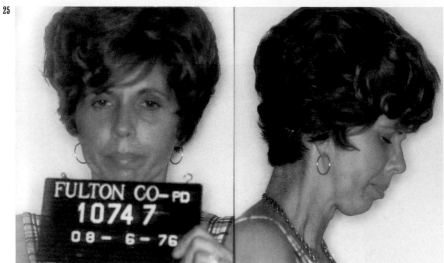

Mug shots of Pat Taylor Allanson taken after her arrest on August 6, 1976 for the attempted murders of Paw and Nona Allanson.

Colonel and Margureitte Radcliffe stuck by Pat during her trial and visited her weekly at Hardwick Correctional Institute.

27

Bill, Susan, and Sean on a visit to Pat at Hardwick. Susan, pregnant with Courtney, was thrilled to see how well her mother looked.

28

Posing on a beach in Florida during a stay with Bill and Susan Alford in 1980, Debbie looked very much like her mother fifteen or so years before.

29

Susan (left) and Debbie together again at the Alfords' new home in Atlanta in 1981. Pat's daughters were as different as night from day.

almost gone. Cindi wept for his pain, but she couldn't be what he needed.

Christmas of 1965 was tense, no matter how hard Boppo tried to make it festive. Kent was so depressed. He had been to Alabama to see Cindi, and even she found him so changed, so bitter.

Gil was often overseas. He had become a shadow husband and shadow father. The tight little family group on Dodson Drive didn't need him; he was as alienated as Kent was.

Kent was living on Dodson Drive, but only temporarily; he was trying to get into an apartment of his own. Pat's kids wanted him around, but his sister railed at him constantly. Boppo was torn between the two of them, but as always she sided with her daughter, guessing that Kent was stronger than Pat.

Kent was dating a flight attendant in College Park, Georgia, in the latter part of 1965. She was beautiful and she really cared for him, but Kent could no longer risk trusting any woman enough to fall in love. When the girl became pregnant, she kept the news to herself, sensing that the timing wasn't right and that Kent's feelings for her weren't strong enough. She bided her time, waiting for the right moment to tell him.

It never came.

On February 1, 1966, Officer M. C. Faulkner of the East Point Police Department received a Signal 59 directing him to 2555 Stewart Avenue, "just in front of Nalley's Chevrolet." A Signal 59 meant a dead body. He expected to see an accident. And, indeed, there was a minor traffic accident on Stewart Avenue. An Oldsmobile sedan parked at the curb had a smashed right front fender and the tire on that side was flat. Nearby, Faulkner saw a station wagon with the tailgate dented.

Officer G. H. Wade told Faulkner that he had been called to the scene by a salesman at Nalley's. In response to their questions, Mary Schroder said she had been driving her 1962 Ford station wagon south on Stewart Avenue with her attorney husband, James, as a passenger. "I was making a right turn into Nalley's when my car was struck in the rear by that Oldsmobile. I think it's a '62 too. The car then passed our car and pulled to the curb."

James Schroder picked up the strange account. "The driver looked back at us as he passed. I got out and started to walk over to his car and then I saw him slump over in the seat."

A Nalley's salesman said he had heard a loud report—"like a

gunshot"—just before the accident, but another witness told the officers that the Oldsmobile had passed his car just before the crash and that the driver, a young man, had been smoking a cigarette.

Just when the gunshot had occurred was a moot point. The driver of the Oldsmobile was dead, his body stretched out across the front seat with his head resting near the right front door. His feet, clad in Hush Puppy shoes, still rested next to the accelerator and brake. There was no blood apparent; he might have only fallen asleep. But a .22-caliber pump-action, single-shot rifle lay on the floor on the passenger side on a pile of crushed newspapers. The recoil had left it pointed at the dead man's knee, but its single shot had done its work.

On the slight chance that the young man might be alive, he was rushed to Grady Memorial Hospital, but he was dead on arrival. A driver's license and Social Security card in a wallet found on the dead man identified him as Reginald Kent Radcliffe, twenty-six, of 2378 Dodson Drive.

Sergeant Haines of the Fulton County Medical Examiner's Office arrived to take charge of the body. The ME's office classified Kent's death as "violent" and as a suicide. He had suffered a "pressed contact gunshot wound to the mid-chest through the clothing." He would have died almost instantly. A blood alcohol test revealed that the percentage of ethyl alcohol in Kent's system was .13. In most states, .10 is the standard for legal intoxication.

Investigators removed Kent's belongings from his impounded car. His wallet held $2.40. There was an athletic bag, a cigarette lighter, cigarettes, two ballpoint pens, a second lever-action .22 rifle, his glasses (in the backseat), and, also in the rear seat, a partially empty pint bottle of rum.

There was no sophisticated forensic science test that could determine just when Kent had fired a bullet into his heart. Was he dead, or even dying, when he hit the rear of the Schroders' car with his right front fender? Probably not; James Schroder was sure the driver had glanced back at them after the collision.

Had Kent intended to kill himself sometime that first day of February? Had he driven around East Point with the gun poised and ready? Or had the traffic accident been only the final straw to a man who believed that his life was without joy? Had he grabbed the gun and fired in a fatally impulsive gesture?

The East Point investigators even considered the possibility that there might have been another passenger, that Kent might have been murdered. His glasses were unbroken in the backseat. He was so nearsighted that he could not have seen to drive without them. No, it was more likely that the force of the blast knocked them from his face and over the seat. They dismissed the murder theory. Too many people had observed Kent's car after the accident, and no one had emerged and run away.

Kent had destroyed himself.

✦ ✦ ✦

It was early evening when the notifying officer knocked on the front door at Dodson Drive. Margureitte answered, feeling a premonition; no one but strangers ever came to the front door. When she saw the uniform and before the officer spoke a word, she cried out, "My God! Kent's killed himself!"

Pat stood down the hall, watching. She tried to hug her mother, but Margureitte pushed her away, inconsolable. Colonel Radcliffe went to the morgue to make the formal identification.

Kent's death made no headlines; there was only a short article on the back pages of the *Atlanta Journal*. His obituary was even shorter. No mention was made of the manner of his death. Survivors were listed as his parents, Colonel and Mrs. Clifford B. Radcliffe, East Point, and a sister, Mrs. G. H. Taylor, East Point. On Thursday, February 3, 1966, services were held in Hemperley's Funeral Parlor and Kent was buried in Onslow Memorial Park in Jacksonville, North Carolina. Cindi Alan slipped a ring on his finger before his casket was closed. It was engraved, "To Kent from Jessica."

But there would never be a Jessica. Nor would there be another baby, one that Kent had not known about. The flight attendant who had been carrying his child had an abortion. She grieved terribly, but not for very long. Six months later she was a passenger in a two-seater private plane. It crashed, killing her and the pilot on impact.

Pat *was* an only child now. Kent was gone forever. The only obvious reminder of his existence was a picture of him as a shy grade school boy that Margureitte kept constantly in view. Margureitte had borne three children. Two of them were dead. She refused tranquilizers. "Why do I want to numb the pain?" she asked hopelessly. "Kent's dead. In the morning, he will still be dead. Nothing will change. Why numb the pain?"

Pat grieved dramatically for her brother, sobbing about what a tragedy it was. She blamed Cindi. "She killed him with a broken heart!" But Margureitte was not unaware of the rancor that Pat had always felt for Kent. She stared blankly at her daughter's tearful face.

Margureitte now devoted all her energies to Pat and Pat's children. Besides Clifford and her sisters, they were all she had left. And now Pat had her mother all to herself. None of her histrionics and machinations had done real harm to anyone before. Rather, she had been just an inadequate young woman, self-absorbed and hysterical, who seemed her own worst enemy. But now, with her brother's suicide, her overwhelming selfishness had, quite literally, drawn blood.

22

Life went on on Dodson Drive.

It was 1966 and Pat was twenty-nine years old. The war in Vietnam raged far away. Gil Taylor, cut adrift from his family, spent a large chunk of his life in that war. "From the time I was eleven or twelve," Susan recalled of that year, "we mostly lived on Dodson Drive with my grandparents. My father dropped in occasionally and he sent money. We kids missed him."

Pat used Gil's money for her own needs; she told her parents that he contributed nothing to his family's support—a lie. Boppo and Papa supported her and the children. The Taylor family made sporadic attempts to reunite, but they were always back with Pat's parents within a few months. Gil signed on for another tour in Vietnam. On their fifteenth anniversary, he sent Pat a picture of himself in fatigues standing outside the mess tent. On the back he wrote,

6 Sept. 1967. My Darling, Lt. Levine took this of me this morning. ANNV. PRESENT. Ha! I love you. Happy Anniversary, My love.

Pat had not lived with him for more than a fraction of those fifteen years.

Colonel Radcliffe retired from the army and dabbled in real estate. Margureitte decorated the Dodson Drive house so that every room pleased her. There were three bedrooms and a den. Ronnie, seven, slept in Pat's room; Susan and Debbie had shared a room until Kent moved out, and then Susan got his room. After he died, she had bad dreams. She cried for him for a long time. But no one spoke about Kent very much. Certainly no one discussed why he had killed himself. What was the point?

Through her granddaughters, Margureitte lived out her old dreams of being a horsewoman. She prevailed upon the colonel to invest in a horse, not much more than a plug. They named him Sam, and Susan, Debbie, and Ronnie rode him. Margureitte's job as a receptionist for a local dentist provided money for her grandchildren's riding lessons. Pat took lessons too, reveling in her image, but she had no real flair for riding. She could ride sidesaddle and look pretty, no more than that. Her children were good—particularly Susan and Debbie. They studied with some of the most prestigious trainers in the South, and learned English-style riding, jumping, and equestrienne. Seeing her granddaughters in their jodhpurs, tailed jackets, and fedoras, Boppo beamed. She never missed a competition if she could help it and was very proud when they won blue ribbon after blue ribbon. "My girls always pinned high," she recalled fondly. There was something so refined about this sport; the best people in Georgia participated.

Debbie and Susan got along as well as most teenage sisters. Susan's two-year advantage in age gave her more privileges, which Debbie resented mightily. Neither girl inherited her mother's green eyes; they had dark brown eyes. Susan had thick, almost black hair, and Debbie's was light brown. They were both very pretty. Susan tended to be quiet and Debbie feisty.

Many years later, Colonel Radcliffe laughed when he recalled that Susan and her girlfriends used to sneak out on the porch so they could peek at him while he was in the shower. An adult Susan shook her head in bewilderment. "We *never* did that. Why *would* we? Why would he say that? Maybe my girlfriends would have liked to peek at *Kent*—but they never did. And they sure didn't want to see my grandfather naked."

Ronnie's seizures continued sporadically, and many times his grandparents and his mother held a tongue depressor between his teeth, wrapped him in blankets, and sped away to the hospital. "They would never tell us what was wrong with him," Susan said. "And, after a while, it didn't happen anymore."

The girls' weekends were taken up with riding lessons and shows. Sam was relegated to pasture, and they rode their own Morgan horses now: La Petite and Biscayne. Debbie and Susan were so good that they rode in shows for other owners too. They went to the best tack shops for their English riding uniforms and had them tailored to fit. Pat drove them to their lessons and competitions and Boppo and Papa paid for everything. They bought the horses and took care of their board and vet bills.

"I was the Georgia youth champion for riding Morgans when I was fourteen," Debbie remembered. "And then the world youth champion. I was riding someone else's horse when I won; it was Lippit Moro Alert, owned by Ronald Blackman." But Biscayne threw Debbie and she broke her arm. Despite the pressure at home, she refused to ride her again. Susan felt the push to win too. Although she loved the jumping events because they made her feel "free," she was often frightened on the obstacle courses. "I faked it once—if my mother had found out, she would have killed me because it was a very elite show in Atlanta. Biscayne and I made the first few jumps, but we were coming up on a solid brick wall and I just knew she couldn't spread out enough to make it. I was terrified, and I clamped my knees down and made it look like *she'd* balked. Everybody blamed her but *I* was the one who was scared. I felt guilty about humiliating her that way."

With time, the pain from Kent's suicide became less acute for Margureitte, although she never truly recovered from the loss. But she still had Pat and the colonel, who accepted her grandchildren as his own. He called Susan "Poogie," Debbie "Diddle," and Ronnie "Sam Houston Texas Taylor." As for Pat, she was so much more serene when she lived with her parents. Her own parenting sometimes seemed quixotic. She continued to sew for her daughters, wonderful special dresses that would have cost hundreds of dollars in a store, and she encouraged their efforts. "She was always telling me I could do anything," Susan said. "She was so proud of us when we did well."

But there were times when Pat's maternal talents were not quite so genteel. Susan recalled riding in a car with her mother when she was twelve or thirteen and asking a question about sex. "We were driving in the car and my class had been studying the population explosion. I didn't know the first thing about sex, and I said, 'Well, nobody should blame somebody because God put a baby in her stomach.' My mother laughed and said, 'Don't you know *anything?* The man puts his penis in the woman's hole and wiggles up and down.' She went on telling me about sex in the ugliest, most graphic terms. There was nothing about love or no birds or bees—just a blunt explanation of what men *did* to women. I was stunned. I don't know why she told me that way. When I was older, I told Boppo about it and we both laughed."

All in all, the years living with Boppo and Papa were good. Neither Debbie nor Susan remembered them as unusual in any way. They adored Boppo. And Boppo told them constantly how much she loved them. Boppo herself was happy. She had her daughter and her grandchildren. Her sisters were an easy drive away and she saw them often. Mama Siler was eighty-six and frail—but still with them. The Silers continued to meet every August at White Lake, North Carolina, for the annual reunion. Aside from missing Kent, life was as good as it had ever been for Boppo. She had never had a house she loved as much as the one on Dodson Drive. She never wanted to leave it—and, apparently, neither did Pat.

✦   ✦   ✦

Sergeant Gilbert Taylor was nothing if not persistent. He still loved Pat, and in his mind, it was only a matter of time until he gathered his family around him again. He knew what it would take, and when he transferred back to Fort McPherson in 1969, he was prepared to give his wife what she wanted. Pat had always dreamed of a house finer than any house a Siler had yet known. Hell, she still wanted her Tara. She always had and she always would, and if he ever hoped to get her out of her mama's house, he was going to have to find a way to give her what she demanded.

They went out driving in the country looking for likely properties. Finally, they found some land for sale on Tell Road.

They could have missed the place so easily; it was west of East Point in the Ben Hill district, beyond No Name Road, and dead-ended at the Atlanta city limits. It didn't look like city at all. It was deep country with thick trees up to the road and wetlands that some homeowners had dammed up into algae-covered ponds. The piece for sale was way back in, past a log cabin-like place inhabited by a maiden lady of indeterminate age named Fanny Kate Cash, who had lived there all of her life. It was Fanny Kate who was selling off the back piece of land.

There was no house, no road, nothing but trees. But Pat wanted it. Here they would build their mansion and create a wonderful riding ring for horse shows. She would give riding lessons to help meet their bills. She assured her husband that the spread at 4189 Tell Road S.W. would be known in horse show circles all over the South.

Gil had to work three jobs to pay for it: his regular army assignments, of course, and then as a caterer loading meals on airplanes *and* for the J. C. Penney Company. He had always had dark circles under his eyes, but now they turned almost black. Fearing the pace was going to outright kill him, he tried to explain to Pat, "Honey, I can't make it. I'm only getting four hours to sleep at night."

She shook her head impatiently. "Sure you can. You just have to try harder."

He did—and they bought the Tell Road property. They cleared and graded a spot for a riding ring and put up bleachers, bright lights, and fences. However, the mansion Pat visualized was far beyond their means; that would have to wait. In the meantime, they found two houses that were being sold dirt cheap because they had to be moved. One was white and one was red brick, and they were eased precariously down Tell Road past Fanny Kate Cash's place and up to a knoll back in the woods.

They soon learned that putting the two houses together would be far more costly than to simply *build* a house on their land. It didn't help that Pat insisted on the very best in lighting fixtures, flooring, and fancy trim. When Pat wanted to pave the long gravel driveway, even Boppo threw her hands up and said, "Good Lord! Your mother's lost her mind! Does she have any idea what that would cost?"

The road stayed gravel, but Gil had masons lay a red brick foundation under the white frame house and he built a long veranda that faced out on the show ring. They planted boxwood shrubs out in front and hung black shutters like the ones found on the best homes in Atlanta. It wasn't enough. When it was done, they could see that they didn't have the mansion that Pat had pictured. All they had was a mishmash that just looked like two houses stuck together. Worse, they had two mortgages they couldn't keep up with and they were about to go bankrupt and lose it all.

Pat went to her mother and stepfather in tears. They *had* to help her. As usual, she blamed Gil for their troubles; he didn't know a damn thing about building and she should have realized that, but it was too late now. She promised Boppo and Papa that she would take care of them in their "golden years" if they would only help her save the Tell Road place.

Of course, her parents said they would help her as they always had, and the malignant money drain began. In the end, it seemed the only way Margureitte and the colonel could come up with enough money to bail Pat and Gil out would be to sell their Dodson Drive house and move into the Tell Road place with them. It would be a profound loss for Margureitte. She didn't want to leave her elegant home to move into a half-finished, jerry-built excuse for a house that was so far out in the boon-docks that it took almost an hour just to get to a grocery store. She didn't want to leave the lovely neighborhood just off Head-land Drive and have afternoon tea with Fanny K. Cash. "I just want to live in my own house," she wailed, "and have my grand-children come to see me like other grandmothers do. I don't want to move."

But she finally acceded to Pat's pleas. She wanted Pat to be happy. How could she deny her daughter her dream?

"My mother always used guilt on my grandmother," Susan remembered. "She would start an argument by saying, 'Mother, why did you go off and leave me all alone with Mama Siler? Who was my father? Didn't you love me? Why did you leave me?' And Boppo would say, 'I had no other choice,' but it hurt Boppo. I always remember my grandmother saying—even when I was a grown-up: 'Why *can't* your mother be happy?' "

The Dodson Drive house was snapped up as soon as the Radcliffes put it on the market. They wondered if they should have listed it at a higher price. Boppo and Papa moved out to Tell Road and into Ronnie's bedroom, sharing the rest of the unfinished tacked-together house with Pat, Gil, Susan, Debbie and Debbie's boyfriend, Gary Cole, and Ronnie. It was crowded and uncomfortable. Once more Pat was living with her parents, although she felt it was time for *her* daughters to grow up. She could hardly wait for them to leave home.

Debbie competed in her last horse show in Hickory, North Carolina, in the late summer of 1970. She was fifteen years old and she was four months pregnant. "I won," she recalled, "and that was my last show." She married Gary, a husky blond laborer who was just seventeen, and they found a place of their own.

Susan was determined to graduate from high school; she would be the first girl in her immediate family to do so. The move to Tell Road meant she had to go to summer school if she hoped to graduate early from Headland High School. Susan was shy, but she set certain standards that no one could talk her out of. She was not going to marry anyone until she had a high school diploma, and she wasn't going to be pregnant at her wedding. Furthermore, she was truly going to flout tradition by staying single until her eighteenth birthday in March 1971.

Susan graduated from Headland in October of 1970 and went to work at the PX at Fort Mac to help the family budget. She attended a dance at the fort one night in 1970 with her girlfriend, Sonja Salo. "I met this guy I thought was a maniac," she remembered, smiling. "He was good-looking all right, but he was dancing with another girl, and he kept turning her around and winking at me and making faces behind her back. He was a show-off and a wild dancer too. I finally asked Sonja what on earth was wrong with him, and she laughed and said, 'Oh, he's okay. That's just Bill Alford. He always acts like that.' "

Alford, a first lieutenant, left a note on Susan's car a few days later and they met at Sonja Salo's apartment, which was in the building where he lived. Reluctantly, Susan agreed to go out with him. He was six years older than she was, and he was far too much of an extrovert for the shy, soft-spoken Susan. Still, his exuberance was contagious, and in spite of herself, she was soon utterly captivated by the brash young lieutenant.

So was her mother. Pat took one look at George L. "Bill" Alford and decided he was perfect for Susan. "My mother was the matchmaker," Susan recalled. "She said if she was younger, she'd take him herself. I believe that—but I also think she was clearing the decks. When we came home from our *first* date, I was mortified to hear her ask Bill if he'd given me an engagement ring! She wanted us all out of the house and on our own. She had plans."

On November 6, 1970, Fort McPherson photographers took a picture of Miss Susan Taylor and Colonel John H. Calloway, the base commander, as they pinned the insignia of Bill Alford's new rank on his uniform. He was Captain Alford now. Pat was pleased. An army captain, still in his early twenties and already on his way up, would make a fine husband for Susan.

They were married on March 27, 1971, in the Fort Mc-Pherson chapel, the same chapel where Susan's mother and father had been married eighteen and a half years earlier. Pat had been pregnant with Susan then.

Susan and Bill had a beautiful wedding. The groom and the father of the bride were in full-dress uniform; Susan wore a white dress with a long veil edged in lace, purchased at Rich's Department Store, and she carried white roses and stephanotis clustered around a huge white orchid. Everyone smiled happily for the photographers with the exception of Margureitte. Her face was fixed in the familiar crystal gaze of the Siler sisters. Perhaps she knew what was about to happen.

"My reception was a disaster," Susan recalled many years later. "My mother chose my wedding day to announce to everyone that she was leaving my father. She had a restraining order against him and he had to leave at once. He was absolutely dumbfounded. He didn't see it coming. Even twenty years after, I think he still wondered what he did wrong. He was there, giving me away, and then he was gone. Banished. My mother had a new life planned, and he didn't belong in it."

Her dramatic announcement at her daughter's wedding was vintage Pat. She did not like anyone else having the spotlight. At some point in the months after they all moved into the house on Tell Road, she had apparently come to the realization that Gil could never provide her with what she needed. He had worked three jobs, complaining all the time. He was a fool. He had been so enthusiastic about the new place, and it turned out to be just an ordinary house in the woods. He had no vision; he had no sense of grandeur. Besides, she didn't like the way he drank beer. She decided he was probably an alcoholic, while in reality he was only a moderate drinker. When she found a cache of beer cans he had buried out in back, she was sure she was right.

Both her daughters were married now, and she was only thirty-three years old. She could do so much better.

23

Pat became a very young grandmother only two days after Susan married Bill Alford. Debbie was hugely pregnant at her sister's wedding and went into labor a day later. Every generation of Siler women in memory had included fifteen-year-old mothers, and the latest was no exception. Her mother advised her to stay home as long as possible; complications developed and Debbie had to give birth by cesarean section to her baby girl, Dawn.

Later, five generations of Siler women posed for Susan's camera; Mama Siler was eighty-six, Boppo was fifty-two, Pat was thirty-three, Debbie was fifteen, and Dawn was a month old. Oddly, not one of them smiled.

Pat became a grandmother again when Susan gave birth to her son Sean the next year in April. "Mom just wouldn't let me go to the hospital when my water broke," Susan recalled. "She kept insisting that I eat this great big steak and relax. Boppo just paced and smoked, telling Mom I *had* to go. I finally got there less than three hours before Sean was born."

The house on Tell Road was much less crowded now that Gil, Susan, Debbie, and Gary had moved out. Only Ronnie, twelve, was left, and he would have been delighted to live with his father, but Pat wouldn't allow it. Gil had ruined all their plans for a wonderful country home and he didn't deserve his son. Pat allowed Ronnie to do pretty much what he pleased. She bought him a motor scooter, and then, when he was fourteen, she let him fake a driver's license and he was off driving all over Atlanta.

The colonel was now responsible for the upkeep of Pat's "plantation." And Margureitte maintained her air of quiet dignity, smiling her frozen smile as if her life were proceeding exactly as she wanted it to. She would brook no criticism of Pat, nor would she complain about her diminished life-style to anyone beyond Debbie or Susan. They knew how Boppo mourned for the home she had left behind, but appearances were everything and Margureitte made everyone believe that she adored living out in the woods even if her determined smile cracked her face.

Pat and Gil were soon divorced, but that was not the only change in Pat's life. It was the early seventies and long gone were the drab skirts and blouses and the bobbed hair of her twenties. She threw away her glasses and wore contact lenses. She had looked radiant at Susan's wedding in a silver and moss green brocade coatdress that caught the emerald of her eyes, and she really began to blossom now that she was a newly single woman. She teased and back-combed her thick honey-colored hair until it added a good four or five inches to her height. She wore makeup that accentuated her eyes and full lips.

Nobody would ever mistake her for somebody's grandmother. She was a hot-looking woman. In fact, Pat Taylor was already something of a sly conversation piece among the men who moved in the horse show circuit: the owners, trainers, veterinarians. In her slow southern way she was a shameless flirt, but none of them bragged that they had slept with her. If any of them had, they only joked and lied and said that they would like to. They were all married.

Pat's metamorphosis continued. As her teased hair rose ever higher, her skirts grew shorter. They barely skimmed her panty line. She made halter tops and wore them without a bra so that her full breasts swayed like ripe peaches clinging to the tree. She wore tight shiny vinyl boots that drew attention to her slender legs. For herself, she designed some very short wraparound dresses, cutting the bodice in such a deep V at the front that men tripped over their own horses as they peered at her breasts. She also liked Tom Jones and Engelbert Humperdinck. She listened to love songs as avidly as any teenager. She especially loved "Please Release Me" and "What's New, Pussycat?" There was no question about it. Pat Taylor was sending out signals that she was most approachable.

Pat had affairs and fleeting assignations with a number of men. Boppo and Papa pretended they didn't know. Susan and Debbie knew and were embarrassed. But their newly emancipated mother didn't care. In her mind, she had been held back for twenty years, suffocated in a loveless, go-nowhere marriage. Her changed appearance caused ripples at the Siler Family Reunion in August of 1971. The Righteous Sisters—who had always adored her—were shocked at the skimpiness of her bikini bathing suit and the miniskirts she wore. The beautiful little Patty Radcliffe was now the beautiful Pat Taylor. She knew she was a great-looking woman and she believed that men—or rather, *a* man—was the only avenue to her heart's desire.

That's what she wanted, and she went after it. As one of her lovers later remarked, "There wasn't any way you could get away from her, even if you wanted to—which I didn't. Once she made up her mind she was going to bed with you, you didn't have a chance. She liked sex."

Pat needed a man. She wasn't trained to do any kind of work, nor had she ever worked. She was an old-fashioned kind of woman, she always said, content to do her sewing and fancy work. She had only a junior high school education and she didn't read anything but historical romance novels, stories about Joan of Arc and Robin Hood, and Victorian poetry. She could sit a horse prettily, but not as competently as she claimed.

For a southern girl, she wasn't a very good cook. Her own tastes ran to chili dogs, tuna sandwiches, tomato soup, and takeout Chinese food. If her mother didn't cook for her, she would eat bread spread with pimento cheese or peanut butter or a tomato and mayonnaise sandwich for supper.

Pat was no longer a military dependent, and without Boppo

and Papa she would have had no means of support at all. It would seem that the acquisition of a plantation would be the least of her worries; she needed to find a job. "I guess I'll have to work at the waffle house," she often cried to her mother. "I can't do anything else." Working in a fast-food restaurant seemed, to Pat, the depths of degradation.

And then, suddenly, any job was out of the question for Pat. In April of 1972 she fell from one of the horses they still had at Tell Road, and it stomped her. Her injuries freed emboli (blood clots) to float freely through her bloodstream. There was real concern that she might suffer a pulmonary embolism—fatal within minutes if it blocked the flow of blood between her heart and lungs. She complained of such severe pain that it took Percodan and morphine to control it. Her doctors warned Pat and Boppo that she would have to beware of embolisms for some years, possibly for the rest of her life.

Invalidism suited Pat. She looked especially fetching as she rested languidly on the veranda, the heat—or a touch of fever—dotting her upper lip and forehead with moisture. No one urged her to get up and get on with her life—not with a wayward blood clot threatening to end it without warning. Boppo was, of course, even more solicitous of her daughter, catering to her every whim.

Pat finally had surgery at Emory University's hospital. In an extremely delicate operation, surgeons inserted minuscule "umbrellas" through her jugular vein, tiny catch basins that would stop a blood clot before it rushed irrevocably into her pulmonary artery. She spent some time in intensive care but gradually improved.

Another catastrophe befell the family in August of 1972. The Radcliffes, Pat and Ronnie, the Alfords, and the Coles traveled as usual to White Lake, North Carolina, for the Siler Family Reunion, taking several cars. On the way back home, the car carrying the Coles and Ronnie had a terrible accident. "It happened just south of the North Carolina border," Debbie remembered. "We had eaten there, and we changed drivers, and I drove . . . and everybody went to sleep. . . . We were on the back roads and the last thing I remember is going around a curve and the steering wheel locking, and I couldn't do anything. I was going seventy-five miles an hour. I remember waking up on top of the hood on my back with my legs down over the steering wheel and my seat belt was still hooked.

". . . My brother got thrown out of the car completely and his whole scalp was pulled back from the glass. He was in the front seat and he went out, Dawn went under the dashboard, and my husband went from the backseat into the dashboard. . . . Finally someone saw my brother walking around in a daze, but we were out there for six hours before they found us. They took us to two different hospitals. . . . I broke my back, and Gary broke his neck. Dawn had a skull fracture. I was in the hospital in Florence for four weeks, and in another hospital at home for three months after I had surgery to fuse my back in five places. They put in a metal rod. I had three operations."

Susan and Bill were the first ones home from the reunion, and they walked into their apartment to a ringing phone. "I had to tell my mother about the accident," Susan recalled. "I told her that Debbie's back was probably broken, and she snapped at me, 'I don't care about Debbie! I want to know about Ronnie. . . .' That's the way she was. Each of the three of us was indispensable to her, but she took turns. At the time of the accident, Debbie didn't matter, but Ronnie did. I have no idea why."

No one was ever really sure who had been driving. Some family members thought that Ronnie was, and that Debbie had lied to protect him. They were all lucky to survive the grinding crash.

After that, Pat's luck seemed to change. Through her contacts in the riding world, she met the man she had been looking for in the fall of 1972: the perfect lover. Her choice might not have been every young woman's dream; he was as old as Papa—but not nearly as handsome—and he had gray hair, a florid complexion, and a chunky midsection. Put him up next to any one of the men in the horse show crowd and he would come out a distant second as far as looks went. But he had it in his power to give Pat everything she craved.

Hap Brown* was a member of Governor Jimmy Carter's cabinet, the head of one of the most important departments in the state of Georgia. His name was always in the paper, he sat at the governor's right hand, and he kept a fine house back in his hometown as well as lavish lodgings in Atlanta. When Hap Brown walked into the Capitol building with its gold leaf–covered dome, people lined up to talk to him and shake his hand. He was known all over Atlanta—all over the state of Georgia, for that matter.

When fifty-eight-year-old Hap Brown's eye fell on thirty-five-year-old Pat Taylor, he was instantly captivated. She was lush and beautiful, but she moved with a certain class too. Her voice was a soft drawl, a young girl's sweet voice. When she spoke to him, she looked directly at him with her crystalline green eyes, and then, seeming suddenly embarrassed, she looked down. He liked her directness, and he liked her shyness.

And she obviously liked him. He sensed he could possess her if he chose. Hap knew he would have to be discreet—more than discreet. He was not only a member of Jimmy Carter's top staff, he was a married man, and Jimmy Carter, his boss, was not the kind of governor who would tolerate a member of his cabinet fooling around. Even more critical, the money in the Brown family came from *Mrs.* Brown's side. Hap had his salary and benefits, but Cordelia* controlled their true wealth. She would certainly look upon any intimate arrangement with Pat Taylor with far more disfavor than even Governor Carter.

Hap Brown could not help himself. He was soon completely smitten with Pat. She made him feel like a man twenty years younger. She was the most romantic woman he had ever met, and, at the same time, the most sensuous. She wrote him poems that were tender and symbolic, and then made love to him like a brazen trollop.

Like all those who loved Pat, he was concerned about her well-being. She seemed too delicate and too refined to have to go to work each day, but she needed to work, so Hap created a little public relations job for her. She missed a lot of work. She was often ill, sometimes hospitalized, and he visited his pale, wan mistress, held her hand, and promised her that he would take care of her, although she must understand that their affair would be very, very private.

She always agreed and Hap felt safe, pleased that he had found himself a woman both sultry and sensible. Hap's government position meant they could be together almost all the time. He had meetings to go to, political functions, reasons that he couldn't get home in the evenings or on weekends. He and Pat dined out often. His wife was a comforting hour's commute away from Atlanta and it was highly unlikely that they would run into her or any hometown friends.

Since Pat had no office skills and precious little formal education, there wasn't much that she could do for the Department of Energy, but there was a lot she could do for the department head. She and Hap took long lunches and whole days off together, driving around the countryside, watching the verdant vegetation of summer change to gold and orange in autumn.

Hap sent Pat flowers—roses. She adored roses. He bought her a gold cameo pendant and she began to collect cameos. She treasured each of his gifts. "She told me they would go out to the country and have a picnic by a stream," Susan remembered. "He'd put his head in her lap while she read Victorian poems to him. I think she really loved Hap, and she used to tell me that he was going to 'come for her' one day, and she'd be waiting for him. It was as if she expected him to come riding up and sweep her into his arms."

Pat seemed to be truly devoted to Hap Brown. If he was not exactly a knight in shining armor riding to her rescue, maybe she saw him as a father figure who would care for her always. She wanted so much to be the one and only woman in Hap Brown's life. And sometimes, she seemed to be. Hap looked at her with eyes poleaxed by love. Although he insisted on discretion, she suspected a lot of people knew about them. She saw the lifted eyebrows in the office when she slipped away to meet him. She didn't care. The sooner his wife faced the truth the better. Then Hap would be free to come for her.

Hap Brown quickly realized he would get only the frostiest welcome at the house on Tell Road. Margureitte was outspoken in her disapproval of the relationship. The Radcliffes were too proper to confront him directly, and if they had, Pat would have thrown the tantrum to end all tantrums. But the message was there: *We do not approve.*

Pat took instead to entertaining her married lover at Susan and Bill's apartment. She had used the apartment before to meet other married men, but she prevailed upon Susan to serve drinks and appetizers and to "be nice to Hap." Susan saw that Hap was "courting" her mother in the old-fashioned sense of the word. He was gallant and kind and generous. But he was still married, and he seemed in no hurry to change that arrangement.

Pat made no secret of her intentions. Susan remembered her mother pleading, "Take me home, Hap. Take me home to North Carolina." "She wanted to go back with the aunts and back where Grandma Siler was," Susan sighed. "Hap couldn't just leave and take her there, and they'd fight and she'd cry."

Pat enlisted Susan's aid in her campaign to capture Hap, suggesting that she call Hap "Dad." Susan balked at that, and Pat countered, "Well, at least you could say, 'When are you going to marry my mom and be our father?' " Susan already had a father, but she finally got up the nerve to blurt out, "I hear you-all are getting married?"

Hap froze as he reached for an appetizer, drew back his hand, and stared at the floor. He was clearly embarrassed, and for once the voluble politician could find no words. The minutes that followed were awkward. Pat looked away and bit her lip, disappointed and frustrated. Susan was mortified. She could see that Hap Brown had no intention—ever—of marrying her mother.

For all the power Hap had, he was alarmed by Pat's growing possessiveness. He tried to deflect her single-minded thrust toward his divorce and remarriage to her. He put himself out time and again for her and her family. He did his best to help Bill Alford stay in the army when a sweeping reduction in forces hit Fort McPherson. But Bill wasn't regular army, and even Hap's senator friends couldn't buck the trend. Bill left the service in August of 1973 and went to college while Susan managed Colonel Alan's horse farm in Riverdale—the same Colonel Alan who had once posed so proudly for an article about his daughter's engagement to Susan's uncle, Kent Radcliffe.

Over Margureitte's objections, Hap took Pat along on a business trip to Dallas and they had a wonderful time, but she came home no closer to a commitment from him than before. Sometimes—far too often for Pat—Hap couldn't be with her. For all her skill at manipulation and seduction, she was either naive or blind to the bleak realities of stolen passion with a married man. Pat would sit forlornly on the wide veranda her ex-husband had built for her and stare through the dark woods toward Tell Road as if she could make the sound of Hap's car materialize by sheer force of will.

But all she heard was the rain in winter or the cicadas in summer or Fanny Kate Cash calling to her cats.

✦   ✦   ✦

Pat clung desperately to Hap through Christmas of 1972 and into the long spring and summer of 1973. When he was with her she was happy, but when he left, she agonized that he would never come back. She implored him to ask his wife for a divorce. He hedged and gave her reasons why he had to delay such a confrontation.

Miserable, Pat felt her life closing in on her again. She didn't even have the horse-show circuit any longer. Debbie couldn't be expected to jump horses with a steel rod in her spine.

Pat had always been able to coerce Susan to ride no matter what. "She even convinced me to ride when I was five months pregnant with Sean," Susan said. "It was a costume show and Mom had to let out the waist of her long velvet dress and then pin me into it. I was so wobbly and nauseated I thought I was going to pitch forward on my head. Mom was the one who loved costumes, not us."

But by 1973 Pat's daughters were both married and mothers and they had no time for horse shows. Pat herself wore the costume that had once almost tripped Susan up. She had designed it in burnt orange velvet and it had a lace jabot and cuffs. With it, she wore a black felt derby with a two-foot-long ostrich plume. She saved and treasured a photograph from that period of herself and Governor Jimmy Carter in a fringe-topped surrey on the Georgia Capitol grounds. Pat was in her glory, smiling graciously as she sat beside the governor while a liveried driver held the reins of a Morgan horse. It was undoubtedly a "photo opportunity" picture of some sort, but for Pat it was proof that she was meant to move in the highest circles of society.

Hap Brown was her entrée to those circles and she wanted him more than she had ever wanted anything. She beseeched, argued, implored, nagged, even subtly threatened. If Hap Brown didn't divorce Cordelia, she didn't know what she might do. Together, she and Hap could have the perfect life. Why was he too blind to see that?

Pat was hardly a typical grandmother; she was far too involved in her affair with Hap. Boppo *was* the grandmotherly type, and she lavished attention on Dawn and Sean. Debbie and Gary Cole lived with her grandparents sporadically, but their marriage was full of dissension and recrimination. Pat allegedly de-vised a way to keep her daughter's husband in line. Nineteen-year-old Gary Cole was severely shaken when his wife's best friend confided that he should "watch his backside." The young woman whispered that Pat had put out a hit contract on him and was bragging that she had ordered him killed. Gary walked scared and alert for months, but nothing ever happened. He reconciled with Debbie and they continued their uneasy alliance. He told himself the rumors were only the product of a family that thrived on high drama and flamboyant gestures.

Ronnie tended to get lost in the shuffle. He wasn't allowed to be with his father, and his mother, whom he adored, had no time for him. He began to get into trouble at school and minor scrapes with the law. Ronnie had never shone in the family. His sisters were the stars as they rode the Morgan horses. They were both extremely beautiful girls, and he was only an average-look-ing boy.

Spring came again to Georgia, and the woods were full of the pink and white of dogwood and azaleas. Tired of waiting, Pat decided to force Hap Brown's hand. Backed to the wall, he made a choice, a choice that sounded the death knell for Pat's plans. She never told anyone what he said to her, but his answer had clearly been no.

Night after night, Pat huddled tearfully on the veranda, her lace handkerchief a sodden lump in her hand. She neither ate nor slept. "Hap's never coming for me," she cried to Susan. "He's not going to come for me."

Susan tied up the horse she had been exercising in their show ring and looked at her mother. She couldn't understand how such a young and beautiful woman could be so distraught over an old man. "You have your whole life in front of you," she argued. "Hap's an old man. You can have anyone."

But Pat seemed not to hear. "Hap's not coming for me," she sobbed. "Never, never, ever again."

Indeed, he did not. Whatever he had told Pat, it seemed final. Pat took to her bed, and then was hospitalized. Boppo and Papa hovered near, afraid that she would die of a pulmonary embo-lism if she didn't stop grieving so.

Pat had gentleman callers flocking to her sickroom. A man from Social Circle, Georgia, came to see her every day, carrying with him a single red rose. A man she described only as "a millionaire who wants to take me to California in his jet plane" often appeared at her bedside.

It was no use. They weren't Hap.

Risen at last from her sickbed, Pat arranged to send Hap one final message through his secretary. "You go tell him that if he doesn't change his mind and leave Cordelia and his children and his farm and come for me, I'll be married to Tom Allanson in two weeks. You just tell him that." Hap did not respond. When Pat devised a harassment campaign with phone calls to his office and his home, she met with only silence.

She had threatened to marry Tom Allanson. Who, Debbie and Susan wondered, was Tom Allanson? They knew him as their feed man and the blacksmith who came to shoe horses from time to time. But that was all. They hadn't even realized their mother knew his last name. Why on earth would she pick *Tom Allanson* as a threat to hold over Hap's head? She couldn't be serious.

But she was. Pat had decided there could be no better way to get Hap Brown off the dime than to be seen with Tom. Hap was aging and fat and Tom was a magnificent specimen. Pat suspected she could have Tom if she only crooked her finger. She didn't really want him—not in the beginning. She used him to make Hap jealous. Tom was only a means to an end, a hugely virile male symbol, full of youth and energy. But later, when Pat finally accepted that Hap was never coming for her, she looked more closely at Tom and rethought her options.

PART FOUR

JAIL

24

Within the space of less than two years, Pat had soared to romantic peaks few women ever dream of, only to plunge downward into deeper abysses of despair. With Hap, she had come so close to having everything she ever wanted and she cried bitter tears when she finally accepted that he was gone. But then she had found Tom and she knew he would never leave her. He gave her Kentwood Farm and passion and true love, and suddenly all that, too, was disappearing, like smoke in a darkening sky.

It seemed to Pat that fate stalked her, deliberately snatching away every shred of happiness she found. It wasn't fair. Boppo had always told her she was special and a special person deserved to be happy. And yet when she got those things she yearned for, her pleasure lasted no longer than a mouthful of cotton candy. Someone always ruined it for Pat. Something always made her cry. And she didn't know why.

After his conviction and sentencing, Tom went with "the chain"—all the prisoners from the Fulton County jail handcuffed and chained together on a bus—bound for the Georgia Diagnostic and Classification Center at Jackson Prison.

He wasn't there long. On October 25, 1974, Ed Garland filed a motion for a new trial. He cited twenty-nine errors by the court to substantiate his request. It was a standard ploy, something any good criminal defense attorney would do, but Tom pinned all his hopes on the thought of a second trial. The motion for a new trial meant he could be summoned back from prison to the Fulton County jail, and Pat insisted that that be done at once, even though facilities in Jackson were considerably more modern and comfortable than the crowded county jail; she wanted him close by. Fulton County Sheriff Le Roy N. Stynchcombe was given official orders to travel to Jackson and return with Tom Allanson.

Once he got over the shock of his conviction, Tom held on to an impossible dream that he might be released on bond by Christmas, 1974, pending his appeal. He had been locked up in the Fulton County jail for 103 days. The approaching holiday season made things, if possible, worse. His request for release on bond was refused.

Pat had great difficulty accepting the fact that Tom had been found guilty. The shock she showed the night the jury came back with their verdict had been genuine. She lived in a soap opera kind of world, her every perception colored by what she read and what she watched on television. She had always preferred shows like *Perry Mason* and *Burke's Law* where trials ended with a surprise witness and the innocent defendant was reunited with his or her lover. That had not happened. They had taken Tom away from her.

Pat was frantic that she was going to lose Kentwood too, her perfect plantation. She could not bear to have anyone else live in the rooms Tom had remodeled just for her, or to have someone else enjoy her special roses. She went to Susan and Bill Alford and begged them to buy Kentwood—to save it for her. Bill was going to college. Susan's job at Colonel Alan's horse farm in Riverdale hardly paid enough to cover the six-hundred-dollar-a-month mortgage on Kentwood, much less the balloon payments. Nevertheless, they went to the bank and tried to get a loan. They failed to qualify and told Pat there was no way they could help. "I'd rather see it burn then," Pat spat out. "I'll be damned if I'll let anyone else have it!"

In November, Tom wrote to his grandparents every few days, beseeching them to help Pat. He had no money to pay an attorney to work on his appeal. Everything he and Pat had built up was being sold, all the horses and saddles, the buggies and the tack, their tools, farm equipment, Tom's guns. The Radcliffes had mortgaged the Tell Road farm twice and were selling whatever else they could. Kentwood Farm would go back to Hoyt Waller if they didn't come up with thousands of dollars by December. They were already three months behind on payments. "You are our last straw," he pleaded to old Paw Allanson.

Tom truly believed his wife would die if he didn't get out and take care of her. He had never known her when her health was not in jeopardy, and the strain of his trial and conviction seemed to have worn her down like wind against a sand dune. Although Pat insisted to Tom that she would get a job, he begged her not to. She couldn't work; she was far too ill. "We have no other choice," he wrote to Paw. "It all boils down now to a matter of life and death. I love you both, please help me, Tom."

Paw had held tightly to his money for so long, secreting it here and there on his farm, and he had already helped Tommy out quite a bit. But it was hard for him to let go of the amounts of cash that Pat and Tom needed, both for attorneys and for Pat's medicine and doctors. Tom was asking for at least twenty-five thousand dollars for his attorneys, and Lord knew how much more it would take to support his wife.

With growing urgency, Tom sent his letters to Paw and Nona, extolling Pat and damning his aunt Jean Boggs as a money-grabbing "vulture." He bombarded the old people with scare techniques, warning them that there would be no one left to take care of them if Jean ever got control of their money. But he only wrote what he believed to be the truth, what Pat assured him *was* the truth. He did love his grandparents, and if he was freed, he would have taken care of them. He loved Pat beyond all reason, and believed she was slowly dying without him. She did nothing to assuage his worries and prodded him to keep writing to his grandparents.

His letters were transparent, but they worked on Paw and Nona. Tommy was more of a son to them than the son they had lost. Grudgingly, the old couple eventually came through with enough money to pay the lawyers and Pat's doctors. But they would not mortgage their own home to save Kentwood.

✦ ✦ ✦

Just as things seemed to be as bad as they could possibly get, the Radcliffes sustained another blow: fires.

They seemed to come out of nowhere, as if some malevolent "barn burner" right out of William Faulkner were passing through Georgia. They began on Tell Road in the last week of November. Colonel Radcliffe woke in the early hours one morning to the acrid smell of smoke. Throwing on a robe, he hurried by Pat's room and saw her standing at the window, clothed in a negligee. She gazed, transfixed, up past the show ring. His eyes followed hers and he saw smoke billowing from the stables. Pat had apparently been too frightened to move or even cry out.

The stables were two hundred yards away, halfway up to Fanny Cash's place, and the colonel saw tongues of orange flame already licking at the red siding of the U-shaped structure. Although he was in his sixties, he had kept himself in good shape. By running full tilt, he was able to save the two terrified horses inside, but the stables were lost. Pat visited Tom in jail and told him about this latest disaster in their lives. She said she had been hurt helping Papa save the horses. It wasn't true; she had never left her bedroom that night.

That same week, the barn at Kentwood burned too—to the ground. It was fortunate that the only livestock they had left was a lone renegade cow that had been off foraging for herself up in the orchards. And then to bring Tom down even further, he learned that his maternal grandmother, Mae Mama Lawrence, had died. She too had cut him out of her will.

The house that Pat and Tom had loved so at Kentwood also fell victim to flames, just before Christmas. Pat collected insurance on both the house and the barn and deposited the checks in her bank account, ignoring the fact that they required a co-endorsement with the mortgage holder. Then she wrote Ed Garland a five-thousand-dollar check on the account, which bounced. The bulk of the insurance on Kentwood wasn't hers at all, but Hoyt Waller's. The other policies were written not only in her name and Tom's, but also in Paw's, as he had helped so much financially when they bought Kentwood. Collecting on the policies was complicated and prolonged. Pat and Tom's share was gone at once for legal expenses.

The Kentwood sign came down and the blackened timbers of the house and barn were lonely charred relics in the cold December fog. The holly bushes still lined the curving driveway, and the white fence was as pristine as ever, but nothing else was the same. The property went back to Hoyt Waller, and Pat's dream of a Zebulon plantation had disappeared in the flames. Now all she had left was Tom, and she clung to him desperately, fearing he would abandon her too.

Pat came to see Tom in the Fulton County jail as often as she was allowed to, usually on Wednesdays. She walked up the long, long passageway to the old jail. It was built on an incline, the slope steep enough to wear her out. They were not allowed to touch, but talked to each other through a glass partition using telephones. Pat would raise her small hand and hold it up to the glass against Tom's huge paw. She was as loving as she had been in the very first days of their courtship, staring through the glass at him as if her heart were about to break. "It about drove me crazy," Tom recalled. "She dressed in the most revealing, seductive clothes she could."

Tom had introduced her to country and western music and they had a dozen favorite songs that were special to them, ballads of passion and betrayal, of hopeless love and longing, songs like "For the Good Times," "Blanket on the Ground," and "Please, please, don't stop loving me, 'cause I couldn't live with you gone." The lyrics brought back the memory of what Tom and Pat had been to each other. Late at night, she would call disc jockeys and ask them to play special songs "for my Tom." Lying on his jail bunk, he would listen to his tinny little radio, trying to stay awake to hear the songs his wife had selected for him.

Pat and Tom remembered their slogan. "First things first." They both scribbled that phrase on the back of every letter they sent. "First things first. . . ." Again and again Tom promised Pat their love would survive.

As bittersweet as their time together was, dissension seemed to accompany Pat's jail visits. She rarely moved quietly through the security system with the other visitors; every jailer remembered Tom Allanson's wife; she didn't care for their rules and she let them know it. She accused them of deliberately losing some of her letters to Tom and she began to number them so she could catch them at it. Pat attracted attention to both of them. She was impatient and petulant when Tom begged her to obey the jail regulations. But even as she proclaimed her undying love for him, she annoyed the guards who controlled his daily life.

Tom could never be sure what mood Pat would be in. Sometimes she was cheerful and full of enthusiasm about some fancy card or drawing she had made for him. She was so talented artistically, and she loved to make him old-fashioned lovers' cards with lace and hearts and little pop-up figures. He plastered his cell walls with the pretty pictures she fashioned for him. She embroidered on men's boxer shorts and gave them to him for Christmas. Despite the chortles from the men in his cellblock, he wore them.

Sometimes Pat's anger spilled over during her visits. Tom promised her they would be together after Ed Garland got him a new trial, but Pat had come to truly hate Garland. She told Tom he was disrespectful to her and she put up with him only because he was supposed to be the best attorney in Atlanta. "Baby," Tom pleaded. "You just got too much hate and revenge built up that you got to stop."

In between visits, Pat and Tom spoke on the phone. Every evening, the guards in the Fulton County jail carried telephones from cell to cell, and each prisoner had his allotted time to talk. In order to "buy" phone time, Tom traded everything he could to his fellow prisoners. He didn't smoke, but he bought cartons of cigarettes to barter for time. He gave his cell mates the best bunk, his desserts, and other choice items off his food trays. He did chores, read legal papers for the illiterate, and even prevailed upon Pat to call the wives and girlfriends of his fellow prisoners to deliver messages—a task she performed grudgingly—so that he could have some of the other men's phone time.

Their phone talk was so precious to them. They discussed everything from legal strategy to what they would do in the future. Pat recorded their conversations, she told Tom, so she could listen to his voice later and not be so alone. She could never accept that despite all the minutes he collected from other prisoners, Tom's time on the phone was limited. She blamed him when he had to hang up precipitously.

With each legal setback, Pat grew more negative. She reminded Tom in every phone call that he was going to prison for at least twelve years and that she would be "an old woman" when he got out. Her voice was very soft, alternately choked with tears and icily accusatory. His was desperate as he pleaded with her to try to understand. But it seemed there was no way he could win with Pat in their phone conversations. Each time he heard her voice, he hoped they could have a loving, warm call, but she twisted his words, found fault in almost everything he said, and accused him of being cruel to her. Tom was baffled. She knew he would never do anything to hurt her. What more did he have to do to prove he still loved her?

Pat preferred to be Tom's *only* visitor and discouraged even family members from going to see him. She told him that Paw and Nona complained about the cold, the guards, the long walk up the corridor, and that he shouldn't ask them to visit. She even complained on occasion about Boppo. If she *did* allow her family to visit Tom, she wrote out questions she wanted them to ask him. When Susan or Debbie or Ronnie left Tom, Pat debriefed them to be sure that she knew everything they had discussed with him.

Most of all, Pat detested Matthew Rawley,* a college friend of Tom's. He was a minister and tremendously supportive of Tom, who needed all the bolstering he could get. When Rawley first came back into Tom's life, Pat had appeared to like him well enough, although she debated religious issues with him continually. "Show me. Show me where the Bible says that," she would demand. "If there *is* a God, then show me in the Bible." He listened patiently to her arguments and then pointed out his source, but Pat came to hate the young minister when she learned that Tom sometimes asked his advice.

From then on, every time Pat heard that Matt had visited Tom in jail, she pitched a fit. She spent much of their precious telephone time accusing Tom of betraying her by letting him visit. In the end, she demanded that he choose between herself and the Rev. Rawley.

Of course, Tom chose his wife.

✦ ✦ ✦

Boppo and Papa, who had once had every expectation of living a comfortable retirement, were now fending off creditors. The Dodson Drive house was long gone, and it looked as if they were going to lose the Tell Road farm too. Pat and Ronnie were, of course, living with them, and Ronnie was sent to the same military school that Tom had attended. Boppo was very protective of the skinny, quiet boy, and she insisted that he at least have proper schooling, despite their reduced circumstances. He was no student and couldn't maintain the C average the school required. He dropped out in the ninth grade.

Both Susan and Debbie hit rocky places in their marriages. Bill Alford told Susan he didn't want to be married anymore. Susan and her friend Sonja Salo were accepted for training as flight attendants on Eastern Airlines. Susan and Bill were divorced, but they remarried within six months. Bill took care of Sean while Susan moved temporarily to Newark, New Jersey, to attend Eastern's six-month training school. But whatever else was going on in the family, it was of minor importance compared with Pat's predicament. She wouldn't let anyone forget it, or the injustice that was being done to Tom. And as if in confirmation of all the disparaging things Pat and Margureitte had said about Tom's ex-wife, his children, Sherry and Russ, were removed from their mother's custody by children's protective authorities. There was a possibility that Little Carolyn would have visitation rights, if she straightened out her life and found a permanent residence. In the meantime, Big Carolyn's brother, Seaborn Lawrence, was caring for them, despite Tom's wish that they go to Pat.

Ed Garland's motion for a new trial was delayed on February 20. With that piece of bad news and at Pat's repeated urgings, Tom's letters to his grandparents grew more pressured. The same theme wound through all of them. They must not trust Jean Boggs—she was only trying to get their money. They must believe in him and in Pat, who could be counted on to take care of them in their old age. Pat warned Tom of the danger that his grandparents' wills could easily be broken if someone unscrupulous influenced them. That would be a catastrophe for them, she explained, now that he was in jail. He was currently an heir, but *her* name was not on those wills. He was locked up, she pointed out, and if one of his grandparents should die and her name was not specified as executor, whatever would happen to the other? Who would care for the surviving grandparent?

Moreover, they had to be realistic. His grandparents' money and property could quite possibly bypass Tom. He had already lost his birthright, his parents' assets, and now Pat cautioned him that he would probably be disinherited by Paw and Nona because they were old and didn't understand. If that happened, he would *never* have enough money for the legal fight needed to get him out of jail.

She was very persuasive and Tom saw the logic behind her arguments. He wrote another letter. Meanwhile, quietly, subtly, and without much fuss, Pat was moving into Tom's grandparents' lives. His letters made Pat seem like family to them, and she visited them as often as she could, ran errands, sat with Nona, cooked special little meals for them. Even when she wasn't feeling well, she talked to them on the phone every day. It was a bad time for the old people; their son and daughter-in-law were dead—murdered—and their grandson was in jail. Paw and Nona had been semi-estranged from their daughter Jean ever since the trouble when Paw sold his land to Walter instead of her. The old people's lives had a vast empty spot and Pat began to fill it. She carried messages back and forth between Tom and his grandparents. Sometimes she took Debbie with her to help out in the little house on Washington Road, and Boppo often stopped by to visit.

As each new day passed, Pat revealed a different facet of her mercurial personality. With Tom, she was alternately accusatory or loving, "his Pat" who couldn't survive without him. With his attorneys, she was imperious and demanding, and her voice had a stainless-steel edge. When she was with Paw and Nona, she gave them advice and took charge of their lives. With her parents, as always, she was a dependent, spoiled child given to tears and temper tantrums. She worried Boppo sick when, in a fit of anger, she would hop into the watermelon red Cougar they had given her and roar off down Tell Road. She drove like a maniac, leaving a cloud of dust behind her. Invariably, she would then edge her car back down the road and park it where the barn hid it from the house. If Boppo or Papa spotted her there and came out to try to talk sense to her, she'd flick on the lights and speed off again.

✦ ✦ ✦

Pat and Tom usually talked on the phone late at night, and each time Tom hoped they could make it through an entire call without accusations and depressing thoughts. ". . . I love you, darlin'. I miss you more than anything in this world," he whispered one night into the phone. "You're my Pat, and you'll always be my Pat. We gonna make it, Sugar. I need you more than anything in this world. You're my life—my whole entire life wrapped up in my Pat, okay? . . ."

"Okay," she murmured flatly.

It was not going to be a good phone call and he had only a few minutes to talk. "I'll mail you a letter tonight. Shug, I'm going to try to call you back."

"I'll talk to you Monday," she said without one word of endearment.

"I'm going to try to call you back. I love you."

"Okay. I'll talk to you on Monday. . . ."

He had done something to make her angry. She could change so quickly from being sweet to being mad at him, and he seldom knew what he had done to cause it. He lay back on his bunk and listened to the radio. There were no dedications from Pat to Tom.

But, as always after each phone call, Tom sat down and wrote another letter to his grandparents, pleading for them to love Pat, to help her—and to do that, they would have to help him get out of jail. He was worried more about her than about what would happen with his appeal.

Pat had developed some kind of an infection on her hip and was using a crutch to take the weight off her right leg. She told Tom she had a continual fever, and now he had something else to worry about.

"How do you feel?" he asked during one phone call.

"Now that you called," she said, "I feel much better. . . . Well, I've still got a fever . . . and I had a bad night."

"When are you going to the doctor?"

"Monday."

"For sure?"

"For sure, honey."

"I've been living on dreams ever since I met you," he began, trying to cheer her up.

But Pat could not be consoled. "We can't *be* like normal people and think about any kind of future," she said. "We can't even plan other than today. When things got bad, [at least] we could reach out and touch each other."

"We still can," Tom argued.

"I can't touch you, Tom. You are healthy and you know, in all probability, you've got a number of years ahead of you. So therefore, you can hold up if it took ten or twelve years. You will live through that. But let's be realistic. It's wonderful to dream and wonderful for me to say, 'Tom, I'll wait for you forever,' because you know in your heart if I *were* strong, and if I *were* well, I could wait for you forever, Tom."

"You're not going to die anytime soon. . . ."

"The reason I would, would be just from heartbreak and being lonely. . . . I have no one to help me now."

"You've still got me. If you don't think I'm right there with you, look around you . . . look at the letters."

"I know that, Tom," she said softly. ". . . The letters, the flowers, the cards, the statues, the pictures I'm looking at—all of those things cannot hold me when I'm sick. They can't support me when I have to be supported. They can't pay the bills. They can't reach out for me. They cannot protect me. They cannot keep me secure. They can't get me any support or protection at all."

There was a silence. What could he answer? "Pat," he groaned. "You know it's hard for me to be here."

"What you don't understand, Tom, is that before—when I had just accepted the fact that I wasn't going to live very long— I did what I wanted to do and that was it because I didn't worry about it. Then, when you came, I had a desire because *you* were there, and each time that I felt like death was going to come and grab hold of me, you were there for me to take hold of, but you aren't here anymore. . . ."

Tom pleaded with Pat to let him give her the will to live.

". . . For what?"

"For me. For *us!*"

"There is no me—or us—not now, Tom. . . . There is me— or us—in the fact that we love each other, but we're not together."

The conversation stretched on for twenty minutes more, and when it was over, Tom was convinced his wife was dying. He believed every word she said. He was losing her and he felt completely helpless as she slipped away from him.

25

Pat *was* ill. She had painful sores on her thigh, and a larger lesion on her right buttock that had abscessed. They had appeared suddenly and her doctors were baffled about what caused them. And she seemed to be edging once again toward hysteria. She wanted her mother around all the time and that wasn't possible. Boppo had to work, her job more important now than ever as the Radcliffes' finances were strained to the limit. She was an excellent receptionist and popular with both the dentists she worked for and their staffs. But over the years she had lost too many jobs; it was hard for her to concentrate at work because her family had so many emergencies and called her continually.

Pat was thirty-seven and her problems were still the focal point for everyone in the family, the star they danced around, the burden they bore even as their own strength waned. Boppo and Papa, Ronnie, Susan, Debbie, Tom, and all the aunts were the ponies in a merry-go-round endlessly circling the brightly painted mirrors in the center. And all the mirrors reflected Pat.

It was as if floodlights played over her always. She called the shots, alternately preening, sobbing, arguing, and smiling beatifically.

Boppo and the colonel were so involved in saving her from the disappointments of life that they had no time to evaluate what they themselves had lost in the struggle. If they had, it probably wouldn't have mattered. Everything had gone to rescue Pat—houses, horses, money, credit ratings, furniture, antiques, and, if it came down to it, human beings. They had come so far, all the while dedicating their lives to her, that they never thought of shifting the balance.

Tom had always believed his wife was delicate, but in truth Pat was very strong physically. She could lift heavy saddles, and her hand around a wrist was like a vise. Boppo was the only one who dared confront Pat when she started acting out physically. She scared the rest of her family half to death. But Paw and Nona never saw that side of Pat. Her bearing with them was so loving and refined, so caring and helpful that they had come to think of her as a daughter, just as Tom was like a son to them.

Tom's grandparents had each drawn up a will on September 11, 1974, two months after the murders. Utilizing the "marital deduction," which in Georgia divides the estate into two parts for tax purposes, each left his estate to the other. In the event, however, that both should die, their assets were to be divided equally between Tom and Jean Boggs's two children—that is, Tom would get half and his cousins each half of the remaining half. Tom and his aunt Jean were to be coexecutors of that estate.

On March 4, 1975, the elder Allansons added a codicil to their wills. With Pat's help, Paw Allanson contacted his attorney and arranged for Pat to be added as an executor to serve in Tom's place if he was not able to do so. Jean Boggs remained the coexecutor.

✦ ✦ ✦

They all waited that spring of 1975 for word of Tom's new trial. Tom was touched that Pat would attempt the long uphill climb to the visitors' area on crutches when she was in so much pain. On March 10, when the hearing for Tom's appeal was delayed again, Pat was desolate. Both her mental and physical condition went downhill; she didn't seem to take care of herself and Margureitte worried.

On the night of April 9, Wednesday—a visiting night—Pat discovered that Tom had talked to one of his attorneys without her. She was enraged and lit into her husband. How could he even consider doing such a thing? Apparently, Tom had told Ed Garland one thing and she had told him another, and questions had come up that she did not care to answer. "He is a lying son of a bitch," she exploded, referring to Garland.

"Okay, Pat," Tom said, trying to gentle her. "You don't feel any better about the whole case, do you? I'm not in the habit of somebody telling me something and then turning it around."

"You're not in the habit of a lot of things, Tom."

Tom explained to Pat that he was unable to call anyone a liar to his face. He was not about to do that to Ed Garland. He didn't believe it was true, anyway.

"You don't have to *say* they are a liar," she explained, as if to a dolt. "All you have to do is say, 'I'm sorry; I can't see you. We have a rule. That's it. The whole law firm knows about it. . . .' Look, we are sitting up here arguing about something we wouldn't be arguing over if you hadn't talked to him . . . 'cause you've got one story, and I've got another."

And that was the problem. Tom could not tell his lawyers anything about the murders—she had insisted on that often enough. She felt she had to censor her husband's every word. She lived in fear of what he might say, of the areas he might venture into with his attorneys when he discussed the shooting of his parents. Tom trusted too many people. He had no sense of self-protection at all, and no sense of how to protect her either.

After Pat had railed at him for half of their visit, she made Tom promise that he would never "do anything like this again."

"I promise. I promise."

Then, to make things worse, Pat had left some contraband reading material in a visitors' waiting room, meaning to go back and hide it in a letter to Tom. It wasn't there when she went back, and jail authorities abruptly cut short her visit. She turned white with fury. Papa and Boppo were with her that night and tried to stop the storm they knew was coming. Pat was seething and hysterical. She demanded to see the chief of jail operations.

Tom watched helplessly. The more she rocked the boat in the Fulton County jail, the more likely *he* was to be shipped off to prison.

But Pat was completely out of control. With all the histrionics going on in their house, the strain on his wife, the physical confrontations, Colonel Radcliffe temporarily lost his usual detached air and his self-control. Somebody had to shut Pat up. When she continued to rage as they walked down the long passageway from the visitors' area, he suddenly flung his hand back and caught her full in the face, smacking her in the eye.

Pat was struck dumb, and then she started to sob. All the way home, she threatened to move out and go over to Paw and Nona's and take Ronnie with her. When Tom called, she sobbed to him about being struck. "He hit me full force before we even got out of the jail," she complained. "Walking down the hallway. . . . He said I was terrible to you and about everything I did to you, and everything was my fault. I just finally went into tears and said, 'Get off my back.' He said he was going to have me committed to Metropolitan. I told him it would be over my dead body."

"I didn't mean for all that to happen, Sugar."

" . . . I worked so hard to get pretty and everything for you."

"Please forgive me, Shug. First things first, remember."

She sobbed into the phone, but she smiled as she hung up, a smile that Tom, of course, could not see.

✦ ✦ ✦

Pat almost convinced Tom that he should fire Ed Garland. Garland was rarely available to her when she called, would not listen to her suggestions, and she detested him. She phoned another attorney and asked to make an appointment with him. She explained that Tom was still represented by Garland, but she saw no reason why she couldn't hire the second attorney to be *her* adviser. "My father—who used to be with counterintelligence—told me that."

The attorney said he could represent Tom *after* he dismissed Garland, but he explained that he could not ethically sue Ed Garland to get back fifteen thousand dollars Pat said she had coming. He also suggested that Tom's college degree and skill at blacksmithing would make him a natural to teach in prison as part of the new Georgia Youthful Offenders Program. That way, Tom could be outside more, pending any appeal. It would be far easier on him than being locked up in the crowded Fulton County jail. "That would be up at Buford Prison," he added. "It's an accredited high school. He could teach, and it would be better for him. It's only thirty minutes away."

"My physical condition is quite critical, and while he's in Fulton County jail I can see him once a week and talk on the phone four times a week," Pat said, quashing the suggestion at once.

The attorney explained that Tom could have almost unlimited visits and phone calls in Buford.

"His big thing is contact with *me*," she countered. "If he has to go to Jackson [prison] first, he'd be down there for six weeks and he couldn't see me. . . . I could go at any minute."

With a start, the attorney realized this woman was saying she might *die* at any minute. She sounded healthy enough on the phone. It scarcely seemed possible.

Pat never told Tom that he had a choice to go directly to a teaching job at Buford; she simply explained firmly to the attorney who suggested it that Tom would always choose to be near her—no matter what conditions he himself was in. Nor would she tell that attorney specifically who her doctors were. She had many. She had "specialists."

✦　✦　✦

The climate at the Tell Road farm was not good. The one thing that Clifford Radcliffe would not allow was for anyone to criticize his wife. "Reit," as he called her, was the most beautiful woman, the kindest, the most well bred, and his sweetheart. Usually he went along with anything she wanted, and protecting her daughter at all costs was the most important thing she wanted. But Pat's outbursts were wearing her mother down. Pat had chased after both Boppo and Papa with a knife and an umbrella when she didn't get her way. Her behavior at the jail had been inexcusable.

The colonel had to make a trip out of state. It was an unfortunate time for him to be gone. Pat continued to insist that she was moving out and going to Nona and Paw's. Boppo pleaded with her to be reasonable. On April 10, Pat disappeared into her room and slammed the door, and the trouble—at least for that night—seemed to be over.

But then Pat emerged, wearing a diaphanous red nightgown held up with spaghetti straps. She was barefoot, and there were thin crimson stripes of blood welling up on each wrist. Before Boppo could stop her, and despite her crutches, Pat ran from the house and disappeared into the piney woods and quarry area behind. It was April, but it was a nasty evening, full of sleety rain. There was a power company right-of-way back behind the trees, a wide clear swath where the towers that carried the lines pierced the dusk. Pat half-ran, half-hopped, a blur of red in the fading light, over the stubble-cut grass, too fast for her mother who ran behind her, begging her to stop.

Boppo phoned for help and rounded up a number of neighbor men. They hurried to their cars and headed up Tell Road. The only place for Pat to go was along the power lines; a mile or so further on she would come out to railroad tracks and a veterinarian's clinic. The Radcliffes knew the vet well—he had taken care of their horses—but nobody would be there at that time.

After hollering back and forth in the lowering twilight, they finally found Pat, still running and hobbling, her hair streaming behind her and her wrists dripping blood. She had worked herself into an ultimately hysterical state.

Still dressed in her nightgown, Pat was admitted on a court order to the Metropolitan Psychiatric Center in Atlanta for evaluation of her dangerousness to herself. Pat wouldn't be staying in a "psycho ward" in some city hospital; Metropolitan was decorated like a fine hotel, and it was very, very expensive. When she was admitted, she had superficial slash marks on her wrists, and she appeared anxious, agitated, and extremely talkative.

She complained that she could not see out of her left eye because her father had struck her. The clinic physician was more aghast at the festering abscess on her right buttock.

Pat was disheveled and talked a mile a minute, but her response to what was happening around her was flat. She gave the admitting physician a long history of her life. By her own reckoning, she had always been the victim, assailed by bad luck and other people's insensitivity. Her husband was in jail, she said, convicted of two murders he had not committed. They had only been married eleven months, and right after the wedding, she recalled, she had been in a terrible automobile accident. "I've paid my lawyers forty-five thousand dollars and given them property worth thirty-five thousand more to appeal my husband's case to the highest courts," she declared.

Margureitte told the doctor that Pat hadn't been taking care of herself; she was obsessed with getting her husband out of jail. "She's been talking a lot, and she's just had a lot of negative thoughts."

Pat insisted on calling her daughters. "They're trying to kill me!" she told Susan breathlessly. "I was raped when I was only a child," she whispered into the phone, and told Susan she would kill her if she didn't come down and get her out of the hospital. Doctors listening in noted that she was grossly distorting the severity of her injuries to them.

Asked about the abscess on her buttock, Pat said that it and the sores on her thigh had been caused by penicillin shots she had received from her regular doctor, Dr. Taylor. A check with Taylor's office revealed that Pat had received no penicillin shots, but she had been under treatment for the mysterious sores. She complained of terrible pain and was given injections of Demerol.

Pat was admitted with a tentative diagnosis of "Agitated depression with possible thought disorder." It was a catchall diagnosis, not to be found in the *DSM-II,* the *Diagnostic and Statistic Manual of Mental Disorders,* the bible of the psychiatric world. Two psychiatrists did concur that she was "not able to take care of herself at this time."

A physical examination revealed that "the patient is afebrile [has no fever] with no acute infections present. Chronic subcutaneous and muscular cold abscess formations under treatment with incision and drainage, and antibiotic coverage is also noted. . . . There was no evidence of thrombophlebitis . . . there was no evidence of pathological process involving the left eye."

Papa's thrown-back hand had done no real damage to Pat's eye; she could see out of it perfectly well, and even though Pat had convinced Tom that she had only a few years—perhaps months—to live, a complete physical showed that her heart, lungs, blood, kidneys, and all other systems were completely normal. She had no blood clots. Except for the odd abscesses, she was in good health.

Pat received individual and group psychotherapy. During her stay at Metropolitan she demanded frequently to go to the Fulton County jail to see her husband. A week into her treatment she was allowed to visit Tom with Boppo, and she "tolerated this short leave of absence well."

After twelve days in the clinic, Pat was discharged with a prescription for fifty milligrams of Mellaril four times a day, the usual initial dosage for treatment of borderline psychotic patients. She was to be followed as an outpatient and her doctors felt the chances were good for "significant return of function."

Pat took the Mellaril for only a short time, but she doubled her intake of her other prescriptions. If the clinic doctors had picked up on her growing dependence on sedative and painkilling drugs, they did not note it in her records.

26

Once released from the Metropolitan Psychiatric Center, Pat seemed not at all psychotic. She didn't bother to continue psychiatric counseling. Her abscess had begun to heal while she was in the hospital and, for a time, she looked much better. But it was still painful for her to walk up the long slope to visit Tom, so they worked out a way to "be together" over the phone.

Besides sharing their love songs on the radio, they thumbed through the *TV Guide* together and decided what they would watch. That way, Pat explained, it would be almost as if they were really together watching the same shows. Pat quizzed Tom later to be sure he had watched the shows they had selected. Sometimes he had to fudge a little; he couldn't always dictate which channel the jail TV would be turned to. Once he made the mistake of praising Farrah Fawcett Majors's beauty when she guested on her husband's show, *The Six Million Dollar Man*. "Tom!" Pat sulked. "I don't want to talk about her! I want to talk about us."

◆ ◆ ◆

Summer came again to Atlanta. Tom was still locked in the Fulton County jail. On July 8, 1975, exactly one year to the day since his arrival in that facility, his motion for a new trial, so long postponed, was denied. "Having given said amended motion due consideration in the light of the arguments, the same is hereby overruled on each and every ground and a new trial is denied," Superior Court Judge Charles Wofford decreed.

He also denied Tom's application for bail.

Pat had never hired a new attorney. Much to her chagrin, Ed Garland assured Pat that he wasn't going to quit. Getting Tom a new trial had become a "personal vendetta" for him. Having to deal with his client's wife was a cross he bore stoically.

Tom wrote to his grandparents:

I know the disappointing news of the hearing was upsetting, but don't eat my steak. I am going to be home soon, and I can assure you I will devour it. I am just so thankful that my two women and you, Paw, are holding up out there for me. I really have to commend Ma and Pat for being so strong. It has been so hard on both of them. I guess it has been physical hardships on top of all this mental strain that has been so rough. I sure am glad you and Ma love Pat and she loves the both of you so much. I know she has been a real blessing and support to you and Ma. She always seems to gain strength from somewhere when Ma is upset and calms everything down. Paw, I really love that woman. She is so wonderful.

In late July 1975, Pat Allanson called Bill Hamner, Paw Allanson's attorney, and told him that the elder Allansons wished to add a second codicil to their wills. This codicil, dated August 1, removed Jean Boggs completely as executor or trustee of her parents' wills, leaving Pat and Tom Allanson as the sole executors. If Tom were still incarcerated at the time of the Allansons' deaths, then Pat alone would distribute their assets.

Nona and Paw were deemed of sound mind, and they knew what they wanted to do. Nona was confined to bed much of the time, her speech was garbled, and she had little use of one hand. Paw took wonderful care of her, lifting her tenderly and seeing that she was always well groomed. He was a good cook and in relatively good health for a man of seventy-eight. They could manage on their own, but they had come to depend on Pat for backup. Her presence was comforting. Visits from Pat and

Debbie, and often Margureitte Radcliffe, brightened their days. There were errands to run and things difficult for Paw to do. It was hard for Pat too. Her abscess was getting worse again.

Pat had long since stopped taking the Mellaril, although she was receiving fifty milligrams of Demerol four times a day for the pain from her abscess. Demerol is a narcotic drug, and two hundred milligrams a day is a high dosage for anyone to take regularly. Demerol is not routinely prescribed, anyway, for more than ten days for an outpatient.

To her doctors' consternation, Pat's abscess grew larger, deeper, and more purulent during the summer. They could find no reason for this, save the possibility that she was simply a "poor healer." Pat had to use a wheelchair now when she came to visit Tom, and the jail authorities allowed them to visit downstairs in the lawyers' cubicles to save her the agonizing trip to the regular visiting area.

In September, Pat's abscess became an out-of-control volcano. It was as big as a fist, extending three or four inches down into her right buttock. The odor from the wound was nauseatingly putrid. She was in constant danger of going into septic shock from blood poisoning.

On September 12, Pat went to the Bolton Road Hospital in Atlanta. She complained of severe radiating pain and was no longer able to walk. When physicians lifted the dressing from the open wound, they gasped. The thing seemed to have a life of its own. How could this slender woman have stood the pain of such an angry-looking pus-filled lesion?

Pat was admitted to the hospital at once. She would undoubtedly need surgical intervention if she was to survive. For years Pat had complained to everyone who would listen that she was a sick woman, a woman who was not long for this world.

And now that might be true. The doctors at Bolton were puzzled as to the cause of such a deep festering wound, especially when their patient had been taking four capsules a day of the potent antibiotic Keflex. Pat was released from the hospital but only on a temporary basis; she was readmitted pending surgery two weeks later. During this period she sometimes appeared delusional. She became fixated on religion. Lying in her bed in her filmy negligees, she would often rise up suddenly, point her finger at whoever was visiting, and cry out, "May the

Lord have mercy on your soul!" Other than that bizarre affectation, she seemed relatively stable mentally. Susan and Debbie, who were often at her bedside, grimly compared their mother to Regan in *The Exorcist*.

Pat had harassed Eastern Airlines until Susan was transferred from Newark, New Jersey, "for compassionate reasons." She needed all of her family nearby. One evening that September, Susan was on call for Eastern, and she planned to stay the night at the Tell Road farm because it was much closer to the Harts-field-Atlanta Airport than the Alfords' home in Marietta. She carried with her the uniform of an Eastern flight attendant—a blue skirt, blue and white plaid blouse, and fitted red vest with gold buttons and wings over her left breast.

"They called me in the afternoon for a flight," Susan recalled. "And, out of the blue, my mother decided she didn't want me to go. I had my uniform on and I was trying to get out the door when she came after me with her crutch. People never realized it, but my mother was physically very, very strong. She would get right up in your face, so close that it seemed like she could walk right through you. She had me backed up in a corner, poking her crutch in my stomach, when Boppo showed up. Papa had called her. Boppo could control Mom. Boppo almost never got angry, but this was one of the times she did. Mom let me go, but she'd accomplished what she wanted. She wanted Boppo to come home from work—and Boppo was there. I missed my flight, but I managed to make the next one and wasn't disciplined."

Susan recalled that her mother's behavior that summer became increasingly assaultive. Pat turned on her stepfather often. She never drew blood, but it was a frightening time. The only person who had any control over her was her mother; Margureitte could stare Pat down. And, if need be, Margureitte could draw on a few histrionics herself.

"If you keep this up, Pat, I'll kill myself . . . ," Boppo would cry. It was her final weapon. That threat always worked. Emotions were so chaotic among the Radcliffe women that suicide threats were omnipresent. And they were all given to sporadic bouts of melancholy: Susan, Debbie, Pat, of course, and eventually even Boppo.

Thorazine, a potent antipsychotic drug, was prescribed for Pat. For a time, things got somewhat better.

✦ ✦ ✦

Tom and Pat argued in late September; she was interfering in his case, overriding his attorneys again, and it worried him. She had attempted to see police records of the Athens and Atlanta police departments hoping to find some record on Little Carolyn. It was illegal for Pat to do that. When Tom told her that, she flew at him.

As always, he was contrite when he phoned the next evening. "Sometimes you do the wrong thing, darling," he tried to explain. "Do you really expect me to go along with you when I know it's wrong? Can't I correct you some? Don't you understand it doesn't affect our love? . . . I'm trying to keep you from making a mistake. It's not got a thing to do with our love."

". . . The other day, you said you were so proud of me," she sulked. "You can't be when you call me things like you did yesterday."

Pat told her husband she was going into the hospital but she would send him a picture first. "I'm standing [in the picture] without the crutches," she said. "I have a painful look on my face. . . . Did you stay up long enough to hear all the songs I asked for last night? 'I Want You in My Dreams' and 'Blue Eyes'? I did it special because of the way you felt about me yesterday."

To make him even more ashamed of questioning her actions, Pat confided that he had upset her so much that she had had her first blood clot in a long time after their argument, and that she had lost the use of one arm. Neither was true.

"Tom, if I was dead, do you think you would ever be able to find out what's going on? . . . I don't have much longer, Tom."

"I just don't understand," he groaned. ". . . Did the doctors just wash their hands?"

"I'm fighting like crazy when the doctors tell me it's hopeless."

". . . I don't believe that," he said desperately.

"I told you you weren't ready for the truth. . . . I told you what the doctor said. They say there is nothing they can do."

"How long do they give you to live?"

"It depends on how fast it eats up the tissues."

"*Nothing* can stop it?"

"Nothing. They can't do any blood transfers 'cause they've got an open place that won't close, and it never will close because it gets deeper and deeper. . . . Now you can understand the pressure I've been under. You are the only thing that gave my life real meaning. If I do something that hurts you, it tears me up. I been laying here torn up all afternoon," she said softly. "I come up there smiling, Shug, even though I hurt."

Pat's abscess was, indeed, growing deeper and deeper and deeper. Back in the hospital on October 1, she went through myriad medical tests. Cultures of Pat's wound grew out both *Proteus mirabilis* and *Staph aureus* bacteria. She required blood transfusions, and she vomited continually. Given gamma globulin, she had a severe anaphylactic reaction, accompanied by hysteria. Since anaphylactic shock—often experienced by those allergic to bee stings or penicillin—can kill quickly by suffocation as the breathing passages and throat swell, Pat's panic was not abnormal.

Pat had been admitted to Bolton Road Hospital on an emergency basis, and it became evident that the surgery had to be done soon. On October 17, when she was strong enough to withstand an operation, she was given nitrous oxide and a local anesthetic and the huge abscess was excised, along with the granular tissue and the scar tissue surrounding it, leaving a massive permanent indentation in her right buttock. During and after the procedure, the wound was flooded with antibacterial materials.

Judge Wofford signed a judicial order that allowed Tom to go to the Bolton Road Hospital under guard and donate blood; Pat's surgery had required many transfusions and she would be hospitalized for a month or more.

"Patient had extreme pain and required large doses of narcotics and sedatives, and was very difficult to control under these circumstances, but gradually through the team effort of her mother, Dr. P., Dr. G., and Dr. R.—all working together—we convinced her of the benefits of sticking to one regimen and she gradually got better," her hospital records noted.

Pat was finally released from Bolton Road Hospital on November 21. She would have to return every week to have her progress monitored and her dressings changed. At her request, her doctor wrote a letter to the Fulton County jail authorities.

TO WHOM IT MAY CONCERN:
This patient . . . has a deep (3–4 inch) ulcerating lesion of the

*right buttock which renders her bedfast . . . and, as such, she is
in critical condition, and likely to remain so for some time.*

*Her husband is in the Fulton County jail nearby where she
can at least talk to him by telephone and know he is in proximity.
It would be extremely beneficial to this patient if he could remain
there and possibly if it could be arranged at some point for her to
visit him, whereas if he is farther away, she certainly would not
be able to. The emotional upset which has accompanied the trials
and tribulations of her husband have materially affected her
health and continue to. . . . She requires sedation and pain medications. . . . If the problem was compounded by his being removed, it could conceivably have a very detrimental effect on
her general physical health, as well as her emotional stability.
. . . I believe that this could have a life and death bearing on
Mrs. Allanson's case in terms of her mental and physical well-
being. . . . The circumstances are most unusual. Her illness is
also most unusual. . . .*

All of Pat's physicians were bewitched by the beautiful green-
eyed woman who bore such terrible pain. Not one of them ever
isolated just what had caused her intractable infection. In lieu of
a definitive diagnosis, they marked their records: "Chronic non-
healing abscess, secondary to penicillin injection."

✦ ✦ ✦

At home, with her physicians' approval, Margureitte tried to
cut Pat's use of narcotics. She gave her pain shots several times
a day as she had for weeks now, but she gradually diluted the
Demerol injections with water. Pat noticed the difference almost
at once and was furious.

Pat hired a private detective, without consulting Ed Garland,
and had him follow Tom's ex-wife. She suggested that the detective seduce Carolyn to gain more information. "Just pull the 'old
suave' on her," Pat urged. The planned seduction of Little Carolyn never came off. Pat was still operating on *Perry Mason* plot
lines, and the private investigator only humored her. When she
told Ed Garland what she was up to, he shook his head. He
explained to Pat that the only issues left that might help Tom
were: if they could discover new evidence, if they could prove
Carolyn had perjured herself, or if they could prove that Tom's

lineup had been contaminated by the presence of the two fire fighters whom "everyone knew."

Despite all the letters saying that Tom's departure for Jackson Prison would kill his wife, he was definitely headed in that direction—and soon. For the first time, Pat wondered if she might have called the shots wrong in Tom's defense plan. It was humbling for her to bring up, because she had never apologized for anything. "Let me ask you something," she finally said to Ed Garland. "Would we have been better off to drag the cat along and [if we had] told that Tom went there without any weapons and talked to his father?"

"Want my honest opinion?"

"Yes."

"Yes. He would have been better off. . . . It's been my opinion the whole time, based on all my information. . . . We could have got a manslaughter and ten years out of this case to begin with—if only we'd approached it along those lines," Garland said firmly.

With time off for good behavior, that ten years would have come down to only a few. Tom could have been out of prison and back with her long before the seventies moved into the eighties. Pat had truly messed up her husband's defense, and Garland was at a loss to know why. She wasn't stupid—far from it—and she wasn't crazy either. Willful, yes, and strangely secretive. Whatever her reasons had been, it was far too late now to change things. Tom was going up for a very long time.

Pat beseeched Garland to find a way to have Tom incarcerated in Atlanta. "I will never be able to travel the distance to see him . . . that's just like taking a candle and putting out the light. . . . Now, once every four or five days I'm going to be talking to him for ten minutes. That keeps me alive for another four days."

27

Paw Allanson had a heart attack on January 15, 1976. Pat told Tom when he called her from jail. "Yesterday morning, Paw had a heart attack," she said. "He's in South Fulton [Hospital] . . . the doctor is not expecting him to die from it, you know— he's not paralyzed or it's not a stroke or anything. It did some damage to the heart walls; when he comes out, he is not going to be able to do heavy lifting. . . . Ma called me yesterday morning to tell me. She was hysterical—she couldn't tell me anything. . . . I told her to stay calm."

Pat had been confined either to bed or to a wheelchair, but with the news of Paw's coronary she was suddenly up and about. Almost miraculously, she was able to drive again. She needed a cane to walk, but she was in the hospital visiting Paw, seeing to Nona in the rest home and then in South Fulton where she had been placed temporarily, and generally taking over all their affairs. She refused to let their own daughter, Jean Boggs, have any say in their care.

On February 4, 1976, there was a third and final codicil to the elder Allansons' wills. This time, the codicil was far more intricate, but when the details were winnowed out, their daughter Jean Boggs had been completely excluded from inheriting, and Tom had become his grandparents' principal heir. If Tom should predecease Pat, she, as his wife, would inherit almost everything the Allansons owned.

When it was decided that Paw could go home, it was Pat who insisted on being there for Paw and Nona almost every day. She was the liaison between Paw and his attorney. She was the only one who could translate Nona's garbled speech. Pat Allanson was the indispensable woman.

✦   ✦   ✦

It looked as though Tom was going to Jackson Prison and there wasn't a thing in the world to stop it. Even though his case was being appealed to the Supreme Court, he would have to await the justices' decision in prison. Pat had warned him that he might have to go to Reidsville Prison, "where men died all the time." In comparison, Jackson Diagnostic Center was preferable by far.

Pat's whole mien had become one of bitter acceptance. She bombarded Tom with negative thoughts. They both might as well be dead. Every time he tried to inject hope into their phone conversations, she deflected it. "I'm trying to explain to you that I don't have anything to live for," she sighed.

"Oh you *don't?*"

"That's what I can't make you understand."

"You know better, Shug," Tom said, trying to soothe her.

"You just said you've been trying to find something that is important to keep me interested in doing something," she replied softly. "But don't you understand the *only* thing that is important to me is you?"

"I know, darling—but I *can't* come home right now. So what am I gonna do in the meantime?"

"You can't come home period," she countered.

"You really know that is true, don't you?"

"All I know is that you've been sentenced to two life sentences and that is a fact," Pat said, her voice suddenly harsh.

". . . I see you want to argue about this, and we're not ever gonna get anywhere." Tom's voice dropped hopelessly.

"I don't have any reason to live," Pat said. "You are the only reason I have to live. You said life is being concerned with the things that we can feel and touch. We can't feel or touch or see each other."

"Pat, you know what I'm talking about—"

"It's nice to hear you talk about things that you know we can never do," Pat whispered sarcastically. "Like going to other countries or different places. . . . I have a right to tell you how I feel."

"Every conversation, every letter, you talk about the very same thing—about you not wanting to get well, not wanting to live." Tom's voice wasn't angry; he was pleading with his wife to keep trying.

"Are you telling me that you are with me and taking care of me and looking after me and all that?" Pat began to sob. "I just know I can't feel you because I can't touch you. You act like I can feel you—but I can't. I know you love me and 'that's all that matters.' See, Tom—you talk about our life later, but that's going to be *your* life."

"You agree with the part when I said that you're young and still living?"

"Will you talk that way fifteen years from now?"

"Pat. You'll be here *thirty years* from now."

"Not without you, I can't. Oh, I can do anything *with* you, but I can't exist without you."

Behind Tom, the sounds of caged men reverberated against the walls. It took tremendous effort for him to maintain a calm voice, as if he were talking to a child, willing her to live.

"How am I going to support myself?" Pat cried. "How am I going to live?"

Tom was finally defeated. "I don't know."

It was true, he didn't. He was locked up, with no real hope of being outside prison walls for the next decade. Tom tried to tell Pat she could get her horse business back together again. She was still living with her parents; she had a roof over her head and food to eat. She wasn't a destitute teenager. She was almost thirty-nine, and her parents still stood firmly behind her.

"You know you are going to prison, Tom," she accused, as if he were *choosing* to be in prison.

". . . I'm coming home," he promised.

"You may be home in ten or twelve years, Tom—but you won't be coming home to me."

". . . I'm coming home to you. I just hope you'll be there."

One theme and one theme alone began to emerge when Pat talked with her husband as he waited to go on the chain to Jackson Prison. Tom was going away and it would kill her. He might as well accept it; she could not live without him. If he ever wanted to be with her again, and he assured her he did, it would have to be in some other, better world. In death, they might be together; in life, they no longer had any hope at all.

"Shug, you don't know what happens after we die, and neither do I," Tom argued.

She blamed herself. "I wish you could understand how terrible I feel because you're there and I know it is my fault."

Pat had never before alluded to the possibility that *she* had any fault in Tom's alleged crimes—not in their private conversations; certainly not to Tom's attorneys. But Tom wouldn't let her think about feeling guilty. He didn't blame her for any of this. He had hope for his appeal.

"Our lives are dwindling away," Pat cried. She told him that she was fighting his own lawyers to try to keep him close to her.

"Pat, you're not physically able to do that."

"It's the most important thing in our lives. Tom, what good is it if you're gone?"

"Don't you think I'm ever coming home? . . . I'm coming home to you, Pat. I promise you. . . . We'll start over and we'll make it okay."

"I won't even be walking by the time you come home. I won't be much good for anything but companionship."

". . . You're good for everything. You're good for being my wife, you're good for being my Pat. You're my lover. You're my super kind of woman. . . . Age doesn't have a thing to do with it. . . . It doesn't make any difference as far as my love goes whether you're in a wheelchair or you're up running around."

"Are you going to be able to say that twelve years from now?"

"I sure am. . . ."

"I won't live that long in a wheelchair."

Pat always used the wheelchair when she visited Tom, even though she could have gotten by with a cane. The wheelchair meant they would be allowed to meet in the attorneys' cubicles on the second floor, where they could have some contact. Tom didn't realize that Pat could get around just fine with a cane, or that she had no trouble driving her own car.

During her visits, Pat continued to chip away at Tom's belief in the future. When he was down, she pulled him further into the pit of despair. Again and again she told him her own death was imminent. She talked of their perfect love, now broken and hopeless with prison bars about to separate them. There was only *one* way they would ever be together. They would both have to be dead. Man and the law were going to keep them apart.

Tom didn't really take her seriously; it sounded like more of her depression.

✦ ✦ ✦

Pat had always been consumed with an almost unnatural curiosity about what jail was like for Tom. She questioned him continually about what he thought, who shared his cell, what they talked about, and she focused most intently on humiliations he might have suffered, reinforcing those embarrassments in the process. Even locked away from her, he had no privacy with his own thoughts. To his chagrin, she asked him if he masturbated, phrasing it obliquely: "Do you do—*you* know—what men do in prison when they're locked away from their women? You know what I mean?"

"Pat!" Tom barked into the phone. "No. Don't ask things like that."

Pat quizzed him about "the chain," and about the strip searches he would endure, commenting how humiliating they would be for him. She didn't seem to have much sense of tact about how Tom might feel. It seemed like the further down he got, the more she picked away at him. Tom put it down to her own unhappiness; she had no idea what she was doing to him.

To be sure that she was taken care of while he was in prison, Tom willingly acceded to Pat's request that he sign over his power of attorney to her. That way she could handle their affairs and parcel out what little money they had left without having to travel down to Jackson to get his signature. That way she would be making decisions about his children.

✦ ✦ ✦

Before the dogwoods budded out in the spring of 1976, Tom was on his way to Jackson, handcuffed to another prisoner, both of them chained to another pair of prisoners in the bus seat behind them. That was "the chain," and it was as long or as short as the number of prisoners shuffling off to "the walls."

Once Tom was in Jackson, Pat made sure that she would be his primary source of information. She told everyone that only "immediate family members" were allowed to write to him. No one else wrote to him for a long time, believing it was forbidden. Tom viewed all events through his wife's letters. The state of Georgia and his wife controlled his life.

Although Pat's doctors had doubted she would be able to stand the fifty-mile trip down to Jackson, she managed amazingly well. While Tom was still in the "fish tank"—the diagnostic testing that all new prisoners go through—he was allowed no visitors for six weeks. After that, Pat visited, in a setting where they could touch. There, Pat spoke openly for the first time of a plan she had been hinting at. Since Tom would be locked up for so long, she had come to realize that the only way they could be reunited was to pledge to commit suicide.

Initially, he didn't take her seriously.

When Tom finished his diagnostic tests in Jackson, he was put to work as an inmate clerk and became "a pretty good secretary." He did well. Somehow, finally *being* in prison wasn't nearly as bad as the two years of waiting in the Fulton County jail.

Whenever he and Pat visited or talked on the phone, she would mention the suicide pact. Tom always refused to discuss it. Talking softly and fervently to his wife from a pay phone in Jackson, he murmured, "Shug, don't say we'll never be together again. *Never*—that's like a steel door. '*Never* gonna come home. *Never* gonna do this. *Never* gonna do that. . . .' I've gotta have hope, Shug. Pat, I would do anything in this world for you—"

"Almost, Shug," she said, so quietly that he could barely hear her.

"*What?*"

"*Almost. Almost* anything."

He knew what she meant, and he realized she had trapped him.

She kept talking. "Can you do something for me? Say you

love me more than any*one,* but don't say you love me more than any*thing.*"

"Why don't you want me to say it?"

"Because it's not any *thing.*"

He sighed.

"I know you love me more than any*body,*" she argued. "But not more than any *thing.* You love *life* more than any *thing.*"

Gently, Pat reminded him that he had betrayed her in the most basic way. But as she kept talking about it, he had the odd sense that a rabbit had run over his grave. It was not fair, she complained, that he was not willing to kill himself so that he could be with her in eternity. She had no one to take care of her and he was thoughtless and uncaring to expect her to go on alone when, if he truly loved her, they could be together in death. Her quiet sobs echoing in his ears, Tom went back to his cell feeling useless and depressed.

Even so, he was glad for the next call, the next visit. Tom looked forward to seeing his wife on visitors' day and to getting letters from her.

She was his world—all the world that mattered to him.

Her visits, however, were sometimes as upsetting as her calls. Tom was a little chagrined at Pat's behavior when she came to Jackson. Pat waged full-scale war on the authorities who controlled her husband's destiny. She never failed to cause, at the very least, a hassle—and often a scene.

All mail was censored. Tom's letters to Pat had to be handed unsealed to the guard for mailing, and all of her letters were read before they were given to him. Pat's letters were full of references to various prison officials, derogatory and inflammatory comments. It was almost as if she were deliberately taunting them. "Here I was doing my best to be a model inmate," Tom said later, "and she kept making accusations against the system."

Whatever she did, Tom still longed for Pat with a steady ache, and he went to sleep nights listening to the poignant love songs —*their* songs—that bespoke unspent passion and endless frustration. It well nigh killed him that he couldn't be with her—to help her and to take care of Paw and Ma. Pat continued to remind Tom not to talk to anyone. He must remember that he couldn't trust anyone else—not even his lawyers. Sometimes he wondered what the point was. He was in prison, and it looked as if he were going to stay there for a long, long time. His appeals were almost exhausted.

As the months dragged on, Pat was no longer vague about when and how she and Tom should commit suicide. She reminded him constantly that it was the only way for them to be together. "One time, she told me we were going to do it next week," Tom recalled later, grimacing. "She didn't show me what she had, but . . . she even tried to bring some stuff into Jackson, and she wanted me to commit suicide with her right there. It was supposed to be some sort of pills or something. I told her, 'I ain't ready to die yet.' She told me to take them, and then she'd go out and take some herself, and we'd both be dead, and we could be together. I couldn't. It didn't make any kind of sense. Besides, I didn't believe in suicide, and that's what she wanted."

Pat was asking him to make the supreme sacrifice for their love. She was asking him to die for her—and trust that she would die for him. Tom wouldn't do it, perhaps because, for the first time, he was beginning to have serious doubts about his wife.

PART FIVE

NONA AND PAW

28

Dr. R. Lanier Jones had his own practice, specializing in internal medicine, on Church Street in East Point. Nona and Paw Allanson had been his patients for almost a decade. Jones was one of a vanishing breed of doctor; he actually made house calls. On the night of the double murder of Walter and Carolyn, he had gotten out of bed and gone over to see to the elder Allansons.

Old Walter was a brick wall of a man. He had started in steelwork in 1926, farming in his spare time, and didn't quit until he was over sixty-five. Nona, younger than Paw by seven years, had not enjoyed the same robust health. Dr. Jones had treated her for two massive strokes, in 1968 and 1974. Nona's right arm and both legs were completely paralyzed, she had only partial use of her left arm, and she had difficulty swallowing. Her speech was slurred so badly that only those close to her could decipher what she was saying. All of her life she had been active, and she was a proud woman. Now, she could do virtually nothing for herself.

Paw and Nona had been married for forty-nine years. Not openly demonstrative people, they were a quiet love match, and Dr. Jones was impressed with Paw's tender attention to his wife. "He had been extremely strong. . . . He lifted her, turned her frequently through the night, helped her into her chair. [All the] bodily care of her through the years. I thought he was an extremely strong person."

Paw kept his wife spotlessly clean and well fed. He tempted Nona's appetite with his corn muffins and coconut–sweet potato pie. Most stroke patients get bedsores, but Nona didn't. She needed an enema every night, and Paw took care of that with sensitivity and as little fuss as possible.

Paw was not a smoker or a drinker, and he took few pills. "He just didn't want it—didn't need it," his doctor recalled. The old man had suffered stoically through the loss of his only son and daughter-in-law, the conviction of his grandson, and then had borne much of the cost of Tom's defense. But at seventy-nine, the burdens had taken their toll. In the middle of January 1976, Paw called his doctor complaining of a tightness in his chest and some pain. Dr. Jones sent his own nurse out to Washington Road to drive Paw back to his office. Paw insisted he was just fine, but Jones determined that he had had a heart attack and sent him immediately to South Fulton Hospital. A blood clot had blocked a coronary artery and a portion of Paw's heart muscle had died.

Dr. Jones had Nona admitted for temporary care in a nursing home, but she was miserable there without Paw so she was transferred to South Fulton too and placed in a room right next to Paw's.

Jean Boggs learned belatedly about her father's heart attack from her minister. The pastor and parishioners from the Westside Christian Church often visited her parents and kept her informed of their progress. That way, she at least knew how they were. She hurried to the hospital and visited her father. Then she went to her parents' home and found the doors padlocked. When she asked Margureitte Radcliffe about the locks, she was told that her father didn't want anyone inside—not even Jean. Pat was handling all of Paw's business matters.

Jean was hurt to think that her parents would put a relative stranger above her. She had warned her father that he might be sorry for putting his trust in other people, but he paid little attention to her. Now it was clear that both of her parents had somehow become totally involved with Tom's wife and her parents.

Paw was a tough old bird, and Dr. Jones released him from the hospital on February 13, four weeks after he was admitted. He wanted to get out so he could take Nona home again. Paw was given a mild antianxiety sedative, Vistaril, after the heart attack. He used it only occasionally. But *he* knew he wasn't as strong as he had been, and it was a good thing to have Tom's wife to spell him. Pat wasn't well, and she reminded him of that often, so it impressed him even more to see her with her cane, trying to help them, smiling through her own pain.

Jean Boggs was effectively shut out of her parents' life; Tom's letters and Pat's continual warnings about Jean had apparently convinced them that she *was* greedy and that she didn't care about them at all. Besides, they had Pat now.

When Nona was hospitalized with pneumonia in March, Jean went to see her mother and found a note on the door barring all visitors except "granddaughter [Pat] and Mr. Allanson." Jean was hurt, and she was worried. She had a sense of impending disaster, but nothing she could really prove. She asked her pastor to help her get through to her parents, and she complained to Dr. Jones. Jones was well aware that there was dissension between Jean and her parents. "I didn't make it my business to find out why," he said later. All Dr. Jones really knew was that Paw had insisted on several occasions that the doctor was *not* to call Jean Boggs in an emergency. "I was told to call Pat Allanson."

Jean was not needed on Washington Road, although she kept trying to be with her parents. She visited them on Mother's Day in May 1976 and took a gift. Nona barely glanced at it and sniffed, "I already have one of those." Jean tried to smile and said, "Well, now you have two."

At the time, she noted how well her father looked, how alert he was; he was fully aware of current affairs. He was the same ornery, closed-in man she had always known, but it was not Paw who was shutting Jean out so completely. It was her mother. Nona plainly didn't want her there. Theirs was a family in which estrangements were not uncommon, and although Jean was still hurt, she still hoped and expected to make things right with her parents. Jean knew very little about her parents' financial affairs, but she suspected that Pat and Tom might be eating into their capital with their constant need for money for lawyers, writs, and appeals.

There wasn't a thing Jean could do about it.

In the spring of 1976, Pat was out on Washington Road almost daily with Nona and Paw; Debbie, her five-year-old daughter, Dawn, and Boppo and Papa were often there too. It was as if the elderly couple had had a "family transplant"—just as Tom himself had had two and a half years before. As refined and ladylike as she was, Margureitte Radcliffe seemed such a warm, selfless woman. She bustled around Paw and Nona's home, doing the things Pat couldn't do because she was on crutches. And Pat. Well, Pat *was* family.

On Thursday, June 10, 1976, Dr. Jones received a call from Pat. She was concerned because her husband's grandfather was vomiting almost every evening—not a great deal, but she just wanted to be sure it wasn't something serious. Jones prescribed a mild antinausea medication and had it delivered to the house.

The next morning, Pat called and said Paw was no longer vomiting, but she was still worried. "He hasn't been eating properly," she told Jones's receptionist. "And I guess I'd better tell you. He's been drinking a lot of homemade whiskey. Both of them have been mixing up their pills, putting them in different bottles and squirreling them away. You know how forgetful old people can get." The two women agreed that old people certainly could be like that, and that it could also be dangerous.

When Dr. Jones took a look at the Allansons' charts, he was troubled by Pat's comments about Paw Allanson and pills. It was totally out of character. The old man fought taking pills. Jones had to be firm with him to get him to take his heart medication consistently. He called Pat.

"What is Mr. Allanson drinking?" Jones asked.

"White lightning—over rock candy," Pat replied.

"White lightning over rock candy?" the doctor asked, amazed. Mr. Allanson had never been a drinker. He had certainly plunged in with a vengeance.

"He's into it again," Pat whispered, and Dr. Jones could hear frustration in her voice. He could not go over and snatch a drink out of his patient's hand, but he urged Pat to keep an eye on Paw and to watch that no medications were combined with the whiskey.

On Saturday morning, Pat was back on the phone to Dr. Jones. She said she and her parents had gone to Paw and Nona's home in response to a desperate call from Nona. No one answered their knocks on the front door. "We went around to the back of the house," Pat said. "We could see Paw in the back window, without a stitch of clothes on. He was just babbling and not making any sense, and he wouldn't open the door for us to get in. My father had to crawl through a window to get in."

Pat felt that Paw had simply been hitting the white lightning again. He wasn't sick; he was just drunk as a skunk. Dr. Jones weighed putting him in the hospital, but Saturday was a difficult day for admitting patients with alcohol or psychiatric problems. He asked Pat if Paw was eating, and she assured him that she had been able to get him to eat a little, and that he was taking fluids well.

"Well," Dr. Jones said, "if someone can be there with him, to see that the medications and the alcohol are out of his reach, he should be feeling better in a matter of a couple of hours."

Pat said that she and her family would be glad to watch Paw and Nona. She would personally search the house and get all the pills and put them up high. She would keep Paw away from the white lightning.

"Just let him rest. Give him as much fluid as he'll take," Dr. Jones advised. "I'll call you back later and see how he's doing."

Dr. Jones did call back that Saturday afternoon and Pat said that Paw was doing better. He had had a nap, and something more to eat, and he was taking fluids well. She promised to stay all night with the old couple. If either one's condition weakened, she would call the doctor at once.

At nine that evening—despite his vow to keep out of the Allanson family feuds—Dr. Jones took it upon himself to call Jean Boggs. He told her that her father had had too much to drink and was sleeping it off. Jean was baffled. "No, that's not right," she exclaimed. "My daddy does not drink." She offered to go over to her parents' house, suggesting that Pat was somehow behind this peculiar situation. Dr. Jones didn't think that was a good idea at all. If Paw was sleeping peacefully, he didn't need a confrontation between his daughter and his "adopted" granddaughter-in-law.

On Sunday morning, Dr. Jones and his family were preparing for church around nine-thirty when the phone rang.

It was Pat. "I went in to wake up Paw, and he seems to be unconscious," she said. "I can't get him to wake up."

Dr. Jones told her he would be right over.

"It took me about ten minutes to get there," he later recalled. Pat let him in.

"I went to his bedroom and found him in bed, deeply comatose." No one was in the room with Paw, which struck Dr. Jones as odd when he saw how desperately ill the patient was.

The old man was in such a deep coma that nothing his doctor did brought him out of it—not shouting, shaking, or even pinching. Paw had secretions bubbling in the back of his throat and he was lying on his back. Dr. Jones was afraid he would aspirate the mucus into his lungs, and he struggled to turn his heavy patient on his side.

Dr. Jones turned to ask Pat to call an ambulance to get Paw to the hospital. He had to do it himself; Pat was not in easy summoning distance. To the doctor's amazement, he found her in the bathroom giving a sponge bath to Nona. "It just seemed to be business as usual," he said. "While a man was lying in such bad shape in the other room, *gurgling* with secretions like that, it seemed a bit inappropriate that the other household functions would be carried on in what seemed to be such a day-to-day fashion."

Paw was critically ill. As Dr. Jones was examining him and getting an airway open, Pat wandered into the room and said, "You know, he tried to murder Ma a couple of nights ago. He tried to smother her with a pillow."

Dr. Jones looked up at her, aghast.

"See, see there?" Pat said with amazing calm. "See those scratches on his elbows? That's from where she fought him off."

Dr. Jones felt goose bumps rise along his arms. There was no way that Nona Allanson could have fought her husband off—not with one completely paralyzed arm and the other severely compromised by her strokes. It would have been like a butterfly batting its wings against a buffalo. But more than that, he knew these old people too well to believe that Paw would ever, ever hurt his wife. He loved her, and he had cared for her so gently for years.

The abrasions on the old man's elbows weren't scratches; they were the kind of extremely minor abrasions that mark aged skin that has rubbed against sheets. Dr. Jones felt that something was wrong. He didn't have much time to think about it as he fought to stabilize his patient, but the shock of Pat Allanson's accusations against Paw stayed with him.

Maybe there *was* a problem with overdosage. With a patient in a coma, Dr. Jones couldn't overlook that. "Do you have any of his pill bottles?" he asked Pat.

She led him into a little breakfast nook and pointed to dozens of pill bottles lined up. He quickly sorted out those that were sedatives and slipped them into a paper bag to take to the hospital. It would give them a place to start when they screened for a drug overdose in Paw's system.

Pat handed him a single yellow capsule. "I found it on the kitchen floor. When we got in Saturday morning, he was just gobbling pills by the handful. I think this is one of them."

Dr. Jones studied it. It looked like Nembutal, a hypnotic sedative.

Paw? No, that warred with everything the doctor had learned about the old man in ten years. Paw Allanson wouldn't have taken a sleeping pill, not when he had to look after Nona—and turn her several times during the night. But then, the Paw Allanson he knew wouldn't have touched white lightning either. There were so many things that could go wrong—suddenly—in a man almost eighty years old. A massive stroke, perhaps. Another heart attack. Things that could affect thought processes too.

Dr. Jones's sense that something was not right grew even stronger. Why would Paw try to kill Nona? And why on earth had Pat Allanson left the old man all alone, unconscious and gurgling, and calmly wheeled Nona into the bathroom for a sponge bath? Those ablutions were not necessary, and taking care of Paw was vital.

"I was a suspicious doctor," he later commented succinctly.

They heard the wail of an approaching ambulance. Dr. Jones walked from the breakfast nook toward the front door. In the hall, Pat handed him what looked like an old-fashioned whiskey bottle, although it had no label. By tilting it toward the light, he could see a small amount of clear liquid in the bottom.

"This is the bottle Paw was drinking from yesterday," she said. "I found it hidden away out in the garage."

Dr. Jones slipped the bottle into his medical bag. He had already made up his mind to call the police when he got his patient to the hospital. He wasn't even sure what he might be reporting; he would let them sort out the information.

With sirens blaring, the ambulance crew got Paw Allanson to South Fulton Hospital by ten-thirty. Dr. Jones began treating him at once for an overdose of a "sedative nature." He didn't know *what* Paw had overdosed on—perhaps the Nembutal that Pat had pointed out, perhaps something else. The most important thing was to use nasal gastric suction to pump his stomach, and to keep his blood pressure, pulse, respiration, fluids in-and-out, and body chemistry within normal boundaries. Paw was in extremely critical condition, unable to tell Dr. Jones what he had taken. It was quite possible that he would die without speaking.

Back at Washington Road, Pat soothed Nona, telling her that Paw would be home soon and that she would stay right there with her. Boppo and the colonel had rushed to the hospital to be sure that Paw was getting the proper care.

29

Almost exactly two years after the double murder of Walter and Carolyn Allanson, the East Point police received another call to respond to a case involving a Walter Allanson. It was jarring for a moment—until the dispatcher realized that this was Walter Allanson, the *elder*. He dispatched Officer G. W. Pirkle to the emergency room of South Fulton Hospital. When he learned that the patient apparently had taken a massive overdose of sedatives, Pirkle called Detective Sergeant William R. Tedford for investigative backup.

Bob Tedford was introduced to Colonel and Mrs. Clifford Radcliffe. He spoke with them in the waiting room while he waited for Dr. Jones. The pair seemed very concerned about the old man. Mrs. Radcliffe reconstructed the bizarre weekend for the young detective. "Ma called us yesterday morning—Saturday," she began. "She said that Paw was acting strange and wild, and begged us to come over right away and help her."

She said that both she and Pat were on phone extensions and heard Nona Allanson begging for help. They had thrown on their clothes and raced over to the Washington Road house. When no one answered their pounding knocks on the front door, they had gone to the back of the house. Colonel Radcliffe had started prying a rear window open.

The colonel took up the story, remarking that it was fortunate that the ladies hadn't seen Paw without warning. "He was naked except for a T-shirt and an Ace bandage on his ankle." He had shouted for Pat not to look—that Paw was headed toward the door naked as a jaybird. Boppo nodded. "When he opened the door, he was naked, all right, and he had a handful of pills."

All three of them had burst into the kitchen, but Paw had walked away from them, they said, stuffing pills into his mouth and washing them down with orange juice. "He was cramming so many in his mouth that they were dropping out the sides and falling on the floor," the colonel said. "I told him that Dr. Jones wouldn't want him to take all those pills, trying to reason with him, you see. He replied, 'To hell with the doctor!' and just kept on taking pills."

The Radcliffes explained that their daughter Pat was basically the one taking care of the old couple. "Is there any closer relative that I could call about Mr. Allanson's overdose?" Tedford asked.

"Yes. Well, I don't know—they have a daughter, Jean Boggs. But they don't get along. Pat has been staying with them, running errands, this type of thing, for the past several years," Margureitte explained. Detective Tedford's impression was that these people *were* the patient's family—or at least the closest thing to it.

After a tense hour and a half, Dr. Jones came out and said that Paw Allanson's condition was stable and that he could say, albeit cautiously, that the elderly man might survive. It was touchy, of course, treating a man with a history of cardiac problems, but Paw Allanson had always been a tremendously strong man. Even now, although he was considerably weaker since his heart attack five months before, he seemed to be fighting his way back to consciousness.

"What have you prescribed for Mr. Allanson?" Tedford asked Dr. Jones.

"Vistaril—that's a very mild sedative. Nembutal—a barbiturate—and Librax for his stomach. But I suspect he's taken something other than what I prescribed. I found so many empty pill bottles in their home."

Paw's condition could have been an accident, and a fairly common one at that. An old man, confused and perhaps a little senile, had had too much alcohol and too many of the wrong pills. But Tedford was inclined to code it as a possible suicide attempt. Elderly people were often depressed by their diminished capacities.

Dr. Jones called Jean Boggs again. He explained that he had admitted her father to the hospital, and that he was in a coma.

"From *what?*"

Dr. Jones explained that her father had apparently been drinking again and taking pills. He also said that Paw had allegedly tried to kill his wife.

Jean was shocked almost speechless. "This doesn't make any sense at all!" she burst out. "There is something wrong."

Dr. Jones agreed with her. He told her he felt that whatever had happened, it was a matter for the police. Jean immediately called the East Point police and asked for a complete investigation. "We already have a detective on it," she was told.

By the time Jean got to South Fulton Hospital, her father had been taken to his room. He was still unconscious and he had tubes sprouting from every body orifice. "Paw," she said. "Paw, it's Jean. Can you hear me?"

He gave no sign that he was with her at all.

Jean noticed that the Radcliffes seemed to be everywhere she went. She wondered where Pat was—probably home with her mother. That thought gave her a sudden chill.

When she was distraught and frustrated, Jean Boggs could be abrasive and demanding. She had been shut off from her parents for months, and her father might be dying. She approached the detective, who was making notes, and demanded that he investigate thoroughly. A bit ruffled, Tedford assured her he was doing just that. She also suggested that he familiarize himself with her brother's and sister-in-law's murders. Jean minced no words; she flat out accused Pat Allanson of having something to do with her father's coma. "He does *not* drink, and he does *not* take pills," she insisted. "If he's in a coma, she did something to him. She's practically moved in with them, and I think she's after what they have."

Tedford had seen his share of family beefs and rivalries, and he had heard wild accusations tossed around. But there was something about Jean Boggs's words that made the hairs stand up on the back of his neck. After assuring her that he would keep at it until he found out what had caused her father's coma, he hurried back to the ER to ask that the contents of Paw Allanson's stomach be retained for examination.

It was too late. The emesis had already been disposed of.

✦   ✦   ✦

By Monday morning, June 14, Paw seemed to be out of danger but he remained a miserably sick man. Bob Tedford and Detective H. R. Turner drove out to 4137 Washington Road to talk with Nona Allanson. They were not prepared to find the lady as incapacitated as she was. Debbie Cole, Pat's younger daughter, answered their knock and invited them into the living room. From somewhere in the rear of the little house they could hear a woman sobbing and wailing; she sounded as if she were in desperate distress.

"That's Mrs. Allanson," Debbie explained. "She's really upset about everything. If you'll wait here, I'll try to get her out here to talk with you. My mother's with her."

A few minutes later, a lushly pretty woman who appeared to be in her mid-thirties approached. Although she limped noticeably herself, she was pushing an elderly woman in a wheelchair. She introduced herself as Mrs. Tom Allanson, the "granddaughter" of the senior Allansons.

Tedford quickly realized how compromised Nona Allanson's speech was. He couldn't understand a word she said.

"I'll translate," Pat said. "I can understand her."

It was a good thing she could, Tedford thought, because he sure couldn't. Pat repeated what she said the older woman had said. "She said that Paw's been taking pills—too many pills. No, she hasn't seen him, but she says he's been drinking more than usual, and she hasn't seen him eat for several days. She called us Saturday morning and told us that Big Allanson—that's what she calls Paw—was trying to kill her, so of course we rushed right over."

It was apparent that the old woman was growing more and more upset and Tedford stopped the interview. Pat ushered the detectives out onto the front porch, where they could talk privately. She repeated, almost verbatim, the story that Tedford had heard from the Radcliffes the day before. He noticed that her eyes brimmed with tears as she recalled how Paw had gone downhill with the drinking and the pills. She seemed about to break into sobs.

"He tried to run me off the road, you know," Pat said quietly.

"What?"

"He did. He tried to run me off the road."

Tedford recalled the elderly shell of a man he had seen in the ER. He scarcely looked capable of driving a car, much less aiming it at another vehicle and forcing it off the road. "Why would he try to run you off the road?" he asked.

Pat cast her green eyes down and sighed. "When Paw was in the hospital during his last heart attack, he felt he was going to die. He had me send for his attorneys—Mr. Hamner and Mr. Reeves. He told them about a killing in 1974. He admitted to them that *he* did it—not my husband. Personally, I was never so shocked in my life. It just took me by surprise that he would tell that to his attorneys. I sat in the corner, and I started taking notes . . . and he realizes that I know about this. His attitude toward *me* completely changed."

Tedford had read the case file on the Allanson murders. He wondered if Pat was telling him that old Walter had killed his own son and daughter-in-law. If she was, it was a startling—an almost unbelievable—revelation, but she seemed incapable of saying it in so many words.

"I hate . . . ," she began, her eyes still bright with unshed tears, "I hate to know something that will get someone out of trouble but will get somebody else into a lot of trouble."

She looked so forlorn that Tedford felt sorry for her; she was struggling with supressed secrets that she didn't want to tell him. And yet at the same time, he knew, she *did* want to.

Finally she blurted it out. "When Paw got out of the hospital —after his heart attack—I was finally able to set him down one day, and I just outright asked him would he tell me again what he told his lawyers. I guess I needed it down on paper—in case . . . in case anything happened to Paw."

The detectives leaned forward, fascinated to hear what had happened next. What was it that old Mr. Allanson had confessed to? But that was all Pat was going to tell them. She wiped her eyes with her little lace handkerchief and forced a bright smile.

"Oh, never mind," she said. "I guess I was just thinking out loud. I'm just so concerned about Paw coming back to this house. I'm sorry to say I don't want him back here with Ma. I'm scared to death he really will hurt her next time. . . ."

✦ ✦ ✦

Pat Allanson was certainly a handsome woman; the cane made her seem frail, but she had a perfect, full-breasted figure, and she dressed to show it off. Her thick auburn hair was coiled and twisted in what women called a French roll. The detectives knew that her husband was down in Jackson Prison for murder. No wonder she teared up so easily. She must have been through hell.

It was easier—in the beginning, at least—to talk with Pat Allanson, with her sweet, sad manner, than it was to deal with Jean Boggs. Jean was an attractive woman too, slender and tall with silky black hair. She was immaculately groomed right down to her long scarlet fingernails. But she was an angry, bitter woman in a hurry, and she seemed to have little faith in the justice system. She knew the brass in the East Point Police Department, and she wasn't averse to going over the detectives' heads to demand a quicker resolution to her suspicions about her father's illness.

Jean was incensed that the contents of her father's stomach had been thrown out. How were they ever going to prove now what she suspected—that Pat had given him something to make him so sick? She had seen the old-fashioned whiskey bottle that Paw was supposed to have been drinking out of. There was just no way. Years ago, her father had made blackberry wine from the wild berries on his farm, but he hardly even tasted it himself —he gave it away. He was almost eighty years old. Why would he start drinking at this age?

On Sunday afternoon after leaving the hospital, Jean and her neighbor, Sherry Allen, had dropped by the Washington Road house to check on Nona Allanson. They found Pat there, feeding the old lady lunch and fussing over her. Pat asked Jean how Paw was, and Jean said he was still unconscious but unless he got pneumonia or another heart attack or something, he was going to pull through.

Pat shook her head, disagreeing. "It doesn't look like he'll make it."

"Well, we really don't know yet," Jean answered slowly.

Pat had fixed her green eyes on Jean and told her that Jean had no idea in the whole wide world what a dirty old man Paw really was. "You don't know that old man," she said. "He's done things you wouldn't believe. He's not good and kind like you think."

Jean started to shake her head in warning as she glanced at her mother, but Nona just sat there and let Pat rave on about her husband. Although she couldn't speak, Nona was sharp enough. It seemed to Jean that her mother had heard accusations like this before. Nona made no move to correct Pat; she apparently *believed* what Pat was saying.

Jean could not understand Pat's vitriolic attack on her father; he had always been so good to her. Why was she savaging him with her words while he might be dying?

Pat complained about having to get up with him the night before he had taken sick. "It was two-thirty in the morning and he wanted some ginger ale. I took it to him, and *damn him*, he wouldn't drink it! He decided he wanted half-and-half and I took him that."

Pat suddenly changed the direction of her conversation. "I talked with him about death—you know, about funeral arrangements and all. He said he wanted to be put away in a casket with pink satin to lie on. I've got his clothes all picked out. Your boy will be one of the pallbearers."

None of that sounded a bit like Paw, Jean thought. Pink satin indeed.

As Jean and Sherry walked down the front steps, Pat suddenly appeared on the porch. She leaned across the railing and said flatly, "I hope he dies."

"*What* did you say?" Jean breathed softly.

"I said I hope he dies."

Jean walked to her car, stunned.

✦   ✦   ✦

On Tuesday, Paw Allanson's blood pressure dropped so low it barely registered, but medication slowly boosted it back up. He was a very old man, but he was made of tough Georgia stock. He remained in a deep coma for a week, caught somewhere between living and dying.

Jean was sitting by his bedside as he slowly regained consciousness on Saturday. "Do you recognize me?" she asked, truly believing that he would not.

"Sure," he grumbled.

"Who am I?"

"Jean," he said, as if she had taken leave of her senses. Of course he recognized her.

"How do you feel, Daddy?"

He looked at her. "I think I'll be all right when I get over this stroke."

"Is that what you think you had, Daddy?"

"Yes—I feel like I'm taking the flu too. My legs ache me so bad. . . ."

✦ ✦ ✦

Pat maintained her position that Paw Allanson was a dangerous man, octogenarian or not. She insisted that he had tried to kill his wife, and that she had no idea what he might do next. She had retained a new attorney, Dunham McAllister, to work on Tom's latest appeal. She had also asked Paw's attorneys, Fred Reeves and Bill Hamner, to fight any attempt Jean Boggs might make to become her parents' guardian.

Pat told McAllister that she feared for her life; she had in her possession a document that made her very vulnerable. McAllister contacted the East Point police and informed the investigators that Pat had overheard Paw give his attorneys a confession to the murders of his son and daughter-in-law. At the time, Pat had explained, Paw had believed that he would not survive his heart attack.

McAllister was concerned about Pat. If Paw remembered how much Pat knew, and if he survived his current illness, her life was most certainly in danger. McAllister was very worried about Nona Allanson's safety too, citing the alleged smothering attempt only a day or so before Paw overdosed. Pat had confided to the lawyer—just as she had to Tedford—that Paw had treated her coldly ever since he had come home from the hospital in February. She could deal with that—he was an old man and cantankerous—but it was far more than that. When Paw tried to run Pat off the road, she had been hampered by her weak leg and hip. It was all she could do to keep from crashing into a tree or slipping over a gully. She told McAllister that she had received harassing phone calls asking her where she had been, what she was doing, whom she had talked to. She hinted that the old man had watched her constantly to see if she would tell anybody about his confession. If he thought she might, he would kill her without warning.

McAllister's next meeting was with Bill Weller, the assistant D.A. who had successfully prosecuted Tom Allanson. If Paw's confession was true, then Tom had been wrongly convicted. Dunham McAllister handed over what Pat had told him were her roughly typed recollections of "the confession." The actual confession was alleged to be in the possession of Paw Allanson's attorneys.

Although such scenarios are common to TV courtrooms, they rarely happen in real life: a convicted killer proved to be innocent after all, exonerated when someone else confesses to the crime. But it *could* happen. Maybe Tom Allanson *was* doing hard time for crimes he had not committed. *But Paw Allanson a killer?* If the old man was guilty, he would certainly be one of the most unlikely murderers ever to surface in Georgia.

30

On June 21, Investigator R. A. Harris of the Fulton County District Attorney's Office went to the First Palmetto Bank in East Point. According to Pat, officers of this bank had witnessed and notarized Paw's signature on a typed reduction of her own notes on the old man's admission of murder.

An assistant vice-president of the bank, A. V. "Gus" Yosue, remembered a rather odd incident. A woman had come into his bank around six in the evening on a Friday a few months back, asking if she could get some papers notarized. She had explained that all the other banks were closed and that "Daddy"—her grandfather—didn't want everyone knowing his business anyway. Yosue had never seen her before—or since, for that matter. "Daddy" was out in the car when the woman first came in, and Yosue had explained that the old gentleman would have to come inside to have his documents notarized.

Joyce Tichenor, the head teller of the First Palmetto Bank, told Investigator Harris that Mr. Yosue had helped an elderly man to her window. He and his granddaughter had a stack of papers, and Tichenor's cursory glance had told her they seemed to be some type of real estate documents—warranty deeds and the like—most of them apparently standard forms.

The woman, in her thirties and very attractive, had seemed most solicitous of the old man. She had pointed her finger at the bottom of several pages, saying, "Sign this paper, Daddy," or "Daddy, sign here on this line."

Tichenor had notarized the signatures. She had no idea what the documents really were; it was not, she explained, her business to read documents brought to her. Neither she nor Yosue had read the papers. The elderly man had simply followed the directions of his granddaughter, signing without question.

Pat had told Bob Tedford that Paw's attorneys held a white envelope that contained vital information, but she had been tearfully hesitant to say more. Tedford wanted to see what was in that envelope. The East Point detective called Hamner and Reeves and asked if they had such a document. They did, and promised to meet Tedford with the envelope in Paw Allanson's hospital room.

Bill Hamner had wrestled with the question of legal ethics and the plain white envelope he had held, he *thought,* for old Mr. Allanson. Should he have come forward earlier? Should he have waited longer? Hamner explained that it was Pat Allanson who had brought the envelope to his firm. The envelope bore only a few words, scribbled in a shaky hand:

Mr. Walter Allanson
    plese dont open untill I pass out

"I thought it was sort of strange," Hamner said, "but the envelope was sealed. I just stuck it in the file. . . . I probably had the confession six . . . maybe eight weeks total. . . . Pat came up to the office one day. . . . She said she had been riding with 'Daddy' and he had tried to run the car into a tree. He was driving and she was in the passenger seat, and he had tried to hit the tree on the passenger side. . . . [S]he grabbed the steering wheel to keep him from hitting the tree, and she thought . . . he was trying to kill her, maybe. She said this would tie in with the envelope."

Hamner was a civil, not a criminal, attorney and he had urged her to give that information to Dunham McAllister, who would better know what to do about it. Bill Hamner and Fred Reeves had reason to expect some startling revelation in the envelope, but they had adhered to the instructions on the front and hadn't opened it until old Walter Allanson had truly "passed out" and slipped into his mysterious coma.

On June 24, Investigator Harris, Sergeant Bob Tedford, and George Boggs, Jean's husband, went to Paw Allanson's hospital room to ask him about his "confession." Apparently Paw hadn't seen any version of his so-called confession. He was only ten days past a critical coma, but he would have to read the confession before he could confirm or refute it.

Paw was rapidly returning to his old self and was absolutely lucid now, with a keen memory. With his permission, Hamner gave Sergeant Tedford the opened white envelope. He showed it to Paw and asked him if he remembered writing on it. He nodded. "Yeah. I was cooking supper one night, and Pat came into the kitchen and told me that my lawyers wanted me to write that on the envelope."

"Was there anything in it?"

"Nope."

There was something in it now. Five legal-sized sheets of paper on which a very bad typist and speller had typed what appeared to be a confession. Bob Tedford read the contents without speaking, and then handed the pages to the old man in the bed. "Did you write this?"

Paw scanned it, beginning to shake his head almost immediately.

April 19, 1976

My name is Walter Allanson, and I'm telling this to my grand-daughter, Tommy's wife, Pat Allanson, and she's doing it on the type-writer cause I don't write so good anymore since I had the heart attack. This is so if I have a heart attack before Mama dies Tommy won't have to stay in jail for what he didn't do. If Mama dies first then I'll tell what I did. I told all this to pat, Tommy's wife, at the hospital. . . . I thought I was going to die, and I knew nobbody would beleive Tommy if he told em the truth. Then I got better and Pat didn't say nothing, so I didn't say nothing . . . [but] I told her that if Jean didn't quit Bothering

Mama I'd shoot her like I did Walter. . . . Pat started to cry and said I shouldn't talk like that. . . . I said it was the truth, but she didn't beleive me. . . .

The writer of the confession tended to ramble a good deal, hinting that "Tommy" had known the truth all along but had agreed to protect his grandfather and to tell no one. He also took several swipes at lawyers in general, and Ed Garland in particular.

. . . I never figured they'd be able to keep Tommy locked up.

But, of course, they had.

Little Carolyn and Walter Allanson were castigated on page after page.

I told him he'd never give Tommy a chance, even when he was little. . . . Anyway, Walter just laughed and said he'd clean up all this mess before the week-end and then he'd take care of me and Mama. . . . She told me Walter had said he'd kill her if he found she was helping Tommy, and he was going to put us both in old folks home after he took care of Tommy. . . . If I'divae heard Walter when he threatened Mama, then he wouldn't have even lived until the next tuesday. I'd a shot him right there. . . .

The confession was, in its own way, a masterpiece, misspellings and all. Every question a sharp detective might have asked was covered. The writer explained his motive for murder, how he was able to be away from home without raising suspicions on the day Walter and Big Carolyn Allanson had died, how frightened Pat and Nona had been, and then he moved ahead to the actual incident.

I took care of Mama first, and then drove over to where Walter lived . . . went up the driveway. I cut the phone wire with my pocket knife. Then I jimmied the basement door open, and went upstairs to get walters shot gun and some shells. I didn't know he'd bought that rifle or I'd got it too. Jakes's Pistol wasn't there, so I figured Walter had it. I went back down into the basement, and cut the power off and went to waiting for Walter.

The writer had heard cars come home, people talking, Walter coming down the basement stairs, and he realized, too late, that Tommy was there in the basement too.

I didn't figure on Tommy bein thre. He was telling his Daddy that he just wanted to be left alone . . . he said he wann't mad at nobody. . . . Tommy told his Daddy that Pat was at the Doctor. . . .

The document painted Walter Allanson as a wicked man indeed; Tommy had tried to leave—he had said what he'd come to say—but Walter wouldn't let him go. He told Tommy to wait in the basement while he calmed down the women upstairs.

I was hoping Tommy would leave right then out the kitchen way, but he was doing what he always done all his life. He was waiting for Walter to come and tell him it was O.K. He always did what his daddy said, and Walter knew he would. . . . I'd already figured out that Walter was not going to let Tommy leave there alive. He was going to kill Tommy like he was going to kill Mama and me. . . ."

According to the long, rambling confession, Paw had somehow managed to hoist himself up into the "hole" in his son's basement and hide there before his grandson crawled up beside him.

I thought he was going to yell out when he found me in there. I think he was too scared. . . . Tommy said, "Let's get out of here, Paw—Daddy's going to shoot us both. . . ."

But then they had both heard Walter talk to the policeman and refuse to let the officer search the house, and it had all gone downhill from there. The writer said Walter had come back into the dark basement again, right up to the hole, and shouted that he was going to kill Tom, so he might as well come on out.

Then Walter hollered up for Carolyn to bring down the rifle, "I've got him cornered—he ain't gonna get of here ever." . . . I

*told you he was a coward. . . . He walked away from the hole,
and that's when I come up to the opening. Big Carolyn come
down the steps hollering, "I'm going to kill him," and cut loose
with the rifle, right at where me and Tommy was. I shot back
and hit her and she fell. I stepped back to reload, and thats when
Walter emptied the pistol in the hole all around Tiommy. . . .
Then I shot agian and hit Walter, but he didn't fall right off like
Carolyn did. Tommy started saying, "oh my God, oh My God,"
and I told him to get the hell out and get away, and he kept
falling over stuff and ran out the back door. . . . (I didn't want
to kill big Carolyn or little Carolyn, I didn't want to kill nobody)
but Walter was mean and greedy and hateful . . . so I had to get
him first, before he got Mama and me and Killed us or put us
away. . . .*

The writer of the confession seemed to know things that only
someone who had actually been in that basement could have
known. And every so often, he reminded whoever might read it
that Tom was innocent, that Pat was innocent and had tried
only to protect Tom, Paw, and Nona, and that it had been a
matter of kill or be killed. He even tossed in that Tommy had
called him from the liquor store after the shootings to say he was
hitchhiking home to Zebulon.

Paw—at least the Paw in the confession—couldn't come forward to get Tommy off the hook because he couldn't go to
prison and leave his wife. He repeated this over and over.

*MAMA DON'T KNOW WHAT I DID. She might have a stroke
if she did. This is how it happened and how I did it. . . .*

All of his grandson's troubles and the knowledge that Tom
was going to prison for a crime he had not committed had worn
the writer down.

*That worried me and got my brain tired out, and probably made
me have the heart attack. I didn't want Tommy to stay in prison,
but I aint going to prison for Killing Walter, when I had to do it
to keep him from killing us or putting us away. If I tell about it
now, they'll still lock me up, but I'm too old, and that'd kill
Mama, so I can't do it right now. But I"M telling this now so*

that when I die at least they'll beleive Tommy when he tells the
truth. After I"M dead Mama will understand why i did what I
did. I'M gonna sign this in front of a witness to put in a envelope
to give to my lawyers. They can't open it til after I die. . . .
That's all I got to say.

Underneath that voluminous confession, someone had printed
crookedly: "Sworn to and subscribed before me this 16 day of
April 1976. Joyce Tichenor, Notary Public." There was no seal
imprint, but there was Tichenor's official stamp, and she had
verified to investigators that the stamp was indeed hers. The
printing was not.

Paw Allanson's signature was at the bottom. It *was* his signature—he was sure of it. And the initials at the bottom of each
page were his too. But he had absolutely no memory of writing
or agreeing to any of the contents. He seemed dumbfounded—
as well he might. Harris pressed. Was there any truth in this
confession? In any part of it? "No!" Paw snorted.

If Paw Allanson hadn't written the confession, who had? The
details certainly sounded as if the author had been an eyewitness
to the deadly events of July 3, 1974. But *Paw?* He was a sturdy
old man, but would he have been capable of all the actions the
confession described? Tedford figured that was highly unlikely.
Paw was as puzzled as the detectives were. Of course, if he had
died of an overdose, he would not have been able to refute the
confession.

If the D.A.'s office believed that Paw was the real killer of his
son and daughter-in-law, then Tom would get a new trial and
would quite probably be freed. And who, Tedford asked himself, had the most to gain if such a thing came to pass? Tom
Allanson certainly. Tom had sent frequent letters to his grandparents—right up until May—urging them to trust Pat. But as
far as any hands-on action, Tom couldn't have poisoned Paw if
he had wanted to; he was locked up tight in Jackson Prison, and
had been for months.

"Do you remember ever signing any papers for Pat?" Tedford
asked Paw quietly. "Anything at all?"

Paw scratched his head. He explained that he and his wife had
trusted Pat; she had been good to them after Tommy went to
prison.

"Did you ever go to a bank on Washington Road with Pat?" Harris asked.

Paw strained to remember. "Yeah, seems like I did. Pat wanted me to sign some papers—in front of a notary lady." He could not remember actually going into the bank, but he recalled Pat had wanted him to sign some business papers. He hadn't bothered to read the papers.

Sergeant Tedford turned to Hamner and Reeves, Paw Allanson's attorneys.

"When did you say you got this envelope?"

"Mrs. Allanson—Pat Taylor Allanson—came into the office one day in April," Hamner replied. "I couldn't tell you the exact date. She told us that Mr. Allanson wanted us to have it."

This didn't jibe with what Pat had told the East Point detectives as she wept in the shadow of the wisteria vine on Paw Allanson's porch. Both Tedford and his partner had been impressed with her sincerity, her pain, and her helplessness.

"During earlier conversations with Pat," Tedford wrote in his follow-up report,

> she told us that Mr. Allanson's attorneys were in his hospital room when he had had his last heart attack. This is when Mr. Allanson had given this statement. Pat said she took notes during this conversation, and then, when Mr. Allanson was released from the hospital, she had typed another statement from her notes and Mr. Allanson had signed it. The copy of the statement obtained from Dunham McAllister, Pat's attorney, is exactly the same as the original obtained from Hamner and Reeves, and could not *be exactly* alike if she had typed hers from notes. Hamner and Reeves are sure that they have *never* taken a statement from Mr. Allanson in the hospital or anywhere else. . . . [B]ased on this information, this statement is believed to be a forged document. . . .

Tedford suspected other false documents might be tucked away here and there. He made a note to check into the elder Allansons' wills. Paw was in no immediate danger of dying, although he would be in the hospital for some time. The doctors still couldn't pinpoint just what had brought on his collapse and week-long coma.

31

Jean Boggs was a determined woman. She didn't know yet about the confession, but she did not believe for a moment that her father had tried to kill her mother, nor did she believe he was suicidal. Paw was too bullheaded to give up on life, and he had taken exquisite care of her mother for a decade. He would never leave her behind willingly, and he would never hurt one hair on her head.

Paw seemed as puzzled as Jean was by his condition. He had been truly amazed to find that he had *not* had a stroke. He shook his head in bewilderment at the thought that he had "overdosed." He wanted to find out what was wrong with him as much as Jean did.

Two specialists—neurologists—were called in on a consulting basis. Neither could isolate the cause of Paw's coma. They suggested that he have CAT scans of the brain and his upper gastrointestinal tract. The scanning lab was just across the street from South Fulton Hospital. Jean and her son, David, wheeled Paw there. The tests took thirty minutes and the results were inconclusive.

A horror was growing in Jean Boggs. She already suspected that Pat Allanson wanted to inherit her parents' assets. But now Jean wondered if Pat might actually have attempted to hasten her father's demise. Was Pat dosing her daddy with something that made him sick? Jean had heard that two years ago someone had snuck into Little Carolyn's apartment and put something in Tommy's baby's milk. She had been told—mistakenly—that the substance used was arsenic. In fact, the milk had been contaminated with formaldehyde.

Jean was about to become an expert in poison—at least one poison: arsenic. Paw had used it on the farm years back with the animals, not as a poison but as a cure. It was really the only poison she had ever heard about. Jean called the Georgia State Crime Lab and asked to speak to someone about the symptoms of poison. She got lucky; one of the top experts in the South happened to be in the lab that day. Dr. Everett Solomons, with an undergraduate degree in chemistry and a Ph.D. in medicinal chemistry, knew as much about poisons as anybody in the state of Georgia.

"Could you tell me what the symptoms of arsenic poisoning are?" Jean began without preamble. "I really need to know."

There was something about her voice. This woman *meant* it when she said she had to know.

"Well, it could show up a number of ways," Solomons began. "Gastrointestinal upset, vomiting, or flulike symptoms, aching in the extremities—the feet, legs, hands, arms."

"My daddy has three of those symptoms. Is there any way that you can check for arsenic poisoning *after* the person's system has been flushed out with intravenous feeding—I mean, after time has gone by?"

Solomons paused and cleared his throat. "Is this gentleman— is he still, ah, *alive?*"

"Oh, yes."

"Well, then your answer is yes. I can check for you. I want you to do some things for me. Ask your doctor to collect a twenty-four-hour urine specimen. Next, cut some hair off your father's head."

"How much?"

"Oh, about a fourth of a cup."

How much hair makes a fourth of a cup? Jean wondered to herself. Do you pack it in like brown sugar, or let it fluff up like shredded coconut? Solomons explained that the hair had to come from new hair growth around the subject's neck. Thirdly, she was to cut her father's fingernails and place them in a plastic bag.

Jean hurried back to the East Point Police Department and conferred with Assistant Chief Lieb and Sergeant Tedford. She informed them of Solomons' advice. This time, they had every reason to take her seriously. Tedford immediately called Dr. Jones and asked if it was possible that Paw Allanson had been given arsenic.

"It could be," Jones said, his voice suddenly aware of an unthinkable possibility. "The symptoms look like so many other diseases—at least at first."

When arsenic is ingested, it seeks a place to "hide" in the human body. It goes rapidly to areas where phosphorus is stored and replaces it. Human beings need phosphorus for energy. After long exposure to the poison, the extremities ache, circulation is compromised, and eventually paralysis and death occur. In the beginning, arsenic poisoning can resemble a bad case of bone-aching flu with vomiting. Later it can mimic multiple sclerosis and other more serious chronic illnesses.

"We're going to need lab tests," Tedford said. "Mrs. Boggs said we need at least two hundred cc's of urine over a twenty-four-hour period." Jones said he would advise the hospital at once and the urine samples would be collected. Tedford hung up and called the Fulton County D.A.'s Office and informed them of the new suspicions about Paw Allanson's condition.

On June 26, Tedford accompanied Jean Boggs to her father's hospital room. The old man sat patiently as Jean snipped a quarter of a cup of hair and cut his fingernails. Tedford said he would be back the next day to pick up the twenty-four-hour urine sample.

By 8:00 A.M. on Monday, June 28, 1976, Dr. H. Horton McGurdy of the Georgia State Crime Lab was in possession of a brown jug containing 1,000 cc's of urine, a plastic bag with hair and hair root samples, and a similar bag with fingernail clippings. Analysis would begin at once.

◆   ◆   ◆

Jean Boggs was nervous. Now that the wheels were in motion, she hated the thought of her mother alone with Pat out on Washington Road. Scarcely expecting a gracious welcome, she drove there anyway. She found Nona Allanson sitting in the kitchen with a practical nurse Pat had hired. The nurse stared at Jean. "Miz Allanson's went on home to tend to some things," she said coldly. Evidently, she had been told to beware of Jean.

Jean saw tears on her mother's cheeks. She knelt down and took her hand. "What's wrong, Mother?"

"There's nothing wrong with her," the nurse answered quickly.

"Yes, there *is,*" Jean said. "She's been crying."

"She doesn't ever cry unless *you* come around her."

"Mother, what *is* wrong?" Jean asked again.

"I can't tell you," Nona mumbled.

"I can't help you, Mother, if you don't tell me what's wrong."

Finally, Nona sighed and asked sadly, "Why did Daddy kill Walter and Carolyn?"

"Who on earth told you *that?*"

"*Mrs. Radcliffe.*"

"Mrs. Radcliffe? Is she the only one who told you that?" Jean thought surely her mother was confused.

"Pat told me too, and Colonel Radcliffe . . ." Nona Allanson was so upset that her daughter could not calm her down.

Jean got Bob Tedford on the phone and he offered to come out and talk to her mother. Jean had some questions of her own too. When he arrived at the house, the young detective assured the elderly woman that her husband was not a killer, that nobody believed that. He was sick and he was in the hospital, but he would be home with her soon—just like always. Nona Allanson seemed only slightly comforted; she remained apprehensive and tearful.

Almost as a throwaway question, Tedford asked, "You haven't been signing any papers, have you, while your husband is in the hospital?"

Tedford couldn't be sure, but he thought her mumbled answer was, "Yes."

"Oh, my Lord," he breathed. Jean looked up at Tedford with dread. She didn't even have to ask her questions. She could see it in his eyes.

✦ ✦ ✦

At 3:00 that afternoon, the lab called Gus Thornhill. "The screening test on Walter Allanson's urine is complete," Dr. McGurdy said. "We found arsenic . . ."

It would take somewhat longer, the toxicologist said, to test the hair and nail samples. But the first results were more than enough for Thornhill and Tedford. They grabbed their case file and headed for the D.A.'s office. Andy Weathers would be taking over this case. The assistant D.A. was sharp, combative—but with a humorous edge—and terribly dangerous to guilty defendants.

Until now, the case file had been only a few pages thick and the complaint still read, "Overdose." It was growing thicker. The charge would now be "Criminal Attempt to Commit Murder."

And the prime suspect was Patricia Radcliffe Taylor Allanson.

The Georgia Crime Lab had placed Paw Allanson's urine sample in a container with hydrochloric acid, water, and a piece of copper. If certain metals were present—including arsenic—a black deposit would appear on the copper. It had. The urine was further analyzed by a wet oxidation procedure to reduce the specimen to a small amount of clear liquid, free of all extraneous materials except metals. This material was then subjected to reduction by zinc and acid, producing arsene gas in a small tube. A reddish color would indicate the presence of arsenic. The *amount* of arsenic present could then be determined by an electrospectrometer with a laser probe.

The average person's urine would show no arsenic present. Certain occupations caused a low percentage of the poison. Paw Allanson had, in years past, used arsenic on his farm. Would that have accounted for the poison in his urine? No, the lab technicians said. Even if he had used arsenic on the farm recently—which he had not—that would not account for the fact that Paw had *ten times* the amount of poison in his system that a working farmer would have!

Arsenic had been carried in his bloodstream and deposited at the base of his fingernails and at the roots of his hair, an irrevocable process that left a "calendar" of ingestion. Paw Allanson's hair had 1.0 milligrams of arsenic per 100 millimeters; his nails had 5.5 milligrams of arsenic per 100 millimeters.

The East Point detectives swung into action. They called Dr. Jones with the results of the crime lab tests. He agreed that Nona Allanson should be removed from her granddaughter-in-law's care at once and hospitalized. For a long time, Jean Boggs's accusations against Pat had seemed suspect; it was clear to them she didn't like her nephew's wife, the woman who had taken her place in her parents' lives. The East Point officers and Dr. Jones had initially found Pat Allanson a rather nice woman who seemed genuinely concerned about her grandparents-in-law. Just a week before, Nona had suffered from pneumonia and severe bronchitis, and Pat had obediently followed Dr. Jones's every direction. Nona's 103-degree fever had dropped, and she was doing much better. Given the fact that Pat was on crutches or a cane due to her own poor health, Jones had found her especially dutiful.

Now Jones doubted his own judgment of human nature. It was beginning to look as if Pat Allanson was *not* the tender care giver she purported to be, and that Jean Boggs had been right all along. Bob Tedford sent word to Jean that he was on his way to see Fulton County District Attorney Lewis Slaton himself to get a court order to remove Nona Allanson from her home. Every hour's delay might count, and someone should be with the old lady. "Bob says not to let your mother eat or drink anything," the police dispatcher advised.

Jean and her son headed immediately for her parents' home. She was met at the door by a livid Pat Allanson. She had had a phone call from Dr. Jones. "He said they need her there for some testing, and I think that's a terrible thing," Pat ranted. She could see no earthly reason for Nona to go to a hospital.

"Well," Jean stalled. "If he thinks that's the thing to do, then we'd better do it."

Pat wouldn't even consider letting Nona go to the hospital. She had already called an attorney, who advised her that Dr. Jones had no power to hospitalize Mrs. Allanson. Pat was suspicious, but her suspicions were pointed in the wrong direction —at Jean Boggs. She had no idea that a police investigation had rolled into high gear. She assumed that Jean was trying to have Nona declared incompetent so she could take over her guardianship—*and* control Paw and Nona's assets.

Pat fussed over Nona's hair, petting her and reassuring her.

"You don't have to go anyplace you don't want to, Ma. They can't make you and I won't let them."

Jean was frightened. She wondered what was taking the ambulance and the police so long. She was even more concerned when Colonel Clifford Radcliffe showed up. He was such an imposing man, and Jean was suitably intimidated. None of them wanted her there—not Pat, nor the colonel, or even the nurse. The only chance Jean had was to somehow get through to her mother—make Nona understand that she was there to save her life. But how? Her mother seemed to think that Pat walked on water.

When Pat left the room, Jean whispered to her mother, "Mother, listen to me very carefully. Don't tell anyone what I'm saying to you. Don't say anything to Pat—but Daddy has been poisoned."

It was, perhaps, an unwise move. Her mother was very feeble, and they had not been close for months now. Nona Allanson just looked at Jean blankly and mumbled, "What?"

"We just found out about it," Jean whispered. "We have to get you to the hospital to see if *you're* all right. You have to have some tests."

Nona clamped her jaw down and announced she wasn't going anywhere. "I won't go."

Jean begged her mother to trust her, and to speak quietly. The wait was becoming a nightmare. Despite Jean's objections, the nurse brought Nona a 7-Up. Jean couldn't very well snatch it out of her mother's hand.

The phone rang. Jean grabbed it. She lied to her mother and said it was her husband—but it was really Bob Tedford.

"How are you feeling?" Tedford asked.

"Uncomfortable."

"Hang on. I'm on my way."

Tedford had laid out the case for D.A. Lewis Slaton, and Slaton had grasped the need for rapid action. "You've got whatever permission you need. Don't worry about papers. Get that lady in the hospital *now!*"

Tedford had called an ambulance and it was speeding toward Washington Road.

It was 4:00 in the afternoon on Monday, June 28, 1976. And then 4:30. The minutes crept by agonizingly. Then, suddenly, there was a loud pounding on the front door. Jean jumped. She wondered who else Pat might have called for backup. She heard footsteps approaching and was tremendously relieved to see Bob Tedford and another detective walk into the living room.

Tedford made no attempt to soften his announcement to Pat Allanson. "Arsenic has been found in Mr. Allanson's system and we need to take Mrs. Allanson to the hospital for tests."

Pat looked at him without changing expression, not so much as the flickering of an eye. She turned on her heel and headed for Nona's bedroom. Tedford was right behind her.

The little house on Washington Road erupted into chaos. Nona Allanson was already nearly hysterical, unable to grasp what was going on. When Tedford informed Pat that an ambulance was on the way for Mrs. Allanson, she was incensed. Her voice rose, whipping the old lady into a froth of panic. She bombarded her husband's grandmother with dire warnings, every word making the paralyzed woman more terrified.

Nona's mouth worked ineffectively as she tried to form questions, and Pat just kept on shouting at her. "They're going to take you to the hospital for some silly tests! They'll be giving you shots all the time. You can't let them. Your insurance won't pay for it," Pat ranted. "You'll be deep in debt, Ma. I won't be able to come see you. They won't let you have any visitors."

Tedford feared the old lady was about to have another stroke. She looked utterly panicked and begged to stay in her home. Pat kept after her, predicting all manner of disasters if Nona let them take her in the ambulance. Finally Tedford had had enough. He pulled Pat aside and spoke through gritted teeth. "I've heard all I want to hear from you. If you keep this up, I'm going to ask you to leave."

Jean Boggs was the blood relative; she had the law on her side, Tedford told Pat, and *she* would decide whether her mother would go to the hospital or not. Pat was seething. The hatred in the room rose around them like an almost palpable miasma.

Colonel Radcliffe got *his* attorney on the phone and handed the receiver to Tedford. The attorney threatened Tedford with a lawsuit, and the detective replied that that would be just fine. The real defendant would be the Fulton County district attorney, Lewis Slaton—officially, it was Slaton who had ordered that Mrs. Walter Allanson be removed from her home for tests. Nobody in his right mind sued Lewis Slaton.

"Colonel Radcliffe," Tedford continued easily, "since you're here, would you mind showing me where it was that you saw Mr. Allanson taking all those pills on that Saturday?"

The two men now stood in the hallway near the kitchen. "I don't remember any pills," Radcliffe said.

Tedford jerked his head around as if he'd been struck. *"What?"*

"I don't remember any pills."

"Well, Colonel Radcliffe," Tedford began quietly. "This is how the whole case of the overdose got started. It was all based upon your statement to me, Pat Allanson's statement to me, and your wife was there at the hospital too when you told me. All three of you were agreeing at the time. *Now* you're saying that you didn't see him take any pills?"

"That is correct."

"But you *told* me about the pills. You *described* the way he was tossing them down."

"You're confused, Sergeant. You're lying."

"Fine, then," Tedford said grimly. He knew what he had heard the first time, and he found it interesting that Pat's stepfather had had such a sudden loss of memory.

Mercifully, the ambulance finally arrived, and a still-protesting Nona Allanson was carried out on a stretcher. Pat hopped on the jump seat in the back beside her, and Jean sat next to the driver. The old lady was the object of a tug-of-war between them, and neither of them had done much to calm her down. Nona didn't believe what Jean had told her, that Paw had been poisoned. Sadly, she no longer trusted her own daughter. Pat had convinced her that she was going off for some terrible tests, that her insurance wouldn't cover the cost, and that she would be barred from seeing anyone she trusted and loved.

Bob Tedford was completely exasperated with Pat. "I can't stop you from going with her," he stated flatly, "but I don't want you talking to her on the way to the hospital. Do you understand that?" Pat looked back at him defiantly. No one had ever shut her up when she had something to say, and she wasn't about to obey commands now. By this time, Nona Allanson believed everything Pat told her.

Everything.

Over Pat's objections, Jean asked Lieutenant Thornhill to padlock her parents' home the moment the Radcliffes vacated it. Pat insisted that it was *her* duty to live there, that that would make Nona feel more secure, but Jean just pursed her lips and shook her head. She didn't know what it was about Pat that had mesmerized her parents, but she was going to find out. In the meantime, she would try to protect whatever assets they had left.

"Padlock those doors, Gus," she pleaded. "And don't let anybody in unless I say so."

Pat talked continually to Nona on the short ride to the hospital, but once there, the old woman was whisked off to the emergency room, where no one could see her but hospital personnel.

If someone had adulterated Nona's food or beverages with arsenic, it would show up in tests. As doctors worked over Nona, Jean hurried to her father's room to let him know that his cherished wife was now safe in the hospital, only a few doors away from his own room. His attorney, Bill Hamner, was visiting him. Jean demanded that Pat's power of attorney over Nona and Paw's affairs be terminated at once. "She's still using it."

Hamner agreed to see that Pat's control over the elderly Allansons' estate was stopped. Just like Dr. Jones, Hamner and his partner, Fred Reeves, had been impressed with Pat, finding her almost martyrlike in her steadfast care of the old couple. Whenever she had approached their offices, it had always been on matters seemingly instigated by Paw Allanson. She appeared so ill herself, but she never complained, spending her slight energy in caring for the Allansons. Even now, a moment or two after Jean had warned Hamner about Pat, she limped into Paw's room and motioned the lawyer over for a private consultation.

At first Bill Hamner found himself between a rock and a hard place. Jean watched with crossed arms and a baleful glare as he talked to Pat. She thought Pat was an evil, manipulative force in her parents' lives. Pat considered Jean a money-grabbing, ungrateful daughter. In the end, the choice was simple for the attorneys. Hamner and Reeves represented the elder Allansons, and they would do what seemed best for them.

32

On June 29, Paw Allanson gave Bob Tedford a written Consent to Search waiver for his home and property. Accompanied by W. L. Jackson and Jean Boggs, Tedford searched the padlocked house. They removed six liquor and wine bottles, some empty and some full and still sealed. Jean identified some expensive whiskey as long-ago Christmas gifts, and the blackberry wines Paw had made decades before. "Spirits" had always been kept out in the shed, but these were found in the kitchen and the bedroom areas. They also cleaned out the refrigerator of liquids: tea, ice water, prune juice. A syringe was removed from the bathroom and labeled.

None of the items taken proved positive for arsenic.

◆ ◆ ◆

On July 1, Colonel Radcliffe appeared at the East Point police headquarters at Bob Tedford's request. Tedford said calmly, "You are a suspect in an attempted murder," and advised Radcliffe of his rights under *Miranda*.

The ramrod-straight ex-colonel's face blanched, reflecting shock, denial, and perhaps just a trace of apprehension. Tedford didn't yet know enough about Pat Allanson to be aware of the blanket of protection that had been spread tenderly over her by her family from the moment she was born. He didn't realize that Colonel Radcliffe and his wife, Margureitte, had spent much of their married life saving Pat from the pickles, messes, and downright catastrophes she had managed to provoke.

Tedford had seen Pat as a tearful, helpless, beautiful woman who made a man want to protect her—then had watched her change in an instant into a strident harridan. She had been outrageous as she frightened the old lady to keep her out of the hospital, but she had been completely convincing when he and Turner talked to her and she sobbed out her fears and losses. Tedford wasn't sure *which* woman Pat really was. The more he knew about her, the more elusive she became.

Colonel Radcliffe offered no more information on Pat. He stared glacially at Tedford when the detective said he wanted to talk more about the Saturday morning of June 12, the day Pat and the Radcliffes had rushed to save Nona from her "berserk" husband. Radcliffe's memory of that day was not nearly as precise as it once had been.

"Let me ask you, Colonel Radcliffe," Tedford said. "Have you ever gone with your daughter and Nona Allanson to see an attorney, or been present when either of the senior Allansons signed papers?"

"Not to my knowledge."

"Does Pat have powers of attorney from Paw and Nona Allanson?"

"Yes, I believe she does. You would have to ask Pat about that. I don't get involved."

"Have you seen Pat lately?"

The colonel looked vague. "Not for a couple of days."

"Where is she?"

"You would, of course, have to ask her attorney. Look, Sergeant, I have to go back to work." Colonel Radcliffe had taken a civil service desk job at Fort Mac to help stem the burgeoning financial costs of Pat's "problems." "Am I under arrest or not?"

"No, you can go."

The next day, July 2, the results were in on the tests done on

Nona Allanson. Her urine samples proved positive for arsenic, although the concentration was only one-sixth the amount found in her husband's system. Her hair samples also showed the presence of the deadly poison. Her urine had 100 micrograms of arsenic per milligram, and her hair tested 3.5 micrograms per milligrams of arsenic.

Nona had been bedridden, unable to prepare food for herself, certainly unable to go outside her tiny home. Everything she ingested had been given to her by Pat, or by the nurse hired by Pat. Her other regular visitors were Margureitte and Clifford Radcliffe; Pat's daughter, Debbie Taylor Cole; and the Radcliffes' neighbor, Fanny K. Cash. Nona had lost all contact with her own blood relatives.

She had not fared well with her new "family."

George "Homer" Boggs stopped by the East Point police station that same afternoon. He had with him a check drawn on the Allansons' account at First National Bank in the amount of a thousand dollars, signed by Pat Allanson under her power of attorney and deposited immediately in her own account. She had no legal right to do that; the papers giving her power of attorney over the elder Allansons' considerable assets specifically designated that she was to use their money only to take care of them, *or* with special permission.

When Tedford asked him later, Paw Allanson said that he had not given his consent for this check. He *had* gone with Pat to the C&S Bank in late May or early June and arranged a thousand-dollar loan to Pat to help Tommy. That check had its purpose written right on it: "For Tom's Life." The second check for a thousand dollars, however, was news to Paw.

Tom had needed that thousand-dollar loan; he had one last appeal left to him, and Dunham McAllister was trying to see that he got it. It had been almost exactly two years since Walter and Carolyn Allanson were shot to death. For East Point detectives on this new case, it would be the second Fourth of July they had spent investigating the Allanson family while the rest of Atlanta was celebrating Independence Day.

A few days later, Lieutenant Jackson and Sergeant Tedford were poring over the confession for the twentieth time. Suddenly, they noticed that on the last page of the statement, something had been x-ed out. Reading carefully *through* the x's, they could make out the phrase "Dixie Cup Morgan Classic, Stone Mountain." The first seven lines on the last page appeared to have been typed at a different time than the rest of the text. They were indented more than the others and typed at a different margin setting.

James H. Kelly, chief document examiner for the Georgia Bureau of Investigation's crime laboratory, verified that the last page of the confession had not been typed continuously with the other text on the page. "After the first paragraph was typed," he wrote, "the paper was adjusted by either taking it out of the carriage and reinsert[ing it, or it was] moved while in the carriage."

That would make sense; if the notary public *had* glanced over the page she stamped, she would have seen only sentences about ". . . If Mama dies before I do," and nothing at all about guns and murder.

Now the detectives had to find someone who was connected with Morgan horses. And they already knew who that was.

✦   ✦   ✦

Both Paw and Nona Allanson had ingested arsenic, given to them in some way that they could not detect. The East Point police and the Fulton County D.A.'s investigators hoped to trace the source of that arsenic. They began by checking through the myriad prescription drugs that Dr. Jones had gathered up at the Allansons' home. There were over fifty vials, packets, boxes, and bottles. Some of them went back to August 1950, and there were also the drugs that Dr. Jones had prescribed recently. Apparently, the old couple never threw a container of medicine out as long as there were a few pills left.

Eventually, they were all identified. There were pain pills, tranquilizers, diuretics, antivertigo pills, sleeping pills, allergy pills, decongestants, antacids, and antibiotics. Analyzed at the Georgia Bureau of Investigation's crime lab, none of them contained arsenic.

A police sweep of the house had also produced a brown bag containing white powder, a jar with a green cap containing brown granular material, a jar with a red cap containing the same, and a glass bottle with a white cap containing white powder.

None of these substances proved to contain arsenic.

The bottle that Paw had allegedly been drinking from on the morning Pat and her parents broke in to "rescue" Nona *did* contain arsenic. In fact, according to toxicologists Drs. Solomons and McGurdy, it still contained so much arsenic that, if the old man had been drinking from it, a swig or two would have surely killed him where he stood.

Dr. Jones, of course, had never actually seen Paw with that old-timey bottle; Pat had handed it to him.

While arsenic is a poison much beloved by fictional mystery writers, by 1974 it was not nearly as available as it once was. Nor is it a particularly good choice as a murder weapon. Its residue stays in the body for all time. It is also an extremely painful poison. The investigators could not find a case on record where arsenic had been used for suicide; it is just too agonizing and protracted a way to die. If Paw Allanson had planned to kill himself and his ailing wife, there were so many other methods that would have worked more rapidly, and with far less pain.

Bob Tedford began the tedious task of interviewing veterinarians in the East Point area who might have treated the Allansons' or Radcliffes' animals. He finally located the vet who treated the Radcliffes' horses. Asked if he ever used arsenic on horses, the vet replied, "No. Old-timers used to use it to treat horses for worms, but I don't know anybody who does these days. I use a chemical that serves the same purpose. It takes longer, but it's easier on the animals."

The vet did mention a drug used to stimulate appetite in horses: Appitone. As far as he knew, it had been off the market for two years. "It contains arsenic, but I doubt if it has enough to kill anyone. I bought the last dose of it from another doctor because one of my clients requested it."

"Mrs. Allanson?" Tedford asked quickly.

The vet shook his head. "Nope. Someone else. I had to search awhile before I located any Appitone."

Another drug, known as Caco Copper, was used to encourage bone marrow in horses to produce red blood cells. "People say it has arsenic in it," the vet said, "but it doesn't."

"When was the last time you treated Mrs. Allanson's horses?"

"Let's see." The doctor consulted his records. "It was January 29, 1974. I treated one of the girls' horses for a vitamin deficiency. I never gave Pat—Mrs. Allanson—any medicines. And the *only* medications I use with arsenic in them are injectables. I never hand them out to anyone else."

"You know of any doctor still using arsenic routinely?" Tedford asked.

"Nope. It's really an obsolete treatment."

Asked how well he knew Pat Allanson, the veterinarian looked away. "I never dated her. She made it clear that she was available, though. She was trouble. All the vets knew that. A couple of years back—before I was married and my present wife and I were just dating—Pat called her up and caused some real problems with what she said."

Tedford got the same information from a number of local doctors who treated show horses. One vet, who clearly disliked both Tom and Pat, snorted, "She's a real come-on. She throws herself at every man she sees." Another veterinarian looked nervous as he said he had never heard of the name Allanson. Tedford learned later from a confidential informant that the doctor knew Pat very well indeed. He had dated her—but he'd been married at the time, and he was still married. His reluctance to discuss her with the investigators was understandable.

Don Birch of the Georgia State Drug Inspector's Office told a Fulton County D.A.'s investigator that he had checked all the drugstores in Zebulon, Grantville, Griffin, and Barnesville for any arsenic sales to either Pat or Tom Allanson in the prior two years and found no record of such a sale. "Very few of the pharmacies sell arsenic in any form at all," Birch said. "It's not sold in powder form anymore. The only thing anybody uses arsenic for is to kill rats, treat dog mange, and heartworms in horses."

Rat poison came in liquid form—in six-ounce bottles. There were no dusty medicine bottles out in Paw Allanson's barn or shed. If he had ever used old-fashioned preparations to treat his animals, medicines containing arsenic, they were no longer on his premises.

✦ ✦ ✦

The news media had heard rumors about "poisonings" in East Point. On July 8, Detective Sergeant Tedford was close-mouthed, hinting only that "as many as four persons might be arrested." He refused to name those persons. There were too many missing elements of the case yet to be revealed.

One very large segment was added when the investigators learned from Paw Allanson's attorneys, Fred Reeves and Bill Hamner, that there had been no fewer than *three* codicils to the elder Allansons' wills in a relatively short time. The original wills, drawn on September 11, 1974—two months after Walter and Carolyn were murdered—named Tom and his aunt Jean Boggs as coexecutors of Paw and Nona's estates. On March 4 of 1975, after Pat had made herself indispensable to the old couple, the first codicils added Pat as a coexecutor, in case Tom could not serve. The attorneys said they had gone to the Allansons' home and no one else was present as Paw and Nona signed the documents.

The second codicils came on August 1, 1975. Jean Boggs was removed completely as an executor, although she still received certain assets under terms of her parents' wills. Reeves and Hamner had been very careful to see that both Allansons read and understood each section of the codicils. If Pat Allanson was in the house at the time, she was not present at the signing.

On January 20, 1976, after Paw had his heart attack, Pat was given a sweeping power of attorney. And finally, on February 4, 1976, when Nona and Paw were both hospitalized for extended care at South Fulton, the third codicils changed the distribution of the elderly Allansons' fortune completely. Jean was eliminated altogether as an heir. Paw and Nona Allanson's current wills dictated that their assets would be distributed thusly:

(1) Fifty percent (50%) of the trust estate; or all real estate, farm animals, jewelry, clothing, household goods, furniture and furnishings, pictures, silverware, objects of art and automobiles . . . shall be distributed to my grandson, Tom Allanson, if he be in life. If my grandson, Tom Allanson, be not in life and is married to Patricia R. Allanson at his death [a clause that Hamner and Reeves had insisted on] then the property named in this subparagraph shall pass and be distributed to Patricia R. Allanson.

(2) The remaining portion of my trust estate shall be divided equally between my grandson, Tom Allanson, my grandson, David Byron Boggs, and my granddaughter Nona Lisa Boggs.

(3) I have specifically excluded my daughter, Jean Elizabeth Boggs, from any distribution of my estate. I have done this as my

daughter has adequately provided for herself and I have further decided that recent changes and events concerning the Allanson family situation dictate that my estate could best be utilized and would be more beneficial to the aforenamed individuals.

Tom Allanson was, indeed, "in life," but he was also in *for* life. What the third codicils to his grandparents' wills really meant was that, should they die, his wife, Pat, would control 66⅔ percent of a very healthy inheritance. She would have Tom's half of the entire trust, *plus* Tom's third of the half that he shared equally with his two cousins. She would also be the executor. Anything the old couple had *beyond* the trust assets would also go to Pat.

As long as Tom was in prison.

Tom was cut off from his family; his information was controlled by his wife. Her letters and infrequent visits were his only window on the world outside, and she didn't fill him in on all the boring details of wills and codicils. She kept assuring him that she was fighting to get him out. His last chance would be coming up in November.

Tom had no idea how dicey things were at home.

33

All through the melting-hot July of 1976, Pat and the Radcliffes waited for the other shoe to drop. The damnable East Point police were snooping into every facet of Pat's life, asking questions, testing everything they carted out of Paw and Nona's house. The police were so rude; they clearly had no breeding at all. They had been rude to her mother and the colonel too, and it was unnerving to hear Bob Tedford tell the newspapers that *four people might be arrested.*

Tedford talked to one of Nona Allanson's nurses, Juanita Jackson, who had cared for the elderly woman after Paw was hospitalized. Juanita had noticed that Nona seemed inordinately drowsy, and Pat had explained that she was taking some pills and needed one every twenty-four hours. She showed Juanita a bottle of green and gray capsules. But the old woman slept so much that the practical nurse had suggested to Pat, "Let's don't give her any more of this medication." She didn't know whether Pat had taken her advice or not. Mrs. Allanson remained quite groggy.

The sedative Vistaril came in a green and gray capsule in twenty-five-milligram doses, usually given three or four times a day. It had been prescribed for Paw—not Nona—and it was to be given cautiously as it had a depressive effect, particularly when combined with other medications.

"Who cooked?" Tedford asked.

"Pat did some, and sometimes she brought in food. I did some, and the night nurse did some."

The only visitor Juanita recalled in the weeks between June 15 and June 28 was a pleasant, heavyset woman named Fanny K. Cash. But there was another visitor. Mrs. Amelia Estes had been Nona and Paw's neighbor for nineteen years. She was appalled to find her old friend in a sorry state when she called on Nona one day after Paw was hospitalized.

"I found her different from what I had ever seen before," she told Tedford. "You could tell something was wrong because she looked . . . drugged. She didn't really know anybody or know what she was doing or saying. . . . Pat asked her if she wanted to go out on the porch, and we rolled her out there. Pat went to the mailbox and I sat there with her, but she could not hold her head up for any length of time . . . and if she came up, her eyes were rolling and wallowing around. There was something desperately wrong someway."

Mrs. Estes had also been let in on Paw's supposed confession. "I started to leave and Pat asked me if I had a few minutes. . . . She wanted to tell me about Mr. Allanson signing a confession to the murder of Walter and Carolyn! Of course it was a terrible shock to me to think that such had been done. . . . She said she had a terrible time getting him to sign it because he thought if he lived through this, they couldn't pin anything on him. She said that he had confessed to her while he was in the hospital— and she was crying—and said she had to live with this without telling anybody for so long, and nobody would ever know what she had gone through after getting the confession and having to keep it to herself."

✦   ✦   ✦

On July 20, Tedford left a call for Colonel Radcliffe, asking for another interview. Radcliffe returned the call and pointedly asked, "Are you going to be advising me of my rights again?"

"Yes, I will be."

"Well, then I'm not coming in."

"You can have your attorney present during any interview."

"I can't afford an attorney. You'll have to provide one. No, I don't believe I will consent to an interview."

On July 26, Colonel Radcliffe changed his mind. He and his wife came in with their attorney and gave a formal statement to Tedford and Investigator Richard Daniell. As always, the Radcliffes were very proper, very precise in their speaking patterns, and they maintained their position of annoyed dignity, as if it were patently ridiculous for people of their social standing to actually speak with the police. Margureitte Radcliffe was the more talkative—as she always was. Her husband began most of his answers with "To the best of my knowledge . . ." and "Not to my knowledge."

Everything—*everything*—they said dovetailed with their daughter's recall of events at Paw and Nona Allanson's home. Yes, the old woman had most assuredly been terrified of "Big Allanson" and had begged them to come and save her from Paw. They had done what decent Christian people would do.

Margureitte recalled that the bad weekend in June had really begun on Wednesday afternoon, June 9. Nona had called the Radcliffe home on Tell Road to say she had had nothing to eat, she had wet herself, and needed help. "I said I had no transportation at the moment, but whoever got to the house first would come over," Margureitte said. "My husband and I went . . . and gave her some water. . . . I cleaned her up. . . . Mr. Allanson said he was feeling not so good, his legs were a little weak and had been bothering him, and he had not been able to do anything for her."

Margureitte and Pat had stayed that night with the old couple. Things had, of course, been worse on Saturday morning when the colonel had to break into the house. Neither of them had actually *seen* Paw swallow any pills. Colonel Radcliffe thought it might have been Tang, and not orange juice, that Paw had been drinking. They had both seen the old whiskey bottle.

"*I* saw a pint bottle," Margureitte explained, "and I haven't the remotest idea of what it was. . . . By the freezer, there's a mangle thing—there was *a bottle* . . . and the doctor had said, 'Get everything out of his way.' Mrs. Allanson [Pat] said, 'Pour it out,' and before I could say 'beans,' my husband took it in the bathroom and politely turned it up and poured it out. I said, 'Maybe you shouldn't have poured it out—because Dr. Jones possibly will want to look at it.' "

Both the Radcliffes stressed that it was Dr. Jones who had planted the idea of an "overdose" in their minds. Margureitte added some details, however, to Paw's bizarrely assaultive behavior. "She [Nona] . . . said at one point he [Paw] held her mouth and said, 'Drink this coffee!' *But it wasn't coffee.''* Her voice lowered to a dramatic whisper. "Now I said to her, 'Ma, you mean he didn't have anything?' And she said, 'I mean it *wasn't coffee.'* . . . Then she said he had pulled her hair and tried to smother her with a pillow. She said at one point, he had tried to wrap her up in the sheets!"

"Were you aware," Richard Daniell asked suddenly, "that Tom Allanson and your daughter, Pat, at the time back in June —in the event of either Mr. or Mrs. Allanson dying—that they would get almost everything according to the wills?"

Margureitte sighed deeply. "I know Nona's *told* me that she wanted to change her will. I don't know *what* the feelings are in that family, and, frankly, I wish I'd never heard of any of them! I'll be perfectly honest with you; they've really just torn us apart. They don't even like each other—can't even tolerate each other."

The detectives were fascinated to hear the Radcliffes backing off on vital specifics and filling in dramatic details elsewhere in their statements. Most of all, they were interested to see just the slightest fraying at the edges of this couple's facade of elegant detachment. They were protesting too much.

The Radcliffes announced that they had a witness *outside* the family who could back up their recall of old Walter Allanson's aggressive behavior: Fanny K. Cash, their good neighbor on Tell Road. Fanny had, in fact, accompanied them to the East Point Police Department. She too was advised of her rights under *Miranda* and didn't bat an eye. Although Fanny had not seen the elderly Allansons for a month, Pat and the Radcliffes had prevailed upon her to spend that Saturday night at the Allanson home, so that Pat wouldn't be alone. She had agreed to go, as long as they would see she got to church on Sunday morning. She was very active, she explained, in church activities and ladies' circle meetings.

Fanny Kate had packed up her bag, and Pat had picked her

up. It must have been somewhat crowded in the Washington Road house; there were only two bedrooms, and Nona was in hers and Paw was in the guest room. Pat had said *she* had slept in bed with Nona. Fanny K. would have had to bunk on a couch.

Fanny said she had been told that Paw had been taking something that put him "to sleep." "Mrs. Radcliffe is a trained nurse, and she knows when she sees some of these things."

Asked about liquor bottles, Fanny recalled seeing only one. "It was just a plain old liquor bottle with no label on it—and what was in it smelt enough. It would have knocked a polecat down to have smelt it, whatever it was. And I said, 'Well, if anybody drank *that,* they were bad off with something!' "

"Who told you he [Paw] had been drinking out of this bottle?" Tedford asked.

"Mrs. Allanson did—Grandma—did. I asked her plainly. She said she thought he had quit drinking; he had promised her that. And she seemed to be very much disturbed because he had taken it behind her back. . . ."

"In other words, the Radcliffes or Pat Allanson didn't tell you?"

"No."

"Where did you see this bottle?"

"It was there in the laundry room."

Fanny K. Cash said she had known the Radcliffes for almost ten years. "There are no finer people nowhere than they are," she added.

✦ ✦ ✦

July in Atlanta was so hot that even the kudzu vines drooped, and the days passed sluggishly, the only sound on a hot afternoon the buzz of flies and cicadas. The big news in Georgia was the nomination of Jimmy Carter on July 14 as the Democratic candidate for president, with Walter Mondale as his running mate. Carter would be the first major party nominee from the Deep South since the ill-fated Zachary Taylor ran in 1848. Political news eclipsed crime news in the Atlanta papers. Still, for those involved in the Allanson investigation—or fearful of involvement—there was only one story.

Everybody was jumpy. Martha Foster, one of the Allansons'

practical nurses from the Quality Care referral service, had been staying in the empty Washington Road house, in case either of the Allansons could come home from the hospital. In late July, she went to the emergency room of the South Fulton Hospital, vomiting and complaining of terrible pains in her abdomen. She was transferred to Grady Hospital, where Bob Tedford found her. He asked her how long she had been staying at the Allansons' house.

"I've been out there since last Wednesday—the twenty-first."

"When did you get sick?"

"Sunday, yesterday."

"What did you eat there?"

"Just some frozen hot dogs that were in the freezer. The only other thing I had there was the coffee and the Pream—that powdered cream substitute stuff."

Mrs. Foster's urine was checked for arsenic. It was negative. The hot dogs were gone. The coffee and Pream were analyzed. Arsenic in powder form can be white or brownish or yellow—or even red. Test samples proved to be only coffee and Pream. However, another vial of pills was found, a prescription with Nona Allanson's name on the label. There was one capsule inside that was different from the rest.

The capsule had a pill inside; analysis of the pill showed it was mercury. In some forms, mercury can be a deadly poison. *Liquid* mercury, however, is not as lethal. The investigators learned that it had once been an accepted treatment for constipation, way back in the twenties and thirties. Since the old couple had kept pills for twenty-five years, it was possible that they had kept some even longer. But the pill-within-a-capsule was not liquid; it was compressed powder. Deadly. Why was there a single capsule with mercury in it in a modern prescription container?

On July 26, Nona Allanson was released from the hospital and returned to the house on Washington Road. Her daughter Jean would henceforth be in charge of her care. Paw Allanson remained in South Fulton Hospital in fair condition.

✦ ✦ ✦

Dunham McAllister was using old Walter Allanson's confession as the focal point of his strategy to free Tom. On July 30,

McAllister filed a motion requesting a hearing in Fulton County Superior Court to determine whether a new trial was warranted for Walter Thomas Allanson, since someone else had confessed to the crimes for which he had been convicted. The Fulton County D.A.'s Office denounced the confession as worthless. They had Paw's affidavit repudiating it.

Still, the new activity gave Tom the first hope he had had in a long time. There was an irony here; if Tom *should* be freed, would he be reunited with his wife? Or would they be like the old fable—the fox, the goose, and the grain—where one was always onshore and the others in the boat? It was beginning to look as if Pat might go to prison herself.

The time had come to fish or cut bait. Andy Weathers of the D.A.'s office believed that they could get convictions. At least it was worth a try; to simply walk away from a case where two elderly people had nearly died would be unconscionable. How many names would be on the indictments? Four? Three? More than four?

On August 6, 1976, Bob Tedford appeared before the grand jury and presented the evidence his team of detectives had gathered on the arsenic poisonings of Nona and Walter Allanson. Much of it was circumstantial, and it would be a squeaker. He had to show motive, method, and opportunity on the part of someone with murder in his or her heart.

Pat Allanson had had the motive to want her husband's grandparents dead—two motives really: she was both heir and executor of their wills and she needed money to live the life she longed for and to get "her Tom" out of prison. She had had the opportunity: she had the victims' total trust. And she could very easily have had the means. The arsenic in that old whiskey bottle had, perhaps, been "squirreled away" out in the barn, way back in the days when Paw was an active farmer. Or perhaps it had recently been purchased, supposedly to kill rats. The prosecution team couldn't prove either theory; they had never found the actual source of the arsenic. As for what had taken place in the house on Washington Road, four stories matched much *too* closely—Pat's, Margureitte Radcliffe's, Colonel Radcliffe's, and Fanny K. Cash's. Meanwhile, the stories of Amelia Estes, Jean Boggs, and her friend Sherry Allen were diametrically opposed to the first story.

No one knew what might happen behind the closed doors of the grand jury, but that very day in the first week of August, the Fulton County grand jury returned an indictment.

Only one.

The Fulton County District Attorney's Office immediately issued an arrest warrant charging Patricia Radcliffe Taylor Allanson with two counts of criminal attempt to commit murder. At 4:15 that afternoon, Bob Tedford and Richard Daniell from the D.A.'s office drove to the Tell Road horse ranch to arrest Pat. She was not at home, nor was she there when they returned at 5:00 P.M.

Would she run? Had she already left the Atlanta area? She must have known that she was the main target of their investigation, that something was going to come down. Still, the detectives reasoned that Pat Allanson's whole world was contained in Georgia and North Carolina. She had her mother and stepfather, her doting aunts, her three children, her grandchildren, and, of course, her husband, Tom. No, she wouldn't leave.

They didn't realize how right they were. Pat had never been on her own. She *had* to be close to her parents. Even though she was nearly forty, she still needed them to be there, to straighten things out whenever they got out of control. But now her life had finally spun completely off its track and her machinations would not be easy to smooth over and deny.

At 7:00 P.M., Tedford and Daniell drove slowly down Tell Road, turned right onto the rutted drive, and passed Fanny K. Cash's cabin. They drove by the empty stables on the left, and then headed down past the show ring toward the two conjoined houses that Gil Taylor had once tried to make into a grand plantation for Pat.

Margureitte and Clifford Radcliffe stood in the front yard. They stared coldly at the two investigators but grudgingly accepted the warrant Tedford held out. "We are here to arrest your daughter on two charges of criminal attempt to commit murder. Is she here?"

Colonel Radcliffe led Daniell and Tedford into the house and pointed toward Pat's bedroom. She was home. She listened sullenly as the charges against her were read.

"May I call my attorney?" Pat asked.

"Yes, ma'am."

Pat's bubble-cut hair was as carefully coiffed as always. Her makeup was in place. She wore a short pink-and-black plaid sundress, a necklace, and hoop earrings.

While Tedford radioed for a female officer to accompany them on the ride to jail, Pat phoned Dunham McAllister. She spoke to him for about fifteen minutes, and then Daniell and Tedford and Officer Bebe Mozeman left the Radcliffes' house at 7:35 and proceeded to the Fulton County jail, where Pat was finger-printed, photographed, searched, and booked.

She looked straight ahead defiantly as she faced the jail camera, but she bent her head and appeared ready to cry when she was instructed to "look at the wall to your left." The woman who had wanted so much, who had aspired to a life of perfect love, gracious living, wealth, and social acceptance, was—at least for the moment—Prisoner No. 10747 in the Fulton County jail.

She would not stay in jail long. Already her mother and step-father were rallying around her, arranging for money to bail her out, to bring her back to her room in their home. She was their child, their precious daughter, the focus of their lives. It was unthinkable that she should be exposed to the sort of women who ended up in jail. *She* was a special person.

Pat didn't even spend the night in jail. She was released on twenty thousand dollars' bond that evening. Somewhere, Boppo and Colonel Radcliffe had found the two thousand dollars necessary to guarantee that amount.

34

His wife's arrest came as a tremendous shock to Tom. She was his sole source of information about the outside world, and Pat had continued to assure him that she was moving heaven and earth to free him. He had been relieved and proud that she had taken over the care of his grandparents. From all her reports, things were going as well as they could hope for, considering how old Paw and Nona were. Tom had been told about Paw's supposed overdose, but not about the crime lab's findings. Pat had convinced him that it was not unusual for an old man, depressed by his diminishing strength after a heart attack, to turn to liquor and pills.

Tom loved his grandparents; at the same time, he was compelled to see them as his sole source of financial rescue. Given Pat's illnesses and inability to work and the Radcliffes' near bankruptcy, there *was* no one else with financial assets who might help him. Tom had written Paw and Nona scores of letters urging them to trust Pat and to put all their affairs into her hands. *He* had trusted Pat, and he had survived in prison by dreaming about the time they would all live together on a good farm. He had needed his grandfather's backing—but he had every intention of paying him back.

Pat had assured him she felt the same way.

Tom was doing well in prison. Everybody liked him, and he was much in demand as a clerk. He was college educated, smart, and never complained about the work load. He *needed* the work. He had lost damn near everything in his life—except for Pat and his grandparents.

If Tom believed that the charges against Pat were true, it would mean the end of all his dreams. He would be left with no one. He tried to find some other reason for what was happening to her. It was hard going.

Tom had written to his uncle Seaborn and begged that Pat at least be allowed to see his children whenever she could; she was Tom's only link to them. He didn't know that he had already lost his children, perhaps forever. Seaborn had realized he was too old to raise young children, and Little Carolyn refused to conform to the state's requirements for a custodial parent. Pat didn't want the children, and she had already used Tom's power of attorney to sign away all his links to Russ and Sherry. She had convinced him that they were being placed only temporarily in a good Christian home—"for *their* sake." But she had really agreed to put them out for permanent adoption.

All he had left was Pat. From the moment he first became intimate with her, Tom had committed himself to her, to her beliefs, her advice, her plans and dreams. But by the late summer of 1976, even Tom saw that her perfect facade had begun to erode. Resolutely, he fought his doubts back. If Pat was *not* his one true love, he would have to admit that he had let his whole life slip away for nothing.

Tom had quickly realized that nobody in Jackson—from the guards to the administrative staff—liked Pat. He loved her enough that he could ignore the snide remarks and the smirks when he received her daily letters. He took the lacy, fancy-decorated envelopes in his big hands and hurried to read his mail in privacy. But later he would remember that her letters caused him all manner of problems. "We were allowed to get *legal* mail uncensored, so Pat would get some lawyer's letterhead envelopes and then she'd put *personal* mail inside. They caught onto that quick enough, and they'd call me in and say, 'This is *marked* legal mail, but we're going to open it in front of you.' Sure enough, there would be personal mail inside, and I'd get chewed out."

Pat's visits were even more difficult for Tom. She wore her skirts cut up to here, and her blouses cut down to there, and no man in the area could resist swiftly turning his eyes in her direction. She was as inappropriate as she was beautiful. It was agonizing enough for Tom to be shut off from her; her provocative clothes and her Jungle Gardenia perfume about drove him nuts. And then she always had stories to tell him about men who were bothering her. He questioned her—gently—suggesting that a woman as attractive as she was had to be careful of even the appearance of availability. That only made her angry. She demanded to know how he could even *imagine* that she cared one fig for any other man? Was he trying to say she was a slut?

Tom sighed. Pat never saw anything in gradations of meaning; she saw white or black—more often black—and was quick to take offense.

He didn't believe that she would deliberately hurt Paw and Nona. He *couldn't* believe that. The police had been quick enough to jump on *him,* and he remembered how he had been a free man one day and a convict the next. He knew what had really happened that July night two years ago—or he thought he did. The law could twist things and make them seem more menacing than they really were. Pat was only one frail, little woman. She had a temper and she sure wasn't the most reasonable woman in the world, but he could not visualize her really hurting anyone. He did not want to think of her actually putting poison in his own grandparents' food. That was a scenario that shut itself off in his mind the moment he tried to visualize it. He was barely maintaining his equilibrium as it was, and the rush of guilt that came with thinking about Pat hurting Paw and Nona almost knocked the wind out of him.

✦ ✦ ✦

As Pat awaited her own trial, free on bail, she grew more frenetic and querulous. Her prison visits to Tom always meant trouble of one kind or another. Tom both longed to see her and dreaded what she might do next. She wasn't helping his case.

Even the warden at Jackson took an interest in Tom and his incorrigible wife. Tom remembered one day when the warden was leading a tour through the prison. "He came over to me and he told me, 'Tom, you're doing a good job and everything, but your wife is creating one hell of a lot of waves downtown. She's not helping you. Would you please calm her down?' "

That was easier said than done.

Pat's accusations were familiar. Nobody really cared about her, she loved him so, and she tried so hard. She was doing her best for him, even though she was sick and scared to death that they were trying to send her to prison too. If that happened, who would care about him anymore?

It got worse and worse. "She claimed some of the corrections officers raped her," Tom remembered. *"One* of them supposedly did, anyway. She said they followed her in a state car . . . to the expressway, and handcuffed her and raped her. . . . She even came back and said one of them cut her up with a knife."

Tom had seen the marks. Pat indeed had bruises that appeared to be from handcuffs, and numerous cuts on her back, legs, and breasts. Superficial cuts. Tom might have been a fool for love, but he wasn't a plain fool. He had to question Pat's outrageous stories. He wondered how so many terrible things could happen to one woman. When he looked at the wounds she showed him, he wondered even more.

"Every one of them you could tell was self-inflicted—from the direction it went and how deep it was," he later said. "You know, even at the time I didn't believe her because I *knew* those officers and they were good men. They wouldn't do something like that, but I just passed it off as one of 'Pat's things.' "

Not long ago, back when he was free—or even when he had a slight hope of being free—Tom had found Pat's dramatic ways endearing, possibly a little exciting. She fainted the way old-time southern women did, slipping to the ground in a heap. He had liked bringing a single rose to his pale, stricken love as she lay in bed, gently suffering from some mysterious, womanly ailment.

But "Pat's things" weren't so endearing anymore. Not to anyone. She had always used sexual attacks as an attention-getting device. She had screamed rape at the slightest provocation for the past two decades. She had told Susan and Debbie that she had been molested when she was a child. And then there were all the rapes in Germany. Her obsession with sexual assaults was growing shopworn and, in the aftermath of her arrest, she seemed to be getting worse.

One evening in the summer of 1976, when Debbie and Susan had taken Dawn to the emergency room at South Fulton Hospital—she had been wedged between Debbie's car door and the carport—Pat suddenly appeared in the waiting room with her panty hose around her ankles, sobbing and screaming that she had been raped. This time, she accused the East Point police detectives; she said they had pretended they were going to question her, but instead they had handcuffed her and sexually abused her. "How can you *do* this?" Debbie cried. "Get out of here!"

With Boppo on her heels, Pat had leaped into her watermelon red Cougar and driven along the hospital sidewalk. Susan and Debbie were mortified, but nobody took Pat's cries of rape seriously anymore.

Not even Tom.

He still loved Pat, but his head was beginning to clear. His true love now meant only pain. He did fine in between his wife's visits, but every time she came to see him or he talked to her on the phone, he was desolate. His counselor monitored the phone calls—with Tom's knowledge—and wondered how Tom could do his time with any degree of acceptance at all when his wife kept pulling at him with her siren songs. He recommended that Tom stop talking to his wife on the phone and Tom was surprised that he felt mostly relief that there would be no more hysterical conversations.

The letters did not stop; during the fall of 1976 Pat kept up her voluminous correspondence with Tom, holding on to him with stamps and scribbled lines, clinging for dear life. She wanted him to have her letters as quickly after she wrote them as possible. Almost every evening she drove east from the Tell Road ranch to some all-night restaurant along the freeway toward Jackson—a Denny's or a Shoney's or one of the waffle houses. Pat spent hours sipping coffee or a Coke as she wrote love letters on the Formica tabletops, oblivious to the bustle around her. Country and western ballads played in the background over the Muzak systems. She would look up when she heard one of their special songs—especially Dolly Parton and Porter Wagoner in their duet "Is Forever Longer Than Always?" Sometimes, she drove all the way to Jackson to mail the letters. That way, Tom would have them the very next morning.

Those evenings may have helped Pat forget what was looming ahead—that this time the trial was her own. It took so many country love songs, so many letters, so many long drives east to Jackson through the hot Georgia nights for her to force it to the back of her mind. It was unthinkable—but there it was. She was scheduled to go on trial the first week of November 1976.

✦ ✦ ✦

Susan Taylor Alford had been on a plane with her toddler son, Sean, flying back to Atlanta after a wonderful vacation in Key Biscayne at the moment her mother was arrested. The twenty-three-year-old Eastern Airlines flight attendant landed and soon learned the terrible news that the charge was attempted murder. More than the rest of the family, Susan had acknowledged that her mother had a real problem with prescription drugs, a long-standing addiction. Nobody else wanted to say it out loud. Heaven knows, Susan had seen her mother out of control on more than one occasion in recent years. But chasing someone with her crutch, or even running away hysterically in her nightgown, was far, far different from attempted murder.

"I thought that, if my mother had done what they said she did," Susan remembered, "then she was terribly, terribly ill. She couldn't be in her right mind. The drugs were telling her what to do. That couldn't be *my* mother. I kept thinking about the times she told me I was her friend, and how she was so proud of me—that I could do anything I set out to do. My mother could be the most wonderful person in the world when she wanted to."

Susan went to Dunham McAllister and pleaded with him to help Pat. She was convinced that Pat should not be tried on the merits of the case against her; she couldn't have known what she was doing. Someone had to step in and see that Pat was committed to a mental hospital where she could get help. "I thought my mother was sick," Susan later said. "I was so angry with Mr. McAllister when he wouldn't listen to me, when he wouldn't use my mother's illness as a defense. No one—*no one*—could convince me that my mother would have hurt anyone if she was in her right mind."

On October 28, 1976, Tom had his last chance for a new trial. Judge Wofford listened to McAllister's motion for a writ of error *coram nobis,* asking for a hearing requesting a new trial. Wofford read over the alleged confession of Paw Allanson and Paw's signed affidavit swearing that the confession was fake and that he had signed it only "through the deceit of Patricia R. Allanson." Wofford denied McAllister's motion.

Tom had now exhausted all of his appeals. The U.S. Supreme Court had refused to hear his case. He was desolate. He expected to serve "at least fourteen years on each of my two convictions."

✦　✦　✦

The Allansons were no longer relegated to the inside pages of Atlanta area newspapers. Their continuing saga made them front-page, headline news. Each story about Tom included a summary of Pat's pending trial. And each article concerning Pat included Tom's legal history.

But then the December 15, 1976, issue of *South Fulton Today,* a daily paper, featured an article on Pat that made no allusion at all to her postponed trial (it had been put off to January 1977), and had no reference to Tom, arsenic, murder, or anything embarrassing. That may have been because Pat had quietly dropped her married name. She was once again Pat Radcliffe, and a staff photo showed a pretty woman in profile, gazing at two dainty paper nosegays in her hand. In the ultimate rejection of reality, Pat Radcliffe was the subject of only a pleasant little feature story:

A Real Card
Local Resident Sends Old-Style Greetings

South Fulton resident Pat Radcliffe has a solution for persons who can't find the right card for that special person. Ms. Radcliffe designs and makes 18th-Century greeting cards that put most store-bought cards to shame.

A former horse trainer and instructor at Woodward Academy, Ms. Radcliffe has always liked "old-fashioned things" and has an artistic flair. While recuperating from an illness that left her unable to pursue her greatest love—horses—Ms. Radcliffe began making replicas of the 18th-Century cards to give to friends and various charitable organizations.

The article explained that Pat had formerly done portrait painting but had just begun to design her special cards.

"I didn't have any idea in two weeks' time that it would come to anything." Ms. Radcliffe has found that persons of all ages like the cards and are interested in having them done authentically. In making the cards, the Tell Road resident relies on books that show the various types of cards, as well as the help of an older friend, Fanny Kate Cash. . . . Ms. Radcliffe uses tweezers to put lace around the edges of cards and spends hours cutting out the tiny roses and other appliqués on the cards. . . . For a couple celebrating their 50th wedding anniversary, Ms. Radcliffe has fashioned a round card made out of satin and lace from the woman's wedding gown. In the center, hands reach out for a yellow rose, which has a special meaning to the couple.

Apparently, "Ms. Radcliffe" was being deluged with requests for her work, and the feature writer marveled that she also found time to create handmade bookmarks and hand-painted handkerchiefs.

The local resident, a former Hallmark Card employee, puts a message or one of the handkerchiefs in the back pocket of a card or fan. She also letters a verse on the front of the greeting card.

Pat explained that she did her own verses to suit.

Her grandchildren, Sean, 4, and Dawn, 5, also help her out by cutting things out for her and "gluing the simpler things.". . .
    "There are no two alike. People come to ask for something special. I consider them special cards for special people."

Pat had always loved the romance of bygone eras, and she was extremely artistic, although she had never worked for Hallmark as she told the reporter. She had been making dainty cards to surprise Tom ever since he was arrested. He had tons of cards and letters with tiny roses, lace, hearts, and intertwined hands.
    Lisa Richardson, the reporter who interviewed Pat, had not

asked Pat about other interesting aspects of her life, and Pat had not seen fit to mention that her card making might be interrupted soon when she went on trial in Fulton County Superior Court for attempted murder. She was, in fact, terrified of going to trial. She spent her time making cards, sewing dresses that she would wear to court, and placing phone calls to her beloved aunts in North Carolina. She begged them all to come to Atlanta and be with her during her trial. Boppo and Papa would be there, of course, and Susan and Debbie. But she wanted— needed—her whole family around her. The prosecutor was going to be rude—she was sure of it.

Susan, having had no luck at all convincing her mother's attorney to pursue an insanity defense, did whatever she could to help Pat. She delivered the old-fashioned greeting cards to her mother's customers, found new customers among her fellow employees at Eastern Airlines, and listened as Pat talked far into the night about her fears for the future.

The holiday season of 1976 was not a happy time on Tell Road, no matter how hard anyone tried to make things seem festive, at least for the sake of Sean and Dawn. Boppo and Papa had always made so much of Christmas, even dressing up like Mr. and Mrs. Santa Claus. But the specter of the trial ahead hovered over them, and the knowledge that bankruptcy for the Radcliffes was not far behind haunted them too.

Still, nobody blamed Pat. They saw her, as always, as the victim of cruel circumstance.

Largely due to Pat, the Radcliffes' lives had been fraught with loss, change, and upheaval. After staving off creditors for so long, they finally went bankrupt. The house on Tell Road was due to go on the block, a public humiliation that they narrowly avoided when a man who had worked with their horses came forward the day before the sheriff's sale and bought the property. Margureitte's perfect home on Dodson Drive was only a distant memory now; they were no longer homeowners at all. Margureitte and the colonel rented a house at 6438 Peacock Boulevard in Morrow, Georgia, a hamlet south on I-85. There would be no room for horses, no orchards or rose gardens. Just a plain house.

Pat moved with them, of course.

PART SIX

PAT'S
TRIAL

35

Dunham McAllister had originally been retained to represent Tom Allanson in his last chance for an appeal. But Tom had come to the end of his road. It was now Pat who needed all the lawyers she could afford. McAllister, a bearded, rumpled man in his thirties, and his wife, Margo, practiced law together in Jonesboro, Georgia. Because Pat's case was inextricably tangled with Tom's and because her life story was so filled with extraordinary events, McAllister had to immerse himself in research to prepare for trial. There were stacks of court transcripts to read, medical records, dozens of people to interview.

McAllister requested delays several times. Pat didn't go to trial in November, or in January. Indeed, it would be spring again before the proceedings to be known as *The State of Georgia v. Patricia R. Allanson* began on May 2, 1977, in the Honorable Elmo Holt's courtroom. That day, there was an ironic juxtaposition of items in *South Fulton Today:* the defendant's old world next to her present arena. Pictures of the Palmetto High School Horse Show, featuring a pretty young rider on a

Morgan horse, abutted a column headed, ALLANSON TRIAL SET
FOR TODAY.

Andy Weathers, assistant district attorney for Fulton County,
had been relieved by the long delays requested by the defense.
The case against Pat Allanson was no sure thing. Not at all. He
had had his own research to do. Weathers, like his opposing
counsel, was in his thirties. He had a thick shock of black hair
and penetrating dark eyes. His voice was as deep and rumbling
as thunder, and his mind lightning quick. He knew he had to be
ready when he went into court. Judge Holt's trials were jugger-
nauts; once they got going, nobody dared ask for delays. The
Fulton County judicial system was overladen as it was. Cases—
even murder cases—usually went in on Monday and got spat
out to a jury by Friday, even if it meant that court was in session
until long after sundown. Judge Elmo Holt could be a curmud-
geon, especially if he was trying to keep within his own tight
time schedules.

"That trial," Andy Weathers recalled, "was a very unusual
situation, a very *volatile* situation. All the different family members there. The Boggses. The Radcliffes. Everybody. I always
expected the best defense was going to be, 'How could anyone
do this? How [can you believe she would] do that to elderly
people who *trusted* her?' " Weathers felt that normal, caring
people would find the charge so outrageous that it should have
been its own defense.

"But they didn't go for that—the defense just went for trying
to prove that Pat Allanson had *not* done it, period," Weathers
said, still somewhat bemused by that decision. It was, in fact,
the same approach that Pat had insisted on in Tom's earlier trial.
Deny everything.

"We had to hammer in on small details and inconsistencies,"
Weathers recalled of the prosecution's case against Pat. "We had
no history on her behavior—at least she had no *criminal* history.
We had to look for very small things, trying to do a probing
examination. But you couldn't look at it without looking at the
first case—where Tom killed his parents. That put everything
in context. No one really knew exactly what her [Pat's] part was
in that—not from watching her and watching Tom—but she had
the type of personality that it seemed that she would call the shots.

"But the deal about the arsenic was so *outside* what we usually dealt with. What we usually have here in the Atlanta area is passion killings. When you have a situation where someone actually *plans* to commit a murder—really gets down on it—you have situations where you don't have any witnesses. We had no eyewitnesses in this case. What I was trying to do was like building a house—trying to lay a foundation about what had been going on.

"Pat Allanson had a two-pronged motive. There were two things she was trying to accomplish, I thought. She was trying to lay it off on the elder Mr. Allanson, as being the original killer. . . . If he had died, they would have gotten the money *and* gotten Tom out of prison. I think that was the thrust of what she was trying to do."

After studying the case that Bob Tedford, the East Point investigators, and the D.A.'s investigators had put together, Weathers concluded that there had been almost perfect planning on the part of the defendant. "The experts told me there was a lot of similarity between arsenic poisoning and the normal aging process. Jean Boggs was the one who began to see and notice the things that only a member of the family would notice. If you weren't specifically looking for this, it probably would never have been found. Tedford got on things then, and we worked on that case for a long, long time. We got Joe Burton—who's now the medical examiner in DeKalb County—and he knew a lot about arsenic, and there's a toxicologist named McGurdy in the GBI lab. Their testimony was critical."

Even so, most prosecutors wouldn't have taken on the case. It wasn't a sure thing. It was the kind of case that could rapidly lower the percentages on an assistant D.A.'s conviction record.

"Obviously," Weathers later said, "I was convinced in my own mind that Patricia Allanson did it or I would never have tried the case . . . but I was still trying to get it in the form of tangible proof. It took going back and looking at the old liquor bottle, the nuances—just building on minutiae to try to put together a chain of facts. If you looked at each fact independently—if you looked at the wills being changed—"

With his new knowledge about the action of arsenic poisoning, Weathers hoped to be able to pick up on the "little mistakes" made by the defendant.

If, indeed, she had made any.

✦ ✦ ✦

The white marble Fulton County Courthouse took up the entire block and was constantly being refurbished and expanded, so that its bulk hunkered over sidewalks and seemed about to burst into lanes of traffic. There were six huge columns on the Pryor Street side and wide steps leading to three double doors. Bronze pedestals supported a profusion of round white lights, and sheriff's cars and vans nudged the curb in front. Tom's trial had been held there and now it was Pat's turn. But Tom had been locked up; at least she was free on bail. The day Pat's trial began, Monday, May 2, 1977, promised to be hot as summer, and the air was humid and thick. High above bustling Pryor Street, Judge Elmo Holt presided over courtroom 808.

Pat Allanson looked wonderful. She had put on weight once her hip finally began to heal. She had made all new dresses for her trial. She chose a deep garnet–colored sheath for the first day of jury selection, and she wore a large cameo on a gold chain, cameo earrings, and a cameo ring. Her hair was perfect, and her makeup was subdued but elegant. Her cane added just a hint of vulnerability, and she occasionally touched her handkerchief to her forehead and lips as if she felt ill. Although her aunts could not all be with her, Boppo and Papa were there, and so was Susan.

On this first day of his wife's trial, Tom Allanson was brought over from Jackson and into Judge Holt's courtroom. In exactly one week, Pat and Tom would celebrate—if the word fit considering the circumstances—their third wedding anniversary. They had lived together as man and wife for exactly seven weeks and six days. Their anniversaries since had been marked by disaster rather than happy remembrance.

The jury had yet to be picked and Tom was present to answer possible questions in pretrial motions. It was rumored that he might testify. He stared at Pat and she gazed back. And then Dunham McAllister signaled Pat to follow him. She left the courtroom to meet with her husband and they talked for two hours.

Being together was not the same. It never would be again.

Despite the publicity surrounding Tom's trial only a little over two years earlier, a jury unfamiliar with that case was picked on

Monday afternoon—five men and seven women, nine whites and three blacks, white-collar and blue-collar.

The witnesses listed were predictable. For the state, there would be investigators, forensic scientists, toxicologists, Jean Boggs, Paw Allanson's attorneys, the bankers who had notarized Paw Allanson's "confession," and Paw and Nona themselves. For the defense, there would be those people who had *always* defended Pat: Mrs. Clifford Radcliffe, Colonel Clifford Radcliffe, Debbie Taylor Cole, and Miss Fanny Kate Cash (who had postponed surgery to be present). There were whispers that said Patricia Radcliffe Taylor Allanson would take the stand in her own defense. With the prospect of such a happening, courtroom 808 was packed. This might not be a "passion killing," but then again, there were many in the courtroom who remembered Pat at her husband's trial two years ago. They had wondered then what kind of woman she really was; perhaps now they would find out.

Pat looked even more beautiful the second morning of trial as opening arguments began. She wore an emerald green dress that precisely matched her eyes. She sketched and scribbled on a yellow legal pad as Andy Weathers presented the state's position in opening arguments; her face only occasionally betrayed a slight drift of annoyance.

Weathers had won his plea to introduce to the jury information on Tom Allanson's conviction—a most important legal coup. Now the jury listened but gave no sign of what they thought as Weathers described Pat's takeover of the elder Allansons' affairs following her husband's conviction for the murder of their son and daughter-in-law. "There will be introduced into court . . . various documents. These documents gave Patricia Allanson complete power of attorney to sign anything as if they themselves were signing it—gave her complete access to all the bank accounts, papers . . ."

"Arsenic." Saying the name of the poison out loud provoked a ripple in the gallery. Andy Weathers promised the jurors proof —scientific proof—that the old people had had their body fluids and their hair and their fingernails infiltrated with the deadly poison.

Dunham McAllister's opening statement promised that the evidence would show something entirely different. The confession was real enough, he said, dictated by Mr. Walter Allanson to Pat. "She doesn't take shorthand, but she wrote it down in longhand, a lengthy statement which we expect the state to introduce. And this statement was, in fact, notarized.

"He *signed* it," McAllister said emphatically.

Both the state and the defense were going to utilize the same evidence, but each would maintain that it supported its *own* case. Yes, McAllister agreed, there *was* arsenic, a bottle of it, but the liquor in Paw and Nona's house had come from Jean and Homer Boggs. "We expect that the state will have failed to carry its burden of proof of proving beyond a reasonable doubt that Pat Allanson is guilty of anything."

✦   ✦   ✦

Weathers was continually surprised at the civility of the cast of characters in this trial. Colonel and Mrs. Radcliffe were gracious, if reserved. "They were there every day, and they'd come up and talk with me," he recalled. "I really believed that they were sincere in their belief that she didn't do it—at least I believed the colonel. I believe there was a history of mental—*stuff* . . . but the defense didn't know how to use it. Maybe they couldn't have used it—it doesn't usually work in a killing for profit, especially when you have *chronic* arsenic dosage. . . . Still, there was something about the dynamics of that trial," Weathers mused, remembering that sometimes it seemed like a very proper social reception, despite its real purpose.

Margureitte Radcliffe was, first and foremost, a lady. And the colonel was what he always had been—absolutely correct. In public, they never broke; they never even bent. And above all, they were never rude. To many in the courtroom, it seemed inconceivable that their daughter stood accused of a terrible crime. Pat was a lady too, but as the prosecution moved into witness testimony, the picture evolving of Pat's complete control of the elderly Allansons' assets was devastating.

When Dr. Lanier Jones took the stand, Nona and Walter Allanson were wheeled into the courtroom so he could identify them. Nona was used to a wheelchair, but it was an ignominious thing for the old man to have to be wheeled anywhere. His feet and lower legs didn't work anymore—the nerves were permanently damaged by arsenic poisoning. Nona waved at her doctor with her one good hand, smiling but confused by the courtroom scene. When they had left the courtroom, Dr. Jones compared the robust old man he had known with the comatose patient he had examined on June 13, 1976. He repeated more than once that he had been a "suspicious doctor."

Dr. Everett Solomons described the corrosive action of arsenic on the human body, and Weathers moved on to the contents of the whiskey bottle Pat had given Dr. Jones.

"Would you state for the jury the results of the test of that bottle?"

"When we received the bottle, it contained approximately half a millimeter of liquid—3.63 milligrams."

". . . arsenic?"

"Arsenic."

Weathers then called the associate chief medical examiner of Fulton County, Dr. Joseph Burton, and asked his opinion on what was wrong with Walter and Nona Allanson at the time of their hospitalization in June 1976.

"Arsenic intoxication. Arsenic . . . when introduced into the body—by whatever means, accidental, suicidal, or by a homicidal person—it has certain actions it takes. . . . It's rapidly absorbed into the GI tract. It appears in the blood twenty-four hours after ingestion. Within twenty-four, forty-eight, fifty-two hours, one will begin to get urinary arsenic excretion, and, if there is a single dose, this may continue for seven to ten days until the arsenic is cleared from the system. After about twenty-four to seventy-two hours, this arsenic also will appear in the hair and nails of the individual.

"Now, the hair grows at approximately a half a millimeter per month. The nails grow approximately a tenth of a millimeter per month. The white part of your nail is the active growing site that the arsenic would be deposited in. . . . If one finds arsenic in the nail *tip,* that tells you that arsenic has been in the nail long enough to grow from this site to this site here," he said, demonstrating.

Dr. Burton explained that the same progression was true in human hair. Speaking of Paw Allanson, he said, "There have been two episodes of arsenic introduced into the system. . . . It's very rare to find a level this high unless someone has introduced into his system a large bolus of arsenic to give you that level. . . . The same is true for Nona Allanson . . . a very high level of arsenic found. There is no way that these amounts that we see in the nails and hair are within any normal range."

It was Burton's opinion, given the Allansons' medical histories and based on his tests, that someone had administered arsenic to the elderly couple about six months before their hospitalizations in June and July, and then again just before they were hospitalized. "This is consistent with *chronic* arsenic intoxication . . . " Burton said.

"Let me ask you this," Weathers continued. "If someone were taking . . . arsenic in their system—bearing in mind respective ages of the people . . . would this have any effect whatsoever on their mental stability?"

"It could," Burton replied. "Arsenic has been proven to cause changes in one's mental attitude, capability, thinking, and reasoning; it can cause neurological complaints and GI symptoms, headaches, muscular aching, weakness, affect peripheral nerves and changes in sensation of the legs and feet."

"With the type you found, would that be consistent with arsenic being ingested through milk, orange juice, food preparation?"

"It can be ingested through any number of mechanisms or methods. In most forms, it is an odorless, colorless, tasteless process where one does not know that they are ingesting arsenic."

Asked if he had ever seen a case of suicide by chronic arsenic ingestion, Burton shook his head. "No, sir."

"Never?" probed Weathers.

"No, sir . . . I have never seen one documented. Several people have committed suicide by the *acute* ingestion of arsenic, but each individual's susceptibility to arsenic varies. It would be hard to predict on a chronic basis how much one would have to take . . . to induce sickness or death. . . . Oftentimes, an individual becomes very sick and it's a very unpleasant . . . If one got very sick, he might be hospitalized. He might be treated and survive . . . unpredictable."

"Is not *pain* one of the manifestations of chronic ingestion of arsenic?"

"Yes, sir." If a would-be suicide chose to end his life in one gulp, Burton stressed, the pain would be intense, even unbearable. It would be prolonged agony when administered slowly.

On cross-examination, Dunham McAllister did his best to shake Dr. Burton, to show that arsenic is all around, everywhere, easy to ingest accidentally, easily misdiagnosed. He maintained that many diseases might have the same symptoms as arsenic poisoning. Burton did not dispute that.

"So it's possible," McAllister said, "that arsenic poisoning can be misdiagnosed for different ailments?"

"Yes, sir."

"More than a dozen?"

"Possibly, yes."

"What about a stroke? Could it be misdiagnosed as a stroke?"

"Yes . . ."

Paw was wheeled back in to testify. "Mr. Allanson," Weathers began. "I am going to ask you just a few questions, please, sir. Can you understand me, sir . . . ?"

"Yes."

"Did you give yourself arsenic?"

"Nope."

"Did you give any to your wife?"

"*No.*"

"Do you know how it got into your system?"

"Nope."

"I have no further questions."

"Never seen any . . ." Paw trailed off.

On cross-examination, McAllister tried to connect Paw's long history of farming with the supposition that there must have been poison on his property. But he didn't seem to have the heart to bear down. Cross-examination fell flat, showing only the tremendously hard labor old Walter Allanson had performed for six decades. The witness could never remember using or seeing arsenic preparations.

"No further questions."

Jean Boggs took the stand next, and if she felt a certain triumph to find herself in a courtroom where Pat Allanson was being prosecuted, it was understandable. She allowed her eyes to flicker over the defense table from time to time.

Andy Weathers used Jean's answers to catch the jury up on the violent history of the Allanson family. "You know, of course, Mr. and Mrs. Walter Allanson?"

"Yes, sir, my mother and father."

"Now, I believe you also had a brother?"

"Yes, sir . . . Walter O'Neal Allanson."

"And was he murdered in Fulton County?"

"Yes, sir."

"Trial held in Superior Court of Fulton County?"

"Yes, sir."

"Who was convicted in your presence?"

Dunham McAllister objected. "It's irrelevant to the trial in this case."

"I intend to show motive," Weathers argued. "I intend to stand by that."

"[There's] been absolutely no testimony about motive at this point," McAllister countered.

"Fixing to be some," Weathers said agreeably. "That is why I am offering it."

The defense's objection was overruled. Jean was allowed to say that Pat was the third wife of the man convicted of his parents' murders—Tom Allanson.

Jean went on to describe her growing suspicion that something was wrong in her parents' home. Dr. Jones had alerted her that her father had been drinking moonshine whiskey. "My father doesn't drink," Jean said. She also recalled her conversation with Pat on the front porch of the Washington Road house. "She [said she] knew what funeral arrangements that he wanted and that he wanted to be put away in a pink satin interior casket, which didn't sound like my father. She picked out the clothes and my son was [to be] one of the pallbearers. It didn't make sense to me. . . . When I started to leave . . . she leaned across the rails and said this to me, says, *'I hope he dies.'* "

The prosecutor was also able to elicit testimony from Jean that showed the utter devotion Walter had shown toward Nona, the confusion and upheaval that Pat Allanson had brought to their household, and the fact that the old man neither drank nor took pills.

"Have you ever seen your father—has he beaten your mother?"

"Oh, my goodness. No," Jean gasped.

McAllister suggested on cross-examination that Jean had neglected her parents, visited them infrequently. She explained that she too had been ill in 1973 and unable to drive. No, she had not visited often after she recovered. She admitted that it had not been pleasant visiting her parents. There had been "a coldness" after Tom's trial in 1974. No, she had never been close to her brother, Walter—not even from early childhood. "We were just two different personalities."

When Weathers objected to the line of questioning, McAllister said he *was* striving for materiality. "It is a most complex family. . . . I'm trying to elicit from this witness some illumination of this family, some *explanation* of this family."

They wrangled, and Judge Holt finally ruled that Jean's relationship with a brother who had been dead for two years was irrelevant and sustained Weathers's objection. McAllister pounced. Based on the judge's ruling, he again insisted that no allusions at all to the double murder *or* Tom Allanson should be made in this trial.

Judge Holt ruled against him again.

McAllister kept Jean Boggs on the stand for a long time, drawing forth the information that she and her husband were now serving as her parents' guardians, paying their bills, hiring their nurses. He ended his cross with "*You* asked the police—or I believe you said you *instructed* the police—to carry out a full investigation, to go to the crime lab with it? Is that correct?"

Jean sat up straighter. "Certainly."

Andy Weathers had only three questions on redirect. "Since Pat Allanson left that house—answer this question 'Yes' or 'No' —has there been any problem with your father as far as overdose of alcohol?"

"No, sir."

"Any problem as far as overdose of pills?"

"No, sir."

"Any problem of *arsenic?*"

"No, sir."

"No further questions."

Jean had done well, but this trial would, in the end, cause her pain. She would be portrayed again and again as a neglectful daughter. Perhaps if relationships had not been so strained in her family, all this would never have happened.

✦ ✦ ✦

They recessed for the day at 6:45 P.M. and began again on Wednesday morning, May 4, at 9:30. Pat wore a lilac-colored dress that day. She listened as Bill Hamner described the steady progression of documents that ultimately disinherited virtually everyone but Tom and Pat. The old people had been very closemouthed about exactly what their assets were, but Hamner knew they had been in excess of two hundred thousand dollars at the time of the first wills. No one knew what remained. Jean Boggs's children's portion had dwindled to one-sixth, and *that* was under Pat's control.

If the spectators had expected titillating revelations, they were disappointed on the third day of trial. The witnesses were dry, and their testimony was rife with dull detail about technicalities. Hamner and his partner, Fred Reeves, went through the many, many changes and codicils to the elderly Allansons' wills. Joyce Tichenor, who had notarized Paw's supposed confession, and her bank manager, Gus Yosue, testified about the single time they had encountered the defendant and her grandfather-in-law.

The evening of April 16 was not totally clear in their memories; there was no reason for them to remember it. Yosue recalled the young woman helping the elderly man into the bank, and her insistence that he didn't want people knowing his business. Tichenor remembered that the top papers on the stack that she notarized had appeared to be warranty deeds with plats, blocks, lots, and measurements on them. She remembered six or seven sheets of paper that were "just turned up from the bottom a little way by her [Pat], and she would say at each sheet, 'Sign here, Paw.' "

Tichenor had not used her seal, but had merely stamped the pages. "The date and the signature were my writing," she said. "I did not write that 'Sworn and subscribed to before me' on there." She had routinely jotted down the specifics of the ten-minute transaction in her log and forgotten about it—until subpoenaed as a witness. She had had no idea she had notarized a confession to double murder.

Andy Weathers hated to do it, but it was necessary. An ambulance was sent to bring eighty-year-old Walter Allanson back to testify. He denied that he had any part in the murders of his son and daughter-in-law. He remembered the murder day of July 3, 1974, well. He did not clearly remember signing the papers at the bank, or, rather, he remembered that April night in mismatched segments. He recalled "signing papers for Pat," but he felt sure that he had never gone into the bank itself. "I never talked to no lady—just a man come out to the car."

Jim Kelly of the Georgia Bureau of Investigation's crime lab, chief document examiner and handwriting expert for the state, was called to the stand by the prosecution to explain the peculiarities in the confession. Only the last of the five pages had been signed, and that last page had not been typed continuously. The confession was rife with typographical and grammatical errors, although someone had gone through it with a blue ballpoint pen, correcting some of them. Kelly pointed out that, while the date of the notary's signature on the last page was April 16, the date typed at the beginning of the alleged confession was April *19*.

Odd. And suspect.

McAllister asked only one question: "How many pages were in the confession?" The answer was "five."

Wisely, the defense attorney left it at that.

Weathers then recalled Dr. Everett Solomons of the crime lab and asked him about the liquid found in the antique whiskey bottle. "Say, right here in front of this jury, I took normal swallows of this arsenic—are you with me so far?"

"Yes, sir."

"What would happen?"

"I would expect you to have to be hospitalized in order to live."

"How many swallows of this would kill you—*normally,* how many?"

"I would expect two swallows."

Weathers was so intent that he did not see the incongruity of "normal" swallows of arsenic. Solomons was adamant that two swallows was a lethal dose. No human would live six months, or four months—or *four minutes*—if he did that.

✦ ✦ ✦

Pat drooped like a wilted rose as the trial progressed beyond 5:00 P.M. that day. During a jury recess, McAllister asked if they might stop. "Your Honor, at this point I would move that we recess for the day based upon the fact that my client is suffering from certain physical disabilities. At the late hour yesterday, she suffered from dizziness. Double vision. She has told me today she has a problem with blood clotting. I know she has problems with her heart. She's been in the hospital three times since the first of this year. She is not in any condition, in my professional opinion, to continue in this trial and to continue to aid me. It is my expectation that we will be ready to go forward tomorrow morning."

Judge Holt peered balefully at Pat. "What *is* the problem with your client that at five o'clock in the afternoon she can't go on?"

McAllister was stumped. He didn't know the specifics of Pat's sinking spells. "I do not know if there is anything inherent about five o'clock or not. But I do know she's unable to continue today in a meaningful way to assist me."

Holt suppressed a snort. "What do you *mean* she's not able to continue in a *meaningful* way?"

"Your Honor . . . it's impossible for me . . . to really converse with her."

"You *have* been conversing with her."

McAllister referred to the physical strain on Pat, who, according to Colonel Radcliffe, was suffering from a "severe blood clot."

"Being on trial would put anyone under a physical strain, Counselor," Judge Holt said. "We can get a doctor up here to look at her."

McAllister backed down. His client had her own doctor.

Holt was not about to rein in his speedy trial. He had trial commitments the next week. But not long after his decision, the state rested its case. It was near 6:00 P.M. on Wednesday, May 4. Although he wasn't happy about it, Holt recessed for the day. They would go longer tomorrow—unless the defendant was truly ill. If she was, she would have to let him know.

The defendant looked surprised. No one had ever doubted her frail health before.

Dunham McAllister rose to begin the case for the defense. "Your Honor, I call Patricia Allanson to the stand."

The gallery murmured. Whatever Pat's physical disabilities of the night before, she had apparently made a miraculous recovery. She wore the emerald green sheath again. She had gained weight and the cap sleeves showed her plump short arms, the bodice tight across her full breasts. She seemed calm and self-possessed, not at all nervous.

Her mother and stepfather looked at her with pride; Margureitte's chin lifted and the colonel's bearing was ramrod straight and tall. Only Susan seemed nervous.

Pat answered her attorney's questions easily, giving her address in Morrow and her former address on Tell Road.

"Have you ever lived at Walter and Nona Allanson's residence?"

"No, sir. . . . Normally, I went when Mrs. Allanson called me."

"How often was that?"

"In the earlier . . . period . . . it was not in excess of three times a week because of my own inability to get around. After I got better, she called me an average of about four or five times a week and asked me to come."

Pat was prepared—even eager—to discuss her own precarious health, but Andy Weathers objected. He could see no bearing on this case. Judge Holt sustained.

McAllister moved ahead to the time of Walter Allanson's heart attack in January of 1976. Pat rolled her tongue in her mouth, wetting her lips with its tip as she recalled her visit to his hospital room.

"He had a nurse to call the house and say that he had some very important information he wanted to speak to me about. . . . When I got there, I went in and immediately he asked me to call for the nurse. My mother was with me . . . he told the nurse that he had gotten approval from the doctor to have a private conversation with me, and he wanted the curtains closed and everything. . . . That was when Paw—*Mr. Allanson*— I'm sorry," she said apologetically, "I can't help but say 'Paw' because I have called him that so long."

McAllister nodded encouragingly, and Pat continued.

"He thought he was going to die, and he had something that had to be told. . . . He told me that Tommy—he calls my husband Tommy—he said that Tommy did not do what he was put in jail for. He said, '*I* did it.' And that is as far as he went because I stopped him. I didn't believe him in the first place, and in the second place, I had been told by the doctor he didn't need anything to upset him or excite him, and I thought *that* was a pretty upsetting and excitable subject—so I didn't pursue it."

Even though Pat had been frantic to have her husband free, she had thought first of his grandfather's health and allowed a confession to murder—which would have saved Tom—to hang in the air, unsaid. From time to time during her testimony she had looked modestly down at her lap. Now, she lifted her green eyes to her attorney.

When Paw returned home, Pat said, he worried about the nurse giving Nona medication. Pat had gone over to help out and they had had another conversation. "He was very, very irate at Mr. and Mrs. Boggs . . . he said [they] had been bothering Maw. . . . He said, 'I want to keep Jean and them away.' He said, 'If they don't stay away and leave her alone, I'm going to blow her head off *just like I did Walter's and Carolyn's.*' . . . So that night, he went into everything. He told me every single thing he done."

Pat was very earnest, very definite as she described how torn she had been between concern for Paw's health and her need to know the truth. She had permitted him to give her details "only after he was released from the doctor's care and I saw that he was all right then."

As she recalled, she had committed the old man's statement to paper about three weeks before it was notarized. "Mr. Allanson wanted me to bring the typewriter over to the house and type it up. And I am not a typist in the first place. The typewriter was too heavy for me to move because I was still on crutches." She said she had explained that to the old man, and he had agreed she could just write down what he told her. "He still said, 'I'm not going to the police about it. It will upset Mama, make her have a heart attack.' He had been using this on me a long time to keep me from going to the police after he told me. And he said, 'I'll tell it to you now the way it really happened.' "

"And did he?"

Pat looked toward the ceiling, as if searching for guidance, and then rolled her tongue again in the familiar gesture. "Yes, sir," she said with emphasis. "He did. . . . I don't know how to describe it unless you could say . . . that the more he told me, the more I wrote down what he said, the more excited he became as he was telling it. . . . I questioned him *numerous* times throughout it . . . you know, like, 'How could you have *done* that, Paw?' . . . I wrote down verbatim every word that he told me. . . . He wanted me to type it up because he could not read the handwriting. . . ."

"Was it typed?"

"Yes, sir, it was. . . . My mother typed it, because I can't type—except one finger."

"Now," McAllister continued, "between the time it was stipulated and June 13 of last year, what was your contact with the Allanson home?"

"Between the time this was signed and the thirteenth?"

"Yes."

"Very few, because I was *afraid* to go back. I would say probably four or five times at the most. Instead of going every day, I only went those times when Ma called me and begged me to come. I always went—but I always took someone with me, from the very day that he told me that. . . . From that date on, I never went back to that house alone."

Pat recalled the unsettling weekend of June 12–13, shuddering at the memory. Her facial expressions and gestures were very dramatic. "Ma had called us that morning. She was hysterical. She said Paw tried to kill her. [That] he was drinking, that he had gone crazy. . . . She didn't know what to do and she was frightened."

Pat and her parents went to her rescue, of course, she said. Once inside the house, someone had called Dr. Jones, and "against my wishes," Pat explained, the old man had remained out of the hospital. She asked her good friend, Fanny K. Cash, to stay the night for protection, as if a sixty-seven-year-old woman would be much protection against the out-of-control admitted killer Pat had described.

On Sunday morning, Pat said, she had to call Dr. Jones again.

"What were you doing when Dr. Jones arrived?"

"When he arrived that Sunday morning?"

"Yes."

"Oh, I remember," Pat said suddenly. "I was bathing Ma, and because I knew I had left her only partially clothed in the bathroom and it was cool, I had to hurry back to her. So I just ran up real quick and answered the door and Dr. Jones followed me back, and I showed him which room Paw was in."

McAllister had a most important point he had to get across to the jury. He wanted to show, through Pat's testimony, that she had nothing to gain, and much to *lose,* if Paw Allanson died. If Paw had died, he submitted, she might never have been able to use his confession to free Tom.

Weathers would not let him ask that directly. He maintained in objection after objection that McAllister's questions on the matter were all leading. When the defense attorney tried through another door, Weathers objected again. At length, Judge Holt allowed McAllister to get at the subject in a roundabout way.

"Did *I* give you certain legal advice concerning your husband's case?" he asked Pat.

"Yes, sir. You did."

"Would you tell the jury what that advice was?"

"Well, you told me that the *worst* thing that could possibly happen would be for Mr. Allanson to die from his heart or anything else, because it was very important that he be alive and that he be able to testify to what he told me. . . ."

"Do you know anything about how arsenic got into the body of Nona Allanson or Walter Allanson?"

"No, sir."

Pat said she had heard nothing about anyone suffering from arsenic poisoning until June 28, when they had come with an ambulance to take Nona away. "There was a lot of confusion going on. And I don't know whether I overheard it or whether it was said directly to me. It seems like Mr. Tedford is the one who said it—it seems."

"Do you know *anything* about the presence of arsenic on or about the premises of Walter Allanson's place?"

"No, sir. He didn't let people ramble around his house."

"Who prepared the food?"

"Oh, Paw did all the cooking . . . he wouldn't let anyone else."

"Was that true on every occasion?"

"Every one until he went to the hospital. Then, of course, there were different nurses who cooked and everything."

"Thank you."

Andy Weathers rose to cross-examine. Questioning a defendant who was attractive, intelligent, and frail—with her cane next to her chair—was not going to be the easiest thing in the world. He knew that even Bob Tedford had initially felt sorry for Pat. Weathers had studied her during this trial and watched emotions flicker across her face. Concern. Boredom. Pain. Fear. Confidence. And sometimes a kind of supercilious annoyance— even with her own attorney. Pat strove, it appeared, to come across as an almost royal presence who, for God only knew what reason, found herself in a temporarily untenable and distasteful situation.

"You just stated . . . ," Weathers began without preamble, "that Mr. McAllister gave you some legal advice as your attorney. I assume by this you mean he was already retained as your attorney at this time, and gave you legal advice about this document not being any good. Is that correct?"

Pat blinked. "Pardon, sir? I couldn't hear."

"You just stated to the jury, did you not, that Mr. McAllister gave you some legal advice concerning the validity . . . of State's Exhibit No. 1 . . . ?"

"Yes, sir. . . . I don't quite understand the question—"

Weathers repeated his question, which emphasized that the confession was worthless. Pat explained that it had not existed when she first went to McAllister in March. At that point, Paw had only told her verbally that he was the real killer of his son and daughter-in-law.

Answering Weathers's questions about her marriage, Pat agreed cautiously that she and Tom were "very close . . . very, very close."

"You're stating to the jury that Tom Allanson never told you one word about his innocence in this case."

"Yes, sir . . . he told me he was innocent and I knew that if he said he was innocent, he was innocent."

"In fact, you knew a lot more," Weathers said, moving closer. "Isn't it a fact when Mr. and Mrs. Allanson were killed, the police saw *you* directly outside the house when Tom Allanson ran outside the house?"

"No, sir. I was not." Pat's face flushed, and she watched Weathers warily.

"You were not in the car?"

"I was in a car not far from there. Not a car, I'm sorry—in a jeep."

"Not far from the murder scene?"

"Depends on what you call far." Pat was slowly regaining her composure.

"Okay. *You* tell me how far."

"A block, block and a half. That is where my doctor was. I had just come from the doctor."

"At the time Walter and Carolyn Allanson were killed, you were approximately one block from that place?"

"More like two." Pat backpedaled and decided that she probably had been *more* than two blocks away from the double murder scene.

"Did you see Tom Allanson run down the street right after the two people were killed?"

"No, sir."

"Were you *aware* that he was seen running down the street?"

"I was afterwards, yes."

"So that puts both of you all within two blocks of the murders."

"It puts *me* in the doctor's office two and a half blocks away, yes."

"I believe you said a minute ago you were in a *jeep?*"

"Yes."

Weathers was tripping Pat up on details, the "minutiae" that he knew he had to have, the string of small lies, exaggerations, the minimizations.

"Now, I believe you stated that this document [the confession] is verbatim—I believe the word you used—*exactly* what Walter Allanson told you about how he went about killing his son and his son's wife? Is that true?"

"Yes, sir."

"And I believe you just testified to this jury that your mother typed this because you couldn't type?"

"That's right."

"Then why does it say in the first sentence, 'My name is Walter Allanson, and I'm telling this to my granddaughter, Tommy's wife, Pat Allanson, and she's doing it on the typewriter because I don't write so good anymore'?"

Pat looked at the prosecutor as if he were totally dense. She explained that Paw had said exactly that—that he had assumed she would be the one to type it.

Weathers switched to the third codicil to the elderly Allansons' wills, dated February 4, 1976. "You heard Mr. Reeves and Mr. Hamner testify that if Walter Allanson died first, and Nona Allanson died, that everything they had would be left to you and Tom?"

"I heard him testify that is the way it was—but I was not aware of it at the time."

"Well, didn't you also hear him state you were *present* there when this explanation was made?"

She shook her head with slight irritation. "I was present *part* of the time. I was not present the entire time in the [hospital] room because the attorney got there before I did, and he was explaining the document to Paw."

"Did you hear Mr. Hamner say you were present in the room when he explained it?" Weathers pushed.

"I will have to beg to differ with Mr. Hamner," Pat said firmly.

While she claimed that her memory was better than the attorney's, Pat was actually quite vague about the details of the Allansons' wills, knowing only that the "percentages" were to be divided up between her husband and the other grandchildren. She insisted that most of what she knew about the wills and codicils she had learned only during the current trial.

"Didn't you hear him say there was a catchall provision that if the estate was worth more than the trust, *everything* in that estate—Mr. Hamner testified—would go to Tom Allanson? [That] if he was married to you at the time, and if something happened to him and *he* was not able to inherit, *everything* in that estate would go to you? Did you hear that testimony?"

"I heard the testimony, yes, sir. I have been sitting here."

Pat clearly wanted the jury to believe that she had had no interest in or understanding of the final disbursement of Paw and Nona's considerable assets. Indeed, she professed to be basically ignorant of such folderol as wills and codicils.

Weathers asked Pat if she recalled using her power of attorney over the Allansons' assets. "You don't recall withdrawing anything from these people's account?"

"There was no necessity to use it," Pat replied.

"Do you recall withdrawing . . . money [from] Fulton Federal Savings and Loan Association [by writing a check] made payable to Walter and Mrs. Nona Allanson dated June 23, 1976, in the amount of one thousand dollars?"

Pat could not really recall putting that amount into her own account the next day, signing Walter Allanson and Patricia Allanson on the back—but she did admit the endorsement was her writing.

Finally she said, "All right. Yes, I did." But she had, she insisted, done it for Nona. Nona wanted cash. Pat refused to admit that she had used the thousand dollars to pay for Tom's legal costs.

Weathers changed tactics and returned again to the way Walter Allanson's confession had been recorded. "Is this an exact account of what Walter Allanson told you transpired?"

"It was as exact as I could possibly get," Pat said. "I don't think I missed too many words. I just—I'm just a slow writer."

"Don't you think," Weathers said in his deep, resonant voice, "it's rather unusual that . . . [when] Fred and all these lawyers you know personally—that [with] something of this *significance,* you take this to a bank in front of people you had never *seen* and have it notarized after a long day of shopping? Just stop by to have a murder confession notarized? Isn't this stretching things?"

Pat sighed. "It was *not* a long day, because we started the day late in the afternoon, and it was only to get groceries and take care of having that signed."

"So, in having it signed, you go to people who don't know any of you-all and just say, 'Sign, Paw. Sign, Paw'?"

"I did not say that."

"Then Mrs. Tichenor's memory is incorrect?"

"Yes, I am afraid her memory is."

So far in her testimony, Pat had found many prior witnesses' memories to be faulty, including Bill Hamner's, Fred Reeves's, and Bob Tedford's. Now, finally, she questioned the testimony of notary Joyce Tichenor. Everyone was out of step save Pat.

Weathers moved to the twenty-eighth of June, the day Nona Allanson was rushed to South Fulton Hospital to be tested for arsenic poisoning. Pat had no memory of Bob Tedford telling her that Pa Allanson had arsenic in his body. "Mr. Tedford did not mention arsenic at the time."

She had just contradicted her own earlier testimony without realizing it.

"Mr. Tedford's recollection, you say, is incorrect again?"

"I don't recall what Mr. Tedford's recollection was. . . . That was not right because I had already found that out earlier at the hospital."

It was another contradiction of her own memory. Weathers noted it, but let it pass.

"Well. . . . If you knew that that man had arsenic in his body," he said, "if you loved that woman, the *first* thing you would want for her . . . would be to get her somewhere where somebody could save her life. It's possible *she* had arsenic."

Again, Pat denied that anyone had told her Nona might be in danger of arsenic poisoning.

Dunham McAllister objected, insisting that Tedford had never mentioned arsenic in his testimony, and asked for a directed verdict of acquittal. He suggested that the state had failed to prove its case.

Weathers responded, "The state thinks this has been a very carefully planned scheme. . . . [She had the] opportunity. She stated to Tedford she was the only one who took care of them. She was the one who had the arsenic. She's the one who had the most to gain. The statement—the *so-called* statement—has been completely refuted by Mr. Allanson. He said he never wrote it. He never did anything to his own child or his child's wife. We think we are far, far beyond a directed verdict in this case, Your Honor."

Judge Holt ruled against McAllister and the trial ground on. Weathers asked the court reporter to read Bob Tedford's earlier statements. The court record verified Tedford's testimony that he had told Pat on June 28 that the old man had been poisoned with arsenic and that the old woman might have been poisoned too.

Pat remained on the witness stand, listening as her testimony was undermined. She seemed unimpressed.

"Do you recollect him telling you that?" Weathers pushed.

"No, sir."

Weathers pushed even harder. "What possible purpose could be served . . . by telling this nearly eighty-year-old woman that insurance wouldn't cover her going to the hospital?"

"I never said that." Nor could Pat see that there was any reason for Nona Allanson's welfare to be a police matter. She suspected it was a guardianship fight.

"You are stating that he [Tedford] just showed up in the middle of the day and said, 'We are taking her to the hospital'? Not going to say anything else—just, 'Let's go'?"

"That just about sums it up. Yes, sir."

Pat was not shaken by the obvious discrepancies between her testimony and the testimonies of a number of prosecution witnesses. She looked petulant and occasionally glanced toward her parents for their support, but she wasn't ruffled. Weathers's skillful questioning had built the "basement" of his "house," and he was working on the superstructure. A pattern of behavior was emerging. Even when he caught Pat in an outrageous, inappropriate response, she simply denied that black was black. She stepped away from this messy business of a trial. Her memory

—the memory she bragged about—was suddenly full of gaping empty spaces.

Weathers forced her back again. Sighing, she related that the confession had been given to her three times—in the garage on Washington Road, in the old man's hospital room, and in his home. She had written it down in her own hand.

"You have that writing with you?" Weathers asked suddenly.

"Gosh, no, sir. I don't."

"You don't have it?"

"No."

"Where *is* it?"

"Thrown away, I guess. I don't really recall where it is. It's probably thrown away because it was only my own writing."

"A *confession* to a murder in your writing as a man dictates it. You threw it away?"

Pat didn't know where it was. "He could not read my writing that well, so it was typed up. And until then, I didn't see that it made any difference the *way* I wrote it out. So long as it was typed properly. It was used to type that document you have in your hand. It was taken from mine."

"The last page of this document has the signature 'Walter Allanson' on it," Weathers said. "Why did you take this out of the typewriter and then reinsert it?"

"I told you, sir. I didn't type it."

Pat denied that she was in the room when Margureitte typed the confession, at least not "the entire time." The last page had been typed on some old stationery left over from when her mother was secretary for the Dixie Cup Morgan Horse Show, but Pat had no idea why that final page had been dated and notarized three days before the first page was typed. Asked if she thought Paw had tried to commit suicide, Pat said it was quite possible. But if he had been suicidal as she hinted, she could not explain why a man who had as many guns as Walter Allanson had not killed himself with one.

"Doesn't it seem strange a man would kill himself with the ingestion of arsenic over a six-month period of time?" Weathers asked.

"Nothing seems strange with him anymore," she said crisply, her voice edged with irony.

The witness stand was no longer a comfortable place for Pat.

She stared coldly at Weathers as she said she had no idea why Paw might have chosen to kill his beloved wife of forty-nine years slowly with arsenic. She did not, after all, know that much about arsenic.

Weathers walked away from her, then turned back suddenly. "I almost forgot to ask you something, ma'am. You *are* the one that told Detective Tedford that what was wrong with Mr. Allanson was he had been swallowing pills by the handful?"

"I might have repeated this to him after Dr. Jones repeated it to me."

"Did you tell Detective Tedford?"

"I don't recall."

"Ma'am," Weathers asked with exasperation in his voice, "how in the world could Dr. Jones have said this? He wasn't even there. Didn't you recall his testimony was based on what *you-all* told him at the hospital? He stated he had trouble getting the man to take pills. Don't you recall *that?*"

"I recall that in testimony. . . . Perhaps I didn't understand your question."

"Did you tell Detective Tedford this man—Mr. Walter Allanson—was taking handfuls of pills and drinking whiskey?"

"Words to that effect—I had told him at one time, yes."

"And do you recall telling Jean Boggs on the fourteenth day of June, out there in front of that house, that you hoped this man died?"

"No, sir. I did not say that."

Nor had she told Tedford—on the very day that hospital personnel felt Paw was going to die—that her husband's grandfather had tried to run her off the road, and that she lived in fear for her very life. "Not running off the road," she said querulously. "I told him something else—but not running off the road."

"And—as to the death of Walter and Carolyn . . . ," Weathers asked, "isn't it a fact that shortly before Walter Allanson died, you made a complaint that Walter Allanson exposed himself to you?"

"Yes, I remember that."

"We are speaking of the dead man. Do you recall doing that?"

"Yes, I think I did."

"You think you did. . . . You make the complaint and your husband said, 'I'm going to kill that son of a bitch'?"

"No, sir. . . . He didn't say anything except to say what could be done about it legally."

"And it is a fact in summation—my last question to you—at the time both of these people were killed, back in '74, *you* were in a jeep within two blocks of that area?"

"I was either in a jeep or in a doctor's office."

Weathers turned away. "I have no further questions."

37

Margureitte Radcliffe followed her daughter to the witness stand. Everywhere Pat went, her mother was close behind her, supporting, mopping up, fixing, rearranging. If Pat had been queenly in her bearing, Margureitte was an empress. Serene and self-contained, she gazed down at her daughter's attorney almost benevolently.

The five-page confession looked perfectly familiar to her, she told McAllister. She had typed it herself, approximately a year earlier. She recalled that she had typed it just after she and her husband, Colonel Radcliffe, had returned from the funeral of his brother-in-law in New York State. They had been preparing to leave for a happier celebration, the fiftieth anniversary of one of her brothers. The Radcliffes were clearly family people, involved and supportive.

There was not a scintilla of Pat's testimony that her mother did not substantiate. Margureitte remembered each facet with crystalline clarity. Certainly Nona Allanson had called them, panicked, needing help on June 12, 1976. Absolutely Nona had said Paw had tried to smother her and then had tried to force her to drink something—something *not coffee.*

Margureitte herself had witnessed it all.

On cross-examination, Weathers wondered why the dates on the confession had been so disparate. It was *her* fault, Margureitte admitted; she had not bothered to check a calendar when she began to type page one. The anniversary they were headed for was on a Sunday, but the celebration was on a Saturday. If Mr. Weathers had a 1976 calendar, she could probably figure it out.

Perhaps not. A glance at a 1976 calendar showed that the sixteenth of April—the day the confession was notarized—was a Friday.

"Do you think this was more than a few days off? . . . Do you think it was above or behind?" Weathers asked.

"It was prior to—it was ahead of time."

"You mean like starting back eighteen, seventeen . . ."

"Yes," Margureitte answered, oblivious of the jury's puzzled looks. "It was more than—in other words, I didn't date it. It was like a—postdated, I would say, would be the proper word. That date is postdated. Is that not correct to be forward?"

She never gave a good reason why the confession had two different dates. The unspoken supposition was, of course, that Paw Allanson had been told to sign some vital documents on April 16, and the confession had been typed in three days later by a mother and daughter working together.

Margureitte had typed the confession in the study of the Tell Road house. In April of 1976. She *was* definitely sure it had been April.

"And how did you go about reducing— *Did* you reduce this from notes?"

"I didn't *reduce* it. I wrote it verbatim."

"You took it from something else and put it on here?"

"That is correct. Yes."

"And who provided you with—"

"My daughter, Mrs. Allanson."

"My question is this," Weathers continued. "Everything there that you put in these papers was provided to you by Pat Allanson?"

"I didn't change it, if that is what you mean."

"I am not trying to imply that at all. . . . In other words, *everything* you know about what's on here is through information provided by your daughter?"

"No—I knew that Mr. Allanson had confessed prior to that, yes."

"Who told you that?"

"Mrs. Allanson."

"Mrs. Allanson told you that also?"

"Yes."

"When did you have this conversation with Mrs. Allanson?"

"I can't give you a date on that. I have to be very truthful. I have to be perfectly honest."

Margureitte Radcliffe was fifty-six, only seventeen years older than the daughter she was trying, as always, to protect. She was still beautiful, and she lifted her chin ever so slightly and surveyed the courtroom with her "crystal gaze." It was essential that she be perceived as very truthful, perfectly honest, and always, always correct.

"Were you aware that they were both full of arsenic?" Weathers went on, using phrases that clearly shocked Margureitte. "Were you aware that they had such a level of arsenic in their bodies [as] to alter their human structure, that [it] would have resulted in death if arsenic ingestion continued?"

"I heard the laboratory said that," Margureitte replied. "I believe last week I saw the lab report, but prior to that I had not."

Arsenic was not something that Margureitte would have chosen to discuss in detail; it was obviously burdensome for her, but Weathers kept alluding to the poison. He established that Margureitte had had "training in nursing."

"You would generally be familiar with the fact arsenic would cause death if ingested in sufficient quantities?"

"The only thing I know about arsenic actually is that it is a poison. I have no personal knowledge."

"I'm not implying for a moment that you do. I'm just asking you as a technical question—would you be aware that arsenic is a poison?"

"I would think it was very dangerous. Yes, *very*."

Margureitte blamed the myriad typographical errors in the

confession, the occasional lines that were capitalized, on her own inexperience. "I'm really not that good a typist."

Weathers had another point he wanted to make. Paw's alleged confession had too many details about the murders of Walter and Carolyn Allanson to be simply guesswork. It had to have been written by someone who had been there, or who had been *told* what had happened that terrible night. Paw had emphatically denied any part in the murders. He had repudiated the confession. Who, then, had written it?

Weathers went about asking that question very subtly. In so many places in the confession, there were references to Paw Allanson's concern for his wife, to his fear that Mama "might have a stroke" if she knew. Why on earth would Paw have told anyone that he was a killer? It could have cost him what he held most dear. Nona.

Margureitte Radcliffe agreed that Paw Allanson most definitely wanted the document kept secret to spare his wife's health.

"So," Weathers asked, "if the knowledge of the confession came to someone . . . it would not come from Walter Allanson. . . . It would have come from some *other* party?"

"I'm not sure I follow you," Margureitte said slowly. "I'd like for you to make that statement again."

"Take the position the *third party* was there in that basement or right outside that area when it took place, knew exactly the details, *wasn't* concerned about Mrs. Allanson's health. That third party or whoever else was in that basement could have put something—or *everything*—down on this piece of paper as to the way this happened. Could they not?"

"I do not follow you at all." Margureitte flushed as she spoke, wary.

"I withdraw that," Weathers said.

"I don't know what the basement has to with what we are talking about, sir!"

Margureitte's testimony was interrupted by a lunch break that Thursday in May of 1977. It was just as well for the defense. The scarcely acknowledged ghost of another crime haunted Pat's trial. It was the *crux* of this trial, really. The double murder of Walter and Carolyn Allanson was what old Paw Allanson had supposedly confessed to; it was the event described in detail in this strange document full of typos and x-ed-out sections. Tom

Allanson was in prison for that crime, but Pat Allanson had said on the witness stand that she had been "one," "one and a half," "two," "more than two" blocks away at the moment the fatal shots were fired. She had been a suspect in those murders. She had never been charged, but that old investigation remained alive and rife with dangerous questions. No one on the defense side of this case wished to see those questions arise in courtroom 808.

✦ ✦ ✦

Margureitte Radcliffe's afternoon testimony was taken up with her typing of the confession, the choice of paper, the crossed-out portions, the manner in which she had inserted the paper into her typewriter—all questions from Andy Weathers. She couldn't recall why she had made such choices. She had no idea whether one would normally start typing from the very top of a sheet of paper, block out the stationery heading and go on, or whether one would start in the middle, and then type the top of the page.

Did the jury see the significance of the different dates, the different margins, the different paper on Paw's confession? There was no way of knowing.

Weathers asked Margureitte about July 26, 1976, the day she and her husband had come to East Point police headquarters with her attorney to give a formal statement about their recall of events in the Washington Road house. Their statements were taken just two weeks before Pat was arrested and charged with criminal attempt to commit murder. "Did you at any time in this statement tell the police, the district attorney's office—or *anyone* in law enforcement—that *you* had typed a confession of murder signed by Walter Allanson?"

"No, I did not," Margureitte said.

"I have no further questions."

✦ ✦ ✦

Colonel Clifford Radcliffe followed his wife onto the witness stand. In response to a question from McAllister, he recalled finding the whiskey bottle—*a* whiskey bottle, although he could not say if the bottle in evidence was the same bottle. The color of the cap looked different to him now. He attempted to say that his wife had told him to "dump it out."

Susan and Pat in
Florence, Alabama,
1986. Susan had her
mother back at last, and
they were closer now
than they had ever been.

Assuming the duties of a
nurse, Pat took care of
one of the "righteous
sisters," Aunt Liz (left),
who barely recovered
from her near-fatal
illness. On the right is
Aunt Thelma.

32

33

The James F. Crist estate on Nancy Creek Road in Atlanta. Pat and Debbie were employed by the Crists as nurses aides for a year in 1987 and 1988.

Susan and her son Adam in early 1990. Tended by her mother, Susan had been confined to bed for four months with an illness doctors could not diagnose.

Dawn's wedding, March 10, 1990: Pat (left), Boppo (right) with Pat's granddaughters Courtney and Ashlynne between them. Debbie and Susan stand behind the two girls, and although she was smiling, Susan was deathly ill.

34

35

Finally released from prison in 1989, Tom married Liz Price, the woman who had truly loved him all his life.

Andy Weathers, veteran Assistant Distict Attorney, Fulton County, had met Pat Taylor Allanson in a courtroom before and wanted to meet her again.

36

37

Bill Akins, Assistant District Attorney, Fulton County, Georgia, was assigned a hauntingly familiar case, and was forced to make an agonizing—and unpopular—choice.

38

Michelle Berry and Don Stoop, Investigators for the Fulton County District Attorney's Office. Stoop was a master at "oddball" cases; Berry would start her Fulton County career with a case she would never forget.

39

Pat, 52, in her room at Margureitte and the Colonel's house in Mc-
Donough, Georgia. Once again her life was about to take a bizarre turn.

Margureitte and the
Colonel at Christmas.
They had spent their
entire lives making
things easier for Pat,
and "for those who
need us the most."

40

Thanksgiving 1989. Left to right: Pat, Boppo, Ashlynne, and Adam.
The family would never be this happy again.

Susan and Bill Alford at a
business convention. They
did what they thought was
right, and it almost
destroyed them.

Pat's world had been reduced to her priceless collection of antique dolls, repaired, dressed, arranged, and tended with loving and obsessive care.

The valuable pearl necklace and bracelet and an antique
cookbook that Pat had given away as gifts would return to
haunt her.

Mug shots of Pat Taylor after her second arrest in April 1991. "I can't
understand why anyone in this whole wide world would think Pat got
whatever she wanted," her mother said in dismay. "She never got *anything* she wanted. Her whole life has been tragic. Why can't people understand that?"

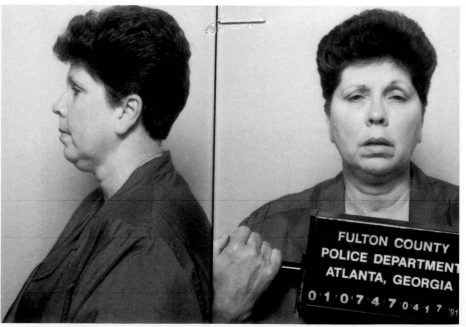

Weathers objected on the grounds the statement was hearsay.

The colonel hastened to explain that Dr. Jones had told Mrs. Radcliffe to tell him to dump out the bottle's contents.

"Your Honor, that's hearsay on hearsay."

After a wrangle between attorneys, Judge Holt allowed the first hearsay but not the second. McAllister asked what the witness had done with the bottle.

"I smelled the contents," the colonel replied. "I smelled the alcohol. . . . I dumped the contents down into the toilet and then I gave the bottle to my daughter to put with the . . . medication we were accumulating in the house to give to Dr. Jones."

He agreed with his wife and stepdaughter that Nona Allanson had called them for rescue on June 12.

"Did she state anything to you in person when you arrived?" McAllister asked.

"Yes, sir. . . . If I may—not only to me, but several times thereafter to other people who came to the house."

"What did she state?"

"That her husband had tried to kill her."

"Thank you, sir."

During cross-examination, Weathers deliberately allowed the jury to once again hear the story of the terrified old woman, the assaultive husband who was drinking and gulping down pills, the trio of rescuers who left Tell Road and rushed to Nona Allanson's aid. Colonel Radcliffe explained easily that he had never actually *seen* Paw taking pills—he might have told detectives that, but he had corrected himself. "I did not actually see him, but there were open pill containers on the counter."

"I am asking," Weathers suddenly took the offensive, "did you tell the detectives when they came out there that he was gulping down handfuls of pills?"

"That was my assumption at the time I first saw him."

Colonel Radcliffe had accused Bob Tedford of lying, of being confused about who said what about the pills. And now, once again, he had reversed himself.

Weathers brought the colonel back to July 26—the day of his formal statement. "Had your wife communicated to you at this time that she had typed a document . . . signed by Walter Allanson admitting the murder of his son and daughter-in-law?"

"At that time, I believe that she had indicated that she was typing a document."

"Did you *see* the document?"

"I had seen it, but I had never read it."

"You were aware that your wife was typing this document purported to be a confession of murder and *you never read it?*"

"That's correct, sir."

"You never *mentioned* that to the police at that time?"

"What, sir?"

"The fact that there was a purported murder confession?"

"I don't recall that I did."

Weathers was astonished. He walked a bit closer to the distinguished-looking colonel. "Well now, certainly, sir—I ask you to search your memory. Would you not recall telling the police whether or not you had information to a double murder where a man and his wife had been *killed* in the basement of a house? You don't recollect whether or not you told the police?"

"Was this supposed to be included in my statement of the twenty-sixth of July?" Radcliffe asked.

"I'm asking, on that statement you gave the police—did you give this information?"

Colonel Radcliffe was as calm and as flat as a windless lagoon. "I believe I *did* mention that there had been a confession."

He had fallen into a prosecution trap and never realized it. He had never mentioned the confession.

✦　✦　✦

Fanny Kate Cash was the next witness for the defense. A heavyset, disheveled woman, she peered at the gallery through thick glasses. Fanny Kate explained that she had lived all of her sixty-seven years at 4185 Tell Road. She had not married. She had once been a secretary and a bookkeeper, but when her mother passed away, she had to take care of her father.

Out there, before there were any other houses, Fanny Kate had lived with her aged father, who lay like a man already dead on the chaise longue on the veranda. She had done sewing and baby-sitting. And then she was alone, except for her church circle. She sold a piece of her acreage to Pat and Gil Taylor. Seeing them tow those two houses in and watching the horse ring and the red and white stables being built must have been a happy thing for Fanny Kate. With the advent of Clifford and Margureitte Radcliffe, and all of Pat's children moving in and out, the neighborhood certainly livened up. Fanny

Kate didn't even mind that Pat had never paid off the land contract.

Fanny Kate had become a part of Boppo's, Papa's, and Pat's lives, and she had lumbered down the road to their house often for lemonade or watermelon. They were so gracious to her that she hated to ask about the land payments. Their home was so lovely and clean. Fanny Kate's life was more basic. Cooking and heating in the cabin where she lived was accomplished by a huge coal stove, belching smoke, and Fanny Kate's home and person smelled of soot. She didn't care for Pat's children, who were terrified of her—their noise and their rambunctiousness set Fanny on edge—but she adored Pat. She had always tried to do her best for that poor, sickly woman. Fanny Kate had almost come to the point where she was going to give Pat her bedroom set, which Pat had long coveted—all carved with cupids and hearts on the headboard.

Fanny Kate testified that she had become a frequent companion and confidante to the Radcliffes and eventually spent much time at the Washington Road home of Paw and Nona Allanson. She substantiated all the testimony given by Pat and the Radcliffes. She had seen it herself.

Fanny Kate was off and running, relishing her place on the witness stand, eager to support her neighbors. She recalled that *she* had heard Paw Allanson talk strangely about his son and daughter-in-law's murder way back in March of 1976. "Grandma was saying she had a dream, and he interfered with her about the dream. It was about the murder. And he told her it wasn't right . . . and so he drew the basement . . . on the back of a magazine and give full details of the basement, where the hole was, where the furnace was, and then the stairway which came down . . . and he said the police never did state the truth about Carolyn and the way she was lying on the steps . . . and at that time, I says, 'Well, where was the one that shot Walter standing?' He said, 'Right there.' And it was *in front of the hole*." Fanny Kate was full of recollections about what Paw had told her.

"Was that the end of the conversation?" McAllister asked.

"He caught himself and realized that he had talked too much, and he shut up then. Shut up like a clam."

Weathers was on his feet. "Your Honor! This is the most pure conjecture I have ever heard—"

It did sound as if Fanny Kate was, perhaps, embellishing her testimony. But then again, perhaps she *was* remembering accurately. She was not, however, responsive to questions. She was away and gone on her own, settled into the witness chair as if it had been designed for her.

Judge Holt again ordered the jury to disregard her statements. But Fanny Kate would be heard. She was, she announced, a witness to Paw's confession to Pat. If not an eyewitness, she was most certainly an "earwitness." She said she had been with Pat the very day Paw dictated his confession. "Mrs. Allanson got restless and wanted to know what they were doing out back, and I went to see. And as I stood at the jalousie door that goes to the garage, I overheard the conversation. Pat begging him to slow down—that she couldn't take the notes so fast. And he become irritable with her and spoke up. His voice raised and says, 'I killed Walter and Carolyn. I didn't intend to kill Carolyn. But I did it in self-defense!' " Fanny Kate said she didn't hang around to listen but had gone back to Nona Allanson's room.

On cross-examination, Weathers asked Fanny Kate about her allegiance to the Radcliffes and Pat Allanson. She allowed she was "close" to Margureitte and Clifford Radcliffe, and "very close" to Pat.

"How long after you heard someone admit to . . . a double murder case was it that you called the local law officials?"

"I didn't understand the question."

"How long . . . from the time you heard this did you contact any law enforcement official?"

"I didn't contact any law enforcement at all."

"When is the first time since this date in 1976 that you have furnished this information to any law enforcement?"

"I furnished it to Mr. McAllister, the lawyer."

"That is not my question. When was it, please, ma'am, that you have given this information for a double murder case to anyone in law enforcement?"

"I didn't *give* it to any law enforcement at all."

"When is the first time you gave it to anyone in the district attorney's office?"

"Not at all."

"When is the first time you tried to contact any judge or any superior court?"

Fanny Kate wasn't catching on yet. "Not at all."

"Well then, *this* is the first time that any of these people have had any opportunity to hear this today, is it not?"

"I turned it over to Mr. McAllister."

"That is not my question."

"I haven't told anyone."

"That is my question. . . . No further questions."

It was clear to the most casual observer that Fanny Kate Cash would do anything possible to help Pat out of a jam. She was not nearly as subtle as the other defense witnesses, and she tended to embroider, but her loyalty was unquestionable. Dunham McAllister could see the problems inherent in his witness. He approached her warily for redirect examination and was rewarded with an incredible story that he would just as soon not have heard.

She said she and Pat had gone to the house on Washington Road with a message from Tom "warning Grandma to be careful. Her life was in danger. . . .

"And that night, between eleven-thirty and twelve o'clock, [my] phone rang and I answered it. *And it was a disguised voice—*"

"Miss Cash," McAllister said quickly, "I don't want to go into that. I think Mr. Weathers probably would object to that."

Mr. Weathers objected to Mr. McAllister's assumption of what he might object to.

"Go ahead," McAllister said, a trace of apprehension in his voice.

"I answered the phone and there was a disguised voice, saying, 'What did you tell Mama?' The word 'Mama' gave the voice away. And *I* coolly answered, and said, 'What did I tell—what did I tell Mama?' and the phone went up. *I recognized that voice, and it was Walter Allanson's!"*

Fanny Kate had a scenario of her own. If the case on trial had not been so serious, her testimony would have been hilarious. But no one laughed.

Andy Weathers caught her again on recross. If Miss Cash had been so fearful for Nona Allanson's life, if she had gone there to deliver an alleged message from Tom warning her that her life was in danger—this pathetic old woman in a wheelchair with the use of only one of her limbs—then *when* had she called anyone in law enforcement to warn them of the great danger this invalid lady was in? Had she told anyone?

"No one, no," Fanny Kate responded. "Not at all."

McAllister demanded to see all of Tom's letters to his grandparents and asked for time to analyze them. Judge Holt would not pause. He had warned the attorneys that he had only a week for this trial. He suggested that McAllister's wife, Margo—his co-counsel—could go over the letters.

They moved ahead, the trial staying afloat but getting bulkier and bulkier, listing to port with its heavy load of objections and legal arguments.

✦   ✦   ✦

Deborah Taylor Cole was the next witness for the defense. She was Pat's second daughter, the one who had married at fifteen and never left Georgia. At twenty-one, she was a slender young woman with brown hair, pretty—but without a vestige of the regal carriage of her mother and grandmother. Debbie spoke so softly that it was hard to hear her beyond the first row of the gallery. She answered with as few words as possible. In Debbie, Dunham McAllister had yet another witness who had spent time in Walter and Nona Allanson's home, and who could verify Pat's statements.

"I worked for them . . . [for] three weeks." Debbie wasn't sure just *when* she had worked for Nona and Paw Allanson. "It was summer. It had to have been June—somewhere around there." She remembered that she had been there the day before Paw was taken to the hospital. Yes, she had had several conversations with Nona.

"Did she say anything about Mr. Walter Allanson?"

"About which incident?" Debbie asked. "I mean there is a lot of things she told me about her husband."

"Did she say anything on that day about anything that he had done to her?" McAllister encouraged.

"Well, she's—I came in and she was crying . . . and you have to get up real close to listen to her because she has—she can't talk very well. So I went real close and asked her what was wrong. She said, 'Paw tried to smother me.' And I said, 'Well, how did he do that?' She says, 'He just did.' "

Debbie's recall was remarkably similar to her mother's, her grandparents', and Fanny Kate Cash's.

When Andy Weathers approached to cross-examine Debbie, she watched him the way a possum watches a hunting dog. He asked her about Nona's condition. Was she not very weak, capable of using only one hand? And wasn't Walter very strong, able to carry his wife from room to room?

Debbie insisted that the old woman was "very strong as far as her side that she could move. She was very strong on that side."

"She would be unable—if she was on the bed—to get up?"

"She was also able to answer the phone if it rang," Debbie added, without answering the question.

"She would be unable to get out of bed?"

"No, she can't get out of bed."

"Don't you really think that if that man wanted to do something to hurt that woman—a man of his strength, a woman weighing less than a hundred pounds, a woman who'd suffered a massive stroke—if he *wanted* to do something to harm her, he could have done it with the greatest of ease?"

Debbie looked trapped, and she ducked. "I really can't answer that question."

Weathers didn't push her. His point was made. In response to further questions, Debbie Cole described the people present in the Washington Road home on June 12, the day before Paw was hospitalized. "I think I was with my mother . . . Mrs. Allanson and Mr. Allanson . . . my little girl."

"Any other people there?"

"No."

"Are you positive?"

"Not to my knowledge," she replied, giving the standard Radcliffe answer.

Amazingly, Debbie had forgotten the bombastic presence of Fanny Kate Cash, who had sworn right in that courtroom that she had been there that day to protect Pat and "Grandma."

"No further questions."

There was redirect and recross, but it was apparent that Debbie was not a very good witness. She often answered, "Huh?" or "I don't remember."

✦   ✦   ✦

Debbie Cole was the last witness. The defense rested without calling Tom Allanson to the stand. Although the gallery had held stubbornly onto their seats in the expectation of seeing

Tom, he had long since been returned to Jackson Prison. Dunham McAllister wanted nothing or no one who could tie his client, however tenuously, to the 1974 double murders on Norman Berry Drive. If Tom had appeared on the stand, Andy Weathers would have had a field day on cross-examination.

To the defense team's chagrin, Weathers did the next best thing by calling a former Fulton County assistant district attorney to the stand on rebuttal. Tom would not be in the courtroom to relive the night of July 3—but William Weller, the D.A. who had prosecuted Tom, was. Weller had recently left the D.A.'s office for private practice and was currently the chairman of the criminal law section for the Atlanta Bar Association.

Although Paw Allanson's confession had already been fairly well discredited, Weathers wanted the jury to see that he could not possibly have shot his son and daughter-in-law, and that Pat had tried to sacrifice the old man to free her husband. Over McAllister's vigorous objections, Weller sketched a rough depiction of the basement on Norman Berry Drive, pointing out the kitchen steps and the "hole." He recalled examining the interior of that aperture and seeing the bullet marks all over the inside.

Bill Weller said that the "window" into the hole was at least as high as his own waist. "It wasn't an easy chore for me—as a *young* man—to lift myself up and get inside that hole," Weller said. "The basement was very difficult to walk around in—just so much debris. About the only area where you could walk, there were rugs and kinds of planks and things all over the floor."

He had made his point. There was no way that Paw, close to eighty, could have physically done what the confession said—run around that basement jammed with junk and then lift himself on the weight of his arms and jump nimbly in and out of the hole. As an expert in criminal law, Weller testified that he "did not buy" the document purported to be Paw Allanson's confession.

"Could this [confession] possibly be used to get a new trial?" McAllister asked him on recross.

"Yes, sir."

"Your answer was yes. It's your opinion that this could be used to get a new trial?"

"Almost anything can be used to get a new trial."

McAllister tried again; he didn't want to leave the jury with the impression that Paw's confession would *really* have helped Tom get out of prison. He needed desperately to remove this motive from Pat's case. "If the person who made this were *dead,*" he asked Weller, "would this be admissible at that new trial?"

"If the judge wants to hear it," Weller said implacably, dashing McAllister's thrust that a dead Paw Allanson would be useless to Pat. "He [the judge] has full discretion to do what he wants to do in a new trial."

Weathers stepped forward to box the defense in further. "If a trial judge wished to accept this document as being true, Mr. Weller, and Mr. Walter Allanson was not there to object, is it not a fact that all charges could have been dismissed that day, and he [Tom] could walk out of the penitentiary the next day, if the trial court judge saw fit to do it?"

"If he wanted to do it," Weller agreed.

McAllister would not give up. "What you're saying then is that, under the law in Georgia, a Superior Court judge has infinite power in the trial of a case?"

"Yes, sir," Weller agreed.

"But such a statement as this is inadmissible, is it not?"

"As a general principle of law," Weller said, "it's inadmissible. But it depends on what you're using it for. If you are using it for *impeachment,* it may be admissible. If you are using it as direct evidence, it would probably be inadmissible, depending on the circumstances."

✦ ✦ ✦

Testimony in Pat Allanson's trial ended near 7:00 P.M. on Thursday, May 5.

Final arguments began Friday morning with Andy Weathers painting a devastating picture of a conscienceless woman who had planned a double murder deliberately. He offered no eyewitnesses. "Ladies and gentlemen . . . when somebody plans a murder and is cold enough to put arsenic in people's food and drink, the state can never bring in someone who watched them do it. They are far too careful."

Weathers listed the outright lies, the evasions, the omissions that permeated Pat Allanson's explanations for everything. A prosecutor who usually argued only for "about five minutes," he talked much longer. So many segments of the defense case didn't match up.

Dunham McAllister argued that the state had not proved its case beyond a reasonable doubt. Why had Nona not testified? Where were the tests of Paw's gastric juices? Why weren't they saved? Was Walter Allanson weak or strong? Since Tom's cousins still got one-sixth of the elderly Allansons' estate, albeit with Pat as the executor, didn't that prove she wasn't behind changing their wills three times?

McAllister fought hard, striking at relatively minor points to deflect attention from the glaring gaps in Pat's testimony. He even went so far as to suggest that, according to the experts, no one knew if arsenic was a poison or a drug, and that it was possible that the poisoning of the Allansons "was just a pure and simple accident." He enlarged on that bizarre theory: ". . . and then he [Paw] takes an overdose of drugs and does strange things and tries to feed Mrs. Allanson something. Maybe tries to feed her liquor that's got arsenic in it. That's just one possibility."

McAllister was an excellent criminal defense attorney, reminding the jury again and again that they had to be *sure*. "Twelve people have got to cut everyone off and say the *only* thing that could be in this case is the guilt of that lady over there. You have got to decide whether they have cut those things off or not." He submitted that the state had failed to prove Pat Allanson guilty to a moral certainty. If the jury agreed with him, Pat would walk free.

It was almost over. Andy Weathers rose to speak for the final time. It was patently ridiculous, he maintained, to consider old Walter Allanson a killer—by shotgun or by poison. Pat Allanson was the guilty party, a woman who had first tried to foist off a phony confession to free her husband from prison and then attempted murder so that she could inherit a fortune. And a fortune it was. In the best light, the Boggs children would receive a small portion of the *trust* portion of the Allansons' estate. *"She* has the power of attorney. *She* has to make no accounting. If she depletes the trust estate, this paragraph number two here only comes into effect *if* there is anything remaining in the trust estate. . . .

"The motive she had is right here," Weathers concluded. "She inherits the whole thing. . . . Pat Allanson is guilty of what she's charged with doing. She's guilty now. She was one block away when her husband was in that basement doing that killing. And you have this confession [Paw's]. . . . You will note in here that Tom Allanson . . . is caught right close by. It says he's *there* while his grandfather does the killing. *Now ladies and gentlemen, if Tom Allanson was there and could refute this, and his wife is on trial, why in the name of God didn't they put him up?*"

Why indeed? It was likely that Tom had not been put on the witness stand because he had refused to lie about his grandfather. Yes, he wanted out of prison terribly. He would hate to see his wife convicted and sent to prison. But he loved old Paw, and he would not get up and lie and say his grandfather was a killer—not even to save his own skin and Pat's.

Perhaps the woman on trial had underestimated her husband.

Dunham McAllister was outraged by Weathers's final statement. He asked that the question about why Tom hadn't testified be stricken from the record and that the jury be instructed to disregard it.

Once again, the two attorneys turned to the law books.

Andy Weathers won.

"I am going to let the Supreme Court say it," Judge Holt barked. "I'm not going to say. I overrule your objection."

"For the record," McAllister asked, "might I also make a motion for a mistrial?"

"Yes, sir—and I overrule your motion for a mistrial."

The jury went to lunch. They would begin deliberating at 2:45 on Friday afternoon, May 6, 1977.

38

Susan Alford was terrified that they were going to send her mother to prison; she was angry with Dunham McAllister for not pursuing a defense of mental illness. She believed that her mother was addicted to drugs and should be in a hospital, not in prison. But it was too late now. The young Eastern Airlines flight attendant, her friend, Sonja Salo—who was also an Eastern flight attendant, but who was saving to go to law school—and her sister, Debbie, waited with Pat, Boppo, and Papa for the jury's decision. Mr. McAllister had warned them that it might take a long time, and if it did, that would be good. If a jury came back quickly, it usually found the defendant guilty. The longer the better.

Susan had a presentiment of doom.

Pat, Sonja, and Susan went over to the Underground to have something to eat. Pat ordered lunch and iced tea, but Susan and Sonja, unable to choke down food, ordered drinks. "We were scared shitless," Susan recalled, "terrified of what was about to happen. I felt in my bones that this was going to be the last time

—maybe ever—that we would be together like that. I kept thinking that my mother might be sleeping in jail that night. I didn't see how she could survive if they found her guilty."

As for Pat, she seemed oblivious of the fact that her fate was being decided across the street and eight floors up.

They hurried back to the corridor outside courtroom 808. Two hours into deliberation, Judge Holt called the jury in and asked them if they were making any reasonable progress toward a verdict. They felt that they were. He offered them a choice about supper. If they went out to eat, they would have to go together on a bus; it would take almost two hours. Or they could order food in.

The jury voted to have Varsity hot dogs sent in.

Susan winced. Her mother loved Varsity chili dogs. Pat was so childlike in her food preferences, and so picky too. My Lord, Susan thought, if her mother went to prison, there probably wouldn't be anything she could stomach. Sonja Salo agreed. She thought Pat was one of the nicest *and* the most fragile people she had ever met. She had seen only bright fragments of Pat's personality; when she visited Pat in the hospital, she had found her very brave. Sonja idolized Pat. Although Sonja herself had very little money, she had eaten peanut butter sandwiches so that she could buy a dinner of steak, baked potato, and salad to carry into the hospital for Pat. She was as worried as Susan was. It seemed incredible that the woman who was so near death a year and a half before was even well enough to go on trial.

They waited. Outside, it was Friday evening, the beginning of the weekend. Inside, time took forever. Boppo smoked steadily and so did Debbie, lighting each cigarette from the one before it. But then, Boppo always smoked a lot; it was part of her. Television crews waited with them, poised and ready.

It had been a little more than seven hours since the jury was charged, but they had taken time out for lunch and supper. They had deliberated for only about four hours. At five minutes to nine, Judge Holt called them into his courtroom to see if they could reach a decision that evening. If not, he would dismiss them until morning.

Robert Hassler had been elected foreman. He said that they were just about to ask a question. They needed some explication of the terms "circumstantial evidence" and "hypothesis" as listed in the fifth instruction to the jury: "To warrant a conviction on circumstantial evidence, the proved facts shall not only be consistent with the hypothesis of guilt, but shall exclude every other reasonable hypothesis save that of the guilt of the accused."

Judge Holt reread the instruction and explained it to them.

Susan felt icy sweat trickle down her back. She *knew*. Maybe it was the expression on the jurors' faces. Maybe it was the question. They were asking about how they could be sure someone was *guilty*.

Boppo lit another cigarette and Papa paced.

At 9:08, the jury buzzed for the bailiff. At 9:10, they returned to the courtroom. They had their verdicts. Mr. Hassler passed the handwritten ballot to the bailiff, who in turn handed it to Judge Holt. The jurist's face was empty of expression as he glanced over the piece of paper. Then he said, "These haven't been dated." The spectators in the gallery let their breath out slowly as the vital document went back to the jury. Robert Hassler dated it, "May 6, 1977."

It was passed through two hands again, and then to Andy Weathers. Pat Allanson stood, her back rigid, her eyes straight ahead as the prosecutor prepared to read the verdicts. Only a pulse in her neck gave her away, her heart beating so violently that the precious cameo on the gold chain around her neck bounced delicately.

Weathers cleared his throat. "As to Count I: We the jury find the defendant guilty."

Pat showed no expression at all. She didn't sway. She didn't faint.

"As to Count II: We the jury find the defendant guilty."

Debbie broke into loud sobs and shouted, "No!" Boppo, as she always had, pushed back her own emotions and hugged her granddaughter in a vain attempt to comfort her. Susan cried more softly and Sonja Salo turned to help her. Colonel Radcliffe looked thunderstruck. Courtroom 808 was full of sobbing and anguished cries, but the convicted woman seemed to be in shock. Pat, who had always crumpled to the ground at the slightest emotional pressure, stood like a tree, unmoving.

Judge Holt issued a stern warning. "Anyone who cannot control himself or herself must leave the courtroom now." No one left, but the crying was muffled. Judge Holt was ready to sentence Pat immediately. Dunham McAllister rose to ask for a delay. He needed time. He was sure there would be leniency in the sentencing guidelines, but he had to have time to do some research. He was not presently prepared to go forward.

Judge Holt was not amused. "You must have anticipated this," he said.

"I have no excuse. I do ask your forbearance in granting a delay."

"I can't do it Monday. I've got two weeks of civil cases. Sentencing will be on May 16."

McAllister started to ask if his client could be free awaiting sentence, but Judge Holt was ahead of him, even before he got the request completely out. "No. If I did it for one, I'd have to do it for all of them. I won't do it. It creates red tape for my office, the district attorney's office, and every other office involved. The defendant is in custody. Do you understand that?"

Deputies moved toward Pat, handcuffs ready. She turned back toward her sobbing family as she woodenly allowed herself to be cuffed. She looked so lovely in the dress she had made, this one of avocado and cream, her green eyes wide and frightened against her stark white skin. Her daughters cried openly. The Radcliffes were stunned, but they did not, of course, break down. They only watched Pat disappear. It simply could not be that their daughter was going to jail, not to stay all *night*.

Jean and Homer Boggs congratulated Andy Weathers and the lawyers began to gather up their papers. As Weathers turned to leave, Boppo ran after him. "Sir! Sir!" she cried. "You have made a terrible mistake!" Weathers acknowledged her with a half shake of his head, but kept on walking.

The television cameras rolled, catching all the emotion, but Pat's family didn't know that until they saw their images caught on the eleven o'clock news. "I felt like someone had died," Susan remembered, "and Sonja was trying to lead me out of the courtroom."

Already, at Judge Holt's order, the bailiff was turning the lights out.

✦ ✦ ✦

On May 16, Andy Weathers urged Judge Holt to give Pat Allanson the stiffest sentence possible. "She took from them [the

Allansons] everything they had—as well as their mental capacities. . . . Arsenic poisoning is one of the most painful ways for a human being to die. . . . This is a brutal scheme. She showed not one ounce of mercy to these two people she tried to kill one day at a time. And they *would* have died if the scheme had not been detected. I don't think the defendant is due any points. It's a cold scheme. It's a calculated scheme. It's carried out where they would die an inch at a time. They suffered great pain. . . . I'd ask the court to set a sentence that is consistent with this brutality."

Dunham McAllister reminded the judge that "the evidence only clearly established at least one poisoning episode for Mrs. Allanson and two for Mr. Allanson. There was no evidence other than that." He asked that Pat's medical problems be taken into consideration. "I would ask the court to consider a lenient sentence, to consider probation, that Mrs. Allanson is a person who can benefit from a period of probation."

Judge Holt apparently did not agree. He sentenced Patricia Vann Radcliffe Taylor Allanson to two ten-year prison terms, to be served consecutively. Under Georgia statute, it was the harshest sentence he could impose. Pat stared at her attorney as if she didn't understand. Surely this was a mistake. Surely the judge was only saying what he *could* give her; he couldn't mean that he was actually going to send her to prison.

Grimly, Dunham McAllister gave notice of appeal.

"I can't hear it now," Holt said. "You can file it. I'll hear it as soon as I can."

Only three years had passed since Pat had married into the Allanson clan, and in that space of time the family had been well nigh annihilated. Walter and Carolyn were dead; Tom was locked in prison, convicted of their murders; and his children had been adopted, lost to him. Paw and Nona would have arsenic in their bones until they died. They would never be the same. Jean had been forced outside the circle of her own family. The few Allansons who were alive and walking free were full of doubts and recriminations. Pat had seemed to be a frail, dependent woman when she insinuated herself into their midst, but she had fanned each faint spark of disagreement into glowing coals of hostility and distrust that needed only a faint breeze to burst into flames.

She had promised Tom love unlike any he had ever known before. Believing he saw paradise in her transparent green eyes, Tom had taken her as his wife. And she had come close to destroying him and everything he loved. He might better have flung himself into a volcano.

Tom's parents had detested Pat, but her own family loved her beyond reason. Margureitte's devotion was all-encompassing, all-forgiving, blind. And it wasn't just Margureitte. Pat had found love and acceptance wherever she turned from the moment she was born. Mama Siler and all her aunts adored her. Gil still loved her even though she had banished him without giving him a reason. Susan and Debbie and Ronnie cherished their mother and overlooked her eccentricities and her demands for more. Always more.

Pat's family had crumbled at its center, the structure weakening with each new disaster until it was as friable as a cheap Christmas ornament. Everywhere Pat walked she left tears and dissension and death in her wake. She was a catalyst to tragedy, a flawed genius who recognized vulnerability in others. Unerringly, she fixed on weakness and burrowed and twisted until something or *someone* broke. If she could not be happy, then she would not have anyone find joy.

Mama Siler had neglected the other grandchildren so that Patty could have the best of everything. Kent was a suicide, dead for more than a decade. Boppo and Papa had never really had a life of their own; they had lost the house on Dodson Drive, and now even the Tell Road farm. They were bankrupt. Ronnie had been kept from Gil when he needed a father most, and Pat gave him anything he wanted as long as he was there for her. Pat had meddled in Debbie's marriage until it was hopelessly broken. Seeing the danger, Bill Alford hoped to get Susan and Sean away before it was too late for them too.

Until this moment, Pat had walked away unscathed from the havoc she wrought, so self-involved that she never even saw the wreckage behind her. But now she was being forced to deal with what she had done. She was thirty-nine years old and she was going to prison.

That couldn't be. It wasn't fair. It was, as her mother had cried out to Mr. Weathers, "a terrible mistake."

39

Pat would serve her sentence at the Hardwick Correctional Institute in Milledgeville, Georgia, the site of Georgia's first state capital. Southeast of Atlanta and sandwiched between the Oconee National Forest and Lake Sinclair, Hardwick was, indeed, a prison, even though it looked from the exterior like a fine southern girls' school set in green rolling countryside. A huge tree grew in front, shading picnic tables and softening the effect of the fence topped with razor wire. It was new construction, made of beige stucco whose hue was not unlike the tan uniforms its inmates wore.

The custodial complex was small—too small, really; many of the inmates slept in dorms in mobile homes on the back side of the prison. There was no free movement from place to place, and Pat's days were regulated by rules and other people's time schedules. The food was heavy and starchy, the sheets were rough, and the other prisoners were not from the kind of life she had known.

She hated it.

"Even though the walls are painted pretty and it looks nice outside," she told her family, "don't let them fool you. It's still a prison. They degrade you."

Margureitte and Clifford Radcliffe made the eighty-mile drive to Hardwick faithfully each weekend. They would not dream of missing a visitors' day. When the Radcliffes or Pat's children came to visit, they were searched and anything they brought with them had to be checked by a matron. When Pat was ushered down to see them, the matrons had her step into a small bathroom off the visiting area before and after for a body search —as if she were a "common criminal," she said. She had been fascinated with the indignities Tom suffered in prison, urging him to tell her details; now *she* was learning what it was like to be caged.

Pat quickly convinced prison authorities that her health problems made it impossible for her to work in the kitchen. She couldn't lift anything heavy and the smells of institutional food sickened her. The prison kitchen served a lot of fish from nearby Lake Sinclair—fish Pat believed were "poisoned" by pollution. The rest of the menu featured all prisons' ubiquitous oatmeal, grits, potatoes, spaghetti, macaroni, rice, and heavy bread baked by inmates and slathered with greasy margarine.

"It's nothing but garbage," she complained to her parents. "I won't eat it. A lot of the women get sick from eating that fish, and the meat is rotten." Indeed, Pat told them she fasted until the weekends came. Boppo always brought in a cooler full of food. When the matron occasionally demurred at some container or eating utensil, she would argue, "Surely there's no harm in *that*."

Each visit, Boppo and Papa brought Pat a large steak from a Bonanza franchise, hot dogs from the Dairy Queen, a pizza, and whatever else she had ordered. She ate every bit, even though so much food at once usually left her bloated with indigestion. Later, Pat would earn privileges so that she could keep peanut butter, crackers, and instant coffee in her cell.

Susan and Bill Alford visited as often as they could, Debbie came less frequently, and Ronnie only rarely. Ronnie adored his mother, and her incarceration was a terrible blow for him. His alcohol consumption increased, and he suffered intense grief and loss reactions when he broke up with girlfriends. Sometimes, he injured himself with knives or razor blades, cutting into the skin of his chest. Ever since he was a child, his role in his mother's life had been to protect her, to run errands for her. Her absence left a huge empty place.

Debbie was bereft too. Even though she and Susan had complained and laughed at their mother's peccadilloes, Debbie had no anchor without Pat. Her marriage bounced continually from bad to mediocre, and she left her husband as regularly as the weather changed. When life away from him didn't meet her expectations, she went back—but grudgingly.

The first Christmas Pat was in prison was very difficult. Susan and Bill decided to stay home in Atlanta and have their own Christmas morning with five-year-old Sean, and Pat took their defection as a blatant omission of love. When Debbie and Dawn didn't show up for Christmas either, she was crushed.

Her letters home were seldom overtly chiding, but rather masterpieces of artful despair. "Dear Susan, Bill, & Sean," she wrote,

Wish I could have been there to see Sean and all his toys. I really was shocked to walk into the visiting room and see Boppo, when I'd expected to see the 3 of you and Debbie and Dawn. . . . I realize it's a long way though and you were probably all tired and just wanted to be home alone. "Alone" is a word I'm very familiar with. It's very "alone" here and the only things that make it bearable are the visits every weekend. . . . Don't think I don't realize the hardship & sacrifice on all of your time, but there are no words to tell you what it means to me. It's the difference between making it & not making it. Handling it or going all to pieces. . . . I live for those visits. I need all of you or I'm lost.

I already know I've lost Tom because I can't "do" things for him like I could. Who will be next? All I have to offer is my love & my desperate need for all of you. Every visiting day I am dressed & waiting hours before. Silly? No. Necessary to survive in this place. . . . It's so lonely here. Forgive the teardrops.

Susan felt awful. And guilty. Even though they would have had to take a toddler 210 miles to visit Pat in prison, they should have gone. Her mother had felt all alone on Christmas Day, with only Boppo, Papa, and Ronnie to eat with her at the prison Christmas dinner.

Tom *was* gone from Pat's life. And not just in a physical sense. He had been moved to Buford Prison north of Atlanta, where his intelligence and education could be utilized, the opportunity he might have had years before if Pat hadn't blocked it.

His wife's interference with the staff had made him do hard time at Jackson Prison, no matter how much he tried to obey the rules and keep his mouth shut. "I had several people tell me, 'That woman is gonna keep you in here *forever,*' " he remembered later. "I began to believe it. Every time I turned around, it was 'Pat this' and 'Pat that' and conferences in the warden's office about something else she'd done. When I got transferred up to Buford, I said I was gonna start over. With the prison system, you can't escape what's around you, but if you get transferred, you sometimes get an opportunity to get a fresh start."

Now Pat was also in prison, and trying to deal with his wife, her counselor, his counselor, and four-way phone calls between two prisons was hellish. "Her counselor had to call my counselor and then I got to sit there in front of the counselor and carry on an argument on the phone, and this guy is sitting there writing down, making notes of my reactions and stuff. . . . I just didn't need that."

What had begun in a blaze of romantic fervor ended as many such liaisons do, flatly and with little emotion. "I told her 'I can't handle this up here,' " Tom said. " 'The best thing that we could do is go opposite directions.' She agreed to it, and the next thing I know, I got the divorce papers. That was fine, you know. I just cut all ties completely."

Tom was really alone. His children were gone—he didn't know where—his family shattered. His grandparents were too sick to visit him, and in his heart he accepted that Pat had done it to them. Although he could not forgive that, some last vestige of loyalty kept him from condemning her out loud. She was paying. He was grateful to be free of her and let her go her way. Pat's family was gone from him too. Susan and Debbie had liked Tom, but now they backed away. "We had to make a choice," Susan recalled later, "between sticking by our mother or writing to Tom. *She* was our mother, so the choice was already made.

Debbie and I took Dawn and Sean and went to see Tom once—
in 1976, when he was in Jackson—and my mother was so angry
with us. She told us she'd called the state police to head us off.
I think that was an exaggeration, but I'm not so sure. We were
afraid to go back."

Up in Buford, Tom decided to do the best he could; he had
accepted the bleak fact that he would be in prison for a very long
time and that he would be alone.

✦ ✦ ✦

In January 1978, Pat suffered a painful insect bite that turned
out—at least given her proclivities—to be a stroke of luck. She
was bitten by a brown recluse spider, whose venom is often
deadly. Tissue surrounding the bite is subject to necrosis, dies,
and sloughs off. With Pat's history of intractable infections, she
was sent to the state hospital in Milledgeville, which had facilities for treating prisoners. It was a huge, venerable complex, so
old it made Hardwick look like something from the space age.
For months, she scarcely had to acknowledge that she *was* serving time. She was allowed to wear her own negligees, and her
relatives could come and go whenever they wanted to visit;
Boppo and her aunts brought all manner of delicacies. It was
not like being in prison at all, and her family loved having her
there. Pat stayed as long as she could. When she recovered from
the spider bite, she developed other symptoms and it took the
doctors a long time to do all the tests they needed to be sure that
she was in no danger of a stroke or a fatal embolism.

Initially, the Radcliffes had planned to sue the state of Georgia for the pain and suffering Pat had endured because of the
brown recluse bite, but they eventually dropped the idea. Pat
did so much better in the hospital than she had done in prison.
She always had seemed to enjoy her hospital stays. Finally,
though, she had to go back to Hardwick. It was almost worse to
go *back* than it had been to go to prison in the first place.

✦ ✦ ✦

There is a saying among convicts: "No one does more than a
year of hard time. After that, you adjust."

Pat Taylor (she quickly dropped the Allanson after she and
Tom were divorced) adjusted. Her parents and her children
were loyal and supportive, although Pat was shocked when

Susan and Bill Alford were moved to Houston in 1978 by Bill's company. Although Bill never went to law school as he had hoped, Susan had worked until he graduated with a B.A. from Mercer University. She resigned from Eastern when Bill became very successful as a sales executive in office supplies. Pat could not believe that Susan could be so cruel as to desert her.

The Alfords would be transferred to Tampa in 1979, and then back to Atlanta in 1981. But Boppo and Papa were steadfast. They planned all their weekends around Pat. They posed for pictures with their daughter, a service offered by prisons in Georgia on visiting days: for a small price, employees took Polaroid snapshots of inmates with their families.

Despite her complaints about the inhumanity of the Georgia prison system, Pat fared amazingly well. She was still very beautiful, and her hair and makeup were always exquisite. She had to wear the tan uniform, but she did clever things with scarves and brooches and made it look as if it were a hundred-dollar dress. She carried the cane that she would use all through her years in prison. In the slightly blurry photographs, Pat's parents stood beside her and smiled as proudly as if she had just graduated with a Ph.D.

Susan and Debbie and the grandchildren had posed too when they visited, a family united. "In a way, I was relieved. I believed that, without drugs, my mother would be all right," Susan remembered. "I was happy to see her healthy and responding so well. She had had a problem, but now things were going to be all right. I loved my mother, and some of the happiest moments of my life had been spent with her. I just can't describe how good she could make you feel when things were going all right. I told my whole family back in 1977 when she was convicted that, if I *ever* saw any signs of something like that happening again, I would stop it, and I reminded Mom of that in prison. I knew she was all right when she said, 'Well, I certainly hope *somebody* would!' and Boppo agreed."

For Margureitte Radcliffe, there may have been an irony in having her daughter in prison. For the first time in a long, long time she could plan her life. She could play cards and go out to lunch with friends. She had always had a passion for bingo. She was a natural, able to play a whole tableful of cards all by herself, and she thoroughly enjoyed gambling benignly at Fort Mac.

The weekends were Pat's, of course, but the time between

belonged to Margureitte. Her granddaughters marveled that
they had never seen Boppo so happy. She was still at her daughter's beck and call, and there were myriad things that upset Pat,
but her phone calls home could only come in the evening at
Hardwick's pleasure. There had always been emergencies with
Pat. But now, at least Margureitte knew where she was and that
she was safe. She talked often about her "poor, innocent daughter" locked up in prison through a "terrible injustice."

No one dared phone Margureitte on the nights Pat was due to
call. She still had to report all her activities to Pat, who wanted
to know every detail of her mother's days. But with Pat in
prison, Margureitte's obsessive concern for her daughter could
be compartmentalized; for a time, it didn't override everything
else in her life.

Margureitte had always had certain self-indulgences, small
things that perhaps allowed her to devote herself so slavishly to
her family. She adored peanuts—she was never without a jar of
them—and she drank coffee and smoked from morning until
night. "I want to be buried with my cigarettes, my peanuts, and
my coffee," she often said laughingly.

Margureitte's preferred dishes disgusted her daughter: fried
liver, scrambled pork brains and eggs, escargot, chicken giz-
zards, and smoked oysters. While Pat was in prison, she could
cook whatever she wanted, she could sip her coffee, smoke, and
watch her favorite soap opera, *Days of Our Lives*.

The Radcliffes moved from their rented house to a townhouse. It didn't take a lot of upkeep, and they were able to relax.
Far away in Texas, Susan was pregnant again. Debbie was giving her marriage another go. A year later, Ronnie married too,
and he and his wife expected a baby. Without Pat, all the Radcliffes achieved a degree of normalcy in their lives, something
that had been very rare.

It would also be very brief.

◆　◆　◆

For the most part, the guards and matrons at Hardwick liked
Pat. She was a perfect lady, and she gave them little trouble.
She was gracious and concerned about their lives, remembering
to ask about *their* children and grandchildren, and her sewing
and fancywork were flawless. They admired the little smocked

dresses and knit things she made for Susan's new baby, Courtney, and they lined up to have Pat make dainty things for *their*
special babies, bringing her all the thread, lace, and cloth she
needed. Later, when she had earned the privilege, they drove
Pat all the way to Atlanta to a crafts store to pick out the materials herself.

In prison, Pat found a way to shine. Her manners were cor-
dial, but she held herself clearly above the mass of women who
languished behind bars. Many of the other prisoners were illiterate blacks, and she often alluded to the fact that she was the
daughter of a colonel from Atlanta; she had never really associated with blacks. Now that she bunked with a trailerful of black
women, she tried to keep her own space inviolate—without letting them see her distaste.

Heretofore, Pat had insisted that she was not prejudiced. She
had regaled her daughters with a story of the time she had defied
the Ku Klux Klan, marched into a midnight gathering, and
shouted at them that they were wrong, even as they circled a
burning cross in a North Carolina field. Locked up, she used
derisive racial slang.

Pat confided to her family that she had been approached by
lesbian prisoners; she had been frightened, but she had managed
to stay free of any involvement. A woman utterly obsessed with
men for years, she no longer spoke of love or even the possibility
of love. Actually, she seemed more fulfilled by her knitting,
sewing, and craft projects than she ever had been by her passionate sexual affairs.

✦ ✦ ✦

Margureitte and Clifford tried to keep worrisome news from
Pat. Ronnie and his wife divorced, and he was given custody of
his tiny daughter, Ashlynne. The tradition of the Siler women
continued. Mama Siler had raised Pat for her first five years,
Boppo had always been there for Pat's children, and now she
stepped in to raise her grandson's child. Ashlynne was a darling
baby and the Radcliffes doted on her. Papa had always preferred
dainty little girls in ruffly dresses, and he carried Ashlynne
around, proudly showing her off. When she cried, he and Boppo
tucked her into bed between them.

Pat did not approve of Boppo and Papa having Ashlynne.

Like Dawn, Sean, and Courtney, this baby was her grandchild, but she didn't appear to have any feelings toward her. It may have been because she was in prison and didn't have a chance to really know the baby; it may have been because Ashlynne had taken her place at home. And she ruined Boppo's visits too; Boppo brought the baby along all the time and fussed over her instead of over Pat.

Margureitte idolized that baby. Just as Mama Siler had doted on Patty, Margureitte loved Ashlynne with a fierceness that was almost visceral. When Pat called home and heard Ashlynne in the background, her voice took on a hard edge and she asked, "What is *she* doing there?" Even though her mother played down how much Ashlynne meant to her, Pat was suspicious.

There were other things Boppo and Papa didn't tell Pat. On July 13, 1978, Debbie was arrested by two Atlanta Police Department vice squad members, J. T. Cochran and W. F. Derrick, and charged with two counts of soliciting for sodomy, masturbation for hire, and escort without a permit. Debbie explained that she had merely taken a job as a receptionist for the escort service, and that she had no idea what the real business taking place was.

The officers' follow-up report was more specific, and far more graphic. Acts of sexual intercourse and oral sex were offered and agreed to by Debbie, representing "Atlanta's Finest Model Agency," to be charged at a hundred dollars apiece, with an additional eighty quoted to Officer Cochran for "intentional erotic stimulation of the genital organs . . . by manual contact." On her booking papers, Debbie listed her relatives as her husband and her brother. She did not mention her mother or her grandparents.

Boppo found out. She found out everything; she always had. But she didn't tell Pat. Margureitte was a woman who strove to do the "correct" thing, but her equanimity was sorely tried. Her daughter and her ex-son-in-law were in prison, and now her granddaughter had been arrested for prostitution. She was nearing sixty, and it didn't seem fair when she had spent her whole life trying to make her family happy. It was not the way she herself had been raised. "I am a lady," Boppo said often. "My mother and father brought me up not to lower myself—I am civilized. I am a better and bigger person. I am a lady."

Debbie requested a jury trial, and the matter was not adjudicated until June 11, 1979. Debbie pleaded *nolo contendere.* Her grandmother appeared in court, standing proud and tall with Debbie. Boppo addressed the judge, explaining, "Sir, this woman has a child to care for." Debbie was given twelve months' probation on all three counts—to run concurrently. She explained she had pressing medical bills and other debts, and the three hundred-dollar fine was suspended.

Debbie's arrest and the trial were, finally, too much for Margureitte. *She,* who had always been the stainless steel martyr, finally buckled and was admitted to a local hospital. After juggling countless family problems for so long, she found solace and peace in the quiet, white rooms.

But not for long. Debbie stormed in and pointed an accusing finger at her grandmother: "How could you do this to me?" she cried. Even more upsetting to a woman in the grip of physical and emotional exhaustion, Pat was given a compassionate leave and brought from Hardwick to visit Boppo. Boppo turned her face to the wall and wished, if only for the moment, that they would all just go away.

Of course, they didn't. Boppo's children, grandchildren, and husband were her very life. In the main, she thrived on their disasters in need of fixing more than she ever needed peace and quiet. She spent her short time in the hospital and then she walked out the doors, head high, ready to do battle for her family once more.

✦　✦　✦

Pat had written an eleven-page letter to Susan in 1979 that displayed a curious mixture of concerns and rationalizations. She didn't appear to grieve at all over her divorce the previous spring; she might never have known Tom at all. Her life was so busy, and she was doing so much for others. She was teaching classes to her fellow inmates. She worked all day, she wrote, sewing and filling orders for the matrons. She had achieved the status of trusty. "With 28 women to teach (and babysit), I don't have much time. . . . Most of the women are old, physically handicapped and illitorate [*sic*] too. I'm mostly concentrating on 'Therapy' things for them & I do the wood carving & burning to make the money. Plus all the fancy needle work & crocheting."

Susan felt optimistic. This was the mother she had always

longed for. Susan's friend Sonja Salo now had her law degree and was seeking a hearing for Pat for a reduction of sentence. When her mother was paroled, Susan believed, they would all start over.

"Susan," Pat wrote in the same letter, "before I go any farther, Deb told me what she did. I *knew* something was terribly wrong & Boppo did too. . . . I know you've about been crazy over it, for I sure have & so has Boppo. And most of all Debbie has. She *needs* proffesional [*sic*] help."

Pat blamed all her own previous problems on diet pills, Valium, and sleeping pills. "You don't even realize it when it's happening. I know I didn't. I have about 2 years of my life that I'm really unsure of & really to this day don't know how much I really remember & how much has been told to me so many times that I *think* I remember."

Pat explained why Tom had deserted her. "It's for the best, Shug, so don't feel sorry for me. Tom made it *very* clear that, quote, (1) being married to me will keep him from making parole, (2) being married to me will keep him from making Trusty, (3) even writting to me is harmful to him & (4) that no one in the family cares about him . . . so it's better to sever it now & I only wish to God it had never been."

Pat listed the dozens of things she was sewing and crocheting for Susan's family, and asked her daughter to "Pray hard that all this nightmare will soon be over & we'll all be together again."

Pat had truly acclimated. With realizing it, she had slipped into a common convict affectation—drawing little circles with smiling faces instead of periods, and a circle-face with the word "Smile!" For men and women behind prison bars in every prison in America, the smiling circle is second nature, and a dead giveaway.

Pat commented to her daughter that she had written the long letter under "duress"—fights were breaking out all around her, and the mobile-home dorm was full of the angry screams of too many women locked up together too long.

"HELP!" she wrote. "I need to get out of this madhouse!"

40

After a careful study of the case, Sonja Salo was attempting to file an Extraordinary Motion for New Trial based on her belief that newly discovered evidence would prove that Pat had been legally insane at the time of her offense against Paw and Nona *and* at the time of her trial in May 1977. Pat had confided to Sonja that she could remember nothing of the prior two years, that she had only recently come back to being herself. Sonja believed her and was gratified to see that the woman she visited at Hardwick seemed so wonderfully together and well adjusted. So normal.

If Pat had been insane, she was no longer out of touch with reality. She was a whole new woman. She told her new attorney that she knew all too well how much damage heartless people could do. "We don't talk about it much," she said softly. "But I have a sister in North Carolina who has no conscience at all. She doesn't care who she hurts."

Sonja never mentioned Pat's sister to Boppo. Lord knows, the woman had borne enough pain. The young attorney didn't know that Pat had no sister at all—only the poor dead baby, Roberta, who had never taken a breath in this world. Pat brought up her "sister" so often that Sonja wondered when she would meet the evil sibling.

Sonja finally argued her case on December 5, 1980, before Superior Court Judge Ralph H. Hicks. She had only one witness: Margureitte Radcliffe. The rest of her motion was based on a psychiatrist's affidavit and several doctors' reports stemming from Pat's first embolism in 1973.

Andy Weathers objected to Margureitte's testimony, failing to see how her recall of an illness in 1973 would show that Pat Taylor had lost her mind and attempted to commit murder in 1977. Judge Hicks overruled Weathers when Sonja Salo explained that Pat's drug use had begun with that first illness, and that it was her position that the drugs had led to Pat's "insanity."

Margureitte recalled the pulmonary embolism and the abscess that would not heal. She testified that Pat's physical condition was always fragile, but that it had worsened after her husband was arrested. "Her personality became entirely different. She no longer was the person that I knew."

"And how did her personality appear to you?" Sonja asked.

"I'm not a doctor," Margureitte said, pursing her lips. "I'm not qualified in that way. . . . I thought that she was losing her mind. I wanted her to see a psychiatrist."

What Margureitte Radcliffe had to admit next was not easy. It was an enormous lie, a terrible secret she had kept for years. But her words would finally explain what had puzzled Pat's doctors for so long: the cause of her near-fatal hip abscess.

"On the area where she had the abscess and she'd been treated—in and out of the hospital—and I was trying to change the dressings—" Margureitte began. She took a deep breath and continued, forcing her voice to stay firm. "She would take instruments and self-mutilate herself where it had been trying to heal up. She would damage it herself."

"Did you see her actually do this?" Sonja asked.

"Yes, I saw her."

"What did she use?"

"Once she used an instrument that was a leather tooling device. It's with a metal thing about this long [demonstrating].

. . . She was scratching herself with that. Other times, she used a small forceps—about *so* large—that she had."

"*Did* you on any occasion have Pat committed to a psychiatric hospital?"

This had to be agony for Margureitte. She had sat in this very courthouse two and a half years earlier and painted the picture of "Mrs. Allanson," her daughter, the near-saint who had devoted herself to the tender care of Paw and Nona—a woman who was above reproach. She had never wanted anyone to discover that her perfect daughter had engaged in self-mutilation. Margureitte would have said anything to get Pat out of prison, but her words at long last had the ring of truth.

She continued to describe the daughter she had tried to hide from the world, the headstrong, histrionics-prone woman who took whatever she wanted. "On one evening, she had cut her wrists and I knew certainly that I couldn't get her to go on her own free will. . . . I talked with her doctor . . . and I saw Judge Gunby, and I signed the papers and they picked her up and took her to Metropolitan."

"Did Pat ever try to inflict pain upon herself in any other way?" Sonja asked.

"Yes . . . this same abscessed area, eventually the doctors decided to do plastic surgery. I thought she had put acid on it—because it turned black. . . . She would not let herself heal up. . . . I did not see her scratch herself. She would have places all over her, on her wrists, and on her body."

And then there were the drugs. Margureitte had tried so hard, she said, to wean her daughter off Demerol, but it didn't work. "She wanted Demerol. . . . I was asked to give her the drugs and then to gradually reduce them. . . . Eventually, I was adding so much distilled water to the Demerol, and then once, when I no longer had any phenocain—which you could tell has a little burn when this is injected—she knew . . . she was not getting it. She became very agitated. . . . Dr. Gandhi gave me enough so that I could add a little bit of phenocain. . . . I was never really able to get her off it. Somebody would give it to her."

Margureitte described a night when Pat had come home from Crawford Long Hospital after treatment for the abscess. "Colonel Radcliffe was out of state and it was sleeting outside and rainy." She said she thought Pat was safely tucked in bed. "I went back and she was gone."

Margureitte said she had tracked her daughter "like an animal" out there behind the house on Tell Road. "She wouldn't let me come near her . . . she said . . . she would take the same instrument that she had used on her right hip and she would plunge it into her heart." Margureitte sat straight and unflinching as she unveiled one histrionic scene after another, her crystal gaze fixed, daring anyone to think less of her and her daughter.

Sonja Salo maintained that Margureitte's testimony was newly discovered evidence that Dunham McAllister had not known about during Pat's trial. "I think under the law that if she was, in fact, legally insane at the time, she could not be held criminally responsible for a crime."

Judge Hicks seemed a little puzzled. "Doesn't that take some adjudication, to declare one legally insane? She has not ever, I assume . . . been *declared* legally insane, has she?"

Sonja said that that could be decided prior to any new trial Pat would have, but she certainly felt the question of Pat's insanity made a new trial necessary.

"Of course," the judge pointed out, "all of the information you had Mrs. Radcliffe testify to so far today was *known* by Mrs. Radcliffe way back in 1975 and '76 and she was in touch with the attorney, Mr. McAllister, and *testified* as a witness in the trial. . . . None of that information is anything new, is it?"

Sonja explained that this was all new, not only to Dunham McAllister, but to everyone else. Margureitte Radcliffe had not known what to do with her knowledge that her daughter was "insane," so she told no one. "Mrs. Radcliffe is under no legal obligation, if she has problems with her child, to be telling an attorney or anyone else that problem."

Judge Hicks was baffled and a little annoyed. "Well, *who* is the moving party in this case today? Is it the same Patricia Allanson? Is it her guardian? Is it a legal fiction—or who *is* the court reviewing?"

Sonja Salo believed so much in her cause that she may not have seen how specious her arguments were. She had had no psychiatric tests done on Pat, who was the "movant," because "I do not believe Patricia Allanson today is legally insane. This is a very strange situation."

It was indeed.

Andy Weathers cross-examined Margureitte Radcliffe. He quickly elicited the information that she had known that Dunham McAllister was her daughter's attorney for ten months before her trial, but she said she had been so unsure of her legal rights that she had never mentioned to him that she felt Pat was insane. Nor had either she or her husband felt they should bring that out in trial.

To date, Margureitte and Clifford Radcliffe had presented many faces to the world. But, never, ever had they appeared timid and unsure. Weathers's voice was thinly edged with sarcasm as he questioned the witness and drew forth only repetitions of how awed she had been by the Georgia judicial system. Margureitte said she had had no idea in the whole wide world that she should have mentioned her daughter's craziness to anyone, or even that she had the legal right to do that.

Sonja Salo introduced an affidavit from Dr. Ray Loring Johnson, a psychiatrist who had treated Pat at the Metropolitan Psychiatric Center in April of 1975, but who had lost track of her between June and December. He had not seen her again until the next October. He'd seen Pat twice in December 1976, and seven times in early 1977, as she awaited trial. He had diagnosed her initially as having "severe personality disorientation" when she slashed her wrists after being struck by Colonel Radcliffe. She had been obsessed with getting Tom out of jail and felt she and her husband were being mistreated. At that time, Johnson saw agitation, disorganization, and "much paranoid ideation."

Essentially, Dr. Johnson could not diagnose what Pat's mental state might have been at the time of the arsenic poisonings. He hadn't seen her at all during that phase of her life. "It is impossible for me to make definite statements about her sanity at the time of the offense, since this was three or four months after I saw her in December 1975, and six to seven months before I saw her again in October 1976. I *can* say that she was disorganized, suspicious, mistrustful, and, on several occasions, had seemed out of touch with reality during my earlier work with her. . . . I believe that it was quite probable that she was out of touch with reality at the time of the offense." Dr. Johnson did, however, say that he felt Pat had been "unable to collaborate effectively with her attorney in the preparation of her defense. At no time did she question her own sanity, or entertain the idea of making it an issue at her trial."

Next came an affidavit from Dunham McAllister to the effect that he had not been aware that Patricia Allanson was "harboring any legal mental defect." Andy Weathers bought none of it. He argued that it was ridiculous to think that McAllister could have spent almost a year with Pat preparing for trial and failed to notice that she was insane. It was even more ridiculous that she could testify at length at her own trial and that no one from Judge Holt, to Weathers himself, to the jury had found her even marginally mentally incompetent. "Now, the other sort of a shotgun defense that is being raised here is that she didn't know what she was doing at the time she did the act," Weathers argued. "The defense in this case was that she did *not* do it, and she very clearly took part in that defense and testified to that effect."

Pat Taylor's current appeal was based on one of the most familiar defense postures ever used: *I didn't do it—but if I did do it, I was crazy at the time. And now I'm not crazy anymore.*

It seldom worked.

Weathers would allow only that Pat "might not have been operating mentally at peak capacity." That didn't make her crazy.

The family hoped and prayed that Pat would be home with them by Christmas. It was not to be. On December 9, 1980, Judge Ralph Hicks rendered his decision. "It is hereby ADJUDGED, ORDERED and DECREED that said Motion be and the same is DENIED." Hicks did not find that the evidence was "newly discovered." He was not convinced that Pat Allanson had suddenly come to her senses and discovered that she had been insane from 1975 to 1977.

Sonja Salo was a very nice young woman. She had done the best she could for Pat and the Radcliffes, and they had lost. Years later, she acknowledged how gullible she had been to believe Pat's stories; she had even believed in the sociopathic sister hidden away in North Carolina. "I can say now," she concluded wryly, "that Pat Taylor is the most manipulative human being I ever met in my life."

✦   ✦   ✦

Pat's story seemed to be over. She was a middle-aged woman, confined to prison for many, many years, her beauty blurred by too much fasting and gorging and by the passing of those years. She found her pleasure in the pages of a craft store catalog and in bombarding her grandchildren—except for Ashlynne—with handmade presents. She sent Sean dainty, hand-painted hand-kerchiefs to carry to school. He thanked her dutifully, and put them in a drawer. She promised him she would buy him a pony as soon as she was free. (She never did.) Pat had never gone into any phase of her life halfway. She became completely obsessed with Victorian needlework. Her letters could still prickle at the consciences of those who loved her. She moved in their minds always, a pitiful creature who lived a desperate existence while they went about enjoying their lives. *"Please* remember," Pat wrote to apologize for slow progress on a petit point picture in April of 1982, "my day starts at 4 AM & I work from 7AM–8 or 9 PM. Then when I do get in at night, I do have to shower, hand wash & iron my clothes for next day. (I only have 2 uniforms.) Then usually I have a little dress to smock or hem, etc. But I usually spend every available moment (that I have any light) on it."

Pat was horrified to hear that Susan and Bill were moving away from Georgia *again*. She worried about how it would affect her grandchildren. "I realize that I have no right to voice an opinion or offer advice; for who am I? I'm a prisoner *but* I'm also your mother. . . . Yes, I've made a lot of mistakes. Let me say one thing—if I lived to be a 100, I *am* paying. I'm paying for anything I ever did, or thought of doing or would ever do. It's Hell enough to not know if I did or did not attempt to harm those two people. But that's something I have to live with & get straight with God. I know I'll *never* take another pill (narcotic) for you can be turned into a monster & not even know it & then everyone & everything that comes into contact with you is harmed in some form or another. That's a form of Hell in itself, to know that you've done this (& to people whom you love & who love you) & yet you have no real memory of it. . . . If anyone ever has any doubt that I'm not suffering sufficiently, I assure them I am & will continue to do so until the day I die. And the worst suffering is *not* the incarceration, but the knowledge that I'm responsible for destroying the stability of my family."

Pat finally acknowledged to her elder daughter that she herself took complete responsibility for everything that had happened; she only wondered if she would ever have a life again. She had been locked up for five years. If ever a woman voiced regret and appeared sincerely rehabilitated, it was Pat Taylor.

Her letters made her children cry.

41

Tom Allanson had been locked up for six and a half years when Pat's appeal for a new trial was denied. The staffs at both Jackson and Buford prisons and the parole board had labeled him a model prisoner. He had served many terms as president of Buford's chapter of the Junior Chamber of Commerce—the Rock Quarry Jaycees—been the executive state director of the Jaycees, and for several years was chairman of the Institutional Beautification Project. He organized a picnic the Rock Quarry Jaycees put on for the mentally retarded. He was voted the most valuable player on the All-Tournament football team. He wrote a column and articles and took photographs for the prison paper. He was vice-president of the Full Gospel Association, sang in the church choir twice each Sunday, and, most important, on July 31, 1981, he accepted Jesus Christ as his personal savior.

Tom was no longer completely alone in the world. Liz Price, his old neighbor in Zebulon, the woman he had had a crush on when he was sixteen years old, the woman who had carried feed and water to his animals after he was arrested, had written to him for most of the years he was in prison. His abandoned horseshoeing trailer was, in fact, still parked on her farm. It was locked and Pat had lost the key long ago. He had no idea if his tools were still inside, but Liz told him she was keeping the trailer safe for him.

She and Tom exchanged newsy, friendly letters at first; he was still legally married to Pat. "I wrote to Liz first," he remembered. "I was so depressed. I had no idea what was happening at home, and it seemed like everybody had turned their back on me—and she answered, and she would come to see me once in a while down at Jackson."

Liz left Georgia, moved to Florida, and vowed to forget Tom. Unknown to him, she had always loved Tom—at least somewhere in the back of her mind—and she needed to leave behind her all the sad reminders of what had happened. She didn't want him to know how she felt about him, not as long as he was a married man.

For a long time Tom had no idea where Liz was. He missed her letters; she was different from any woman he had ever known. She didn't seem to want anything from him—Liz was simply his friend. After his divorce from Pat in the spring of 1979, they got back in touch again; Liz had moved back to Forsyth County and taken a clerical job in the sheriff's office. Gradually, their letters became more personal. Tom told her he had little hope that he would be out of prison soon, if ever. He expected to serve at least fourteen years. That meant a probable parole date sometime in 1989.

It didn't matter to Liz. She visited Tom regularly, never missing a Sunday evening. After a year or so, they knew they wanted to be married, but the only way they could do that while Tom was in prison was by common law. (Later—too late for them—prison marriages were permitted at Buford.) They presented papers to prison authorities for a common-law marriage. It took persistence, but they finally got permission to get married. There were no conjugal visits in Buford Prison.

That didn't matter either. They had a common-law prison wedding in late 1980, and promised each other they would have another wedding when Tom was free.

Although Tom's applications for parole were turned down all through the early 1980s, he gained a sense of freedom *inside* prison. He vowed that he would not let the years behind bars destroy him. "Prison . . . doesn't mean it *has* to be torture or like the movies," he wrote to a friend. "Actually, it all depends on the individual's attitude and what they are made of. There are many that are miserable here and do everything they can to make everybody else miserable. Personally, I try to live right and follow the rules and make the best of this time."

Buford's warden paid for Tom to take correspondence courses from Clemson, and he received a state of Georgia certificate and license as a water and waste water treatment plant operator and laboratory analyst. Later, he was certified for South Carolina too. He paid for his own correspondence course from Cal State–Sacramento to upgrade his skills even more. He soon ran Buford's water and sewage treatment plant and Tom was the only trusty working outside the plant who had a driver's license. He was outside regularly, running errands as far as seventy-five miles away. He was always back on time, to the minute.

Later, he grinned as he remembered one amusing incident. "One time, we had a busload of prisoners over at the warden's place to help him move—and he got an emergency call that his wife had been in an accident. He took off, running, and yells, 'Tom, take the guys back.' So I come driving up to the prison with a whole busload of prisoners, delivering them all safe and sound."

Since he never had anyone to send him money to buy even the smallest necessities, like shaving cream and toothpaste, in the prison commissary, Tom worked with leather to make belts, purses, and billfolds to sell, and he was good at it—so good that he could even help Liz out from time to time. After a while, he even had his own "house" of sorts—the control building for the treatment plant. It was air-conditioned and had hot water, a shower, a carpet on the floor, a couple of big old comfortable chairs, and a radio. He added a hot plate and adopted two stray kittens for company.

It wasn't a real house, and Tom couldn't stay there at night, but he was on his own from 6:45 in the morning until dark, with breaks for meals at the prison. He wasn't required to work that long, but he much preferred being outside working to being inside. Sometimes, in the early evenings, he cooked up a pot of greens and sat listening to the radio with his two cats asleep on his lap. He had long since learned to appreciate and savor small pleasures. He could have walked away from prison easily. He never did; he never really thought about it. He visited with Liz on Sunday evenings and hoped for the day he might be paroled.

As he later described it, Tom Allanson *"was* the farm" at Buford. He did all the plowing, planting, weeding, and harvesting by himself on the three-quarter-acre plot they gave him. He bought his own seeds. When his crops ripened, he gave away produce to the warden, officers, teachers, and secretaries and, of course, to Liz. He grew watermelons, corn, beans, peas, tomatoes, potatoes, and sweet potatoes in the summer and turnips, mustard greens, collards, and cabbage in the winter. There was an arbor of muscadine grapes. He was most serene when he was out alone "bush-hogging" a watermelon field, working under the Georgia sun until the sweat glistened and rolled off his bare back.

Tom had marked a decade at Buford in August of 1987. He was a middle-aged man. He cautiously hoped to make parole. He had three jobs waiting for him on the outside; his expertise in waste water treatment was much sought after. But once again he was disappointed. After his ten years at Buford, on November 6, 1987, he was suddenly transferred back to Jackson Prison. They needed him to run the sewage treatment plant; it was due to open December 1 and would be five times bigger than the one at Buford. Jackson had no one left to operate a Class II treatment plant. One of their few trained men had tried to escape and been transferred out, and another was due to be released.

Jackson's waste treatment complex was way out on the end of the property and had no fence at all; Tom could hear the rush of the Towaliga River and the roar of cars on the highway. There were no guards out there. He was quite solitary. He was glad that he was still a trusty, but Jackson meant that Liz was a hundred miles away, and visiting was much more difficult for her.

In a way, it was ironic. Tom had worked so hard to improve himself and to get training that would help him find a good job when he was released. Instead, he had made himself invaluable to the Georgia prison system, and it would be a hardship for them to let him go.

PART SEVEN

SUSAN

42

Pat Allanson served a total of seven years. When Tom was transferred down to Jackson in 1987, she had been out of prison for three years. They had had absolutely no contact for a long time. She had told Tom again and again that she could not live without him, that her old life had ended when she met him and that she would have no life at all without her man. A hundred times—a *thousand* times—Tom had pleaded with her to hang on, that they would have a life somewhere down the road.

And she had replied only, "If you loved me, you would give up your life for me, and love me on the other side." Had he surrendered to her demands, he would have been long dead, a suicide at the age of thirty-three.

Despite her dire predictions about her failing health, Pat had not only lived without Tom, she seemed to be thriving. When she left Hardwick in 1984, she went to New Horizons, a halfway house for paroled females in Atlanta, where counseling and training would prepare her to merge gradually back into the world she had left in 1977. Fans were mourning Elvis Presley the summer Pat went to prison, and the world she returned to had made Boy George a star. Miniskirts and big hair were no longer in style, astronauts were floating free in space, Ronald Reagan was president, and, for the first time, a woman—Geraldine Ferraro—was nominated for vice-president.

The romantic, Victorian world that Pat had always aspired to was further away than ever. But she was free—or almost—and her family delighted in her return to Atlanta. She could go on weekend passes from the halfway house, and soon she would really be home, back with Boppo and Papa. Susan, Debbie, Ronnie, Boppo—the whole family—believed that Pat was on the brink of a wonderful new life. Her involvement with drugs was years behind her, and she was young enough to enjoy her life. She was still beautiful, albeit possessed of a more mature beauty. Even so, she looked far younger than her true age.

Pat habitually called her mother and daughters before 7:00 A.M. from New Horizons. If they were a little grouchy at being awakened, they immediately felt guilty; it meant so much to Pat to be in daily touch with them. It was such a luxury for her to be able to call them whenever she wanted. Susan, especially, devoted herself to helping her mother readjust to the world. She saw Pat as almost childlike; she had been cut off from everyone and everything for so long that she grabbed at life with both hands.

"I'd come get Mom at the halfway house and take her to the Varsity—that's Atlanta's favorite place for hot dogs; they're real greasy but they're so good—and she'd get chili dogs," Susan recalled. "When she came to our house for supper, she liked to have me fix her chicken cordon bleu, but even so she always wanted to stop and get a Varsity hot dog on the way home!"

Although Susan and Bill Alford were living in Atlanta in 1984, Bill was about to be transferred once again, the standard peripatetic pattern of the young executive in America. The Alfords were moving to Marion, Indiana, in June, and Susan visited with her mother as much as possible before they left.

As always, Pat was furious with Bill for agreeing to a transfer. "How can Bill do this to me?" she implored. But Pat had made an error in judgment when she put Bill Alford in the category of men she could manipulate. She liked his strength and assumed she could harness it just as she had leaned on Gil, Tom, and

Papa. Indeed, in times of trouble she had often cried, "I want my Bill!" But Pat took Bill Alford's good nature for weakness and never saw that he could be pushed only as far as he was willing. Thereafter, he was an immovable object.

"Just when I finally get home," Pat complained to Susan. "How *can* Bill deliberately take you and the children away from me?"

Of course, he had no choice—save resigning. In vain, Susan tried to explain that. She didn't tell her mother Bill preferred to have at least a thousand miles between himself and Pat. In the time they had left together, she took her mother out to lunch and shopping as much as possible. Despite her huge appetite, Pat had lost a great deal of weight since her release from Hardwick. Susan took her to the Lenox Square shopping mall in the Buckhead neighborhood and bought her all new clothes. Pat was thrilled.

"The last time I saw her before we moved," Susan remembered, "I took her to the bus stop so she could go to work, and we both started to cry. She looked so lost. I hated to leave her."

With the often inexplicable reasoning of the parole system, Pat, who now called herself Pat Taylor, was assigned to work as a companion to the elderly—a "sitter." It had been stipulated in her parole papers that she would work at the Fountainview Convalescent Home in Atlanta. Apparently, no one had researched the crimes that had sent her to prison in the first place. She now cared for wealthy elderly people who lived in their own apartments in the retirement center. She helped them bathe and eat and supervised their medications. On occasion, she even gave insulin shots to diabetic patients. Her clients all spoke highly of her; she became like part of their own families. She seemed to have no emotional life of her own, although she later confessed to Susan her feelings for an Episcopal priest who had supervised New Horizons. "He was probably the only man I could ever have really loved," Pat said wistfully. "But of course, he wasn't free to love me."

In November 1984, when Pat was released from the halfway house and officially paroled, she was forty-seven years old. She had "maxed out." Under Georgia sentencing guidelines, she had been incarcerated as long as she legally could be. The conditions of her parole dictated that she report to a parole officer in Jonesboro, Georgia, and live with Boppo and Papa on Arrowhead Boulevard in Jonesboro. But Pat told her mother she wouldn't live in the Radcliffes' townhouse. "There are too many niggers around here," she said flatly. "I won't live here." So they moved to a little red brick house in the tiny hamlet of McDonough, Georgia. There was an upstairs room with a small bathroom off of it, and that would be Pat's. She was coming home at last.

Pat continued with her nursing job at Fountainview, and she arranged for her daughter Debbie to work the shifts preceding or following her own. Debbie had separated from and reconciled with her husband innumerable times. She was not yet thirty and Dawn was almost fourteen. Vaguely unhappy with her life, Debbie often came to visit Susan and Bill in the lovely homes they owned far away from Atlanta, and Susan listened sympathetically to her younger sister's litany of troubles. Debbie had missed her mother acutely while Pat was in Hardwick, so she was happy they would now be working together. Neither Pat nor Debbie had any formal training as licensed practical nurses or nursing assistants. They were learning on the job.

✦ ✦ ✦

Almost from the beginning there were certain problems with Pat's return to her family. Maybe they were inevitable. For so long, the family had believed that Pat's homecoming would be their happy ending after so many years of bad times, but things didn't work out that way. She still threw tantrums to get what she wanted. "I thought Pat would be happy when she got out!" Boppo cried out to Susan. "She can *never* be happy. I've done everything I can do for her. If there was something else I could do, I would do it. I just want to live my life now in peace!"

First of all, there was Ashlynne, Ronnie's daughter. In prison, Pat had been annoyed to learn that her youngest granddaughter was living with Boppo and Papa. When she came home to live, she had to share her mother with the child, and she resented it. There was no question of sending the little girl to her own mother; two-year-old Ashlynne had been in terrible condition when Boppo started caring for her—unwashed, with diapers unchanged for days, and with head lice. Ronnie lived nearby, but he had been married three or four times—no one was sure just how many—and his life was too unstable to care for his daughter properly. Ashlynne *needed* Boppo, and as Boppo said so often, "How can someone not love a child?"

Ashlynne wet the bed. Every time she did, Pat removed another of her toys and put it away in a closet. Eventually, Ashlynne had no toys left. Pat bought Ashlynne clothes at garage sales—and there was nothing wrong with that, except that she chose the most faded, most threadbare dresses and little shirts on sale. Dressed by her grandmother, Ashlynne looked like a refugee. When Pat wasn't looking, Boppo threw the used clothes in the rag bag. Pat continually insisted that Ashlynne should go home and live with Ronnie, that she had no business at all taking up Boppo's time. All the babies in the family seemed to threaten Pat, as if she feared she would no longer be loved if there were too many of them.

After she came home to McDonough, Pat also became obsessed about her background, nagging at Boppo for proof of who she really was. Boppo threw up her hands and cried, *"Why* are you digging up the past, Pat? I've told you all I know." Boppo would call Susan or Debbie and agonize over the situation. "Your mother is calling all of her aunts and asking questions about her real father. Now she doubts I'm her real *mother,* and that Kent was her real *brother.* All my life I've loved your mother. I just don't know what else I can do. Will she *ever* be happy?"

Susan tried to comfort her grandmother, but there was no softening Boppo's despair at the turmoil in her home. "Your Boppo's very tired, Susan," she said softly. "My body is worn out, and I'm just so tired. I look in the mirror, and I can't believe that old lady with the white hair and lines on her face is me. One thing I know for sure—your grandfather and I have been through so much, but we love each other and always have."

Boppo and Papa *were* old now, but with Pat back, their lives were far from peaceful. It shouldn't have been that way. Not from the way Boppo remembered her life. "I'm happiest when there are children around," she said. "I took the ones that needed me most, and I helped them. I loved them all the same, of course. I just do for the one who needs me most. No matter what happens, they know their Boppo's there for them."

And, as it happened, Pat was *always* the one who needed her most.

✦ ✦ ✦

Pat and Debbie grew even closer. With Susan and Bill's "silly moves all over the country," Pat could count on Debbie staying close to her. Gary Cole, Debbie's long-suffering husband, came home one night to find that his wife, daughter, and *furniture* were gone. Pat had helped Debbie move into an apartment, encouraging her to take everything she needed.

At Thanksgiving, 1984, Boppo, Papa, and Pat drove north to Marion, Indiana, to have the holiday meal with Bill and Susan. Susan was delighted to see that everything seemed to be fine with her mother. But several weeks later, Pat drove up alone. Somewhere in Kentucky she had one of her "sudden attacks," and after several anxious hours Susan learned she had been hospitalized. A day later, Pat came driving up to the Alfords' as if nothing had happened. Susan felt a familiar chill, but she fought it back. She wanted to believe in her mother—probably more than anyone else in Pat's family did—but she had to work hard not to see small, disturbing aberrations.

Pat seemed obsessed with retrieving all the things Boppo had given Susan over the years. She said that she would replace everything with new merchandise that didn't have so much sentimental value. Still, they had a good visit, and Susan enjoyed having her mother there. She had been seeing shadows, she decided, where there were none.

In March of 1985, Pat returned for a long visit. Susan's friends found her charming. "They loved Mom," Susan said. "But when they were gone, she told me she hated them—they took up too much of my time. She wanted me to stay in the house with her all the time."

Pat again insisted on checking through Susan's cupboards, drawers, and storage areas, even through Bill's office, looking for Boppo's gifts. "I'm just straightening up," she explained when Susan asked her what she was doing. "You don't want this candelabra—or this silver service. Now that I'm out, you can give this all back to Boppo."

Susan let her have what she wanted, and Pat did replace a few of the things she carried away, but they came from discount stores, the heavy sterling pieces supplanted by flimsy silver-plated things, nothing like the items she took away. Later, when

Susan and Bill packed to move again, this time to Florence, Alabama, Susan realized how many things were missing from her house. Visiting in McDonough, she saw most of her stuff in her mother's room. She was perplexed, but not really angry. It was all in the family.

Pat and Debbie branched out to private-duty nursing in the homes and condominiums of elderly patients. Susan was immensely grateful that her mother was working and liked her new career. She was in such demand; Pat and Debbie had only a week or so off in between patients. Unfortunately, Pat's jobs had a built-in obsolescence. The age and degree of infirmity of her employers made it inevitable that they didn't live long. Both Pat and Debbie took care of Mrs. Mansfield, an elderly woman who lived in a luxurious apartment in a retirement condo in one of Atlanta's finest neighborhoods. Debbie was with Mrs. Mansfield when she died and cried inconsolably. Pat took it philosophically.

"Debbie really loved Mrs. Mansfield," Susan recalled. "Debbie had a real tender side."

✦ ✦ ✦

Bill Alford's career involved troubleshooting to turn around companies with poor performance records, mostly in the office supply area. It meant moving frequently, but he was good, and he rose steadily in his field. He was happy to be away from Atlanta and the *Sturm und Drang* of the Siler-Taylor-Radcliffe family crises. When they visited, Susan was always shushing him and whispering, "Be *nice* to them, Bill!" It did little good, but his sarcasm was so subtle that it often went over her family's heads.

Pat was a frequent visitor when they moved to Florence, Alabama, in the summer of 1985. The Alfords had a wonderful house, and Susan decorated it in a homey country style, using a number of antiques. Pat enjoyed being there, playing with Sean and Courtney, and having Susan wait on her. The Florence house had a pool and Pat liked to sit beside it on a chaise lounge. She wouldn't wear a bathing suit—despite her initial weight loss at the halfway house, she had since regained it all and considerably more—but she sometimes jumped in wearing her shorts and blouse.

It was in Florence the next spring that Susan discovered she was pregnant for the third time. She was thirty-three, and they hadn't planned on more children, but she and Bill were happy. Her mother was not. "You're too old to have another baby," Pat said firmly. "I think the only thing is for you to get rid of it."

"Mom!"

"It will weaken you, I'll tell you that. You'll never be healthy again. What about Sean and Courtney? If you die, they'll have no mother. You'll cheat them."

One of the main drawbacks of having yet another grandchild, Pat insisted, was that she was already sewing and embroidering full-time for the family she had; she could never, ever keep up with a fifth grandchild. Susan thought her overblown view of the importance of her sewing projects was almost pathetic. Admittedly, for *this* family, conception at thirty-three meant an over-the-hill pregnancy, but Pat's arguments verged on hysteria. She had been a grandmother at that age, although she had always refused to be called "Grandma," and only recently had begun answering to "Grandma Pat."

Despite her mother's dire warnings, Susan carried and gave birth to her second son, Adam, on January 5, 1987. Through complications that had nothing to do with her "advanced age," Adam was delivered by cesarean section. At Susan's request, Pat had been barred from the labor room, but she talked her way into the recovery room by explaining to the doctor that she was a registered nurse.

Susan didn't want her there. "I can't say why—maybe it was because she wanted me to abort my baby—but it was like the time I was little in the Philippines and my hand was crushed. I didn't want to see my mother then, and I didn't want to see her after Adam was born. I just turned my face to the wall. The obstetrician and pediatrician were personal friends of Bill's and mine. They told Mom that *I* was the new mother and they made a policy of letting the mothers have what they wanted."

Perhaps Pat had been truly worried about Susan's health. She made such a fuss over Adam that no one would ever have guessed how hard she had fought to have Susan abort him. She cooed over the new baby boy as if she had never had a grandchild before.

Pat was between jobs right after Adam was born and she spent a lot of time in Florence, driving the five hours between Georgia and Alabama by herself. She seemed completely devoted to her newest grandchild. He was a big strapping baby boy, and Susan dressed him in the lacy Victorian gowns and little bonnets her mother made for him only long enough to take pictures—just to keep peace. Pat loved to see him dressed up, but Sean was indignant, and as soon as the photo sessions were over he would put a baseball cap and a sports sweatshirt on his baby brother.

In June of 1987, Susan took her children and drove to Mc-Donough for a visit with Boppo, Papa, and her mother. She had meant to stay only a week, but she got sick. "It was the strangest illness I'd ever had," she recalled later. "I wanted to head home in July, but I had to stay an extra few days because something was wrong with me. Bill kept calling me and wanting us to come home, and I told him, "I can't drive. My feet won't work right.""

"They ached terribly," Susan remembered, wincing. "And I actually had trouble pushing down on the accelerator and the brake. One morning I decided I could make it. I had to try to get home. Sean had his learner's permit, and I thought *I* could drive on the expressway by setting cruise control once I got up to speed. My mother wouldn't hear of it. She told me, 'You can't make it, Susie. You're sick. You're weak.' When she saw I was going to go, she threw up her hands and said, 'All right! If you want to kill yourself, go ahead.' She always said that. She'd said that when I told her I was going ahead with my pregnancy with Adam."

Susan and the kids headed for Alabama, and they did all right until she got on the expressway. The speed limit was sixty-five miles per hour, and Susan had great difficulty getting past thirty-five. Her foot wouldn't press hard enough on the accelerator. She tried to force her foot down on the pedal. "I finally had to reach down and just take my hands and mash my foot on the accelerator. I thought we'd never get home."

Susan's hands ached too. For some time after she got home she had to hold her hands together and squeeze them, rub her legs, and massage her feet to get some relief. It was the worst, bone-aching flu she had ever had. Her skin turned gray and her eyes stared back at her from the mirror like two dead things. Time after time she told Bill, "I just can't stand the pain in my feet. I can hardly walk."

Susan's doctor tried one antibiotic after another, but she got worse. Finally, he said she was probably overmedicated. "I'm just taking you off antibiotics entirely. You've just got a really bad case of the flu."

"But I had no energy," Susan recalled. "I could hardly even get to the doctor's office. Bill was so worried. He said, 'I've got to get you well, 'cause you've got a six-month-old and two kids at home.' Finally, I gradually began to get better."

It took Susan about six weeks to get back on her feet.

Adam worried the Alfords too. At two weeks, he had had unexplained bleeding from the lower intestinal tract. They were frightened that it might be something really serious. The doctors tested him for everything under the sun and finally put him on a special formula. That seemed to work, but he couldn't digest solid food until he was almost a year old. Since Debbie had also had bouts with bloody colitis, the doctors suggested that Susan and Bill check their families' medical histories to see if there were any other relatives who had suffered from rectal bleeding.

"In 1987," Susan recalled, "I had two projects. The first was to go back through all our ancestors to see if any of them had ever had anything like Adam did; the second was to write a book. I wanted to write a really upbeat, inspirational book about my mother and the family. She had been through so much, and then all those years in prison, and she had a good job, helping people, and she'd even helped people in prison with the classes she taught. The rest of us had suffered too; we were still emotionally exhausted from those bad years. I wanted to write a happy-ending kind of book about a family that had triumphed over one member's mental illness and drug addiction. My family wasn't perfect—nobody's is—and Lord knows we certainly had our eccentricities, but I thought we had come through it all just fine.

"I repressed my fears; I still ignored the warnings. I just wanted so much for us all to be all right."

43

Pat Taylor hit a bad patch in 1987. After Mrs. Mansfield died, she couldn't find another "sitting" job. If she wanted to, Debbie could always work as a receptionist in a doctor's office; she was young and attractive with a terrific figure. It wasn't nearly so easy for Pat. She had only a tenth-grade education and she was fifty. She had put on so much weight that she looked her age and more. Almost overnight, she had gone from a slender, almost ethereal woman of a certain age to a stolid, solid middle-aged woman. She still loved exquisite period dresses with lace and hand stitching, and she had a beautiful wedding gown, circa 1880, on a mannequin in her bedroom in Papa and Boppo's house, a white ghost figure standing in a dark corner. The antique dress was about a size 8, and Pat wore a 22. She reveled in her costumes, but she could no longer squeeze into them. If she dreamed of romance and perfect love, she no longer spoke of it.

Way back in the days when Pat and her children, Susan, Debbie, and Ronnie were living with Boppo and Papa, Pat had often accused her parents of resenting the money they spent on

her and her children. "If we're too much for you to support,"
she would cry, "I'll just go work in a Waffle House!" It was only
an idle threat. Then. For Pat, a job at the Waffle House was the
most desperate strait in which an upper-class woman could find
herself. Twenty years later in 1987, she was forced to take a job
as an assistant manager at a Pizza Hut up I-75 in Stockbridge.
She told her children that she would earn close to twenty thousand dollars a year, if you included benefits.

How she hated it. If anything, it was far *worse* than a Waffle
House. The steel bowls of pizza dough were heavy and hurt her
back. The smell of tomato sauce and oregano clung to her auburn hair and seeped into her very skin. She couldn't get along
with the younger managers and the other workers.

Life didn't seem fair to Pat. Susan had a fine house and a good
husband, Debbie was tanned and wild and sexy as Pat had once
been, and Boppo had a man who loved her beyond reason. But
Pat?

Pat had nothing. She had no love, no future, no money, and
she had lost the only home she ever wanted. She had become
fascinated with antique dolls and wanted to collect them. And
then she wanted to own real antique carousel horses. She wanted
to be a true southern lady. There were so many things she
wanted. Somehow, there had to be a way to get them.

44

"Pat didn't want to go to work for the Crists, you know," Margureitte Radcliffe recalled. "I believe it was their son who called her—because she had such wonderful references from her looking after other elderly people—and he just pleaded with her, *begged* her, to take care of his parents. A very fine old family. Very, very wealthy."

Pat resigned from the Pizza Hut, glad to be rid of the smell of tomato sauce and oregano (despite what her mother later said), and went to work for Elizabeth and James Crist.

◆ ◆ ◆

The Crists had lived for decades in a mansion on a huge, rambling spread of manicured grounds on Nancy Creek Road near Atlanta's Peachtree Country Club. Once, a long time ago, Pat Taylor had designed the kind of estate she wanted, but all her efforts to make it come to life had fallen short. Her dream plantation was very like the Crists' estate. Their home was built of pale green wood siding, three stories high, with wings, dormers, bay windows, a "Florida room." The main house had maids' quarters and an attached garage with room for four cars, and the grounds featured a pond, a pool, a barbecue area, and every other possible nicety for gracious living. The mansion was set at least five hundred feet back from Nancy Creek Road. A circular driveway led through the pine trees, oak trees, holly bushes, and huge rhododendrons that sheltered the vast green stretch of lawn. The view from the rear of the house was into private woods. The Crists were, indeed, "very, very wealthy."

In the spring of 1987 the Crists found they needed assistance. James Crist suffered from Parkinson's disease. Betty Crist called a friend of hers who worked at the Peachtree Plaza and asked if she had any suggestions. "Yes," the woman answered. "There's a woman named Patricia Taylor who's supposed to be awfully good."

Armed with Pat Taylor's phone number at the Radcliffes', Betty Crist called her and arranged an interview. The buxom applicant seemed competent and intelligent. She had a certain air of quiet good breeding about her, and seemed unimpressed by the plush surroundings of the Crists' home. Pat Taylor was hired. She would receive, as a beginning salary, ten dollars an hour and meals. She began working for the Crists on May 1, 1987. Debbie soon joined her, working the night shift.

The Crists had two sons and a daughter and they agreed that Pat Taylor seemed to be the perfect solution to their father's health care. He would be able to stay in the house on Nancy Creek Road and wouldn't have to go into a nursing home.

Elizabeth Crist was seventy-six, a cheerful, healthy, and intelligent woman. She needed no care at all herself—but she had a bad knee and had suffered herniated spinal disks in the past so she couldn't lift her husband. They had been married a very long time and loved each other devotedly. Having Pat on duty would allow Betty to be with her husband for company in the days he had left.

✦　✦　✦

Susan and Bill Alford were still living in Florence, Alabama, in 1987, and they breathed a sigh of relief when there was a period of respite from the family problems that usually bubbled up out of Georgia. Pat seemed to adore Adam and grudgingly agreed that childbirth hadn't killed Susan after all, although Susan *had* had that one bad "sinking spell" six months after his birth when she visited at Boppo's. No one had ever diagnosed what had caused her illness.

Susan and Bill were also pleased to learn that apparently both Pat and Debbie had jobs they liked, working as nurse's aides for a wealthy couple near the Peachtree Country Club. That was good news. Susan was hardly worried when she got a phone call from Boppo.

"Susan," her grandmother asked, "do you know how much money your mother makes where she's working?"

"No, she's never mentioned it."

"Well, Debbie says she makes a lot of money—that your mother is making as much as Bill does."

"Oh," Susan said. "I don't think so. You know how Mom exaggerates. Debbie does too. I'm just grateful they both have a job they like and they can work together."

Pat did seem to be making a little more money than she had in the past. At that summer's Siler Family Reunion at White Lake, North Carolina, she proudly announced that *she* was taking care of her mother and father in "their old age. I have a big glass jar and I keep it filled with money. Mother can reach in there anytime she wants and get herself a handful of money."

Susan knew that was ridiculous. Despite the fortune they had lost in legal fees for Pat, Boppo and Papa were *still* supporting her mother. The money she made she spent mostly on herself. There *was* a money jar, but Boppo dipped into it only to please Pat. Susan tried not to borrow trouble. Her mother had a tendency to be grandiose and there was no way that Pat could be supporting Boppo and Papa; maybe it made her mother feel important to tell all the aunts and cousins that she was. Pat was over fifty, and she had always been dependent on her parents. If she put some quarters and fifty-cent pieces in a jar for Boppo, what real harm was there in that?

Pat also became suddenly generous with the rest of the family, giving them little bits and pieces of jewelry and old books—the kind of things *she* liked. She gave her grandchildren funny old-fashioned toys that they soon discarded for plastic fads from Toys "R" Us. But her own collection of treasures of another era was growing larger. Besides her Victorian cards and her dolls, she added another collection: antique hatpins. She said the late Mrs. Mansfield had given her—and Debbie—so many things they admired.

Through the fall and winter of 1987, Pat worked longer and longer hours at the Crists. She explained that Elizabeth Crist's health had begun to fail too so there was a lot more work to do. It no longer sounded like the ideal job; Pat and Debbie both complained that the elderly Crists were penny-pinchers, pointing out how "common" it was the way they lined their garbage cans with newspapers instead of plastic trash can liners. They said they had no place to sleep except a lumpy little couch. Still, Pat and Debbie stayed on the job. It was the longest-running job Pat had ever had.

It ended in mid-June of 1988. Pat explained to her family that it was unfortunate, but there had been a problem with the Crists' medical insurance. "The company just refused to pay for aides anymore," she said. "So the Crists couldn't keep us on."

Colonel Radcliffe turned seventy-five in July. The whole family showed up at a restaurant to honor Papa. Pat had saved up to get him a wonderful surprise, an eighteen-karat gold lapis stone ring. He was very pleased. He held his hand up for Susan's camcorder and described the ring, right down to the intricate carving beside the blue stone.

Papa didn't look seventy-five. He barely looked sixty—fit and handsome—as he posed for yet another group of happy family pictures with Bill, Susan, Debbie, Pat, Sean, Courtney, Adam, Ronnie and Ashlynne, and Boppo. They toasted each other with iced tea in Mason jars. It was a happy night.

With no further practical nursing prospects in sight, Pat started her own business in her parents' home in McDonough. She called her enterprise Patty's Play Pals and had business cards made up. She sewed doll clothes and worked on antique dolls, restoring them to their original condition. She was wonderfully clever with her dolls. Boppo and Papa gave her the room off their recreation room and it soon became a "nursery" of sorts.

Dozens of dolls, their fixed eyes bright and staring, filled that room. Being there was like stepping back in time—to the 1930s and then further and further back until this century seemed not to exist at all. Pat seemed happiest in her doll room, or in the windowless closet adjoining it that she turned into a stuffy little sewing room. She sewed far into the night, her work area lit by a bare light bulb swinging from an extension cord.

On weekends, Pat carefully packed up her Play Pals and drove to hobby shows, swap meets, and flea markets. "That made me sad," Susan remembered. "To see my mother at her age going around to flea markets with her dolls. It seemed so humbling for her—almost worse than it was when she was working at the pizza parlor. She'd go to those tailgate sales or swap meets and she was selling her doll things out of the trunk of her car."

Although there were no more men in Pat's life, she made a very close woman friend, a teacher named Miss Loretta.* Miss Loretta also collected antique dolls and they had much in common. They were both plump, middle-aged women with lonely lives and unfulfilled dreams. Miss Loretta had never been married.

Pat rapidly became as possessive of Miss Loretta as she had once been of Hap Brown and Tom Allanson, and as she *still* was of her mother. She had never been able to hold lightly onto important people in her life. It was no different with Miss Loretta. Pat clutched and clung. She could not bear for "her" people to have lives away from her; she had to know about every detail of their activities.

Although some of Pat's exquisitely restored dolls sold for hundreds—even thousands—of dollars, Patty's Play Pals wasn't a consistent source of income, and Pat had to take another job. She went to work for the Golden Memories shop in Stockbridge, a pawnshop and consignment store that sold old jewelry, small items, and just plain junk that people brought in, keeping a percentage. At least it was more in keeping with Pat's interests than making pizza. The pizza parlor was right across the street, and she shuddered to think she had ever worked there. She made forty-five dollars a day at Golden Memories. At the end of each day, she would open the cash register by punching the No Sale key, and pay herself in cash. She had grown so heavy that it was hard for her to be on her feet all day. Pat bought herself a folding chair at the Wal-Mart Drugstore and sat on that between customers.

If Tom Allanson had walked into Golden Memories, he probably wouldn't have recognized his former wife. The frail and beautiful southern belle had long since been buried under folds of flesh. Even the sweet voice that had once reduced him to tears was vastly changed. Pat either gave imperious commands or she sighed with dull fatigue, her voice harsh and flat.

But, after fourteen years, Tom was still in prison. And he was married—at least common-law—to another woman. Surprisingly, he held no grudge against Pat. He was not a man to hold grudges. What might have been more devastating—if she had known about it—was that Tom never thought about Pat at all.

45

Once, in a moment of searing revelation, Margureitte Radcliffe had confessed to Susan her own worst fear. "I have nightmares about being accused of a crime—falsely—and being sent to prison. That's what I'm most afraid of."

Susan wasn't surprised. Sometimes it seemed as though her mother and grandmother shared one brain. Although Boppo could hold a stubborn grudge against even one of her own sisters, she had always forgiven her daughter *anything,* and she had always absorbed Pat's pain. Of course Boppo feared the worst thing that had ever happened to Pat. Wherever Pat's emotions plunged, her mother's followed. She had practically gone to prison herself when Pat did.

Susan didn't confide *her* worst fear to Boppo—she didn't dare. Boppo would have been outraged. "It wasn't a rational fear," Susan admitted. "At least I didn't think it was then. I was afraid that Bill would die, and my mother would move in and take over my house and my life. I could picture her locking the doors and not letting anyone in to see me—and not ever letting me out. It was a suffocating feeling."

Bill Alford was transferred once again—this time back to the Atlanta area. The Alfords bought a lovely home in the Brookstone Country Club area. Sean was in high school; he had grown up to be a tall, extremely handsome young man who often played golf with his father at the Brookstone private golf course. Courtney played golf too, the only girl in her age category, and she took ballet lessons. Adam was an adorable little blue-eyed toddler.

Pat was still working at the Golden Memories consignment store, and she kept her doll business going, sewing far into the night as she had done at Hardwick. She visited Susan's new house often and complained how she hated having to work all the time. "I just want time to spend with my grandchildren," she sighed. "I can't stand working anymore. It's just too hard." Locked up in prison, Pat had missed most of the growing-up years of her older grandchildren. But she seemed to dote on all of them, with one exception. She still had no affinity for Ronnie's daughter, Ashlynne, and argued peevishly that the child had no business living with Boppo and Papa. Boppo ignored her complaints. Ashlynne was going to stay living with them, and that was that. Ashlynne was the only thing Boppo defied her daughter about. "I think Boppo loved Ashlynne the way she once loved Mom," Susan later mused. "And my mother knew it."

When Adam had his tonsils out in November 1988, his grandma Pat was right there with him, holding him and promising him ice cream. She sat beside his bed in the hospital whenever Susan had to step away for a moment or two. Susan's eyes misted when she thought how happy she was that her mother was *able* to be with them again.

She hadn't made much progress on her book about her mother. With all the moving and resettling, she found it difficult to get going. She had sent for as many family birth and death certificates as she could track down. She knew now how hard Boppo's teenage years had been, and about her three early and difficult pregnancies. She verified what she had always really known—that her uncle Kent had been a suicide. She found no medical records of other relatives with a history of rectal bleeding, but that didn't seem so important. Adam had outgrown that frightening symptom.

Bill Alford was working as a vice president in upper management in a company that seemed as solid as the marble in Stone Mountain. But then came a buy-out. Just before Christmas, 1988, he suddenly lost his job. Susan and Bill had already invited the whole family for Christmas dinner, and they never let on what they were going through. Photographs taken of that day's celebration gave no hint that anything was wrong: four generations of a truly beautiful family, bowing their heads before Christmas dinner.

"It was rough," Susan remembered. "But we made it. Nobody knew what had happened. Bill got another job. I worked two part-time jobs."

During the day, Susan was on call as a substitute teacher. She taught at every level from elementary to high school—particularly special education classes. Evenings, she worked in store security for department stores, Macy's and then Sears. She grew adept at changing her appearance by wearing wigs and dark glasses. She wasn't very big, but she was fast and had a good eye for telltale movements on the part of "shoppers." Working with male security officers, she chased scores of shoplifters and caught them in the parking lots. Susan's college credits were in criminology and psychology; she didn't have a degree, but she still hoped to get one. Her mother thought that policemen were low-class: "They're so stupid, they couldn't find work anywhere else," Pat often said. But Susan seriously considered a career in law enforcement.

Bill's new job looked promising and they breathed a sigh of relief. Like so many couples in their thirties, they were living well, perhaps too well. The Brookstone house was as nice as, or nicer than, their home in Florence, and the mortgage payments were hefty. Their children were used to having extras, and Bill and Susan were happy that they could still provide them. Sean got his own truck on his seventeenth birthday—not a brand-new truck, but one that any seventeen-year-old boy would be thrilled with. Bill and Susan decorated it with banners and balloons.

Even though Susan was now working hard herself, it still hurt her to see her mother sitting on the wobbly folding chair at Golden Memories. Debbie was working as an office manager and nurse for Dr. Francisco Villanueva.* Susan wondered sometimes why Pat and Debbie didn't go back to their nurse's aide jobs. Pat could certainly have made more money doing that, but neither of them seemed interested in returning to that career.

Pat became obsessed with worry about her future. What would become of her? She asked Bill to promise her that she would never be alone. If he and Susan assured her that they would build a little house for her in back of their house, and take care of her when she got too old to work, she would feel so much better. Susan saw that her mother wasn't as strong as she pretended to be. She realized that she could not survive if Boppo weren't around, and Boppo and Papa were growing older. Pat needed protection and care, and the Alfords promised her that she didn't have to worry; they would take care of her.

Pat told them she was worried about Sean and Courtney too. She urged them to rewrite their wills and name her as the children's guardian and as executor of their wills if anything tragic should happen to both of them. She apologized for the years of chaos. "I understand why you couldn't put me in your wills before—I wasn't myself, I was sick—but that's different now. I suppose you have Boppo and Papa in there to take care of the children?"

Susan half nodded. Actually, she and Bill had listed his brother and sister-in-law—her family was always in such upheaval—but she didn't want to hurt her mother's feelings.

"Well," Pat hurried on, "just change that and put *my* name first. They're getting older, and it would be such a mess if I wasn't listed first. Put me down, then Boppo, then Papa."

Pat brought up the subject of the Alfords' wills often, but Bill always managed to steer her away from the topic.

Sometimes, Pat talked about her own death—as if it were imminent. She bought herself a plot up in North Carolina where Grandma and Grandpa Siler—and Kent—were buried. She asked Susan if she might have the full-cut turquoise maternity dress that Susan had worn when she was pregnant with Adam. Of course Susan gave it to her mother. It had fit her loosely when she was nine months pregnant; it just fit Pat, who had now gained over a hundred pounds.

"There," Pat said. "Now I have my marrying and my burying dress. Whatever happens to me, I'm ready."

Susan bit her lip. It was sad to see her mother settling for so little in life. There would be no "marrying" for Pat—not any-more; she never went anywhere, except with Miss Loretta or to visit family.

✦   ✦   ✦

In February 1989, Pat's aunt Liz Porter in North Carolina wasn't feeling well, and Pat insisted on going up to take care of her. Aunt Liz had always been her willowy, beautiful aunt, the sweet aunt who couldn't balance a checkbook to save her life. She had raised her son, Bobby, alone after her husband disap-peared into the woods. Until the mid-1980s, Liz was a strikingly attractive woman. But she was well into her seventies now and quite frail.

Pat moved in to care for Aunt Liz—just in time, she soon said, because her patient grew frailer rapidly. Liz had been am-bulatory, but she became so weak that she could no longer walk. Pat rented a wheelchair and tenderly pushed her aunt around. She explained to Liz's doctor that she was well experienced in dealing with the losses that accompanied advancing age.

Pat took complete care of Aunt Liz for six weeks, virtually shutting her off from the rest of the world. She explained to her cousin Bobby and his wife, Charlotte, that his mother was far too ill to have visitors. She discouraged them from coming by so often, assuring Liz's family that she would recover much sooner if she could only have complete rest and quiet. Pat was her aunt's only care giver and companion. She also advised Liz on her legal affairs and urged her to have a proper will drawn up.

For a while, it seemed that Elizabeth Porter would not sur-vive. Her physician was appalled at how rapidly his patient was degenerating. When Pat returned to Boppo and Papa's, it seemed likely that she would not see her aunt alive again.

Pat complained to her mother that no one even thanked her for the tender care she had given her aunt. Boppo was insulted by their lack of appreciation. "Your mother," she told Susan and Debbie, "has always been *especially* kind to elderly people, chil-dren, and animals. Everything your mother does is always taken the wrong way by her cousins, and *I* don't know why. If it was anyone else saying or doing it, it would be *perfectly all right*— but not with your mother. Your poor mother had to leave all upset, and drive all the way back. I'm shocked at how her cousins treated her, and all she wanted to do was help. Your mother works harder than anyone I know, always busy with something in her hand, up all hours of the night sewing—"

Susan couldn't see how her mother's sewing all night could have helped—or harmed—Aunt Liz, but apparently there had been bad feelings in North Carolina, and Pat was no longer wanted as a nurse for her aunt.

Happily, and much to everyone's surprise, Elizabeth Porter gradually improved. By full spring she was walking again and seemed far more alert. Although her illness had visibly aged her, she was able to be with her sisters at the Siler Family Reunion in the summer of 1989. Bobby and Charlotte Porter, Liz's son and daughter-in-law, had felt a decided coolness in the family, however, since they had sent Pat away. Prudently, they chose not to go to the White Lake reunion. They had criticized Pat, and Boppo would not permit that. With the exception of Bobby's mother, Liz, the surviving Righteous Sisters sided with Boppo.

✦　✦　✦

Susan was still working her two jobs that summer. Adam was only two and a half and she hated to leave him with strangers. Bill was working many evenings, Sean loved his little brother, but he had an evening job too; and Courtney was too young for so much responsibility. Boppo and Papa agreed readily to look after Adam three days a week and have him stay over two nights.

Pat was clearly annoyed by the arrangement. She hadn't wanted Ashlynne living with Boppo and Papa, and she didn't want Adam there either. At long last, Pat's reasoning finally became apparent to her oldest daughter. "I didn't want to believe it," Susan said later. "I wanted everything to be all right with my mother, but I finally had to acknowledge that anyone —anyone—who took attention away from her was her enemy. My mother had to be Boppo's little girl. It didn't matter if Mom was fifty-three years old. Ashlynne—and then Adam—were standing in her spotlight. She enjoyed Adam at my house; she didn't want him at her house."

One night when Susan, Sean, and Adam were at home together, Adam started hitting Sean—and then himself—in the face and whispering, "Shussh! Be quiet!"

"Mom?" Sean asked. "Where's he *getting* that?"

"Adam," Susan asked, "what *are* you doing?"

He looked at her, hit himself in the mouth again, and mumbled, "Grandma Pat."

Sean was furious. Although he was a teenager, beginning to pull away from the family, he adored his little brother. The thought that anyone had hit Adam—even Grandma Pat—made him terribly angry.

Emotionally, Susan was pulled in two directions. She loved the mother who had always told her she could accomplish anything, the mother who had written her such wonderful letters and whose handiworks of love were evident in every room of Susan's beautiful home. She loved the mother who had been taken away from all of them for seven and a half years, and now was home again. At the same time, Susan had finally acknowledged that her mother was selfish, jealous, immature, and consumed with the need to own more and more *things*. Pat was sixteen years older than Susan in years; in truth, Susan was the grown-up.

Because she loved her mother, Susan had trouble accepting her suspicion that Pat had punished Adam physically. She put that out of her mind, believing that her little boy had only been cuffed lightly. Perhaps he had tried to play with her dolls; Susan knew her mother couldn't stand to have Adam or Ashlynne touching her dolls.

Just as Susan was of two minds about her mother, she had a similar dichotomy of feelings about her only sister. Susan loved Debbie but she disapproved of some of the things she did. The two sisters were as different as night and day; they always had been. But they were buddies, so close to the same age, giggling over the weird—but predictable—antics of their family.

Debbie claimed to detest sex, and yet Susan had seen her lift her blouse and flash truck drivers as the women drove past big rigs on the freeway. Debbie had a sensational figure and she sometimes worked as a cocktail waitress in the most minuscule costumes the law would allow. She was either bubbly or depressed, depending on how her love life was going at the moment. Her marriage had been only a convenience for years. Dawn, a teenager now, was as beautiful as the rest of the Siler women.

For years, Susan and Bill had listened to Debbie's lamentations about her marriage and her off-and-on relationship with Mike Alexander, a married man who sporadically promised to get a divorce and marry her. The Alfords' home had always been a haven for Debbie when her world crashed. She had an insouciant air about her that made her endearing even when she was outrageous. Whatever she did, she was still Susan's sister, and Lord knows they had stuck together through some treacherous times.

They had long since learned to laugh about their mother's histrionics. Pat often took offense at something Debbie or Susan said to her during a phone call. They would hear the receiver drop, and then dead silence. Pat was brilliant at timing the "interrupted phone call," because invariably her daughters would hear the sounds of a car door and then a house door slamming—Boppo and Papa arriving home—and next their gasps as they discovered Pat crumpled on the floor in a faint, the phone receiver still clutched in her hand. Boppo would pick up the phone and demand, *"Now* what have you done to your mother?"

Debbie and Susan had learned to suppress their giggles; they knew their mother was perfectly fine. But Boppo apparently still *believed* each fainting spell, each sudden illness. If Miss Loretta, Pat's special friend, was late in calling, Pat was sure she had had a wreck on the freeway and was lying stone cold dead in a ditch. Loretta always called, and things always turned out all right. Hysteria was merely Pat's way, and Boppo played right into it.

Debbie sometimes called Susan to report on one of Boppo's phone calls. Both of them could imitate their grandmother perfectly, but they were smart enough not to do it in front of her: "Debbie [Debbie imitating Boppo], your mother has taken ill on the way to [or from] Susan's house. She's at the hospital," or "Debbie, your mother has been in a terrible, terrible rainstorm coming from Alabama. We are staying in constant contact with the state patrol for any word of her." Debbie would tell Susan, "I'm so goddamned sick and tired of hearing about the state patrol. You and I know Mom's doing this on purpose—just to get attention."

And, of course, Pat was. She would invariably show up eight or nine hours late and make a dramatic entrance. But after Ashlynne started staying with Boppo and Papa, nobody seemed to be as worried about Pat. When she showed up, dripping wet and exhausted from her encounter with yet another "awful, utterly terrifying thunderstorm," and found Papa calmly rocking Ashlynne to sleep and crooning to her, Pat would flush beet red and demand, "What's *she* doing here?"

"Ronnie has to be out tonight," Boppo would say soothingly.

"Well, he can goddamned well come and get her! She's his child. Not yours!"

Pat clearly detested her own granddaughter. And Susan suspected that Adam was no more welcome.

46

On October 25, 1989, Tom Allanson was finally released from prison. They hated to see him go down at Jackson; he knew more about the internal workings of the prison's physical plant than anyone on staff. More than that, he was a nice guy who got along with everyone. He had been behind bars for more than fifteen years, long since forgotten by the Radcliffes and family, except for Susan who had continued to write to him occasionally. Nona and Paw were dead and Tom and his aunt Jean estranged. His son, Russ, had come to see him in Jackson when he turned eighteen and they had tentatively begun to get to know each other again. But Tom had no idea where Sherry was.

Tom had a good job waiting for him; his expertise in waste water management made him eminently employable. His new boss had held the job open for him for a year, and he handed Tom the keys to the company truck the day he walked out through the prison gates. He also had a bride waiting for him. Tom and Liz were already common-law married, of course, but they wanted a regular wedding. They got married the day Tom

was freed. He had never been good at dates; he didn't realize
that October 25 was the same date he had married Little Carolyn
more than two decades before. It wouldn't have mattered. That
might as well have been a hundred years ago.

Tom didn't think about Pat either. She was a *thousand* years
behind him. She had become only someone he had known once.
He didn't hate her. She was no longer important enough to him
to hate.

✦ ✦ ✦

Susan's growing fears about having Adam stay with Boppo,
Papa, and her mother soon became moot. She was the next
family member to fall ill and she had to stop working. In December of 1989, Susan contracted what seemed to be a stubborn
kind of flu. She had headaches, joint pain, and couldn't keep
anything on her stomach. She stayed home with Adam, but she
couldn't keep up with him, and she couldn't even start her
Christmas baking as she had hoped to do. After the first few
weeks, the pain in her joints settled in her hands and feet, a
bearing-down agony as if her extremities were caught in intractable vises.

It was a familiar pain—not unlike what she had felt in the
summer of 1987 when she had had such a terrible time driving
home from Boppo's house to Florence, Alabama. But this time,
it was worse. "I just had to keep rubbing my hands, kneading
them, trying to work that terrible aching out of them. They hurt
so bad I'd wake up at night with the pain."

Pat drove up to Brookstone from McDonough and announced
that *she* would take care of Susan. "Mom wouldn't let me do
anything," Susan remembered. "She took care of Adam, she
cooked for Bill and Courtney and Sean, and she tried to be sure
I didn't get dehydrated. She'd fix me soup or tea and come and
sit by me until she saw that I was swallowing it. I didn't know
what I would do without her."

Bill and Sean were hardly grateful. They made fun of Pat's
cooking; worse than that, they made jokes (behind her back, of
course) about being afraid she would poison them. It was an ill-
kept secret that Grandma Pat had been in prison for arsenic
poisoning, and Bill and Sean shared a certain perverse sense of
humor.

"Mom was no star in the kitchen," Susan admitted. "She tried, but—and I hate to say it because it sounds mean—my mother is not known for her cooking. Sean and Bill wouldn't eat what she made. Her 'famous tuna' still had the oil in it and then she added mayonnaise besides. She never skimmed the grease off of spaghetti [sauce] or chili. She liked it that way, so she assumed everyone did."

Susan begged Sean and Bill to be more considerate of Pat. But they just laughed and scraped their plates down the disposal when Pat's back was turned. Their eyes would meet, and, as if by prearranged signal, the two of them would sneak out to eat in a restaurant.

Susan appreciated having her mother there; she was so weak that she could no longer take care of Adam or the house. Her weight dropped by twenty pounds or more. At first, she only had dark circles under her eyes, and then her eyes themselves appeared sunken in her skull. She had been ill before—those terrible six weeks in Alabama—but not as bad as this.

Pat banned Bill and the children from Susan's room, warning them that she was far too ill for company, but Sean was crafty at sneaking in to see his mother. "Mom," he asked her more than once, "do you think maybe she's giving you something to make you sick?"

"Sean!"

"Well, she did it to people before. She won't let us see you. She's down there banging pots and pans around like she's mad at somebody. When is she going home?"

"I need her, Sean," Susan explained patiently.

"I wish she'd go home. And *I'm* not going to eat what she cooks. Neither is Dad."

Susan was too weak and sick to argue with him. There were many nights when Bill was out on the road and she needed another adult in the house to help her care for the kids. She was too weak and sick to realize that she was actually *living* her own worst fear. Her mother kept her completely isolated most of the time.

Her mother had taken over her house.

No one came to visit Susan and she wondered why. She didn't know that Pat refused to answer the door, had drawn the drapes so that the house looked deserted. She passed on no phone messages to Susan. "I found out later," Susan recalled. "My sister-in-law said she had come over many times to see me, but no one came to the door.",

It was Pat's way. She isolated people in her care. She had kept Jean away from Paw and Nona, and Bobby Porter from Aunt Liz. And now she had virtually locked Susan up in her own home, shutting her off from everything outside her bedroom.

✦ ✦ ✦

Christmas came and Susan was too sick to cook dinner. Everyone went to Boppo and Papa's. It was another holiday where everything seemed idyllic. Pat had spent countless hours painting and refurbishing an incredible dollhouse for Courtney. Sean quickly dubbed it "South Fork." It had four tall columns on the veranda—wrapped with red ribbons for a candy-cane Christmas look—additions on each side of the main house, lace curtains in all the windows, and black shutters. It was the sort of thing Pat loved to work on. Dolls and dollhouses, little worlds of her own creation.

There was no dollhouse for Ashlynne, which was unfortunate since the girls were almost the same age. Courtney thanked her grandmother politely, but she was a little girl far more interested in sports than in dollhouses and miniature furniture.

As they sat down to eat, Adam's "Grandma Pat" moved his highchair four feet back from the table so that he was sitting against the wall, his view of the family blocked by an antique china cabinet. Susan could see he was about to cry, his face bereft at being banished. She nudged Bill and he moved Adam back.

The food was wonderful and Susan tried to eat, but she felt queasy after a few bites. At home later, Bill took a picture of her sitting in an easy chair in her nightgown. She looked like death itself, her eyes sunken, her skin the color of thin parchment.

Susan hadn't been able to take care of Adam for a month, and in the months ahead she felt no better. Her hands hurt so badly that she could scarcely use them. Bill insisted that there had to be something more wrong with her than the flu. On January 19, 1990, he took her to the emergency room at Kennestone Hospital in Marietta for testing. Her doctor had no idea why she was so sick, but he listed a tentative diagnosis: ".079.9: Viral Syndrome."

A complete blood count, a sputum culture, and a urinalysis

yielded no information. Susan was dehydrated from vomiting; she was given intravenous fluids to stabilize her condition and then released. Bill wanted more testing. He wanted hair and nail clipping analysis; he wanted testing for arsenic. Susan absolutely refused. "I couldn't even think of that. I would not believe that my mother would do that to me. Not deliberately. That was too awful to contemplate."

Pat continued to care for Susan. She wasn't living with the Alfords in their home in the Brookstone Country Club but she might as well have been; she was there almost all the time. Susan was grateful; she didn't know what she would have done without her mother. She began to wonder if she had hepatitis or mononucleosis—or even cancer. She had been sick for three months and she just wasn't getting any better. Adam was such a chunk of a toddler that she wasn't sure she could lift him. Her mother wouldn't even let her try. Pat was very, very firm about that. She would not let Susan go near the baby.

Adam missed his mother. And Susan missed him so much she could hardly stand it. One night as her mother moved quietly around her bed, Adam woke up and Susan could hear him down the hall, crying. He played for a while in his crib, and then he started to cry again.

"Mom," Susan begged. "I've got to go reassure him."

Pat glared at her daughter, exasperated. "Do you want to kill him too? Is that what you want?"

Susan got out of bed and braced herself by holding on to furniture as she moved toward the hall.

"Go back to bed!" Pat ordered. "I'll take care of him."

"Mom," Susan said, "he just wants to see me. I've *got* to go in there and see him."

"You want to put *double* work on me, taking care of two of you? How much more am *I* supposed to take?"

Susan gave up. She crawled back into bed, but she could still hear her little boy down the hall. She waited until her mother was in the other end of the house, then she crept down the hall to Adam's room and picked him up. "He was *so* happy to see me. He put his little arms around me, and he just patted my face and looked at me. I think he thought I'd gone away forever."

Susan didn't hear a sound beyond Adam's joyful noises; she was so happy to be holding him again, and he was chuckling with glee to see his own mother. "I didn't hear a movement," she said, "but I half turned and she was there—just staring at me. I don't know why, but it frightened me. I jumped a foot and I said, 'Mom! You scared me half to death!' "

"What are you doing up?" Pat asked coldly.

"Mom, he just misses me. I've got to hold him."

"Go ahead, if you want to kill yourself and kill him. I've already got you to look after. Nobody ever thinks of me."

Susan lowered Adam into his crib and walked slowly back to bed. The house was warm, but she felt chilled. Why hadn't her mother said something instead of standing in the doorway so quietly, staring at her? Her expression had been so awful, so full of hate. Evil. For the first time, Susan was actually afraid of her own mother.

By morning, the feeling had passed, leaving only a smoky hangover of dread in her mind. She had been sick so long it was sometimes hard to think straight.

◆ ◆ ◆

By March, Susan was still sick. Her feet hurt so much that she hadn't worn shoes, much less high heels, for four months. And then, ever so gradually, she began to have good days interspersed with the bad. She was far from well, but she was better.

Continuing the tradition of teenage—and pregnant—brides in the Siler family, Debbie's eighteen-year-old daughter, Dawn, was getting married. Debbie asked Susan to take the pictures at the wedding and Susan promised she would, all the time wondering how on earth she was going to get dressed up, wear heels, and stay on her feet throughout the ceremony and reception.

Dawn's wedding was March 10, 1990. She was a beautiful blond bride, and although she was a little queasy with early pregnancy, she was not as nauseated as her aunt Susan was. Somehow, Susan managed to take a complete set of wedding pictures and stay on her feet. Barely. "I didn't think I'd make it," she said. "But I did. I plastered on makeup to give me some color, but I could see it didn't work in the few photographs I was in."

Susan wore a white silk dress that was way too big for her, but she cinched the belt over four notches. The circles under her eyes made her look ten years older than she was. Boppo wore

a lovely pale pink crepe dress. Pat wore her "marrying and burying dress"—the turquoise dress that had once been Susan's maternity dress. Debbie wore a very expensive white satin brocade
and lace dress. She wore it very carefully; she returned it to the
store the next day.

It was, Susan acknowledged, a typical family wedding, at least
for *her* family. On the surface, everything seemed lovely. Underneath, there were secrets, lies, evasions, and fears eating
away at the very foundation of the family.

✦ ✦ ✦

Although not one of them would ever have admitted it, Susan
and Bill Alford and their children had lived a life-style that all
of the Siler-Radcliffe clan envied. None of them knew how very
close the Alfords had come to losing it all at Christmas, 1988. It
was a matter of pride with Susan and Bill that they had handled
their own problems, pulled out of their economic quicksand,
and gone on.

They almost made it. But by the spring of 1990, there was
not much about the Alfords' lives that their relatives would have
wanted to emulate. Bill's *new* company was in the midst of a
buy-out too, and Bill and Susan doubted that they could survive
another job loss—even after Susan's health improved enough
for her to go back to work. They argued continually, and one or
the other would storm out of the house. They were scared,
worried sick about finances, worried about Sean's mediocre
grades, and worried about the future. The emotional tension
was crushing.

"We grounded Sean too much and made him study," Susan
remembered regretfully. "But we thought we were doing the
right thing. He was sick of the tension and the fighting in our
house—and I didn't blame him. It was such a bad time."

Sean was in love, and far more caught up in his girlfriend's
family than his own. He graduated from high school in June,
and Bill—who found it difficult to let go of grand gestures—
rented Sean a Cadillac to drive to the prom. Sean posed in his
prom tuxedo for his mother's camera.

It was to be one of the last happy pictures. When he turned
eighteen, Sean moved into his girlfriend's family's home and
completely turned his back on his own family. He wanted noth-

ing more to do with them, with their arguments, their worries, their lives. "We wouldn't let him take his truck, and I felt guilty about that—that was wrong—and I lost my temper and screamed at Sean," Susan said, her voice full of pain. Sean was her firstborn, her beautiful little boy grown to manhood, and he was gone; he stepped out of his family's life as if he had never been part of it at all.

Next—and very rapidly next—the Alfords filed a Chapter 7 bankruptcy petition. They had no other choice. The wonderful house in the Brookstone Country Club complex was gone, and Bill was back on the road as a salesman. "We had no place to live," Susan said. "We had no place to go—except to Boppo and Papa's. I was depressed. Sean and everything we'd worked for was gone, and I'd had to see Adam and Courtney give up their rooms, their home. When I was a little girl, Boppo was always the one who came to our rescue—but we were grown-ups and it hurt so much to have to move in with them. We were so ashamed."

Boppo and Papa's little house in McDonough was already crowded. Pat had her wing, of course—her doll room, her sewing room, her bedroom and bath upstairs. She refused to let anyone walk through *her* entrance, so Papa quickly built some rudimentary steps of unpainted two-by-fours outside the kitchen sliding doors.

Ashlynne was still living with Boppo and Papa five or six days out of seven, and she still slept in their bedroom. She had a room of her own, but Pat insisted it wasn't Ashlynne's room; she called it "the guest room." There weren't any other bedrooms. The only place the Alfords could stay was in the formal parlor. There was no privacy, just a room with oriental carpets and all the collected treasures from the Radcliffes' tours of duty. They would live there at Boppo's house, the eight of them—Boppo, Papa, Pat, Ashlynne, Bill, Susan, Courtney, and Adam—until Thanksgiving Day. And it would be the prelude to the unfolding of a nightmare.

Susan had always believed in her grandmother no matter what, but this time if Boppo helped her, she would be at cross purposes with what Pat wanted. From the moment they moved in, Pat made it clear that she didn't want Susan and Bill and the children in *her* mother's house. Perhaps it should not have been the shock that it was. But Susan had clung to the belief that a mother—any mother—would help and protect her child. She was wrong. Pat viewed Susan only as an enemy, a competitor for Boppo's love.

"My mother was outraged when we moved into Boppo's house," Susan said. "She didn't want us there. I had no idea how angry she would be. She was my *mother,* and we needed help. But we were intruding on her territory. Just like Kent had. Just like Ashlynne was. She didn't want us there. She especially didn't want *me* there."

Adam missed his big brother, and he missed his own room. He didn't understand why they had to leave his house and all live in one room. He was a very sad little boy. He sat for hours in a chair by the front window, his head on his folded arms, watching for something—or for some*one.*

Susan was even sadder. Her losses had piled one on top of another over the past year and a half, and she had been mysteriously and dangerously ill for four months. Her body was well —she no longer suffered from crippling pain in her hands and feet—but she could not seem to stop crying.

At first, she tried to help with the cooking and the chores, but she could not please her mother. Pat watched her constantly and criticized everything, from the way she washed a cup to the way she fried an egg. "I just gave up," Susan recalled. "I finally just stayed in the living room, sat on the couch, and cried. Bill looked after the kids, he washed dishes, he did errands. He would sit around the kitchen table and talk with everyone, and he could still make himself laugh. He was wonderful. I knew that he was feeling terrible too, but I couldn't help him. I was paralyzed."

Susan had seen what her mother did to people who invaded her territory. She attacked where she knew they were most vulnerable. She capitalized on weakness, homing in on whatever would hurt the most. Even though Susan had been only a young teenager when Kent committed suicide, she remembered how savagely her mother had attacked him.

And now she herself had become the target.

Susan's only defense against her mother's abuse, her sharp tongue, and her constant criticism was to hide in the living room, appalled at how increasingly depressed she felt. When she looked into her mother's eyes, she saw the same eyes she had seen the night she tiptoed down the hall to pick up Adam when she was sick, eyes full of hate.

Susan was so tremendously sad and so tired that she could scarcely move. She no longer cared to live. But she had children to raise, and she was frightened that she might do something irreversible just to escape the pain she felt. "I checked myself into Clayton Hospital," she said. "In the old days, they would call what I had a nervous breakdown—but they called it depression. I sure didn't disagree with them. I was there for five days and I will never, ever forget that day I came home. My mother walked in, glared at me with loathing, and said, 'What is *she* doing back here?' "

It got worse.

Shortly before Thanksgiving, Susan noticed that Adam had a big bald spot on the back of his head. She pulled him over to her and examined it more closely. It looked as if someone had deliberately taken scissors to his mop of curly hair and cut out a chunk of it. She showed Boppo, who peered at Adam's hair and said, with a straight face, "I don't see anything, Susan. It looks perfectly fine to me. Cliff, look here—do you see anything wrong with Adam's hair?" Papa didn't see the big bald spot either. If Susan hadn't been so depressed, she might have laughed.

On Thanksgiving, as everyone was trying to make the best of a difficult holiday, Pat brought up the subject of hair. They had just finished their meal when she stomped off and returned carrying two of her dolls. She insisted that Susan had deliberately butchered their hair in the back. There were, indeed, sections of the dolls' wigs missing. The backs of their heads looked just like Adam's.

"Susan did it," Pat said icily. "Susan's been back there deliberately mutilating my dolls."

Susan stared at her mother and began to shake her head. And then, with a horrible clarity, she realized what was happening. The dolls were not Pat's best dolls; they were the cheapest ones. She knew that her mother had deliberately cut off their hair to incriminate her. She knew too that her mother had cut Adam's hair just as deliberately, the sharp points of her scissors against his tender neck.

"I didn't know why Mom hated me so much," Susan said. "But I knew she wanted us out of the house, and I saw what lengths she would go to. Adam wasn't hurt. But the thought of her doing that to his hair to get at me gave me chills."

It was the last day the Alfords would spend in that house. Boppo and Papa turned as one to Bill and Susan, and Susan recognized the look. She had seen it before when they had ordered Kent out of their home—because he was upsetting his sister. Now, *she* was the expendable one.

Bill and Susan grabbed Courtney and Adam and left Boppo and Papa's house. They couldn't move far—the only house they could get into immediately was around the corner and on the main street of McDonough. They had saved just enough for the rent. The house was old, but it had a big backyard and a nice landlord.

And it would be their own, with doors to shut and lock.

"I wasn't well yet," Susan acknowledged, "but I know I was starting to get well, from that time on. I just didn't know what I was going to have to face. Our family had had arguments before, but things always worked out. This time was different."

Susan was *still* too close for Pat's comfort. "It began when my mother would pull into our driveway and just sit there," Susan said. "She didn't get out of the car, and she didn't come to the door. She would park there for a while staring at our windows, and then she would back her car out and drive away."

✦ ✦ ✦

By the Christmas season, a month later, Debbie was divorced and remarried—to Mike Alexander, who had finally divorced *his* wife. Ronnie was married to Kathy and collecting state industrial insurance from an injury suffered on a construction job. He had suffered a number of such injuries on the job, which, fortunately, had always been covered by state industrial insurance. Susan and Bill were fighting simply to stay afloat.

In December, Susan got a bizarre phone call from her sister. It took her a minute to figure out what Debbie was talking about. Debbie and Pat hadn't worked for the Crist family since June of 1988, but two and a half years later, Debbie was calling Susan to blame her for their dismissal. "You ruined it for us," Debbie said angrily. "We know that you called Mrs. Crist and told her lies about us. You made us lose our jobs. And I'll never forgive you."

Susan was baffled. As far as she knew, her mother and sister had been let go because the Crists' medical insurance ran out. That was what her mother had said. Why on earth would she have called the Crists? She didn't know them. And she and Bill weren't even living in the Atlanta area at the time.

The more Susan thought about Debbie's phone call, the more she felt an ominous sense that a Pandora's box had been opened —and she didn't want to know what was inside. When she told Bill, he stared back at her, puzzled. Susan wanted to forget it, but she knew that if Bill were pushed, he wouldn't look away. He would find out what the hell was going on. One thing they both knew. Neither of them had ever called the Crists.

On December 26, all unaware, Bill called Dawn Slinkard, Debbie's daughter, to ask that an antique crib that the Alfords had lent her be returned. Debbie answered the phone, and she was still furious with her sister. She told Bill never to call again. "You and Susan have ruined my life. Susan made the Crists fire us. Susan has always ruined my life."

Bill looked in the directory for the Crists' listing and punched in the number. Elizabeth Crist answered the phone. Bill didn't know that the date was special to her; if her husband had lived, it would have been his ninetieth birthday.

"Mrs. Crist," Bill began, "have you ever received a phone call from my wife, Susan Alford?"

"I've never heard the name."

"Well, let me explain. My wife's mother and sister worked for you a few years ago. What I really wanted to ask was whether my wife ever called you about her mother, Pat Taylor Allanson. You may know her as Pat Taylor?"

There was a long silence at the end of the line, and then Betty Crist began to tell Bill Alford "things I didn't want to hear."

When Bill told Susan what Mrs. Crist had said, she was sick at heart. Despite the way her mother had treated her, she still hoped the "trouble" was all over. "But sometimes," she recalled, "there had been things said over the past few years—even the jokes that Sean made, or some question my grandmother would ask—and in spite of myself, I would wonder if my mother was still dangerous. I'd wanted so much for her to be normal that I overlooked a lot of things. But I had told myself—*and* my mother and my grandmother—that if I ever felt my mother was hurting someone else, maybe even trying to *kill* someone else, I would have to go to the authorities. I swore that before she killed somebody, I would stop it—even if I was disowned from the family, with nobody wanting anything to do with me. I guess I always knew that it would blow the family completely apart."

Susan placed a call to the Fulton County District Attorney's Office.

PART EIGHT

OLD SECRETS

47

Don Stoop got all the oddball cases in Fulton County. He was the only investigator in the D.A.'s office eager to dig into cases that seemed, at the outset, to be fairly routine, but might take interesting detours. He was remarkably adept at exposing what lay under the surface.

Stoop was a walking paradox. Nobody ever knew exactly what he was thinking at any given moment. He was a wiseass with a sentimental streak. Most of the time, he appeared to be the ultimate macho cop—and yet, he knew exactly when to stop pushing and the precise moment to listen attentively. An irrepressible tease, he knew when to quit.

Stoop was anathema to crooked cops on the take; he had cleaned out a half-dozen corrupt police departments around Atlanta. His office was upstairs over a restaurant, kitty-corner from the Fulton County Courthouse; nobody could find it without a map and an invitation. It was just large enough to hold a desk and a bookcase, but he was never there, so it didn't matter. A connoisseur of beer, he also kept a candy dish on his desk for his sweet tooth, but he jogged calorie for calorie and never had a spare inch around his middle. He sported a moustache that would be the envy of any member of a barbershop quartet and his ties were hardly inconspicuous.

Don Stoop was born in 1952. He was an army brat and he never really grew up in one place. The closest thing he had to a hometown was the area around Red Bank, New Jersey. As a towheaded youngster, Donnie Stoop spent vacations there with his favorite uncle, "Fritz" Fitzpatrick, a detective for the Freehold Police Department. Fritz was patient and encouraging, a good cop who could recognize the seeds sprouting in the kid. If there is such a thing as a born detective—and there is—Don Stoop was destined to become an investigator. He questioned everything; he wanted to know all the whys and hows, all the details of the cases his uncle Fritz worked on. Why did people do bad things, and how did his uncle know they were guilty? He could not imagine that there could be a better job than to be a policeman.

When his uncle Fritz died, he left his badge to Don.

Stoop had a half-dozen years in the service behind him, a B.A. in police science, and two two-year degrees in criminal justice and philosophy. From the first moment he put on a police uniform in Cedar Grove, Florida, he loved it; it was what he had always wanted to do. A few years later, in 1980, he moved up to Georgia and "started policing for the city of Atlanta." He was still as blond as a Scandinavian, looked about eighteen, and worked a car in the most thickly populated black ghetto areas of the city. The people who lived on Atlanta's meanest streets liked him. He was a no-bullshit kind of guy. He stayed with the Atlanta Police Department for five and a half years.

While he was working in Atlanta, Stoop met his future wife, Theresa Hempfling, when they worked undercover stakeouts together. A lovely, dark-haired woman, Theresa was a federal agent for the Alcohol, Tobacco, and Firearms branch of federal law enforcement. She was in charge of the Zone 6 Project in Atlanta, seeking out "armed career criminals." She was as good at her job as Stoop was at his, and could trade quips with him toe to toe. Stoop was making 92 percent of the arrests in the Zone 6 campaign, and Theresa was seeing the cases through to conviction.

But what Stoop really wanted—what he had always wanted—was to be a detective like his uncle Fritz. The Fulton County D.A.'s investigative unit gave him plenty of opportunity to do just that. He had occasion more than once to "rethink" dispositions of cases marked closed by local police departments. One was the bloody death of a fifty-year-old man whose case had been closed as a suicide by the investigating agency. But there were aspects of the case that disturbed the dead man's family and they asked for an investigation by the D.A.'s office.

Reading over the autopsy report, Stoop saw that the victim had succumbed to several bullets in the chest, fired by an old .445 Webley cavalry pistol. The city detective investigating the case had surmised that the dead man had shot himself many times in the chest, walked around the living room, and then gone out into the hallway, where he shot himself a final time. That, the report read, would account for the proliferation of blood all over the floor.

That it would, Stoop agreed, if a man with his chest full of bullets were capable of walking around. Stoop recalled asking the detective, "Would it surprise you that all that blood in the living room isn't *his* blood?"

The city detective didn't believe the D.A.'s investigator.

"Look at his shoes, then," Stoop suggested.

The victim's shoes didn't have a speck of blood on them. "I think he died right here in the hallway," Stoop said. "And I think somebody else shot him."

✦ ✦ ✦

Stoop's investigation unearthed the fact that the dead man's girlfriend had been stopped by a patrol unit for erratic driving late on the night of the shooting. She had bandages on both wrists. "She told them she'd cut herself accidentally," Stoop recalled later with a grim smile. "And they let her go. She had tried to commit suicide by slitting her wrists after *she* shot him. That was *her* blood that was all over his living room; the lab identified two different types of blood left in his hallway and living room. Evidently, the girlfriend changed her mind about wanting to die—and went to Grady Hospital and got sewed up. We thought we had a case. But they acquitted her. The jury felt if it was murder, then the first investigators should have known it. It didn't make sense, but you can't second-guess a jury's reasoning."

Stoop was a busy man. Not only was he working for the Fulton County D.A.'s Office, but he was available to other agencies that didn't have investigators. On top of that, he still worked with two federal task forces: the Bureau of Alcohol, Tobacco, and Firearms, and the FBI's Drug Task Force. But he was never too busy to take on another oddball case.

When Susan Alford called the Fulton County District Attorney's Office, she had asked to talk to anyone who might know about a current case charging Patricia Taylor Allanson with crimes involving the James Crist family. She was still hoping that maybe Mrs. Crist had exaggerated. Her call was taken by Chief Investigator Ron Harris, who remembered Pat only too well from her 1976 conviction. He had worked on the case. The bizarre situation of a husband and a wife going to trial separately for murder and attempted murder within the space of a few years was hard to forget. No one in the D.A.'s office had ever settled the question of Pat Taylor Allanson's actual involvement in the murder of her in-laws.

"You aren't Pat Taylor's sister, are you?" Harris asked Susan.

"No," she said, wondering if her mother was *still* talking about her "wicked, sociopathic sister"—the imaginary sister who lived in North Carolina.

Susan did not tell Harris who she was in that first call, but he was intrigued. Why would someone be asking about Pat Taylor? The woman would be—what?—in her fifties by now, and she probably was out of prison. Harris checked the computers and found there *was* an open case, with a complaint filed by a Mrs. James F. Crist. But there wasn't much to go on. The only thing that the case file consisted of was a manila folder with one yellow sheet from a legal tablet in it.

Harris called Don Stoop into his office. Stoop had never heard of Pat Taylor, but the single sheet of paper led him to the Atlanta Police Department's Larceny Unit, which had filed away the Crists' complaint in 1988, marked "all leads exhausted." The city dicks had never gotten enough evidence together to charge anyone.

That made it Stoop's kind of case.

✦ ✦ ✦

It was February 5, 1991, when Don Stoop was officially assigned the Crist case. He was instructed to look into the "possible homicide of an elderly gentleman under the home care of two females who were, allegedly, Registered Nurses." James Crist had been dead for a little over two years. His death had been considered natural; he had suffered from Parkinson's disease and he was eighty-eight years old when he died. The question now was: Had someone hurried him along?

Stoop asked for Michelle Berry as his co-investigator. She had no experience as a homicide investigator; the Crist case might give her some. Michelle resembled a college girl more than a working detective. She was in her twenties, but she could easily pass for seventeen, an attribute that made her extremely valuable on her first law enforcement assignments. When she graduated from North Georgia College with a B.A. in criminal justice, she was hired by the Georgia Bureau of Investigation as an undercover narcotics investigator and was sent out to buy drugs from some of the seamiest characters in Georgia's narcotics underworld. She could look like a schoolgirl or a hippie or a confirmed addict. "At the time," she remembered, "it didn't even strike me as dangerous. I was a detective on a detail, and that's what I wanted to be."

Michelle's career as a narc went along swimmingly until she fell in love. "My job didn't sit too well with Jonathan," she said. "He told me, 'Either quit and marry me, or keep doing what you're doing and leave me alone.' " She loved him too much to leave him alone, so, reluctantly, she resigned her job with the GBI and they were married in December 1989.

Six months later, Michelle knew she couldn't give up law enforcement completely; that was what she had studied for. Much like Stoop, helping to keep the law was her life's ambition. Her husband understood, but he didn't want her back on the streets. They compromised. "I got a desk job."

Michelle's desk—and office—were neater than Stoop's, and her objets d'art were not nearly as eccentric as his, some of which were unmentionable. They made an interesting team.

Don and Michelle read Pat's and Debbie's rap sheets, and then did a little background checking on the Crist family. They learned that James F. "Jimmy" Crist had earned the huge house on Nancy Creek Road. If one single man could be said to epitomize the emergence of electric power in the South in the twentieth century, it was James Crist.

Jimmy Crist had started out climbing poles, his spurred boots digging into swaying shafts of tarred wood in winter storms and in the burning southern sun. In 1927, he worked as an apprentice lineman for the Alabama Power Company. He later became a sales representative, and then moved on to the South Carolina Power Company and stayed nineteen years. In 1946–47, Crist helped form the Southern Company, which was incorporated to operate four southern electric companies—Alabama Power Company, Georgia Power Company, Gulf Power Company, and the Mississippi Power Company. Crist was listed in *Who's Who in America* and wrote a book, *They Electrified the South,* about the emergence of electrical power in the first half of the century.

James Crist and his pretty wife, Elizabeth Courtney Boykin Crist, had belonged to the most exclusive inner circles of Atlanta *and* Charleston society. When Crist retired as the executive vice president and director of the Southern Company on January 1, 1966, he was lauded as a true pioneer of his industry and given credit for much of the prosperity of the New South. The thirty thousand employees of the Southern electric system saluted Jimmy Crist.

The Crists had had two grown sons and a daughter, a good marriage, and all the time in the world. He looked forward to playing more golf at the Peachtree Country Club. Crist remained an advisory director of the Southern Company until 1977, but as he entered his ninth decade, he began to show symptoms of Parkinson's disease, a progressive neurological malady that is sometimes connected to arteriosclerosis in an elderly patient. Symptoms began with tremors in the limbs, a masklike expression, a shuffling gait, and a kind of "pill-rolling" movement in the hands. It was a tragic illness for a man who had been so active all his life, and in time, Elizabeth Crist needed help in caring for him.

Jimmy Crist had died in 1988. Elizabeth Crist survived him and was in excellent health for a woman her age.

48

Don Stoop and Michelle Berry met with Mrs. Elizabeth Crist, her daughter, Betsy Chandler, and her sons, Bill and Jim, Jr. in the exquisitely appointed mansion where Mrs. Crist still lived. Betty Crist was attractive and intelligent and seemed younger than a woman in her late seventies. The D.A.'s investigators knew they would have to revive painful memories of Jim Crist, Sr.'s death when they asked his widow to recall the occasion of her meeting with Pat Taylor, but it was the only reasonable spot to begin their probe.

Betty Crist told them that Pat Taylor had come to her highly recommended. She had introduced herself as a registered nurse, just retired from the Army Nurse Corps, and she said she could bring in her daughter Deborah, who was also an RN, to work the second shift. Like her mother, Betsy Chandler had found Pat "very likable" during her employment interview. Pat had explained to Betsy and her brother Jim that she was so recently retired from the army that she had not yet received her Georgia nursing number, but she assured them that the requirements for her army rank were far stricter than the state of Georgia required. She gave them her credentials as "U.S. Armed Services Medical Services: ID No. NA-15-753," and added that she had once supervised all the nurses at Atlanta's Piedmont Hospital.

Jim Crist recalled that Pat had appeared to be about sixty, a stolid, no-nonsense type of woman with bobbed brown hair and glasses who probably weighed about 145 to 150 pounds. She said she lived in McDonough and gave her phone number. She offered references from former employers and Jim had checked those, eliciting only glowing reports. Pat Taylor had struck him as a very "take-charge" kind of woman, perfect for the role of charge nurse, supervising all of his parents' aides. He supposed an army nurse would have to be that way.

Pat's duties were to "take care of Jimmy," Betty Crist said, "take blood pressure, temperature, etc., and fix the meals. Jimmy was not bedridden when Pat was first hired." Nor was Betty Crist. She had been perfectly healthy—but not for long. "I became bedridden after Pat had been here about one month. Then she had to give me my medicine and bring trays up to my room to eat." Pat was indeed a "take-charge" kind of woman. "She would never let me and Jimmy spend time together," Betty Crist said. "She kept me upstairs, and Jimmy had a hospital bed set up in the den."

Betsy explained to the investigators that the family's whole purpose in hiring nurses was so that they could keep her father at home with her mother where he felt safe and as serene as a man so ill could be. "We knew he'd die if we put him in a nursing home—we just didn't want to do that."

"How was Pat paid?" Don Stoop asked.

"I paid her by check every Saturday," Betty Crist said. "When she first started, the fee was only ten dollars an hour. Then by the end of it all, I was paying her much more. I was sedated . . . and I just wrote the check. I paid for her and Debbie."

Betty Crist said that both Debbie and Pat had worn nurses' uniforms, and they certainly appeared to know what they were doing. Pat drove a red pickup truck to work, and Debbie whipped in and out of the Crists' long circular driveway in a white Camaro. Pat had driven Mrs. Crist to all of her doctor's appointments in the Crists' vehicle.

Betty Crist still wasn't sure how their prescriptions were obtained; she had never heard Pat calling them in, but she knew the drugstore made frequent deliveries of medicines and sick-room supplies. Betty Crist's eyes clouded as she recalled that her life had changed drastically almost from the first week she hired Pat Taylor. While before she had dealt with her husband's illness with tragic acceptance, spending long quiet hours sitting beside him, she had suddenly found herself almost totally blocked off from him. There were always "good" reasons why they should stay apart, and as Betty Crist grew weaker, she had less strength to argue with her charge nurse.

Pat worked days, and her daughter Debbie soon had the eve-ning shift, so one or the other of them was in the Crists' home from seven in the morning until eleven at night. Mrs. Crist had noticed that she grew terribly sleepy after she had eaten. "Pat would always tell me to just stay in bed and sleep. . . . For some reason, I grew very afraid of Pat and what she might do. Jimmy and I were always separated and we could never have visitors. Pat complained about being hired to care for one person and having to care for two."

Alone with her two elderly charges, Pat had ruled the Crist household and made her displeasure at small things apparent. She had conveyed her anger with a look, a sharp intake of breath, or a shuddering sigh. When she was truly annoyed— which had been often—she slammed the kitchen cupboard doors and banged pots and pans together.

Jim Crist said that he and his brother and sister had become concerned about Pat Taylor's care of their parents because it seemed extremely "regulated." Visitors were discouraged. When the Crists' grandchildren telephoned, they were always told their grandparents were "too tired to talk." At first, when Betsy or Bill or Jim, Jr., called to visit, and Pat explained their parents were napping and she hated to disturb them, they found her conscientious and caring and said they would come back another time. Later, they tried to pop in at unexpected times and were distressed to find that their parents were *always* indisposed.

Pat had not gotten along at all with the rest of the nursing staff, hired to fill in on her weekends off and on the graveyard shift. One way or another, they had all failed to meet her stan-dards. At her insistence, most of them were fired. The Crist children had assumed that the negative remarks the fired nurses made about Pat were sour grapes. Pat always seemed so efficient, so knowledgeable, and so concerned about their parents' welfare.

They had *expected* that their father's health would grow progressively worse, and that he might be confused from time to time, but there were incidents that were unsettling. One day, Jim Crist received a phone call from his father. That was highly unusual; his father couldn't have reached a phone without help. He could no longer walk unaided.

"I've been thinking about giving away our Civil War relics," his father began. "They're just taking up space."

"Give them away?" Jim Crist asked, amazed. "Give them away to *who?"*

His father said that the nurses would like to have them. Jim explained that the priceless artifacts were already listed in his father's will, earmarked for his grandchildren. He thought privately that someone must have deliberately urged the old man to call, the same someone who had helped him to the phone. His father had mentioned giving the artifacts to Debbie a few times after that bizarre call. Betty Crist nodded. Her husband had called her once when she was in the hospital for tests and horrified her by saying he thought Debbie should have the Civil War pieces.

In January or February of 1988, Jim Crist, Sr.'s Rolex watch was taken to be cleaned. When the shop called to say it was ready, Debbie had gone in to pick it up, but she had come back without it, explaining that it wasn't there. "When I called," Jim Crist said, "the jewelers said that Deborah Cole had picked it up —and signed for it. I have the receipt."

Bill Crist told the D.A.'s investigators that he had begun to notice a dramatic change in his mother's behavior early in 1988. Where she had always been vibrant, she had become sluggish and befuddled. Her words slurred as she talked to him, and she forgot things she had always remembered. He was baffled by the changes. Betsy Chandler saw it too, and wondered sadly whether her mother's age was catching up with her. That, and her mother's depression over her husband's condition, could account for her diminished state.

Jimmy Crist wasn't doing well either. The elderly man had developed an irritating rash that covered his whole body. He had never had anything like that until Pat and Debbie came to work.

He was totally bedridden by this time, and he complained of terrible, intractable pain in his feet. His physician told them that wasn't an expected side effect of Parkinson's disease, although the rash was.

Pat had never produced a Georgia nursing registration number, and she continued to mark her vouchers for the insurance company with her army number, signing them, "Pat Taylor, RN." After she brought Debbie aboard as the night nurse, she simply doubled the hours and explained that she would pay Debbie from her own check.

Later, when Don Stoop and Michelle Berry obtained copies of Pat's pay vouchers, they noted a markedly steady progression in her income. For her first week, she put down 40 hours at $10.00 for a total of $400. By December 1987, she was charging for 79 hours for one week at $12.50 an hour, and for 6 hours of "holiday pay" at $18.75 an hour—for a week's total of $1,100! But she was just gathering steam. Since the insurance company paid Pat immediately, the Crists assumed that her credentials were adequate. In January, Pat's voucher listed 108 hours at $12.50: $1,350. By May, she was charging $15.00 an hour for 132 hours: $1,980 for a week. Pat's final voucher showed that her week's salary due was $2,040! Although Debbie's name was never listed, she was reportedly getting some portion of this insurance money. Between the two of them, they were receiving close to $10,000 a month.

Pat and Debbie had not been released from the Crists' employ because their insurance had run out. Not at all. The medical policies provided to James Crist by the Southern Company were ultimately comprehensive, although underwriters had questioned the soaring nursing costs. Pat and Debbie had been raking in a small fortune. Even so, Don Stoop and Michelle Berry learned that it wasn't the exorbitant pay that resulted in their dismissal. It was what was happening to their patients.

Jim Crist explained that he had visited his mother unexpectedly as she was having lunch one day. She was eating a salad when he noticed there were tiny white tablets sprinkled on the lettuce. "Mother!" he said sharply. "Don't eat that." He took the plate away from her and did the first thing that came into his head; he threw the food away.

Shortly after—in February 1988—Jim took his mother to the

hospital for gastrointestinal bleeding. She stabilized within a few days. While she was in the hospital, she was given no medication except for a mild pain reliever for her headaches. She was soon her old self again, alert and competent. She left the hospital in very good condition, and they were all relieved.

But then, two weeks later, Betty Crist was back the way she had been—sleepy all the time, confused, depressed.

When Jim Crist discussed his concerns about his mother's health with her nurse, Pat surprised him by agreeing that something should be done—and soon. She said that his mother was becoming very hard to take care of. "She doesn't seem to know what she's doing at times." Pat also confided that she feared Betty Crist was drinking heavily, taking far too many drugs, and was becoming careless about leaving large sums of cash around the house. Incredible. This was not the mother Jim Crist had known all his life.

The Crists told Don Stoop and Michelle Berry that Pat's war with every other nursing aide save Debbie had continued. When she wanted to fire the family maid, who had been with the Crists for many years, Jim Crist had put his foot down, and he decided to keep a closer eye on Pat.

Pat had agreed readily to take Betty Crist to her doctor for a checkup. Just as the family became suspicious, she became perfectly cooperative and seemed truly concerned. She assured Jim Crist that she would make an appointment with Dr. Watson immediately. When Jim spoke to his mother, Betty Crist agreed with her son that she wasn't feeling like herself. She was sleeping far too much, and she often felt muddled in the head. By this time the family was so suspicious that they wanted to give Pat no prior warning of what they intended to do.

Jim Crist called Dr. David Watson, the Crists' family doctor, and said he was terribly concerned about his mother. Watson said he had begun to grow worried too.

"How much should my parents' monthly drugstore bills be— just for their prescriptions?" Crist asked.

"Oh, I'd say roughly two hundred to two hundred fifty dollars a month," the doctor estimated.

Jim Crist called the drugstores he knew his parents patronized and asked if he might have a printout of the prescriptions on file for Betty and Jim Crist, Sr. The printout showed that prescriptions for the elder Crists were averaging between seven hundred and eight hundred a month.

Something wasn't right.

Jim Crist dropped by his parents' home the first week of June 1988—apparently casually—and said he was going to take his mother for a ride. Instead, he took her to the hospital for a complete blood workup. When the results came in days later, they revealed that her system was loaded with triazolam, the generic name for the sleeping pill Halcion, in doses far surpassing recommended treatment.

Without telling Pat about the blood tests *he* had arranged, Crist asked her if she had ever taken his mother to see the doctor. Pat said that indeed she had—earlier that very day— and that Betty Crist had passed with flying colors.

"Was a blood test done?" Crist asked.

"Of course. Everything was fine." Pat indicated that the results had come back while they were still in the doctor's office. Jim Crist *knew* it took longer than a day for blood test results, and he felt a chill. He was armed with the devastating results from the *real* blood test.

Later, alone with his mother, Crist casually asked how Dr. Watson was. Dr. Watson was her internist.

"I don't know," she answered. "I haven't seen him in quite a while."

"Did you go to the doctor today?"

"We stopped by Dr. Hardin's."

Dr. Hardin was a dermatologist who was treating his father for his stubborn rash.

"Did they take some blood from you, Mother—for a test?"

"No, of course not." His mother looked at him as if he had taken leave of his senses.

That was enough. Crist fired both Pat and Debbie.

But that wasn't the end of the matter. Betty Crist told the investigators that weeks later she began to discover that many items of jewelry were missing. Over the years, her husband had bought her some beautiful pieces, and she had had some heirlooms too, handed down through their families.

Her jewelry losses were summed up succinctly in Complaint No. 815G2682 in the city of Atlanta's Bureau of Police Services, filed July 15, 1988:

One fifteen-inch strand of pearls with a pearl clasp—valued at
$1,100.

One matching bracelet of pearls—valued at $430.

One pearl ring with a small diamond on either side—$325.

One fourteen-carat gold mesh bracelet—$1,500.

One large oval lapis stone man's gold ring—$420.

One "tulip" ring with a double shank and double diamond flowers
—$990.

One "eternity" ring with a full circle of small rubies, channel set in
fourteen-carat gold—$290.

Betty Crist said she kept her jewelry in a case, hidden high up
on a back closet shelf. After she was confined to her bed under
Pat Taylor's care in January of 1988, she had brought it all down
and kept it in her dressing table "under a lot of petticoats, because I wanted it there. I mean, I couldn't wear it, but I wanted
it there."

Asked about a possible burglary of her home, Betty Crist was
positive that had not happened. With her husband so ill and
then with her own sickness, she had had round-the-clock nursing
help. Not one of them had ever reported a break-in. Hesitantly,
Betty Crist admitted that she had had her suspicions about two
of her nurses. Her son had fired Pat and Debbie, but she said
she hadn't filed formal charges because she was worried that a
court case would be terribly hard on her husband. His Parkinson's disease had progressed fast enough as it was; she hadn't
wanted to subject him to the stress of questioning by the police
and a possible trial.

Her insurance claims agent had written a detailed report of
the circumstances of the loss/theft, and closed by saying that the
Atlanta police had assigned the case a "D" classification. This
meant, in police lingo, that leads had run out. None of the
jewelry had turned up in area pawnshops, and there was no way
to link Pat Taylor and Debbie Cole to the thefts conclusively.

The Crists had decided not to press further. They were com-
pensated for their losses and the matter was dropped. The Atlanta Police Department was awash in larceny and burglary
complaints, and the thefts were buried under piles of new cases.
But Betty Crist continued to discover possessions that were
missing. Many of them were things that Pat Taylor had particularly admired: antique laces and hand-stitched linens; James

Crist's priceless Civil War artifacts; his Rolex watch, of course; her antique cookbooks; and a tiny cut-glass chandelier designed to fit a dollhouse.

But they were only *things*. The real loss was time. She had missed so much time with her Jimmy while she was feeling dizzy and confused. They had scarcely seen each other for months and then she lost him at Christmastime, 1988. It had always been such a special time, with Jimmy's birthday the day after Christmas. James Crist died of acute renal failure in Piedmont Hospital two days after his eighty-eighth birthday. His memorial service was held on December 30 at the Cathedral of Saint Philip, and his body was cremated.

49

On a Tuesday morning in March 1991, soon after their conversation with the Crists, Don Stoop and Michelle Berry drove south of Atlanta to the little village of McDonough to talk with Susan and Bill Alford. Although Susan had not left her name the first time she called the D.A.'s office, Bill had convinced her that they had to come forward and they had called back. The investigators hoped to learn more about Pat Taylor and her daughter, Debbie. They didn't know what to expect. Ex-spouses often called the authorities about each other; daughters rarely reported their mothers.

Susan Alford was a pretty woman, Stoop noted, with thick dark hair and intense brown eyes. She was shy, but she seemed resolute, although it was obviously painful for her to review her mother's and sister's histories. Bill Alford was more voluble, a natural salesman, a man who laughed easily.

"As we got into the case, and as the facts emerged," Michelle Berry recalled, "I had to remind Don that, no matter how outrageous Pat Taylor's behavior had been, this was Susan's *mother,* and there had to be feelings there that still hurt."

"Susan Alford laid it out—this incredible story," Stoop said. "At first, I couldn't believe it. But Susan obviously needed to tell what she knew. And she knew a lot. At that time, however, even Susan wasn't aware of all *we* had found out. There had been so much secrecy in that family."

The Alfords said that they had never doubted Pat and Debbie's explanation for being let go by the Crists—not until Debbie's vituperative phone call just before Christmas, 1990. "She was accusing Susan of making them lose their jobs, and it didn't make sense," Bill said. "That's why I called the Crists. And Mrs. Crist told me that Debbie and Pat were fired because she had been drugged—and because they stole her blind!" Bill said that Mrs. Crist had been "very vivid" about what should be done to Pat and Debbie.

"What did she say?" Stoop asked.

"She said that they should be put in jail."

The Alfords were frank with Don and Michelle about the terrible summer of 1990, the reasons behind their moving in with "Boppo and Papa," and the Thanksgiving Day blowup. The investigators exchanged looks as Bill described the episode of the dolls' hair. Pat Taylor was not going to be your everyday suspect.

Asked to go back to the time Pat and Debbie were working for the Crists, Susan described her grandmother's concern about their sudden affluence. Debbie had bought a new yellow truck for cash, and her mother had bought Persian rugs, jewelry, and things for her dolls. "My grandmother worried; she didn't think my mom and Debbie could make that much money as sitters."

"Your mother and sister are registered nurses?" Michelle asked.

Susan shook her head. "My mother and sister haven't even graduated from high school. My mother *was* trained to be kind of a nursing assistant—more like a sitter—when she was in the halfway house. . . . They came to visit us in Florence in 1985, and Debbie was flashing money around. I said, 'How much money do you and Mom make? Boppo has been asking me about it. Is everything up-front?' And Debbie said, 'Well, I don't know. I'm kind of worried about it myself.'

"A doctor had asked her about her credentials," Susan went on. "Mom told Debbie to say she went to the University of

Munich. I asked Debbie, 'Don't you think that's a little strange?' and she said, 'I don't know.' "

It would have been strange. When Debbie lived in Munich she was four years old. Susan handed Stoop and Berry a handwritten resume Debbie had given her. Her "accomplishments" certainly *looked* impressive.

> Teacher-Elem. Sc.—Riding Instructor—Equitation
> Nurse, Surgical Assist., Private Duty—(Geriatrics)
> Manager of Medical Office with Following Duties:
> * Personal & office corresp.   • payroll
> * depositories   • billing
> * records   • hired, trained, supervised a
> * bookkeeping   staff of 5
> * collection

Debbie described herself as

> dependable, efficient, amiable, adabtable [*sic*], competant [*sic*]. Traveled abroad extensively as a child with parents and exposed to many cultures and ethnic groups.
> Education: Universite of Munich, Germany (Bad Toltz), Degree in Nursing
> Continuing Education—Refresher courses in French and Spanish

Susan said that Debbie was currently working in a doctor's office and seemed to be doing well. She and Pat had given diabetes shots in their "sitters' jobs," and Debbie still gave vitamin shots to their grandfather, Colonel Radcliffe.

Susan felt that her sister would not have planned any complicated subterfuge, but that Debbie always went along with their mother. She explained that her sister had had a sad, hard life, that Debbie had always yearned for something beyond the teenage marriage she felt trapped in.

"Was your mother ever in the armed forces?" Stoop asked.

Susan shook her head. "Only as a dependent. My grandfather is a lieutenant colonel—retired—and my father was a sergeant."

"Do you know," Stoop asked suddenly, "if they *targeted* these people? How did they come across these people who were dying or elderly?"

"They had a good reputation—like Mrs. Mansfield's son, Lawrence, heard about them from Sue and Hudden Jones. . . . Everyone just loved them."

Susan said that Debbie had been concerned early on that their mother was simply taking what she wanted from her patients' rooms or homes. "Debbie would deliberately set something in a certain position, and lots of times it would disappear." Later, Susan feared Debbie got into the spirit of things with her mother. "My grandmother said I was a fool to think Debbie wasn't involved. She said, 'Honey, you can bet that Debbie knows exactly what she's doing.' "

"What about jewelry?" Stoop asked. "Mrs. Crist said there was a large quantity of jewelry missing."

"I know that Debbie and Mom felt justified taking some things. Sometimes, they would say that they were given to them."

"What type of things are we talking about?"

"Small items. Jewelry. Sterling. Knickknacks. My mother liked antique-looking things. . . . Hatpins. She gave me a pearl necklace—more of a choker, and I believe it has two strands. Then there is a bracelet. It has a big gold clasp on the pearls, and they're gorgeous."

Stoop's ears perked up at that, but he didn't change his expression. The pearl set sounded like the one Betty Crist had reported missing. Susan said she had the set in her room and she could show them. In fact, her mother had given the family a number of beautiful pieces of jewelry. A gaudy jade ring for Boppo. A solid eighteen-karat gold man's ring with a lapis stone to Papa for his seventy-fifth birthday. Her mother kept a cedar chest full of miniature sterling pieces and antique pillboxes for herself.

Stoop knew a lapis stone ring had disappeared from the Crists'. "You know anything about a Rolex watch?" he asked.

"No. My sister would have gotten that if there was one."

"Why do you say that *Debbie* would have gotten that?" Stoop was fascinated. He knew that a Rolex was missing from the Crists', but Susan didn't. He also knew that Debbie was the one who had signed for it at the jewelers. "My mother would have had no interest in a Rolex. . . . Debbie would have gotten a Rolex in a minute. . . . Debbie had a shoplifting problem in the past. She justified what she did by the stores' high prices. She's a store detective's nightmare."

Susan had not seen a Rolex watch, however.

"The lapis ring?" Michelle Berry asked carefully. "Does your grandfather still wear that?"

Susan nodded. "And I think I have some video from his birthday party where he's wearing it. *Why?*"

It was apparent that Susan was vacillating between a certain sense of relief that her suspicions could be validated and a wrenching awareness of what her mother had done. Her eyes often filled with tears, and she cleared her throat frequently.

"Let's get back to the idea that Debbie and Pat—your mother —were registered nurses," Stoop said. "Did they ever tell you that they prescribed medicine or called in medications and picked them up?"

Susan shook her head. "What they did tell me was that Mrs. Crist had her medicine delivered to her home . . . Debbie took one of Mrs. Crist's pills one time, and it zonked Debbie out . . . she slept for the whole night when she was supposed to be up. When she woke up, both of them were hollering for her."

"Who is both of them?"

"Mr. Crist and Mrs. Crist."

Susan said that although she had worried enough about the small items her mother and sister had brought home from their nursing jobs, and by the money they flashed, it had never occurred to her that they had been dispensing medicine on their own. Don Stoop and Michelle Berry could see the revival of an old nightmare reflected in her dark eyes.

50

Don and Michelle had thoroughly familiarized themselves with Pat's earlier encounters with the Georgia justice system. They recognized the eerie similarity between what had happened to the Crists and to Paw and Nona Allanson. When Pat told Jim Crist about his mother's "drinking," she had repeated almost verbatim what she had said about Paw Allanson a dozen years earlier.

Susan and Bill Alford had led Don and Michelle back through the eighties and into the seventies, reprising the horrible double murder of Walter and Carolyn Allanson, the near-fatal poisonings of Paw and Nona Allanson, and the glory that was once Zebulon. The investigators were eager to take a closer look at those cases. Pat had been convicted in the latter case—but she had walked away free as a butterfly in the double murder.

But first they had to deal with the current case. It didn't matter how many people *said* that Pat and Debbie were no more registered nurses than they were brain surgeons; Stoop and Berry had to prove it. They had to trace and identify the medications used to render Betty Crist almost immobile *and* find out how they were obtained. And, perhaps the most difficult task of all, they had to try to find the myriad treasures that had disappeared from the Crist mansion on Nancy Creek Road.

It was now almost two years after the fact in the most *recent* case involving Pat. The D.A.'s detectives didn't even want to think about what it would be like to go back two decades on the homicides.

✦ ✦ ✦

Don Stoop began by checking with the Naval Investigative Service, the Department of the Army's Criminal Investigation Command, the Georgia Board of Nursing, the Georgia Board of Licensed Practical Nurses, the Florida Board of Nursing, and the North Carolina Board of Nursing. He was not particularly surprised to find that neither Pat Taylor nor Debbie Cole Alexander was licensed in any of those venues as a registered nurse, licensed practical nurse, or even licensed nurse's aide. One doctor in Florida that Debbie had given as a reference, claiming she had assisted him as an RN in the operating room, apparently didn't exist at all; at least, no one by that name had ever been licensed to practice medicine in Florida.

Pat Taylor *had* been trained at Horizon House to empty bedpans, give sponge baths, and keep her elderly charges company. Debbie Cole *had* worked in a number of physicians' offices and had often called in prescriptions to drugstores on her employers' instructions.

Don Stoop obtained permission to speak to the Crists' attending physicians. Dr. Fred Hardin, their dermatologist, said that he had indeed prescribed a lotion for Jim Crist's rash. He had not, however, seen Elizabeth Crist as a patient since March 1988.

"Would you have drawn blood from either of them in the treatment you provided?" Stoop asked. "Did you ever prescribe medication that would be considered a controlled substance?"

"No, not at any time. Dr. Watson is their internist. He would have done all blood tests—and prescribed that kind of medication, if it was needed."

Dr. David Watson knew the Crists well. Like everyone connected to the case, the internist had found Pat Taylor competent enough on first assessment. She seemed conversant with the proper medical phraseology and, in an insurance assessment conference, she had spoken out confidently about her worries for her patient. She explained that she kept a monitor with her at all times so she could hear Mr. Crist if he needed her. She seemed very protective of her patient and refused to allow anyone else to prepare his meals. She felt that the weekend nurses "agitated" him, and that she was far more capable of assessing his needs. She watched him constantly because she feared he was suffering "small strokes" and might fall and hurt himself.

Dr. Watson's early favorable impression of Pat Taylor had wavered, however, when he saw Elizabeth Crist in 1988. She had been his patient since April 1985. She was a vibrant woman who had always seemed years younger than her age. It was *Mr.* Crist who was ill; his wife was, naturally, stressed by her husband's condition, but she usually managed to keep cheerful.

Checking his notes, Watson told Don Stoop that Betty Crist's sons had brought her to his office on June 6, 1988. "There is a real question," he said, looking up from his notes, "of whether she and her husband were being oversedated by the nurse that was working with them most of the time." Watson told Don Stoop he had scarcely recognized his longtime patient. Betty Crist was dizzy, pale, nauseated, she spoke with a slur and lost her train of thought often.

He had ordered a blood screen immediately. The medication that he had prescribed for hypertension would not have done this to her. The test results were essentially normal—all except for the excessive percentage of Halcion in her bloodstream.

"Had you prescribed Halcion for Mrs. Crist?" Stoop asked.

Watson nodded. "A single prescription—in April. As I recall, I made a house call to *Mr.* Crist, and either Mrs. Crist—or the nurse, Pat—requested it because Mrs. Crist was having trouble sleeping."

Halcion was a very potent sedative. And Betty Crist had been loaded with it. Her physician said he would never have prescribed so much. At most he would have had her start with a dosage of a half pill a day—from a thirty-day supply.

When Dr. Watson worked with the Crists' sons in checking on the number of prescriptions called in to the two drugstores the family patronized, he said he had found that someone had ordered 120 Halcion tablets in a thirty-six-day period from just one of the drugstores. He would never have authorized that many sleeping pills in so short a time. Never.

Don Stoop found that the procedure used by physicians to call in prescriptions was fairly standard. Each doctor had a DEA number that identified his office. His nurses used that number when they called a pharmacy. Written prescriptions bore the same number. It became clear to Stoop that anyone who had once been in possession of a written prescription and who was familiar with office protocol and terminology could call in a prescription and would probably get away with it—unless an alert pharmacist picked up on a pattern of excessive use.

Stoop was convinced that either Pat or Debbie had done just that. On May 11, 1988, someone using Dr. Watson's DEA number had called in a Halcion prescription (thirty pills) to the Reed Drug Store—with *five* refills—for Betty Crist. On April 29, Wender and Roberts Drugs had a phoned-in thirty-pill prescription, another thirty on May 17, and still another on June 3.

Someone had had enough Halcion delivered to the Crist home to sprinkle it in salads, throw it around like confetti, and have more than enough left to sedate Betty Crist to the point where she would ask no questions and cause no trouble.

Stoop also knew that Betty Crist, long back to being herself again, had reached for something in her closet and her hand had touched a bottle of pills, hidden far back. Curious, she had stretched to get it and looked at the label; it was Placidyl, a sleeping pill that had been prescribed for her three or four years before. The pills were two-thirds gone. She had always felt that Pat had given her more than the Halcion; she had been sleepy from the first few weeks Pat came to work in her home. She had probably been slipped the Placidyl too. Lord only knew what else.

When the D.A.'s investigators talked to the Crists' other nursing employees—or, rather, former employees—they verified their suspicion that Pat had been more than the charge nurse of the Crist mansion. She had been the ruling monarch; none of the other women had lasted long after Pat was hired, and all of them said that she had been well nigh impossible to get along with. She had made it clear that *she* was the only nurse allowed to interract with the Crists—except for scut work—and that she would see to all meals and medications. She had explained that Betty Crist was "senile and crazy," and not in any state to give orders. Pat would do that.

It appeared quite probable that Mrs. Crist had been heavily drugged five days a week. From Monday morning to Friday evening she stayed in bed all the time, and no one but Pat or Debbie saw her when she was, at least technically, awake. The night nurse saw only a heavily sleeping patient.

One nurse's aide, Lynn Battle, told Don Stoop that she had been puzzled when she walked into the kitchen one morning and found Pat dissolving a blue tablet (Halcion is blue) in Mrs. Crist's juice. Startled, Pat had recovered quickly. "*You* couldn't do this. You don't have an order for it," she said with her usual touch of superiority.

Lynn wondered why Pat hadn't just let Mrs. Crist swallow the tiny pill, and she wondered more why she was giving her Halcion, a sleeping pill, in the morning. "Then too—well, it was strange . . . ," Lynn began.

"What?" Stoop prodded.

"Pat told me Mrs. Crist got in her way, that she was always hiding medication around the house. I mean, I never saw any medicine anywhere but in the kitchen where it was kept. Pat said she had to search Mrs. Crist's room for drugs, and she was always hinting that Mrs. Crist was crazy."

Lynn Battle hadn't lasted long after Jim Crist, Jr., asked her if she would like to work full-time. "Pat didn't want that. She set me up," Lynn said succinctly. Pat had claimed she had lost an envelope with the money from her paycheck in it. "She called me at the Crists' and asked me to look for it. I did, but it wasn't on the downstairs dresser where she said it would be. She called early the next morning, Saturday, and came out to look for it. She checked everyplace—even the refrigerator."

A day or so later, Lynn's agency called her, brought up the missing money, and told her she was not wanted back at the Crists' home. And yet, after Debbie and Pat were fired, she was rehired and worked with them for the six months until Mr. Crist died.

"It was funny," Lynn said. "All that time after I lost my job, Debbie and Pat were calling me and telling me that they were trying to talk Mrs. Crist into hiring me back. But I knew Pat had set me up. She didn't want any of us there more than two or three days a week."

There appeared to be a good reason for that.

The weekend nurses noticed that when they arrived on Friday, Mrs. Crist was usually shaky and confused, but she grew steadily more alert while they were there. By Monday morning, when Pat came to work, she seemed completely unlike the woman she had left. But within a few hours after Pat came on duty, Mrs. Crist was napping all during the day.

Ruth Garrett had worked the evening shift from time to time. She told Don Stoop that Pat had fired her when she called in sick one evening. "She told me that Mrs. Crist said I 'bothered her.' " Ruth Garrett hadn't particularly liked the head nurse at the Crists, finding Pat bossy and unfriendly. "Pat was in charge of all medication and food. . . . One time, I saw that poor Mrs. Crist looked like death warmed over. Her eyes were sunken, her skin color was awful, and she couldn't even hold her own head up. I told Pat how bad Mrs. Crist looked, and she just said, 'I'll take care of it,' and she called the doctor's office for some new medicine. Pat ordered all the medicine."

✦ ✦ ✦

As Don Stoop and Michelle Berry continued their questioning of the Crists, their physicians, and their other employees, it became tragically, unbelievably, clear what had happened. Betty Crist had been systematically drugged with medications obtained from forged prescriptions, and she had been robbed—of her dignity, of her health, and of her treasured belongings.

But most of all, she had been robbed of the few months of precious time that remained for her to be with her husband. As she slept away the days in her stuffy room through the spring of 1988, her Jimmy was far away from her, and his illness was progressing with those days, taking him still farther from her. She would regain her dignity, her health, some of her treasures —but she would never in this world find again those lost days with her dying husband.

Nor would Don Stoop and Michelle Berry ever be able to prove what they suspected was true. James Crist had complained of agonizing pain in his feet, the most classic symptom of arsenic poisoning. But there was no body to exhume and test for arsenic.

James Crist had been cremated just before the New Year, 1989, two years before.

In checking with criminalists, Stoop learned that arsenic is one of the very, very few poisons that can still be detected in the cremains of a human being. Because it is so insidious, leaching into the hair, nails, and eventually the bones of its victims, arsenic remains long after the person is reduced to ashes. The Crist family had been through so much pain. When Don Stoop approached them about the possibility of having James Crist's ashes tested for arsenic, they could not do it. It seemed a sacrilege.

No one would ever know if the old man had been sedated, tranquilized, *poisoned*.

51

Despite setbacks and disappointments, the case against Pat Taylor and Debbie Alexander moved forward. Don Stoop and Michelle Berry worked relentlessly, gathering a bit of evidence here, another interview there. Their spirits rose when Elizabeth Crist and her daughter, Betsy, positively identified the pearl necklace and bracelet set that Pat had given to Susan. They both recognized at once the gold flower clasp with the single pearl in the center. It was the same with a leather-bound antique cookbook, another thoughtful gift from Pat to her daughter. It had not been hers to give; it was part of Mrs. Crist's Williamsburg cookbook collection.

There were still myriad items missing. Sooner or later, Stoop knew he would have to get a search warrant for the little red brick house in McDonough—Boppo and Papa's house.

✦ ✦ ✦

Susan Alford had some bizarre documentation of the way her mother's mind worked, something she had never sought out, something she was hesitant to turn over to Don Stoop. But the knowledge that it existed burned in her mind.

Years before, in 1977, as Boppo was sorting through hastily packed possessions from the Tell Road house, she had come across a grocery sack with an old tape recorder in it. She gave it to Sean, who, at five, wasn't enthused about the gift. The Alfords had carted the bag and the tape recorder around with them in their many moves from Houston to Florida and back to Atlanta. No one ever bothered to check what was rattling around in the bag.

One day, they were unpacking after yet another move, and Susan lifted the old-fashioned recorder and saw that the bottom of the bag was full of old tapes. "Let's put some country music on," she said to Bill, "and get into the spirit of unpacking."

When the first sounds filtered into the room, they stared at each other, almost embarrassed. They recognized the voices on the tapes, and realized they were inadvertently eavesdropping on an intimate conversation of long ago.

" . . . I love you more than anything in this whole wide world, Sugar."

"Don't say that, Tom."

"Huh?"

"You love me more than any*one*. You don't love me more than any*thing*. You love life more than you love me—"

The tapes Pat had routinely made of her phone calls in the mid-seventies crackled with age and the dust of more than a decade, but the human emotions were still caught there. Pat and Tom's conversations were as filled with manipulation and frustration as the day the words were first said, the male voice deep and laced with pain, the woman's light and full of unshed tears. Bill and Susan felt like voyeurs. They switched the recorder off.

They hadn't really listened to the tapes—only long enough to see what they were: Pat's phone calls from Tom in the Fulton County jail. Susan hadn't wanted to hear more; the voices brought back so much hurt.

"A long time later," Susan eventually said, "I got them out and listened to all of them. And they were frightening. I hadn't known that my mother tried to get Tom to commit suicide. There were so many things I had never known."

At the time, Susan said, she had managed to deal with the

content of the fifteen tapes by reminding herself that her mother had been under the influence of drugs, that this wasn't her *real* mother talking and conniving and playing with Tom Allanson's emotions. This was a stranger addicted to mind-altering drugs.

Now she could no longer retreat to that theory. Until she learned of the episode at the Crists', Susan had always believed her mother's claims that she had no memory of the period when Tom's parents were murdered and when Paw and Nona were poisoned. Susan didn't believe that any longer. She believed that her mother remembered *everything,* and that she had no regrets at all.

Susan turned the tapes over to Don Stoop and Michelle Berry. Most of them were Realistic Supertapes and there were some old J. C. Penney labels too. "Tom" and the dates—mostly in 1975—were written in Pat's hand on the labels. That they had survived the Alfords' numerous moves, the heat of sixteen summers, and the cold of as many winters defied explanation. A few were twisted, but they still played. Hesitant to risk breaking the precious tapes, Stoop took them to an expert to have them copied and enhanced for clarity before he allowed himself to listen.

It was all there, all caught on the thin brownish plastic strips, winding round and round. For years, Susan and Bill had packed and unpacked, moved again and again, and they had always carried with them, unawares, the sounds that finally explained exactly how the mind of a woman without conscience worked.

Tom's voice was deep and concerned, and Pat's was alternately girlish and seductive. Stoop had not yet spoken to Pat Taylor, but the woman on the tapes sounded nothing at all like the charge nurse he had come to know through others' descriptions. Almost every call had a single theme: Tom trying to cheer and placate his distraught wife. Tom forcing down his own concerns to keep Pat serene. Tom agonizing over the mysterious infection he was told would soon take Pat's life. Tom refusing to give up as Pat predicted only doom and despair. And, finally, on one wrenching tape, Tom breaking down at last into sobs that still held so much raw pain this long after.

Pat's manipulation was skilled, honed, and absolute.

There were other conversations that only pointed up further how she had used Tom. Stoop's eyes widened as he heard how entirely changed her voice was when she jousted with attorneys —one moment imperious, the next ever-so-slightly flirtatious. He heard Pat veto the possibility that Tom might become a teacher in prison and avoid hard time at Jackson. Voices of the dead were there too: Paw Allanson, who sounded like an aged Tom, calling to inquire about Pat's health; and then Nona, her speech impaired but sounding worried about Pat.

Stoop knew how Pat's "fatal" infection had occurred; he had read Boppo's testimony in her appeal, her description of how Pat herself had continually opened and irritated the wound in her hip. She had used the emotions of all these people who feared for her life; she had bent them and twisted them and squeezed bloody anxiety from them.

She had orchestrated it all.

Stoop heard Pat's voice threatening Tom's ex-wife and wondered why she hadn't bothered to erase the damning evidence. Stoop knew that Little Carolyn Allanson had been scheduled to be one of the strongest witnesses against Tom. It would have been shortly before the trial when Pat dialed the drugstore where Carolyn worked and asked in a light, sexy voice to speak to someone in the hair dye department, Carolyn's section. Stoop heard Carolyn answer and Pat's voice drop as she hissed, "Be careful." Then she slammed the phone down.

This woman *had* hurt other human beings physically, and Stoop listened to the way she worked insidiously to erode their last vestiges of serenity. He wondered which was worse.

The most devastating tape of all included several twenty-five-minute conversations between Tom and Pat when he was about to be transferred from the Fulton County jail to Jackson Prison. He had borrowed and bought time from the other prisoners so that he could talk longer to his wife. And what did he get in return? A woman who whined, wept, accused, and predicted nothing but doom. She timed her responses meticulously. It was so obvious to a detached listener. When Tom was beaten down too low, she whispered, "I love you, Sugar," and he managed to come back.

She was like a cat. She let the mouse go just far enough, and then she pounced and impaled her prey on the unsheathed claws of her words. On the rare, *rare* occasions that Tom spoke firmly or harshly to Pat, reacting to too much jabbing, she burst into sobs and said that he didn't love her, she was worthless, and she had just wanted him to be proud of her. And he was abjectly apologetic.

Despite her tears, one thing was patently clear. *She was enjoying herself.* The Pat on the tapes reveled in every minute of her conversations with her husband, listening to him twist in the wind, hearing his voice drained of power. These weren't phone conversations; they were contests. And she always won. She was Delilah and Tom was Samson. Each day she rendered this man of such strength helpless with her words.

Tom came close to the real truth once, although he was speaking metaphorically. So close that Pat gasped.

"Tom, when they take you away, I won't know if you're alive or dead."

"Pat," he pleaded, "[in your letters] you're just so eaten up with hate. You're just so bitter. . . ."

"Tom!" she sobbed. "Can't I do anything right anymore? You won't *love* me—"

"Pat, you've got to keep digging at it like a sore; you'll just make it worse—"

"What?" Pat's voice was shocked from its petulant whimper. Stoop, knowing what he now knew, realized that Tom had inadvertently made Pat believe he had somehow found out about her self-mutilation.

"Sugar," Tom soothed, unaware. "I mean it isn't gonna get any better by your hating everyone."

Stoop could hear Pat release her pent-up breath in relief. She hadn't been caught at all. Stoop also realized that there must have been secrets that Pat wanted Tom to keep. But what were they?

If Tom mentioned *anyone* but her, Pat grew petulant and gave orders. "I love you, Tom. I *love* you, Sugar. I don't want anyone else in our lives."

Clearly she did not, Stoop realized. If Tom had no one but Pat, then he would do exactly what she instructed. If he believed she alone loved him and was working desperately to set him free, even though she was "near death" herself, then he would do anything she asked. But what did she want him to do—or *not* do? Stoop realized, too, that if there were secrets that were dangerous to Pat, an isolated Tom would be less likely to give them away. And if he had agreed to her suicide pact and carried out his part, then a *dead* Tom would have given away no secrets ever.

At some point, Don Stoop knew he would have to talk with Tom. He wondered what the man was like now. He had been locked up for more than fifteen years, and free for only a little over a year. Had prison crushed him? Of one thing Stoop was fairly sure. Tom Allanson wasn't going to relish talking about Pat and the decade of the seventies.

And who would blame him?

When Don Stoop questioned Debbie Cole Alexander's ex-husband, Gary, he didn't care to discuss Pat either—beyond describing his former mother-in-law as a "vicious, scheming, evil bitch." He recalled all too well when he had been informed that Pat had hired a hit man to kill him. He had believed it at the time, and he still half believed it. Gary Cole wanted nothing to do with Pat and Debbie. He was still afraid of Pat, and he made no excuses for it.

✦   ✦   ✦

By March of 1991, Pat and Debbie were aware that they were being investigated. They were uneasy, apprehensive about someone unseen retracing their lives, and had angrily accused Susan of "betraying" them.

And Boppo, of course, rose up to defend her daughter. She ran into Bill Alford at the riding stable where Ashlynne and Courtney took lessons. Although she had come to think of Susan as the pariah of the Siler clan, and an ultimately evil person, Boppo still looked upon Bill as someone she could count on. While Susan gave away her every emotion in her face, in Boppo's eyes, Bill was the opposite. His slight, sardonic smile betrayed nothing.

Boppo suggested to her grandson-in-law that he hook up a tape recorder to the Alfords' phone—his *own* phone—so that she could keep track of what Susan was doing. She reminded Bill that Susan was undoubtedly crazy; she would have to be to turn on her mother the way she had. Poor Pat. Everyone knew, Boppo said, that Pat had suffered so all her life, and now she had to deal with an ungrateful and treacherous child!

Bill solemnly promised Boppo that he would hurry home and

hook up a tape recorder under the house to monitor Susan's phone conversations. He had no intention of doing any such thing, but he did not want the Radcliffes to become aware of how comprehensive the Fulton County district attorney's investigation was, or that *both* Bill and Susan were cooperating with Don Stoop and Michelle Berry. If there was any evidence left, any of the items missing from the Crists' house, Stoop wanted it left right where it was.

✦   ✦   ✦

By the end of March 1991, Stoop had proved to his own satisfaction several of the possible charges against Pat and Debbie in the Crist case, but he ached to connect Pat once and for all to the shooting deaths of Walter and Carolyn Allanson. There was no statute of limitations on murder.

Rounding up witnesses from seventeen years before was not easy. Michelle talked to Jean Boggs, whose memory of Pat was as lucid as if she had seen her only the day before. Jean was very helpful in giving background information, but she had avoided contact with the Radcliffes—and even her nephew Tom—for years. She had no current knowledge of their activities. No one had ever convinced her that Pat was not in some way part of a conspiracy that had ended in the murder of her brother and sister-in-law.

Stoop found the receptionist who had worked for Pat Allanson's doctor in East Point in July of 1974. In fact, she still worked there, and she promised to check the appointment book for July 3. She remembered seeing Pat that day. It was, after all, a day to remember. Pat *had* been in the office, just as she told the East Point police the night of the shooting. However, the appointment book proved that she had not had an appointment to see anyone, and records showed that she hadn't had her collarbone X-rayed as she had claimed. To the best of the nurse's recollection, Pat had merely come into the office, greeted the staff at the desk, and left. She had been seen, Stoop thought. She had made damn sure she had been seen by witnesses.

Stoop read and reread the old Allanson case, completely absorbed. He had little doubt that Tom Allanson *had* been in that basement on the evening of the shooting, but he wondered who had cut the phone line and pulled the circuit breaker. He wondered how the gun had happened to be in the "hole" in the basement, and he was particularly intrigued by the ubiquitous Pat. She had been as close to the site of the double murders as next door, she had circled the block in her jeep, and she had bought fried chicken to go and waited with it and her Fourth of July costume, sewing in a darkening parking lot just a block down Norman Berry Drive. But she had claimed that she never saw Tom that day after he let her off at the doctor's office.

What, Stoop asked himself, would Pat have had to gain if her in-laws were dead? And, taking it a step further, what would she have gained if her bridegroom perished in a gunfire storm too?

Zebulon.

The Allansons had disinherited their son, but Pat had never believed that. She had always been convinced that Tom, as their only child, was their true heir. After all, *her* parents had forgiven her *everything*. She could not have even imagined parents who didn't sacrifice for their young. She had to have believed that Boppo and Papa's martyrdom was the way things were in all families. And, if she labored under the premise that Tom would inherit everything Walter and Carolyn Allanson had, she would naturally have believed that she, as Tom's wife, was Tom's heir and would inherit whatever came to him. There had been the huge mortgage on Zebulon, with balloon payments looming on the near horizon. A wealthy widow could handle all of that.

There was another sorry thing to consider, especially after Stoop had heard Tom pledge his love and devotion on fifteen tapes to a whiny, manipulative woman whom most men would have long since grown weary of. Pat was rumored to have been bored with him within weeks of their *Gone With the Wind* wedding. Susan remembered her mother's growing disinterest well. Pat had dodged being alone with Tom. Instead of joining him in bed, she had sat on the swing with her aunt. It was only after he was arrested that she had become the complete tragic heroine, pining and mourning for her lover. Stoop suspected Pat would have been just as happy—probably happier, and certainly less apprehensive—if she could have mourned Tom in widow's weeds.

He grimaced. *Victorian* widow's weeds, of course. Stoop had grown to know the lady's preferences and obsessions all too well. Maybe she even supposed that if she had Zebulon paid off, and if she were a widow, then Hap Brown would leave his wife and come back to her with his hat in his hands.

There was only one other person alive who would know what had actually happened in and around the Allanson home on Norman Berry Drive on July 3, 1974.

And that was Tom Allanson.

52

With the assistance of Tom's parole officer, Don Stoop and Michelle Berry met with Tom Allanson in the Canton office of the Georgia Board of Prisons and Paroles. Legally, Tom no longer had anything to fear. No matter what had happened on the night of his parents' murders, he had paid with fifteen and a half years of his life. He could not now be put in double jeopardy. He could never be tried again for those shootings. He didn't have to talk with the D.A.'s investigators, and they wouldn't have blamed him much if he had refused, or if he was annoyed at the intrusion into his new life. But he had agreed to be interviewed.

They had seen pictures of a young Tom, and this giant of a man seemed not so different—older, but not as old as they knew he was. He was almost fifty now, but he had scarcely any gray in his hair and his arms were muscular and tanned. If he was not pleased to be called in to talk about the woman who had carved a big chunk out of his life, he was, at least, obliging. He reached out his massive hand to shake with Don Stoop.

Stoop probably knew the story of Tom and Pat as well as anyone did now. He had immersed himself in their lives—from the first interviews with Susan and Bill Alford, the voluminous court transcripts of trials and appeals, newspaper clippings, the endless Pat-and-Tom tapes, from talking with Andy Weathers, and from Michelle Berry's interviews with Jean Boggs. So many of the players in the old script had told their stories, and at first, the whole scenario had seemed too incredible to be real. Now, Stoop felt as if he had known the story all his life. He threw out a few questions to hear it again, this time from Tom's angle. Stoop wondered if even now, even after all Pat had done to him, Tom could somehow still be attached to the woman he had loved so desperately, the woman he had sworn to stand by until death —but not, Stoop reminded himself, enough to commit suicide for.

His first questions were about how they had met. The answers were familiar and came in single sentences. Tom obviously didn't remember dates. He admitted he had been obsessed with marrying Pat all those years ago. "I don't know if she wanted to marry me or not," he said. "I was the most insistent one. She kept telling me, 'No, you don't want to marry me.' And I wish I hadn't. . . . My head wasn't screwed on right at the time."

Stoop didn't comment. Pat had known her quarry well. She knew exactly how much demurring it would take to reel Tom in.

"This is going to be a hard question," Stoop said, easing into the meat of what he wanted to know, "but I need you to think and answer as precisely and factually as you can. We need to know, what was Pat's involvement with you in the 1974 murder case? I'm talking about what started it, what led up to it, what transpired during the trial, and *after* the trial while you were in jail."

"That is a hard one to answer," Tom began. "My parents did not like Pat from the very beginning. . . . She wasn't the *reason* for the divorce. She was the outcome. . . . She hated my parents and they hated her."

"Okay. At any time did she feed the fire?"

Tom allowed that Pat had gotten his parents worked up and then started on him. He said the shooting at Lake Lanier just about made his father go "crazy."

"Do you think Pat did it?"

Tom shook his head. "She was with me . . . shoeing horses down in Lithonia. . . . They [the police] took my rifles and checked, and there was no way my rifles could have done that. . . . He [Tom's father] got all bent out of shape and went out and bought a gun . . . and he told all those people that it was gonna be over by the weekend. I was supposed to be in a parade in Atlanta. The only thing I could figure out was he was planning on shooting me in the parade."

"What did Pat say about all of this?"

"It was a long time ago." Tom frowned with the effort to remember. "She just kind of stirred it up and made it worse. . . . Pat was a very headstrong, manipulative type person that would do *anything* to get what she wanted—and you not know she was doing it. She could take a married man and turn him completely around . . . and talk him out of thirty years of marriage and him not even know it. . . . Unless you'd been there, you couldn't imagine what it was like. Pat would have some idea in her mind and she was going to get her way. If she came at you one way and you didn't do what she said, she'd find another way. She'd just keep at you until you gave in to her."

Tom recalled that it was brought up in his trial that phone calls had been made to his father the afternoon of the murders. "But I didn't see or hear her make them," he said.

Stoop asked Tom if he believed now that his father had exposed himself to Pat.

"Naw. My father was not the type of person to do something like that."

"Why do you think she said that?"

"To get me stirred up."

"Did it work?"

"Well, it got me upset, but then . . . I was scared to death. I didn't know what was fixing to happen to me."

Tom's eyes clouded as he remembered his trial. "It was a farce . . . she was sitting there punching me in the ribs, and punching Ed in the ribs, and the judge was having to tell her to be quiet and if she didn't stop trying to run his courtroom, she was gonna have to leave."

"Okay. Let's go up to the murder itself," Stoop said. "You and Pat drove up on that particular day together. Correct?"

"I took her to the doctor."

Stoop could sense Tom's retreat; he would have to backpedal on his questions and wait a while on the murders. "Did she, in fact, go to the doctor?" he asked.

"I guess she did."

Stoop urged Tom to re-create the rest of that day to the best of his recollection, to take his time.

"Okay. I went over there. My mother and father were very systematic type people. . . . You knew when they were going to get off from work, when they came home. . . . So I went over there late that afternoon to talk to Mother, and I thought she would be home round about then. So I didn't drive over there 'cause I dropped Pat off and she had the car. . . . I walked maybe half a block or a block—something like that—I was going to try to get her to talk to him, to get him to calm down a little bit, and I couldn't talk to her at the office. . . . I definitely couldn't talk to her on the phone, since he wouldn't let her talk. . . . He was very hard at the house. He ran the place. . . . And so the only way of trying to get anything done was to talk to my mother without him being there."

Tom said he sometimes suspected Pat didn't really want his relationship with his parents resolved. "She was doing every-thing she could to get them turned against me."

"Did Pat know you were going to talk to your parents?" Stoop asked.

"Yes."

"She *did* know that?" Michelle Berry echoed.

"I believe that I was set up on this." Tom leaned forward. "I really believe that . . . under normal circumstances, I could have been there and talked to my mother. But my mother was a little late. The back door was locked, but the *basement* door was open, so I just went in the basement door and said, 'Well, I'll just wait down here.' I wasn't going to sit on the doorstep in case my daddy came home. . . . My ex-wife and my children came over at the same time, and that kind of messed things up a little bit . . . so I just got more or less trapped. They said the basement door was broke into. I did not break in the basement door; it was open."

Tom was indeed trapped. His ex-wife, whom he described as a "not very rational woman," was upstairs, his father was due home soon, and he was down in the cellar of a house he had been banned from.

And then, to make matters worse, his father came home early, something he never did.

"What about the lights and the fuse box?" Don Stoop asked.

"I don't know anything about that."

"What about the telephone wires?"

"They said [during the trial] that was cut. . . . I didn't cut no wires either."

"Okay. You stated this was a complete setup. You thought you were set up?"

"That's what I was getting to. My father don't usually come home early, and during the trial it said he got a phone call. . . . I believe to this day that she called him from the doctor's office and told him I was over there. I have no proof of that. That's my opinion."

"When you're in the basement, you can hear people upstairs talk. Correct?"

"No."

"So your father didn't come in yelling, 'Is Tom here?' or anything like that?"

"No. He came down in the basement, looked around, and went back upstairs. I was hidden behind some stuff back there, trying to figure a way to get out. Then he called the police. . . ."

"How did he call the police if the telephone wires were cut?"

"Well, we got neighbors. . . . [When the police came] he went out and talked to . . . I think it was Sergeant Callahan—right there—and I heard the conversation then because he wasn't more than ten yards away. That was the time I was planning on leaving, right then—with the police there. I thought, 'Well, this would be a good time, until he [Tom's father] pulled the rifle and the pistol out of his car."

Tom said he had hunkered down in the basement and heard his father refuse to let the police search his house. He would have been relieved to have the police find him. Instead, he heard his father tell the officer, "I got this rifle here. I know who it is, and I'm going to take care of it myself."

Tom sighed. "I don't think Pat cared whether I got killed or not, to be honest with you. 'Cause she had the car and it was almost paid for. . . . When [my daddy] pulled this gun, I felt like if I run out that door, he was going to shoot me right there. I was in a state of complete panic at the time."

Stoop planned to wait until Tom was more at ease to discuss the actual shootings. He shifted the focus of the interview. "I'm getting at Pat's direct involvement, okay? . . . Were you aware that Pat had been driving around the neighborhood waiting for you?"

"*No.*"

"She never told you anything?"

"No."

"You know anything about her going to a liquor store where you stated that you wanted to make a phone call?"

"During the time that I was locked up . . . [in the] East Point jail, I was scared slapped to death. I had no idea what I was going to do. . . . I always depended on my parents, and I had never been in trouble before anyway. . . . So she comes to the jail and tells me, 'I'm taking care of this. I got everything taken care of. Don't worry about it. You *don't* tell them.' What she had done is fabricated a string of people up and down Cleveland Avenue that was supposed to have seen me. . . . She convinced Ed Garland to go on the fact that I was never there because there was no eyewitness. I wished I had gone on self-defense and I wouldn't have spent fifteen years in prison for it. . . . She came up with these people at the liquor store, said they saw me there, and I didn't go that way. Once you start telling a lie to a lawyer that's trying to help you, it seems like it snowballs into a mess. . . . Then he'll quit—which he did quit later."

Stoop asked Tom whether he had expected to go back and meet Pat at her doctor's office or whether she was supposed to pick him up.

"I was going to stay long enough to talk to my mother. Then I was going to come back to the doctor's office. This was not even scheduled to take more than fifteen or twenty minutes . . . and it ended up a lot longer than that . . . but as far as her coming to pick me up? Absolutely not."

After Tom was locked up, he had no information except what Pat told him. "Pat told all my friends that I was not allowed . . . to receive mail from anybody but immediate family. And that's a lie. 'Cause she didn't want anybody telling me anything except her."

"So she controlled what information you got about everything?"

"She controlled *everything*. The money. I was fool enough to give her power of attorney. She controlled the money. She controlled the lawyers. She controlled the farm. She controlled everything that was stolen and done away with. I had no idea about anything."

Tom allowed that he had had his doubts when the house and barns in Zebulon burned down. He had no idea there was insurance on them. He didn't know until Stoop told him that Pat had cashed a check meant for the mortgage holder.

"While you were in jail," Stoop asked, "was anything mentioned about a 'suicide pact' between you and Pat?"

Tom nodded. "You know, she even tried to bring some stuff into Jackson, and she wanted me to commit suicide with her right there. And I said, 'No way.' "

"What did she bring into the prison?"

"I don't know. She didn't show me. But it was supposed to be some sort of pills or something, but I told her, 'I ain't ready to die yet. . . . ' She told me that she was going to do it the next week, and when she came to visit that next day, I said no. . . . If I had done it, I don't believe that she would have took an aspirin. See, she had too much to win and I had too much to lose. And if I was gone, she had the farm again and that fifty-two acres.

The scales had fallen from Tom Allanson's eyes. It was obvious that he had been seeing his ex-wife clearly for a long time, but he still saw Boppo as a paragon.

"Mrs. Radcliffe—to me—was always a real sweet lady and everything . . . Pat could do *anything* and she wouldn't find any fault with it, but I always thought Mrs. Radcliffe was a super person as far as a human being goes. . . . I didn't have any idea what was going on with the family because I was only told one thing, and Pat could walk ten miles to tell a lie, but she couldn't take two steps to tell the truth. . . . Maybe I shouldn't say that, but she is a habitual liar."

Stoop began his next question carefully. "Do you think she's crazy, or do you think she is calculating every move that she does? . . . Do you feel that she thinks everything out . . . that she calculated your reaction—that she knew how to manipulate you? . . . Correct me if I'm wrong. I think her main goal was to keep you in prison, to keep you shut up as long as you were there."

"Like I said," Tom sighed, "she didn't care whether I was living or dying in there. . . . I don't think she cared two hoots and a holler about me getting out or anything else."

Asked about any insurance he might have had on his life, Tom recalled that he had some—New York Life, he thought—but he had no idea what had happened to it.

When he married Pat, Tom said, he could never have foreseen that his problems with his parents would end in violence. "I thought it was just going to be separation from the family. Our family goes through these separations. . . . You know, they [my parents] were upset about the divorce, but I didn't ever think it was going to go this far."

As for his father's supposed threats, Tom said they all came down to him through Pat or Boppo. That was how he learned it "was all going to be over by the weekend."

"In your belief, . . . do you think Pat helped kill your parents?"

There was a long silence. Tom looked down at his hands, debating. "I wouldn't say that she helped kill them, because the only way they died was in a case of about thirty seconds of self-defense. . . ."

Stoop explained that he was speaking in the broader sense.

"I think," Tom said slowly, "that if she had never been in the picture, they would still be alive. Put it that way. I mean, if I never got involved with her, dated her, or anything like that . . . I think my father and I probably could have worked out our differences. . . . I just wish I'd never met her. I'd be a lot better off."

Tom still wasn't ready to talk about the shooting. The investigators could sense that. After all these years, it remained a source of intense pain, and why wouldn't it be? He did, however, reveal a bit of information that was highly intriguing. Pat had always insisted that she had never seen Tom on July 3, 1974 —not after he said goodbye to her at her doctor's office.

In his panicked state after the shootings, Tom told Stoop and Berry, he had run toward the freeway, toward the King Building. "Pat had parked in the parking lot of the King Building,"

Tom said, unaware of the surprised looks on his interviewers' faces. "I told her what had happened, and I said, 'I've got to go home.' And she said, 'My parents are coming.' She called them or something, and I don't know what she had called them for."

"Okay," Stoop said, struggling to keep the excitement out of his voice. "This is important. Let me back up. You are telling us now that once you ran, you did, in fact, find her parked at the King Building?"

"Yeah."

"How did you happen to find her at the King Building?"

"I went right by it."

"You just went by it. And you looked up and you saw her. What was she doing when you went up to her?"

"Sitting in the jeep."

"What did she say to you?"

"I was telling her what had happened. I said, 'I got to go. I don't know what to do. I'm scared and I'm going home.' And she just said, 'Well, I called my parents.' I don't know why she called her parents. She said they were on the way, and I said, 'I ain't waiting. I'm gone.' . . . I don't know what reason she had to call them. Far as I knew, she already knew about it [the murders] when I got there. From the way it sounded. And so I left and hitchhiked home and I did not go down Cleveland Avenue. I got home and my grandfather called me and told me that these four police had come over and had a warrant for my arrest. I said, 'Well, call them and tell them where I'm at.' And I didn't give them any problems and Sheriff Riggins called me—Mr. Riggins and I was good friends—and he said, 'I don't want any problems,' and I said, 'I will not cause you no problems. Come over here.' I just more or less gave myself up."

There was an electricity in the room. Perhaps Tom had never before allowed himself to recognize all the careful planning that must have gone into the apparently spontaneous shoot-out. He *had* done a lot of thinking in prison. Fifteen and a half years of thinking. And that, combined with Stoop's and Berry's questions, had sifted stark truths out of all of Pat's lies and diversionary techniques.

Slowly, Stoop began to list the "coincidences" involved in Tom's burgeoning troubles. First, there had been the formaldehyde in Tom's baby's milk. Pat hated Little Carolyn and anything that connected her to Tom. "We know that Pat works with horses, like you," the detective pointed out to Tom. "We know she had access to formaldehyde because you had it to treat your horses.

"Then," Stoop continued, "she tells you your father drove all the way down there [to Zebulon] and exposed himself. . . . Whether you liked your father or disliked him, you know he would never do anything like that anyway. Eventually it was proven he was still working in his office. You were going to go resolve this with your mother because you knew your father was working, so you felt that was the best time. But Pat didn't want you to resolve anything. Correct?"

"I assume so."

"You both parked at the doctor's office. You go one way. She goes the other. You show up at your parents' house . . . the basement is unlocked. Correct?"

Tom nodded.

"Little Carolyn with the kids comes home. Your mother comes home. You're stuck in the basement, and suddenly your father shows up. Testimony shows that some woman called your father. . . . All of a sudden, the shooting occurs. You run by the King Building. Pat is sitting there, and you tell her what happened, and she says, 'Don't worry about it. I already called my parents, and they're on their way up here.' She stays and you leave. What do you think all this means to you, now that you're looking at it?"

In spite of all the thinking Tom had done on the tragedy that had changed his life forever, it was apparent that for the first time it had all come together with a terrible atonal clang in his mind. "It sounds," he said, "like something she had sat down and planned out, you know—but I don't know how you could *do* that as far as the other people involved."

Clearly, Tom saw the tragedy from the viewpoint of a man who had never deliberately set out to hurt anyone. He was not a devious man. He was not a man who understood willful cruelty to other human beings.

Don Stoop pointed out all the antagonizing, all the real or imagined slights aggravated to major proportions—just as Pat had exacerbated the terrible wound in her own buttock. She had been brilliant at driving the wedge between Tom and his father, and then at setting the little fires of worry and rage that would certainly grow to a conflagration no one could stop.

Quietly, Don Stoop wondered aloud if maybe Pat hadn't believed that she had seen her husband alive for the last time when she kissed him goodbye at the doctor's office. "She could have possibly watched you walk away, given you ten or fifteen minutes, called, and all of a sudden, your father showed up—knowing good and well how you and your father were getting along. And then. . . . boom.

"BOOM!"

The three of them sat there in silence, the two detectives and the very tall man who had given Pat Taylor Allanson two decades of his life. The clock on the wall ticked so loudly that it too might have been going, "Boom BOOM!"

✦ ✦ ✦

Finally, Tom was ready to talk about what had happened in the basement. He began by saying that he had told Pat exactly what had happened, and he had explained the layout of the basement. Against Pat's wishes, he had told Ed Garland too, but by then it was far too late for his attorney to change his defense tactics. No one would have believed that the man on trial wasn't a liar—a man who had lied once might lie again. Tom and Ed Garland were trapped in the legal maze Pat had forced them into.

Tom's deep, pleasant Georgia voice began the story, and Stoop and Berry listened. Tom hadn't been much of a talker until now, but his mind had temporarily stepped out of this interview room into the dampness of an old basement in a time long gone by, and his words continued in a stream of consciousness, remembering.

"He came down with the pistol to look around in the basement, and he went over to this area . . . where he stored all his camping stuff, and he just kind of stepped off and walked in there. And there is one light in there—which didn't work—and I guess I might have been standing there breathing hard or something, and he comes over and hollers upstairs, 'I got him cornered in the hole!'

"And he sticks the pistol in that little area, which is not much bigger than a walk-in closet, and starts shooting all the way around the wall, and not far from me. And he starts over here, and the next one is over here, and the next one is over here, and he ran out of bullets before he got completely around. Pieces of concrete and pieces of bullets were flying and everything. I'm thinking all this stuff hit, plus I'm looking at this gun, and he hollers to my mother to bring down the rifle. Right before the steps, there is a big light bulb—two-hundred-watt light bulb—that hangs down. If you look when you come down the steps, you can see it across the room. And I had no idea where he was at or anything, and I just stumbled across this shotgun in there [in the hole] in the meantime—that he had reported stolen—and it was just sitting up against the wall. It was a single-shot shotgun—"

"Was it loaded?"

"Yeah, he always kept it loaded in the house."

"Even with the grandchildren around?"

"Well, he always had this shotgun in his closet—even with me around when I was a little kid."

"Why did it all of a sudden end up in the basement?"

"Well, he reported it stolen along with his other pistol." Tom had no idea why it had ended up in the hole in the basement.

"Okay," Tom went on, putting his memories into a flood of words. "So he had emptied his pistol right in there, and by this time it's like being in a barrel and somebody shooting in a barrel, you know, and I stumbled across the shotgun, and I said, 'Man, it's time for me to get out of here, 'cause he done called for that rifle.' My mother never shot a rifle in her life. So she comes down the steps panicking and everything—'cause she hears the shooting down there—and she runs down there and she throws the rifle up just as I'm coming out the door, and I got the shotgun down here, not shooting or anything. Just as I come out the door [the hole entrance], this big flash goes and I jump back and [my] shotgun goes off. I had no idea that I even hit them. I surely wasn't shooting at her. . . . Evidently, she [shot] something and it hit my daddy, because there was blood from right there at the door and around the basement. I didn't shoot him. . . . And [my] shotgun didn't hit him, because he was not standing in front of the door. [And at that range, the shotgun Tom found in the hole would have literally blown Walter Allanson apart.] So evidently she hit him. And so everything is ringing up here [Tom tapped his head]. I just reached down on the floor and picked up another shell, and loaded back, and poked it out the door. I don't know how long this was. It may have been a minute; it might not have been that long. And just as I started out the door, he was standing up, throwing the rifle up over there, and I just shot in that direction. Then, at the same time, when I looked out the door, I saw my *mother* laying on the step, . . . and I see the movement of him over there."

Again the room was silent.

Finally, Don Stoop asked Tom if he had ever heard his father mention his name.

"All I heard was, 'I got *him* cornered in the hole.' . . . I don't think my mother knew I was down there."

"Do you think your father knew . . . ?"

"Yep. 'Cause that is what he told the police—that he knew who it was that broke into his house and he was going to take care of it."

Stoop asked Tom several times, in several ways, why he thought his father's shotgun and the shells had been down in that basement cubbyhole. And he had no idea, no explanation. His grandfather had called him two weeks before the shoot-out and asked him if he knew who had stolen his father's shotgun and pistol, and he had been just as bewildered then. He had a whole rack of his own guns; Tom had no interest in his father's guns.

Don Stoop switched back to Pat's adamant refusal to let Tom tell his attorney about the way the shootings had really happened. "Did you ever ask her why she was upset about the truth?"

"Well," Tom said, "because it was contradicting to the story she told. I mean, she started building the lies from that night, and once you build, you can't remember every lie. You forget it. Of course, I don't think *she* ever forgot anything. But, you know, if she is telling one thing to the lawyers and everything, and I'm coming up telling them something else, then the lawyer's gonna say, 'Wait a minute.' A lawyer's got any sense, he would sit there and figure out who was behind all this stuff. And I guess you could say that's why she didn't want it brought out."

But Tom had never betrayed Pat. He had taken the whole punishment. Until this interview, he had never told anyone that he had talked to his wife moments after the shoot-out, and she certainly had told no one. Pat had not offered to drive him home —or anywhere. She had let him run, alone, through the rainy Georgia night, to make his way home sixty miles away, any way he could. And she had waited for her mother and father, for Boppo and Papa, to come pick up the pieces just as they always had.

Don Stoop and Michelle Berry were quite sure that for Pat the sight of Tom running toward her in the rain must have seemed like a ghost materializing through the twilight. They both believed that she had set him up to be shot dead. She had never expected to see him again that night.

Or any other.

✦ ✦ ✦

There were still unanswered questions, even after the interview with Tom Allanson. There always would be. Stoop had his own theories on how Walter Allanson's shotgun and shells got in the hole in his basement. He knew Tom hadn't carried them with him on that July day as he went to try to work things out with his mother. The East Point fire fighter who knew Tom well had seen him walking down the street toward his parents' home. He had seen no shotgun.

It was possible that Walter Allanson himself had put the old shotgun in his basement. He was a man running scared, just as his son was—each of them convinced that the other was plotting bloody murder. Walter could have stashed the gun in the hole so that it would be handy if he were attacked while he was in the basement. It could have been his "downstairs gun" and the new high-powered rifle his "upstairs gun." The borrowed pistol would have been a gun to carry with him at all times.

Why then would Walter have reported the pistol, shotgun, and a suitcase as missing in a burglary? That was a hard one. He was so bitterly angry at Tom. Would he have reported him as a burglar out of revenge? Stoop even pondered the possibility that Walter Allanson had cut his own telephone line and thrown the circuit breaker. If he then called the police about Tom, as he had, it would have given him some concrete example of Tom's culpability, perhaps assuring that he would be thrown in jail and would no longer be the threat his father believed him to be.

It was just as possible that someone outside the home had stolen the guns and the suitcase. The same person or persons might have cut the phone line and thrown the circuit breaker.

Pat? Hardly. In all the mysterious fires—conflagrations that in some way benefited Pat—she had been able to prove that she was nowhere near the house and barns when they burst into flames. She was far away when the ambush at Lake Lanier occurred. It had not been Pat herself who placed harassing phone calls to Hap Brown's wife, but rather a friend. The purported plan to have her son-in-law killed was by contract.

Pat did not get her own hands bloody, or dirty or soot-stained, Stoop figured. But she certainly had had a number of people who had practically turned themselves inside out to "help" her. The woman could be charismatic, seductive, threatening, or pathetic—whatever it took to get her way. But no one would be able to prove at this late date that her fine hand had ordered ambushes, burglaries, line cutting, or anything else.

The times that Pat *had* carried out her own plans, she had been caught. The arsenic poisonings of Paw and Nona had netted her a long prison term. And if Stoop had his way, her machinations at the Crist estate were about to net her another; that crime he could prove. But he wasn't as solidly grounded trying to prove her involvement in the Allansons' murders—although he didn't believe for one moment that their deaths had surprised her.

Her only surprise had been that Tom hadn't died too.

53

They were getting close to going to the grand jury for an indictment. They knew where their quarry was. Pat was still selling old brooches and necklaces at Golden Memories, and Debbie was working in Dr. Villanueva's office.

Judge Sandra Harrison of the Magistrate Court of Henry County, where the village of McDonough was located, gave Don Stoop and Michelle Berry a search warrant for the little red brick house on Bryan Street. Accompanied by McDonough's police chief, M. Gilmer, and his assistant chief, E. Moore, Don Stoop and Michelle Berry knocked on the front door of the Radcliffes' residence. They hoped to find missing jewelry, perhaps more antique Williamsburg cookbooks, the miniature crystal chandelier, the hand-stitched linen, the antique Civil War books and artifacts—something they could tie to the Crists' long list of missing belongings. But they were also realistic enough to know that those items probably had long since been sold on consignment through Golden Memories or out of the back of Pat's car at a swap meet.

Approaching Margureitte and Clifford Radcliffe in their own home and asking to search their premises was akin to confronting Queen Elizabeth and Prince Philip at Buckingham Palace. Colonel Radcliffe accepted the search warrant with glacial civility. Margureitte and her sister, Thelma, stared at the interlopers. It was apparent that Don Stoop would take most of the heat, and it bothered him not at all. Michelle Berry, who was just as much a sworn officer of the D.A.'s office as Stoop was, was viewed as a sweet young lady who had the misfortune to accompany him on his rude errand.

They started searching slowly through the immaculate house. There were so many antiques, artifacts, mementos, photographs, and pieces of jewelry, it seemed well nigh impossible to sort out what they were looking for. And time had been on Pat's side. Stoop glanced sideways at Colonel Radcliffe's hand and saw that he no longer wore the lapis stone ring that he had worn in the videos and photographs of his seventy-fifth birthday party.

They moved through the kitchen, the dinette, the recreation room into the "doll room" and stopped, astonished. Susan had tried to prepare them for this room, but they could see now that it would be hard for anyone to describe. "My mother is, in many ways, like a child," Susan had explained. "Her dolls are *her* children because they don't mess up. They can have their tea parties, but they don't make a mess."

The doll room was every little girl's dream—and every collector's. There were dozens of dolls, scores of dolls. They sat in wicker, wooden, velvet, and silk chairs. They sat in rocking chairs, high chairs, chair swings. They lay in cradles, beds, buggies, and hammocks. Some of them had plates and spoons, some had blocks, some had their own dolls or teddy bears. Not one of them had been manufactured before 1930, certainly, and some looked to be over 150 years old. They were dressed in the finest white cotton and linen, lace and dimity, satin and silk. Their little hats were of straw, ribbon, and crocheted wool. There were rocking horses, carved horses, wooden horses, stuffed horses. Everything was in doll scale from the tiny piano to the stools, steamer trunks, and hall trees. The pictures on the walls were of idyllic little children and, of course, dolls. There were tea sets, music boxes, tops, hoops, and fans.

Don Stoop and the McDonough officers stepped lightly, truly bulls in a china shop, and Michelle Berry turned around and around, bemused by the huge collection. She could not imagine how much money and how many years it had taken Pat to gather this perfect doll family around her. When they began to open the drawers and cupboards, they jumped back in surprise. There were body parts there: dolls' arms and legs and heads, dolls' wigs, every conceivable part needed to refurbish and repair. There were big swatches of fabric and tiny, tiny precious bits of cloth. Buttons. Eyes.

There was a sensation of eyes throughout the room, glass eyes and painted eyes following the intruders who had interrupted their naps and their play. It was daylight on a warm spring morning, and it shouldn't have been spooky. And yet it was. The investigators could not help but consider, if only briefly, what human misery must have been inflicted while gaining the means for this collection.

Pat's sewing room was in the closet off the main room. It too was packed with doll parts and squares of cloth. "Everything you might ever need to make a doll," Michelle Berry remembered. "Even eyelashes."

The search warrant listed items that were so small that the searchers had the legal right to look into drawers and cupboards —wherever the stolen treasures might be hidden.

"If we were looking for a nineteen-inch television set," Berry explained, "we couldn't look into a dresser drawer. But there was so much we were searching for. It was an older house, with all these cubbyholes and closets—and all of them were packed with things. And Pat's parents weren't being cooperative. They weren't telling us where the cubbyholes were, so we had to find them ourselves."

Pat's room was up a narrow stairway over the doll room. It too seemed to have come from another era, with a spool bed with a lace spread, ruffled chintz curtains and lampshades, and the wicker dressmaker's form with the bride's dress on it. Michelle searched through a big old brown leather suitcase. It was packed with Pat's mementos—horse show pictures and ribbons and certificates. "There were report cards for Debbie and for Ronnie, old birthday cards and Mother's Day cards from them —but I didn't find anything of Susan's. In that brown suitcase, at least, it was as if Susan didn't exist, as if Pat had only two children."

Berry and Stoop made a good team; he was abrasive and businesslike, and she was soft-spoken and ladylike. "People usually warm up to me before they do Don," Berry said. "I don't know if it's because I'm a woman, or because I talk softer. Mrs. Radcliffe was very distant at first, but she finally began to talk to me. She told me how they took care of the dolls. She said that every week, she and the colonel and Pat spent hours changing the diapers on every doll. I didn't ask her why. I guess it just seemed so peculiar that I didn't want to know."

While Michelle Berry was going through an armoire in the dining room, an old plaster picture fell out and broke. Colonel Radcliffe was incensed. "He said he was going to sue me, and Mrs. Radcliffe stuck up for me. She told him, 'Colonel, she couldn't help it, and you don't need to report it, and it wasn't anything anyway.' But if *Don* had broken it, hell would have broken loose because *they* did not see eye to eye at all. She complained to him that in all her years of living, she had *never* seen anybody come in and take over someone's *personal* property and ransack it. And we weren't, of course."

It must have been a terribly demeaning experience for Margureitte Radcliffe, too, close to the reenactment of her worst nightmare, accused by the police of a crime. Don Stoop had become the focal point of all the years of accumulated rage she felt toward people who had threatened her Pat and her own dignity. She was a lady, and Stoop was, she would say later, "a terrible, terrible, rude man."

In the end, the investigators found nothing they sought. They took away with them a blue photograph album, a brown leather photograph album, hand-stitched linen cloths, a pair of lace gloves, some letters, an antique dictionary, and a pearl necklace in a Ziploc bag.

Mrs. Crist could identify none of them. They were returned.

Whatever items Pat and Debbie might have taken from the Crist home had disappeared. Everything was gone, save the pearls and the cookbook that Pat had given to Susan.

As it turned out, it didn't really matter. Based on the commonality of circumstances, and the physical evidence the D.A.'s office *did* have, on April 17, 1991, nineteen grand jurors of

Fulton County charged and accused Pat Taylor Allanson and Debbie Cole Alexander with seven counts: aggravated assault with intent to murder; aggravated assault; violation of the Georgia Controlled Substances Act, Count I; violation of the Georgia Controlled Substances Act, Count II; theft by taking, Count I; theft by taking, Count II; and violation of O.C.G.A., Section 43–26–12. The seventh charge involved the accuseds' impersonating registered nurses.

The arrest warrants were next. Out in McDonough, the household of Colonel and Mrs. Clifford Radcliffe was once again braced for another legal shoe to drop. Their little girl was now fifty-three years old and they had pampered and protected her for all those years. Their home had always been her home, her trouble and pain their trouble and pain. They had sacrificed everything to make her life perfect. Pat could do no wrong in their eyes, and yet the world continued to hound her. When would she be happy?

When in God's name would it ever end?

54

Lewis R. Slaton, district attorney of the Atlanta Judicial Circuit, issued bench warrants on April 17, 1991, for Pat Taylor Allanson and Debbie Cole Alexander. Don Stoop and Michelle Berry would make the arrests. Susan had told them that it would be better to arrest her mother and her sister separately. Debbie would be the weak partner in the duo. *"If* you talk to her without my mother around," Susan said, "she may be honest with you. If my mother is there, Debbie will say whatever Mom wants her to."

It was five minutes to eleven on the morning of April 17, when the D.A.'s investigators drove up to Dr. Villanueva's office in Riverdale, Georgia. They found Debbie at work, standing at a file, dressed in shorts and a halter. Michelle Berry noted that Debbie was very thin; she had huge dark circles under her eyes and a large purpling bruise on one thigh. She didn't resist arrest. Rather, she seemed chastened and frightened. Stoop read the charges against her and advised her of her rights under *Miranda*. Debbie immediately blurted, "The nursing idea was my mother's!"

"Are you a registered nurse?" Berry asked.

"No. I never have been."

One of the charges noted the missing Rolex watch, and Debbie said that she had, in fact, picked up the watch. She refused to say where the late Mr. Crist's watch was presently. She denied administering any drugs to Mrs. Crist. "Mrs. Crist was an alcoholic," she said. "She took all that medicine herself. Besides, my mother was in charge of that. I only gave Mr. Crist his medicine."

Deborah Taylor Cole Alexander was booked into the Fulton County jail.

They found her mother at the Henry County Courthouse in McDonough, a historic red brick building that had stood there on the town square since 1831. Ironically, Pat had gone to testify in Magistrate Court as a complaining witness in a case against a shoplifter at Golden Memories. As Stoop and Berry approached, she turned to look at them without interest, with no sign of recognition of why they were there. The colonel and Margureitte Radcliffe were with their daughter in the courthouse. They recognized the two detectives instantly and watched them warily.

Again, Don Stoop read the charges and the *Miranda* warning. Pat stared at him blankly, then quietly asked him to reread the charges, feigning shock. She told him she knew why she was being arrested; it was all because of Susan and Bill Alford. "Susan is mentally ill, you know. She needs psychiatric care. Both of them have been making threatening phone calls to me. Bill and Susan are sick people. Bill called Mrs. Crist, and he has threatened my life—I can't tell you how many times."

Debbie had paid no attention to the part in the *Miranda* warning about remaining silent. Nor did Pat. She, however, was much more indignant and considerably more talkative than her daughter had been. "Mrs. Crist was an alcoholic, you know," she told Stoop. "They wanted me to sign the insurance claim documents as though I was a registered nurse. I could not do that—I *would* not do that; that would be wrong, wouldn't it?"

With Boppo hovering nearby, Pat sat down and stared out the window, silent for a moment or two. She had already slipped and didn't realize it. Neither Berry nor Stoop had mentioned anything at all about insurance forms being signed by "Pat Taylor, RN." Pat herself had brought it up. "But, gosh," Pat said, almost childlike as she turned to Boppo, "that was three or four years ago, wasn't it, Mom?"

The past had always been negligible to Pat; she erased yesterday continually, save for slights or imagined assaults on herself. Stoop and Berry had not been surprised to see that Pat was accompanied by her parents. Margureitte and Clifford Radcliffe stood beside their daughter, the expressions on their faces almost identical, a subtle blend of indignation and concern. How many years had they done this, Stoop wondered, how many *decades* of being there for Pat?

"I am not well, Mr. Stoop," Margureitte said, "and Mrs. Taylor is under a physician's care. She is being treated for hypertension and heart complications and she is on medication."

The two investigators had heard this script before, again and again as they pored over the records of Pat's earlier troubles with the law. She had been "terminally ill" since 1972.

"My mother is dying of cancer," Pat added, "and I am not well."

Stoop thought she looked remarkably well. The pictures he had seen of Patricia Taylor Allanson had shown a willowy, beautiful young woman who might well have been in fragile health. The woman he had just arrested must weigh over 250 pounds, her features suffused in fat. Her once exquisitely chiseled jawline hung like a turkey's wattle, and the neck that "Scarlett" had circled with a ribbon and a cameo was fissured and corrugated with heavy flesh.

"How *is* Mrs. Crist? How is her health?" Pat asked, with seemingly as much genuine concern as Michelle Berry had ever heard.

"She's fine."

"The Crists are very wealthy and influential," Pat said plaintively. "They can do anything. They have lots of money. I don't have that kind of money. What are we going to do, Mom?"

"We'll manage somehow," Margureitte said, squeezing her daughter's hand.

Pat's hands were cuffed behind her and she was led to the government vehicle for transportation to the Fulton County jail.

Michelle Berry got into the backseat with Pat, and Don Stoop drove. Pat complained that she was very uncomfortable. She asked Michelle to remove her handcuffs.

"I can't do that. They're for your protection and ours."

"But my back hurts," Pat whimpered. "And I'm in pain. I don't have my heart medicine with me."

Nevertheless, Pat answered their first questions easily enough: her age, the number of her children. Stoop asked her what her legal name was.

"Patricia Radcliffe Taylor."

"Not Allanson?"

"No."

He asked her how she had acquired the military ID card she carried for the PX and commissary, and she explained that she had been married for twenty-two years to a man who was in the service. She had added three and a half years to her burdensome marriage to Gil Taylor.

"Were you ever a nurse in the military?"

"I did some practical nursing assistance during those twenty-two years."

"You're not a registered nurse?"

"No."

"Ever?"

"No. Never."

But when Don Stoop asked Pat about the circumstances of her 1976 arrest and conviction for the poisonings of Paw and Nona Allanson, she stared out the window at a Waffle House and said, "I think you know all the answers to your questions."

From that point on, the three rode toward Atlanta in silence.

Pat joined Debbie in the Fulton County jail. It was the second time each had been booked into that facility. Once the two women were together, neither had anything further to say to the investigators.

✦ ✦ ✦

Margureitte Radcliffe knew who had caused all the trouble for Pat. It was Susan, of course—Susan, whose sense of loyalty to family seemed to be completely absent. There was no telling what harm she might cause next. Margureitte called her sister

Liz's son, Bobby, in Warsaw, North Carolina. She wanted to be sure that no one up there had complained to the authorities about Pat's care of her aunt Lizzie. Bobby Porter said he didn't feel he could complain to the D.A. in Duplin County, North Carolina, because he hadn't actually been in the house while his cousin was taking care of his mother. However, he would not go so far as to write a letter to the Fulton County D.A. extolling his cousin Pat as a nurse second only to Florence Nightingale and praising her wonderful care of his mother. Nor would Aunt Lizzie herself go so far. Boppo would never be close to Liz again; her sister had refused to come to Pat's rescue.

Shocked and hurt, Boppo also called Bill Alford. "Why in the whole wide world would you talk to the district attorney's office about Pat?" she demanded to know. "Whatever did you tell them?"

"I talked to them," Bill replied. "I answered the questions they asked."

"You had no right, Bill—not after all that the district attorney's office has done to the family. They had absolutely no right to know about Pat's life or about Debbie's life. You know as well as I do that Pat and Debbie never went over to the Crists to kill them. The *only* thing they did wrong was pretend to be registered nurses."

"Did you condone that, Boppo?" Bill asked bluntly. "Didn't you know that was wrong? That was a very sick old man, and he needed a real nurse."

There was a very long silence, and finally Boppo said, "I can't talk to anyone else in the family tonight."

The phone went dead.

✦　✦　✦

On May 13, Bill and Susan received what was intended as an official communiqué "from the desk of Clifford B. Radcliffe." It was from Margureitte and there was no salutation.

I have been diagnosed as having 'Squamus' [sic] non small cell cancer of the left lung. It is inoperable, radiation therapy is complete. The cancer still remains in part. The long term prognosis is poor. Therefore in the event of my death, it is my wish that our granddaughter, Linda Susan Taylor Alford and her husband

George Chester (Bill) Alford, be refrained from attending any Funeral, Memorial or other services for me.

They are also excluded from inheriting *anything* from my estate.

The two of them have caused great tragedy and hurt to so many people, including their son—

Margureitte S. Radcliffe

The letter was signed by a notary public and with it came copies of three letters from her attending physicians verifying that she did indeed have lung cancer.

55

Pat's and Debbie's arrests made news in Fulton County. The *Atlanta Journal*'s headline read, TWO WOMEN CHARGED IN AR-SENIC POISONING ATTEMPT, a startling, if slightly inaccurate, heading. Although arsenic had been Pat's poison of choice in the past, the text of the article pointed out that the only drug defi-nitely tied to her in the current case was Halcion. In the Atlanta paper, the arrests were more newsworthy for the prestige of the victims than of the accused; the Crist name was revered in At-lanta. But Pat was the focal point in the Henry County paper: FULTON COUNTY CHARGES MCDONOUGH WOMAN WITH AT-TEMPTED MURDER. She was the hometown angle.

All news coverage quoted D.A. Lewis Slaton as saying that the two women were suspected of attempting to overdose Eliza-beth Crist with Halcion but were also under a continuing inves-tigation into the possibility that James Crist had died from a drug overdose.

Long before the story hit the media, the word came down in the Fulton County District Attorney's Office that Pat Taylor

Allanson and her thirty-five-year-old daughter, Debbie, had been arrested. Andy Weathers hoped that he would catch the case. It would be his second meeting with Pat on the courtroom battlefield, and it would allow him to pursue his own intense curiosity about Pat's involvement with the murder of Walter and Carolyn Allanson. He had followed Don Stoop's relentless pursuit of Pat with avid interest and had been pleased with his thoroughness. Weathers had unfinished business with Pat.

But it was not to be. At least, Weathers was not to be the Fulton County assistant D.A. who would prosecute in the continuing saga of Pat Allanson; Fulton County assigned cases by computer, and the next name up was Bill Akins.

Akins was an extremely handsome young lawyer in his late thirties; he was a graduate of The Citadel and, like Don Stoop, had been in junior high when the earlier cases involving Pat Allanson took place. He was impressed by Stoop's investigation. That single yellow sheet of paper from a legal pad had grown to a thick file full of old police reports, new police reports, witness statements, newspaper clippings, bizarre anecdotes, photographs, and tape recordings. Akins had never seen anything like it.

"Once I began to get a feel for this case," Akins said, "I realized that, although it wasn't quite on the scale of the William Kennedy Smith case, . . . it was certainly a big case, possibly a case-of-a-lifetime situation. It's got everything; it's got the money, the old cases, the murder. 'Sex, drugs, and rock and roll.' From a prosecutor's point of view, it's got a *splendid* history, a 'career' kind of case.

It was tempting for Akins to take it and run with it. If they went to trial, he and everybody connected with the investigation would be front-page news in Atlanta, the South, the eastern seaboard, and possibly the whole country. If still more indictments came down—the first accusing Debbie and Pat of actually murdering Mr. Crist, and others connecting Pat to the murders of Walter and Carolyn Allanson—there wouldn't be a crime reporter in the country who wasn't beating a path to Atlanta. If they plea-bargained, no one outside Atlanta would know about Pat's crimes.

"But, on the other hand," Akins recalled, "one; I am not a newshound D.A. and don't feel that my ego should dictate what

I do with the case. And two; the most important thing was to see that justice was served, and headlines didn't matter."

Whichever way he decided to handle it, it wasn't going to be an easy case. Given the Crist family's understandable refusal to exhume their husband and father's cremains for laboratory analysis, it would be rough proving murder in that case. Given the almost total disappearance of their missing belongings, it was going to be difficult—but not impossible—to prove the theft charges. As for the Allansons' murders, and the very real possibility that Pat had been part of the very first spate of violence, should an indictment ever be brought, that too would be a real squeaker.

Furthermore, Pat had retained an excellent attorney, Steve Roberts of the firm of Garland and Samuel. Roberts was asking for a speedy trial, something any defense attorney has a right to do. He could, legally, *force* Slaton's office to go into court within sixty days. A defense attorney could always drag his feet and ask for delays—and most of them did—but a prosecutor had to be ready to go into court within that sixty-day period.

If Akins asked for an indictment charging Pat with involvement in a cover-up after the shootings of Walter and Carolyn Allanson, one of the state's witnesses would have to be Edward T. M. Garland, the same Ed Garland who had come to detest Pat's machinations when he tried to defend Tom, the same Ed Garland who had been the object of Pat's derision and scorn all through Tom's trial and afterward. And, of course, the same Edward T. M. Garland who was a partner in the firm of her current defense attorney. That could create a very sticky situation. Ed Garland testifying against Pat would not be a happy thing for the defense, but it was a gleeful prospect for Don Stoop and Michelle Berry. They had listened to those tapes, the hours and hours of Pat slowly barbecuing Tom on her emotional spit, when all the time she had known she could have gotten him out years earlier if she had only listened to Ed Garland.

It *would be* a difficult case to prosecute with only two months' preparation time. Conversely, the threat of being connected to the death of her ex-husband's parents was the last thing Pat wanted. For the state, it meant tremendous leverage in eliciting a guilty plea. For that, Akins was grateful to Stoop and Berry. "I have to give an enormous amount of credit to Don and

Michelle for doing the investigation which gave me the stick—
the real big stick—to hold over Pat's head—and also the carrot."

Pat didn't even want to be associated with the Allanson name.
One of Steve Roberts's first motions was to ask that the charges
against her be in her present name: Patricia Taylor, not Patricia
Allanson. She most certainly dreaded being charged in that long-
ago murder. Akins figured she might very well choose to plea-
bargain rather than risk the connection. She might reach for the
carrot of relative anonymity and prison time to avoid an even
greater danger.

Akins's posture was to be lenient with Debbie and to lean
heavily on Pat. Debbie hadn't had any arrests since the morals
charge years earlier; she seemed to be a follower and not an
instigator. No, Pat was the big fish, whose history showed her
to be the dominant partner in all her relationships. But would
she plead guilty to the seven charges extant, even if it meant a
hefty sentence, rather than risk the publicity circus that would
erupt if Akins moved to add charges of murder and accessory to
murder after the fact to Pat's grocery list of felonies?

Don Stoop and Michelle Berry wanted to go for broke. That
was the way they had always approached this case, working night
and day to trace all the raveled and far-flung ends of it. They
had relived the terrible events of the spring of 1974 that had led
to the murders of Walter and Carolyn Allanson, revisited all the
places where the smell of blood seemed still to cling, and believed that Pat Allanson had been right there in the thick of it all
—not the shooter, but the prodder, the manipulator, the liar.

The instigator.

They wanted to see all the dark corners of Pat's life illumi-
nated. They were detectives. Akins was a prosecutor. The relationship in any county or state office is—and always has been—
both symbiotic and one of natural enmity. Investigators tread
on shaky ground and take chances; prosecutors like to know
where they are and they lean toward predictable odds.

Both want to win. But it might be safe to say that detectives
are more philosophical about losing.

In the end, Bill Akins chose to accept a plea bargain. Pat
Taylor would go to prison. But she would never have to worry
about facing murder charges—at least not in any case up to June
1988. There would be no trial, speedy or otherwise. There

would be no blazing headlines. Don Stoop was livid. He didn't give a hoot for headlines either, but he was a hard-liner on justice. He would remain furious for a very, very long time. "Bill Akins never should have plea-bargained. And I'll never change my mind about that."

Both Don Stoop and Michelle Berry were bitterly disappointed, ultimately frustrated. They had given it everything they had. Georgia passions being what they were, there would be other cases. They devoutly hoped not to run into Pat again, although it was certainly possible that they would, given world enough and time.

56

On June 12, 1991, less than two months after she was arrested, Patricia Taylor Allanson aka Patricia Radcliffe Taylor appeared with her attorney in the Hon. William H. Alexander's courtroom in Atlanta.

A plea had been negotiated in Indictment No. Z-32688.

Pat took the stand and looked stolidly at Bill Akins as he approached her. His questioning was routine. He needed to establish that she was competent and understood what she was about to do, that she felt she had been fairly represented.

"Were you satisfied," Akins asked, "with the services that he rendered on your behalf?"

"More than satisfied."

"Counsel," Akins turned to Steve Roberts. "Do you waive formal reading?"

"Yes, we do."

"Ms. Taylor, do you understand," Akins began, "that you are charged in seven counts in the bill of indictment? Count I charges you with aggravated assault with intent to murder, which carries with it a penalty of one to twenty years in the penitentiary. Count II charges you with aggravated assault, which also carries with it a penalty of one to twenty years. . . . You can't be convicted of both. . . . Count III charges you with violation of the Georgia Controlled Substances Act dealing with being in possession of Halcion . . . one to five years. . . . That is a Schedule IV drug." Count IV was the same. "You can't be convicted of both. Count V charges you with theft by taking, specifically a stainless-steel Rolex watch . . . ten years in the penitentiary. Count VI charges you with theft by taking of some specifically named items of jewelry . . . one to ten years."

Akins explained that the latter two charges were separate. Pat *could* be convicted of both.

"Count VII charges you with unlawfully posing as a registered nurse without a license. That is a misdemeanor, which carries with it a maximum penalty of twelve months in jail and a one-thousand-dollar fine. Do you understand all of those charges and the penalties for them?"

"Yes, I do."

Pat Taylor was prepared, she said, to plead guilty to aggravated assault, to violation of the Georgia Controlled Substances Act, to theft by taking of the specific items, and to posing as a registered nurse: Counts II, IV, VI and VII. She understood full well that she could be sentenced to a total of thirty-six years in prison, and that she had the right to a trial by jury. She was waiving that right.

Pat was eager to make a statement about why she was pleading guilty. Her attorney explained she could do that when the judge questioned her later.

Bill Akins reviewed Pat's long, long history with the legal system in Fulton County, giving a summary of what he would have presented in a trial if there had been one: the violent deaths, the poisonings, the forged wills. Moving into the recent past, he told Judge Alexander that Pat had been paroled, trained to work only in nursing homes. "She also cared for an elderly lady by the name of Mansfield. She essentially worked with Ms. Mansfield through a nursing home and the children didn't have much contact with her. Ms. Mansfield subsequently died and was cremated. And that's really all we know about that."

The Crist assignment was next. Akins described the lies and

misrepresentations, and Pat's constant dismissal of all other employees. "It was essentially she and her codefendant, Debbie Cole Alexander, who were the primary caretakers of the elder Mr. Crist. . . . Mrs. Crist's . . . doctor prescribed a sedative known as Halcion. . . . The doctor prescribed thirty pills . . . to take no more than one pill—preferably just half a pill—at bedtime. Within the span of some thirty-six days, Your Honor, *the defendant acquired an additional one hundred and twenty tablets of Halcion from two different drugstores.*"

The case that Don Stoop and Michelle Berry had built step by step was stunning to listen to. Judge Alexander sat quietly, absorbed, as Bill Akins told of the huge drugstore bills, the Crist childrens' growing suspicions and fears.

"Dr. Watson . . . drew a blood sample [from Elizabeth Crist] which subsequently showed almost double the normal dosage of Halcion, and this was at a time when the elder Mrs. Crist was not as drugged as she was at other points. . . . I would expect the evidence at trial to show further . . . that the overdoses of Halcion that Mr. Crist was getting exacerbated his condition with Parkinson's and accelerated his decline . . . and also harmed the health of Mrs. Crist."

After noting the valuables missing from the Crists' estate, Akins gave the state's recommendation for sentencing. "As to Count II—aggravated assault—twelve years to serve eight, the balance on probation. . . . Count IV, five years to serve concurrent. As to Count VI, ten years to serve eight, concurrent, and, as to Count VII, twelve months to serve concurrent. . . .

"As a condition of probation, Your Honor, I recommend that the defendant receive counseling and that she at *no time* be employed either for compensation or voluntarily in anything which might be remotely a health-related field."

That certainly seemed a given.

Steve Roberts asked for two additional conditions. "He [Bill Akins] has agreed as a condition of this plea . . . that the codefendant, Debbie Alexander, who is Mrs. Taylor's daughter . . . be put into the pretrial intervention program and, upon successful completion of that, that case would be dead-docketed against her and that she will not be further prosecuted." She had also promised to make restitution for Mr. Crist's Rolex watch.

And next, the big carrot. The humongous carrot.

"As a condition of this plea, he [Bill Akins] will in no way attempt to indict Mrs. Taylor for, in connection with, the death of Mr. Walter Allanson, which occurred, I believe, in 1974."

Akins nodded and rose to explain this condition further to Judge Alexander. "Your Honor, that is correct. It came to light during the course of our investigation of this case that this defendant was substantially involved as a party to the murder . . . of her ex-husband's—Tommy Allanson's—parents. It *is* my position that, if she enters a plea as outlined, the state will not proceed further with the indictment or prosecution of that case."

Steve Roberts spoke again. He said that his client was pleading guilty against his advice. He had advised Pat to plead not guilty and go to trial. "My client is entering this plea today. She will tell the court freely and voluntarily she wishes to enter what is in effect an Alford plea."

(An Alford plea has nothing at all to do with Bill and Susan Alford; the etiology of the name is from some landmark case a long time back. It was an ironic match—nothing more.)

Margureitte and Clifford Radcliffe, who were, of course, in attendance, flinched a little at the sound of the name. But they sat as proudly and benevolently as ever, gazing upon their daughter.

"She wishes the court to understand the reasons why she is entering her plea," Roberts continued, "that the nature of the charges made against her and her daughter lead her to the belief that, if the evidence as outlined by Mr. Akins is presented to a jury, that there is a substantial likelihood that she would be convicted, and, if convicted, would receive a harsher sentence than the state is recommending today. . . . The state has indicated it would introduce her prior crimes—which they would contend is a similar crime. Mr. Akins has notified me that he would put up evidence to that effect.

"So all of those things, as well as her intention to put an end to this matter *once and for all*—both with regard to this crime, the crime involving Mr. Allanson in 1974, and her prior offense involving the alleged poisoning—all of those things, Your Honor, are entering into my client's decision to enter her plea today."

Pat lumbered to her feet to face Judge Alexander. She wore jail-issue blue pants and top, and sandals. Fourteen years and thirty-five days had gone by since the last time she was sentenced to prison, but she still had her cheering section. Debbie was there, along with her new husband, Mike Alexander. Miss Loretta was too brokenhearted to come to Pat's sentencing, but she still had Boppo and Papa, just as she always had.

Judge Alexander looked down upon Pat and intoned, "Mrs. Taylor—as to Count II, I will sentence you to twelve years, to serve eight, balance probated. . . . Count IV, I sentence you to serve five years, concurrent with Count II. As to Count VI, I sentence you to ten years to serve eight, and to run concurrently with the others. . . . On Count VII, I will sentence you to serve twelve months. All of those sentences to run concurrently." Adhering to Bill Akins's request, Judge Alexander reminded Pat that she was never again to work in any health-related field.

In essence, Pat was going to prison for eight years.

The deputy guarding her allowed her to step to the side of the courtroom, where she was enveloped in hugs. Margureitte shook her head and muttered under her breath to no one in particular that this was all some terrible, terrible mistake. Pat herself didn't cry. Even facing her return to Hardwick, she may have heaved a sigh of relief; it could have been so much worse.

Later, Margureitte Radcliffe said Pat had only pleaded guilty to save Debbie. "She is the kind of mother who couldn't bear to see her child suffer. She sacrificed herself for Deborah." Margureitte did not mention Steve Roberts' insistence on the condition guaranteeing that Pat would never again have to deal with vexatious questions about the murders of Walter and Carolyn Allanson. Whatever had happened that rainy twilight eve of July 4th, whatever Pat had done to provoke the bloody confrontation in the basement of 1458 Norman Berry Drive, the subject was closed—at least legally closed.

57

From the moment she learned of her mother's first arrest, Susan Alford had dreaded two things, knowing that if she avoided one, she would bring the other crashing down upon her.

Although she doubted that anyone would believe her, she loved her mother and longed for a happy ending. When Pat got out of prison in 1984, it was as if a great weight had fallen from Susan's heart. A whole wonderful future lay ahead of them then. Susan was the daughter who gave her mother so much support while she was in Horizon House, eager to help Pat reenter the world outside prison.

Pat wrote to Susan on November 30, 1984, after her first out-of-state visit while she was on parole. It was a long letter any daughter would treasure.

. . . As each day of our lives together passed, I loved you more and more each one. I have so many beautiful images and memories that will always be with me of you. Oh, how many times I drew on those images and memories all the last 8 years. . . . Trips

*to the beach in North Carolina where you all looked for sand
dollars. Germany, and how all the people thought you were a
little Bavarian girl with your rosy cheeks and long braids. And
as all this time passed, my love didn't stand still either but rather
I just kept loving you more. Every day of our lives (together or
not together) whether the experiences have been painful or plea-
sureful* [sic], *joyful or sad, regardless, each and every one has*
made me love you more. *Neither time, nor distance, not even
the physical seperation* [sic] *of the last 8–10 yrs. can diminish
that love. For every thing we've endured has only made the bond
a stronger one. The baby I loved became the little girl I loved
who became the beautiful and loving woman you are now. I am
so proud that you are my daughter and I look forward to the
many wonderful years and future experiences we'll share. . . .*

The letter had thrilled Susan and made her weep. And yet,
even back then the first niggling doubts had already begun, no
matter that she cloaked herself in denial and rationalizations, no
matter how many times she looked away from what she would
not see.

Susan's worst dread was that her mother would again want
something so badly that anyone who got in the way would be
hurt. It had never occurred to her that *she* might be one of those
hurt. Even when Susan herself had *two* mysterious illnesses that
no one could diagnose, she would not listen to Bill's and Sean's
warnings that her mother was probably poisoning her. She
would not, *could* not, believe that. Maybe she *had* only suffered
from the flu or something equally innocuous. Without specific
testing, no one could say. "But I was lucky at that. I lived," she
said later. "I could have died, like Kent did or the Allansons."

Susan had vowed since 1976 that she would not let her mother
destroy anyone else. And she hadn't, but it cost her.

Her second worst fear was that she would no longer have a
family if she told anyone outside that family about her mother's
crimes. Lord knows, no one had ever acknowledged Pat's dangerousness *inside* the family; if Susan did the unspeakable, she
knew she would be forever beyond the pale. All she could count
on would be Bill and Courtney and little Adam. She had seen
Bobby and Charlotte Porter virtually excommunicated for far
less. They had only refused to write a letter. Although they had

agreed not to prosecute Pat for her alleged mistreatment of Aunt Lizzie, they would not write a letter praising her and they had become pariahs.

In the end, there had been no choice at all for Susan. She could not live knowing that sometime, sooner or later, her mother's eye would fall on something she wanted very, very much. And that disaster would follow.

Boppo had been Susan's ideal for more than three decades of her life, her support, her rescuer, the one person she had always believed she could count on. But when Susan's presence in Boppo's house had irritated Pat, she was out on the street in no time. Susan had no illusions that she would still be part of the family after her mother and sister were arrested. But she could not have realized that she would never be allowed simply to walk away, to begin a new life. Banishment was merely the first increment of her family's revenge.

From the moment they left Boppo and Papa's on Thanksgiving Day, 1990, the Alfords had been on their own. Susan no longer had a sister, a brother, grandparents, great-aunts, uncles, cousins (save the discredited Bobby and Charlotte), or nieces. Her son, Sean, remained estranged—but she learned that he was encouraged to come to Boppo and Papa's house once a week. It was almost primitive. Susan and Bill had betrayed the pack, and the others would never forgive them. Whatever Pat had done, she had always been taken back, not only forgiven but supported and carried above all of them on arms of love. Susan had spoken up only to prevent her mother from doing harm and she was exiled.

The Alfords were becalmed for a year on Main Street in McDonough. Sometimes, they felt as if they lived in a fishbowl. McDonough was so small that they could go nowhere without running into Boppo and Papa. When that happened, they were strangers; Boppo took on her crystal gaze and sailed by them. Susan saw her grandmother often, and she did not look ill, but the doctors' reports said otherwise, and Susan believed them. She worried about Boppo.

It would take her months to hook into the anger deep inside. Naturally diffident, Susan didn't feel rage until she saw her children hurting. Courtney received a letter from Boppo and Papa telling her that they would no longer pay for her riding lessons. Adam couldn't understand why Boppo and Papa had gone out of his life.

Susan heard rumors about her own treachery wherever she went in McDonough. The gossips were busy, and apparently Pat's and Debbie's offenses paled in comparison with Susan's. An "anonymous source" reported the Alfords to the local child protective authorities as abusive parents. The allegations were investigated and dropped when Courtney laughed out loud at the charge that she had been "dragged across the floor by her hair."

Don Stoop and Michelle Berry stood by the Alfords; the case was over, but the detectives had come to like and respect the couple who had done what they felt they had to do. When things got to be too much for Susan, Stoop could usually make her laugh. He didn't tell her, but he was going to be relieved too when the Alfords got out of McDonough. They were objects of such hatred.

On July 8, 1991, Susan and Bill received a letter from Boppo, typed on her old manual machine—the same one she used for everything from suspicious confessions to the official disinheritance of miscreants. Susan and Bill had assumed that their banishment from Boppo's funeral services had been their last official notice. But there was yet another salvo.

Susan Taylor Alford
George C. Alford
  Since this tragedy occurred, I have been trying to find the worrds [sic] *to say to you . . . there are no words that can express the depth of my hurt and thae* [sic] *deep loss I feel.*
  . . . At this point it is impossible that we could ever have any relationship. There are no winners here. But there are many losers. As my Mother said many times, "What has been done is done, and can not be changed, it is written in our page of life and will stand as it is. Only God can forgive you for all of this. With mankind it is a little harder."
  Your Grandfather and I have re-written our wills. So has your Mother. You are both excluded. It is not fitting that you should benefit materially after all the tragedy you have caused. You Susan, will not be getting [the] *ring that Uncle Kent gave to me. I know that he would not think* [you] *deserved same. . . .*

How very sad for your children. Adam saw you, Susan, cry for over a year. . . . What happened? Courtney is old enough to know that I love her. I love them both very much and miss them.

Susan . . . I was in the delivery room the day you were born, and have said that was one of the most exciting days of my life. I could not know then all the grief I would have at the end of my life. How could you do this?

. . . With such deep hurt and more sadness than I have ever known, I say Good-bye to both of you. . . .

I will always love you Susan. BUT I will always detest your actions.

> *Your Grandmother*
> *Boppo*

The Siler Family Reunion celebrated its twenty-fifth anniversary at White Lake in 1991, and Margureitte wrote the memorial booklet, typing it on *the* typewriter. She included, without comment, the Alfords in the listing of descendants, but she did not mention Pat's latest incarceration in a voluminous roundup of catastrophes that had struck various branches of the clan.

Sean attended, but Susan, Bill, Courtney, and Adam were, naturally, not invited to join the rest of the family at White Lake.

✦   ✦   ✦

When Pat was transferred up to Hardwick, Boppo and Papa resumed their weekly visiting, just as they had before. Not long afterwards, Pat was moved to a hospital facility; she had reportedly had a stroke. "She can't speak," Boppo said sadly in October 1991, "and she drags one leg. It's the prison's fault; they didn't give her her medicine for *days*. We're going to sue them." She blamed Susan for everything. The decline of the family had begun, of course, with her treachery.

Debbie and Mike Alexander agreed with the Radcliffes. "Susan needs professional help," Debbie said succinctly. "She cut the hair off Mom's dolls, and one night, when I was all alone in my apartment, Susan came over and cut off all the power and lights to my unit. I looked out the window and saw a dark truck, and I knew it was Susan."

Not likely. Susan was working as much overtime as she could

as a store security officer to make enough money to leave Mc-Donough and the constant surveillance of her outraged family. "Besides," she said with a laugh, "if I wanted to shut off Debbie's lights, I wouldn't have the first idea how to find the thing —the fuse box or whatever—to do it."

Pat's latest conviction appeared to have started a slow winding down of The Family; its gracious facade cracked, and bit by bit chunks fell off, giving a glimpse of what lay beneath. Aunt Lizzie and Margureitte were barely speaking. Aunt Thelma had a stroke and had to be put into a hospital over in Augusta. For a time, Margureitte and Cliff visited her regularly, but she didn't get any better. Thelma's surviving sisters got her power of attorney and sold her house and car. Thelma was placed in a nursing home in Elizabethtown, North Carolina.

Ashlynne still lived with Boppo and Papa; Debbie and her new husband, Mike Alexander, in financial straits, moved in with them in 1992; and Ronnie, disabled by a back injury on a construction job, kept his trailer in their side yard. Boppo and Papa bragged proudly that Sean Alford came every week to play golf with Papa. They did not, of course, encourage him to reconcile with his parents, but urged him to visit his "Grandma Pat" in prison, which he often did.

Letters sent by outsiders to Pat Taylor in prison were not acknowledged. Margureitte reported that Pat was far too ill to be interviewed, and her speech was so compromised that it was hard to understand her. It was ironic; her condition sounded remarkably like that of Nona Allanson sixteen years earlier, when Pat had poisoned her with arsenic. Pat was apparently still able to continue her hobbies, however. In the summer of 1992, her picture appeared in a Milledgeville paper as she proudly showed off a quilt she had made for the prison craft show.

Boppo could scarcely believe Pat was back in prison. "I didn't want her to accept the plea—neither did Mr. Roberts—but they were going to charge Debbie with the 1976 arsenic case, or maybe charge Pat with false imprisonment of her aunt Elizabeth Porter in Warsaw, North Carolina. I can tell you that Bobby, her son, told me that Pat took very, very good care of his mother."

"Pat is hurt so deeply that she can't even be angry," Margureitte said. "She had to sell over eight thousand dollars' worth of her dolls and doll clothing in one day—all heirloom sewing—to pay for an attorney."

Margureitte was still stunned by Susan's treachery. "Susan said her mother was a very good mother. She sang in the choir. She was a *Brownie mother.* The colonel and I bought groceries for Susan and Bill when they were having a hard time, and the colonel invited them to live with us. They left on Thanksgiving. Susan cut her mother's dolls' hair in back, and she called Colonel Radcliffe a bastard!"

Her voice trailed off to a whisper with the shock of it all.

"My own prognosis is not good," Margureitte confided, inhaling smoke. "I have lung cancer, you know. The doctor told me 'two years' last year, and Colonel Radcliffe asked him about that in my last checkup, and he just said, 'I haven't changed my original estimate.' . . . It's terrible to think that I may not have my daughter here to take care of me when I reach my last days."

Margureitte was a woman of a remarkable will and a strong constitution. Although she arrived at the 1992 Siler family reunion at White Lake in a wheelchair, her sisters commented that they had never seen her look better. When the wheelchair wouldn't maneuver in the sand, she abandoned it and didn't use it again during the week-long celebration.

✦   ✦   ✦

Tom Allanson had made the most of his first years of freedom, earning steady promotions and salary increases in his water treatment job—enough so that Liz no longer had to work. They owned a little house out in the country north of Atlanta where they could sit on their back porch and watch the dogwoods bloom and hear the wind in the pine trees. They had a calico cat, a tank of fish, grew roses and vegetables, went to church every Sunday, where Tom was president of the Full Gospel Association, and they seldom thought about the past.

The last time Tom saw Pat was sometime in 1977, before he went to Buford. Shown a mug shot taken at her most recent arrest in 1991, his jaw dropped. The Pat he remembered had been slender and delicate; this woman was hugely fat. "I can't believe it. *That's* Pat?" He shook his head, his thoughts unspoken as he handed the picture back.

Tom saw his son, Russ, regularly, but he still longed to find his daughter, Sherry. "All I know is that she's married and lives out in Seattle," he said. "I'd sure like to hear from her, but I don't know where to start."

Tom had only one faded picture of his children when they were small. He had kept it in his wallet for many years. "The rest are gone," he said. "Pat destroyed every single picture of my children. Russ and Sherry's godparents were professional photographers and we had wonderful pictures of them every few months when they were growing up. But Pat was jealous and she got rid of them without my knowledge."

Tom Allanson had lost his children and more than a decade and a half of freedom for a woman who said she loved him. By rights, he should have double that to enjoy his life with the woman who had truly loved him all through the years.

✦   ✦   ✦

For Susan, there would be no happy endings. Inexplicably, just as the Alfords had regained their financial footing and might have moved out of McDonough—and away from Boppo's ubiquitous crystal gaze—Bill announced to Susan that he was leaving her. He could no longer stand her family. She was dumbfounded; she *had* no family any longer. She had no one at all but Bill and her kids.

Bill moved out, without really explaining why.

Susan had to stay in McDonough, ostracized and alone, for six months. Shy and dependent, married since she was eighteen, Susan now proved to be tougher than she ever realized she could be. She packed up what she could take and had a yard sale with the rest. Courtney sold "South Fork," the dollhouse Pat had given her, for a hundred dollars and gave the money to her mother.

During the yard sale, the family circled the block—not once but five, ten, fifty times: Debbie and her husband and Ronnie, pointing, laughing, and jeering. The colonel and Ashlynne walked by flying a kite. Boppo drove by, again and again, her nose high in the air.

Except for Courtney and Adam, Susan was all alone.

Susan began moving on Mother's Day, 1992, hoping that on that day, at least, Boppo and Papa would be at Hardwick visiting her mother and wouldn't follow her to see where she would be living. It worked, although she later learned that the relatives who disowned her had tried to get her forwarding address from the post office, her childrens' school, and her former landlord. *Why?* Why couldn't they just let her go?

When Susan, Courtney, and Adam pulled out of McDonough for the last time two days later, their truck laden down with the last of their possessions, Susan caught a glimpse of a car that looked like Debbie's in her rearview mirror. She drove a little faster, and switched lanes, trying to lose them. As she headed northeast, and crossed from Henry County into Clayton County, one of the tires exploded. By that point, she had lost sight of the car that looked like Debbie's. She kept the heavily loaded truck in her lane only with difficulty and drove on the rim onto a feeder road, limping to a service station.

"I was afraid I didn't even have enough money left to pay to have the tire changed," Susan remembered. "And then this man came up and helped me. I call him 'My Black Angel.' He just appeared out of nowhere at the Exxon and said he'd help. He put the spare tire on and then he looked at the tread on the bad one and told me it was too thick to blow. He said, 'Take it back where you bought it, and have them look it over.' "

Susan recalled guiltily that the man was shabbily dressed. "He was the kind of guy I would have looked at twice if I was working a store, and that made me feel awful later. He told me, 'Everything will be okay now.' I guess he could see I was beside myself. I offered him the few dollars I had, and he closed my hand over it. I said, *'Please take it,'* and he just smiled and said, 'There are still some good people left in this world. You just take care of those kids.' "

Susan made her way onto the freeway again. As she took the exit ramp a few miles further, there was no one behind her. When she brought the bad tire back to the dealer the next day to ask why a practically new tire should blow the way it had, the mechanic looked at it and scratched his head. "Lady, if I didn't know better, I'd say somebody shot this out."

Looking back over Patricia Vann Radcliffe Taylor Allanson's life, it is only natural to wonder *why* she behaved as she did, why she seemed compelled to cause so much pain for the people who loved her. Was she given to periods of insanity, or was she simply a supremely selfish woman who would resort to anything, even attempted murder, to get what she wanted? There may never be definitive answers to these questions. Unlike many felons, Pat Taylor apparently never did undergo psychological testing. Aside from the diagnosis of Dr. Ray Loring Johnson— the psychiatrist who examined her after she slashed her wrists and ran wildly through the woods in the spring of 1975—no psychiatric or psychological reports exist in her court records. Dr. Johnson's assessment was that Pat suffered from "Agitated Depression with possible thought disorder." She was placed on antipsychotic medication at that time, medication that she discontinued soon after she was released from the clinic. She did not regress.

It was unlikely that Pat was ever insane. Often hysterical, yes.

From the time she was a tiny girl, she whipped herself into emotional tizzies to have her own way. No one ever put limits on her behavior. When Patty cried, the adults in her life gave in. She grew up believing that that was the way the world operated. She viewed herself as special, and why wouldn't she? All of her life, Patty, Patricia, and then Pat was encouraged to believe she was extraordinary. Beginning with "Mama" Siler, who "next to God, loved Patty the most," who gave her granddaughter the last Coca Cola, who could not bring herself to spank her precious baby, and who allowed her to subsist on pancakes, Pat never heard the word "No." When she was five, her mother married Clifford Radcliffe and continued to give Patty everything she asked for—possibly to ease her own guilt at having allowed Mama Siler to raise her child for her first years. Margureitte's indulgence never faltered, not over the next fifty years.

Throughout those years, Pat lied, stole, contrived, manipulated, seduced, and betrayed. She married twice and even attempted murder to get what she wanted. She wanted love and happiness, she wanted money and the things that money can buy, and she usually found someone to give them to her. If not, she set out to get them for herself. No one else mattered; people were merely the means to an end. Yet nothing she attained was enough to fill up the emptiness in her life. She was like a vessel with holes in the bottom; love and things and people and money and happiness seeped away. As Boppo once said, "I can't understand why anyone in this whole wide world would think Pat got whatever she wanted—she never got *anything* she wanted. Her whole life has been tragic. Why can't people understand that?"

In the beginning Pat got her way because the family loved her so; later, they dreaded her sharp tongue, her wrath, and her temper tantrums. In the end, perhaps they could not bring themselves to examine her crimes in a bright light, fearing that they too were in some way responsible. The Radcliffes and Silers always seemed to treat ugly truths like an elephant in their midst. They might comment on the gleam of its eye or the fine ivory in its tusk, but they never acknowledged all of it, only the parts they could deal with comfortably.

Every family maintains a balancing act; some members need more attention, more affirmation. Others are independent or just plain loners. Usually, individual needs change frequently and different family members become the current "burden" to be kept aloft until the balance shifts once again. In a functional family, problems eventually work out and everyone takes a turn at being the bearing wall or the burden. Pat was never the "bearing wall." She was never allowed to take responsibility for her own life. At the first sign of trouble, someone—usually Boppo and Papa—rushed forward to save her.

Pat was always the burden, but as bizarre as her behavior sometimes was, she was far from crazy. When she seemed so, it was a contrived aberrance, which she could slip into when it suited her purposes. Her taped voice in her conversations with Tom, clear over seventeen years of time, alternately imperious and kittenish, and full of throaty laughter, demonstrated the roles she played to manipulate everyone in her life.

If she was not crazy, however, Pat quite likely suffered from a melange of personality disorders. She did not view the world or her relationship to it the way most people do. She knew the difference between right and wrong, but it didn't matter. She had been raised to believe that rules were for other people and what mattered was that she got what *she* wanted.

A personality disorder, once established in the mind, clings like an intractable fungus. It becomes *part* of the thought processes, and trying to remove it would be akin to cutting down a tree to eliminate a fungus. It is better to be "crazy" because crazy can be cured. Personality disorders die with the host, entangled for life in the brain's functioning.

No one knows for certain where personality disorders come from. Most psychiatrists agree, however, that they are not present at birth but, rather, take root in the first few years of life. Normally, a child of three or four will begin to understand that his or her actions can cause pain to a parent, to another child or a pet—that other creatures hurt too. This understanding and awareness leads to the development of the conscience, the still small voice inside that warns humans that certain actions are cruel, insensitive, and against the mores of their society. It is the conscience that provokes guilt, a much maligned emotion that is actually vital to the survival of humanity.

Abused and humiliated children are too busy merely trying to survive to "grow" a conscience or take the first baby steps to empathy. Perhaps children who are never chastised or punished sidestep the conscience-growing process too. Reverend Tasso Siler and his gentle wife Mary were kindness personified and so —according to herself—was Margureitte. Still, one wonders if too much "kindness" cannot warp a child as surely as abuse.

Whatever stunted her emotional development, it is clear from viewing her behavior that Pat was an antisocial personality. Put simply, she had no conscience. That was why she could goad Tom into a disastrous confrontation with his parents. That was why she could feed arsenic to Paw and Nona and could dose Elizabeth Crist with enough Halcion to leave her virtually unconscious day after day. That was why she could drive her own parents into bankruptcy with her ceaseless demands for money. And why she could concoct accusations against her own daughter, a woman in the grip of clinical depression, and drive her out of the house.

She could also write the kind of letters that made Susan cry and filled Tom's heart with love. When there is no real feeling and no empathy for the feelings of other people, it is quite easy to play games with their emotions and their lives. Pat had not the faintest inkling of what they were suffering. She had no desire or ability to connect with other peoples' emotions. Her suffering—even that which she inflicted on herself—was all that mattered, and she used her pain as another weapon to make the people who loved her suffer even more.

A number of personality disorders often go hand in hand, and Pat was probably also a narcissistic personality. Like Narcissus of the Greek myth, who idolized his own image in a pond, she was quite literally in love with herself. She *believed* that she deserved whatever she desired. She was shocked when she didn't always get it. Because she could not have everything, no matter how hard those around her scurried to please her, she was often depressed. She thought she knew what she needed to make her happy—but it never had made her happy for even two weeks. By the time Pat met Tom, she had lost the capacity for happiness, if she'd ever had it at all.

She may have also suffered from another less well known disorder that psychiatric scholars have isolated, one with a long technical name and an impossible-to-pronounce common name: "Chronic Factitious Disorder with Physical Symptoms"— "Munchausen Syndrome." Unlike most people who dread the antiseptic smell of a hospital corridor, those who suffer from

Munchausen's crave medical settings. They truly enjoy the excitement of hospitals, the attention and the drama of being attended by nurses and doctors. They are *so* attracted to this milieu that they actually cause themselves pain to get there.

Munchausen's goes far beyond hypochondria, whose sufferers imagine symptoms of practically every disease they hear about. Munchausen's often involves actual self-mutilation. Susan had seen her mother beat herself with pots and pans until she was badly bruised. The deep fissured scar on Pat's right buttock was the result of her own deliberate and repeated probing at an initially small wound with bacteria-covered instruments. The pain involved must have been almost unbearable—yet she craved attention and excitement so much that she exacerbated that wound over and over and over. At one point, she came perilously close to death from blood poisoning. And she had done it to herself.

Pat's history of illnesses and injuries was lengthy and unique. She cried "Rape!" so often that she eventually became laughable. She collapsed and had to be rushed to hospitals time and again. Only Pat would have almost welcomed the bite of the brown recluse spider. It meant she could spend weeks in a hospital, a pleasant alternative to prison. And, like many who love being hospitalized, she was addicted to drugs—Demerol for one; even Margureitte testified to that. The true state of Pat's physical and emotional health may never be completely known or understood. She herself might have been powerless to control it. But it was among the strongest weapons in her arsenal to exert control over others.

Pat never seemed comfortable in her own skin. Indeed, she attempted to literally destroy her own body. And despite the control she wielded over others, it was quite possible she felt no power at all—except with her dolls. Her dolls always did what she wanted them to do. She was the center of their universe, just as she would be the center of the world she had hoped to create for herself—Zebulon. There she could be Scarlett and Tom her rich and blindly devoted Rhett. Perhaps because her world did not give her everything she ever wanted, Pat could not stand being herself. Scarlett had been full of strength, a woman who could stand alone and fight for what she wanted. In the end, Pat was only a pale imitation.

Pat's effect on what was once a solid—if slightly eccentric—

family was devastating. Even when she was in prison, she called the tunes and kept her mother bound to her. Back in Hardwick for the second time in 1991, Pat was not doing well—according to Boppo, who reported that she had had another stroke and was in a wheelchair, unable to walk or talk. Also in a wheelchair, Boppo was far more worried about her child than she was about her own imminent death. And all around them lay the evidence of the destruction of a family, caused not by the neglect of a child—but by the utter, complete, almost mindless, indulgence of a child.

The only member to survive with dignity was the one they had all reviled—the one who had the courage to do what she knew was right even if it went against the family: Susan. They all quoted Mary Siler, but no one but Susan had listened to her words:

> "What we have done will soon be a sealed book. If it's been good or bad, we can't change it. It will stand as it is. It is sad, for some of us will have marked up pages in our book from many unkind words to someone, or maybe we did not try hard to make others' lives happy . . ."

Mary Valli Siler

◆ A C K N O W L E D G M E N T S

Although the author's name is the only one that appears on the jacket of a book, I suspect few readers realize that we are supported by a benevolent army of editors, agents, publicists, readers, friends, relatives and observers kind enough to share their opinions and recollections. A book of this scope, covering so many years, so many miles, and such a plethora of legal details, would have been impossible without the gracious help I received from so many.

I wish to thank the staff of District Attorney Lewis Slaton of Fulton County, Georgia, particularly Investigators Don Stoop and Michelle Berry, and Assistant District Attorneys Andy Weathers and Bill Akins, the East Point, Georgia, Police Department, and law enforcement personnel from Pike County and Forsyth County, Georgia.

Although there were as many points of view in this true-life saga as colors in the rainbow and few participants agreed, nevertheless I appreciated the time various family members and friends shared with me: Colonel Clifford Radcliffe and Margureitte Radcliffe, Deborah and Michael Alexander, Bill and Susan

Alford, Courtney and Adam Alford, Tom and Liz Allanson and J. C. and Rena Jones. Their perceptions added a great deal to the voluminous public records and transcripts furnished by government officials in Georgia, Florida, North Carolina, and Washington, D.C. From *all* the stories, each interwoven with the next, strand upon strand, emerged one story, the final golden thread that became this book.

Life can sometimes be cold and lonely for a writer at work, and I thank my backup people: My first reader, Gerry Brittingham, and my friend and field assistant on this book, Donna Anders, for their help on the first fledgling research and the roughest draft. And, scattered from Massachusetts to Wyoming, from Michigan to Oregon, in no particular order: Sophie Stackhouse, Laura, Rebecca, and Matthew Harris, Leslie Rule, David Coughlan, Andrew Rule, Michael Rule, Marlene Price, Bruce Sherles, Shirley and Bill Hickman, Lois Duncan, Fred and Bernie McLean, Jeoff Robinson, Jay and Betty Jo Newell, Bill and Maureen Woodcock, Martin and Lisa Woodcock and Don White (who enlarged my office right over my head as I worked), Jennifer Gladwell, Edna Buchanan of Miami Beach, Mike Bashey, Elida Vance, Nancy Hrynshyn, Jann and Sid MacFarland and the houseboat gang, Ed Eaton, Betty May and Phil Settecase, Verne Shangle, Sue and Bob Morrison, Ruthene Larson, Joan and Jerry Kelly, Cheri Luxa, Ginger and Bill Clinton, Hope Yenko, Brian Halquist, Dee Reed, Rose Mandelsberg-Weiss, Elaine and Wayne Dorman, Dr. Peter J. Modde, Anne Jaeger, Marsha MacWillie, Jenny Everson, Dee Grim, Mildred Yoacham, Johnny Bonds of the Harris County, Texas, Prosecuting Attorney's Office, Dr. Martha Krenn, Lola Cunningham, Joyce and Bill Johnson of Mukilteo, Don Wall, Luke and Nancy Fiorante, M. L. Lyke and Susan Paynter, Joyce and Pierce Brooks, Sergeant Myra Harmon and Sergeant Marsha Camp, Charlotte and Austin Seth, Geri and Bill Swank of San Diego, Danny House and Karen Ritola.

To the enigmatic and arcane Northwest B. & M. Society, of which I am proud to be a founding member: Jeannie Okimoto, Judine and Terry Brooks, Ann Combs, John Saul, Margaret Chittenden, Michael Sack, Donna Anders, Don and Carol McQuinn; *and* to the Pacific Northwest Writers' Conference where every writer learns and grows.

To my Ohio relatives—descendants, as I am, of the late Albert Sherman and Florence Stackhouse: Bertha and Bob Mowery (now of San Benito, Texas), Lucetta Mae Bartley, Sherman Stackhouse, David Stackhouse and Glenna Jean Longwell, Neva Steed Jones, and my fellow author, James Steed.

To my Michigan relatives—descendants, as I am, of the late Chris and Anna Hansen: Emma McKenney, Chris and Linda McKenney, Freda and Bernie Grunwald, Donna and Stuart Basom, Bruce and Diane Basom, Jan and Eby Schubert, Karen and Jim Hudson, Jim and Mary Sampson, Maxine Hansen, Christa Hansen, Terry Hansen, and Sara Jane and Larry Plushnik.

Almost two years ago, my editor, Frederic W. Hills, agreed with me that this was a story worth exploring and he has cheered me on all the way. He and Burton Beals have helped me shape, trim, and improve every chapter and have done so with the utmost tact, kindness, and intelligence, never intruding on my own particular style. Even when I balked, I knew in my heart they were right. To Daphne Bien, Fred Hill's assistant, who left us just as we crossed the finish line, and flew off to London. How many of us will miss her! Ed Sedarbaum and Leslie Ellen handled the copyediting and found every comma, date and clause I inadvertently put in the wrong place—or at the wrong time—(or both) and I do appreciate it. To Emily Remes, my legal angel, and to the sales representatives who set out for the far corners of America, carrying books, and came back, hopefully, empty-handed.

To my publicity team, Victoria Meyer and Joann Di Gennaro, and to the "friends for a day"—my escorts on tour who always lead me patiently and graciously around cities I have never seen before.

Again and again, to my much loved agents, Joan and Joe Foley.

Last of all, but truly *most* of all, I thank my readers. You can never know how much your letters mean to an author who has been chained to a word processor for weeks on end. Or how welcome your smiling faces and supportive comments are when I am signing books in some mall, somewhere. *You* have given me that rarest of joys—the chance to earn my living doing something I really love.

Ann Rule

ABOUT THE AUTHOR

Ann Rule, author of the best-selling *The Stranger Beside Me,*
Small Sacrifices, and *If You Really Loved Me,* is one of America's top true-crime writers. A former Seattle policewoman, she
has published 1,400 articles and eight books on homicide cases.
She lectures often to law enforcement professionals on serial
murder, sadistic sociopaths, and women who kill. She has testified before the U.S. Senate and presented a seminar to the FBI
Academy. She served on the U.S. Justice Department task force
setting up the Violent Criminal Apprehension Program (VI-CAP) now in use at FBI headquarters to track and trap serial
killers. When she is not attending trials and researching new
books, she makes her home near Seattle, Washington.